The Economics of American Higher Education

The Economics of American Higher Education

Edited by
William E. Becker
Professor of Economics
Indiana University

and

Darrell R. Lewis
Professor of Educational Policy
University of Minnesota

Springer Science+Business Media, LLC

Library of Congress Cataloging-in-Publication Data

The Economics of American higher education/edited by William E.
Becker and Darrell R. Lewis.
p. cm.
Includes bibliographical references and index.
ISBN 978-94-010-5310-5 ISBN 978-94-011-2950-3 (eBook)
DOI 10.1007/978-94-011-2950-3
1. Education, Higher—Economic aspects—United States.
I. Becker, William E. II. Lewis, Darrell R.
LC67.62.E257 1982
338.4'337873—dc20

Originally published by Kluwer Academic Publishers in 1992
Softcover reprint of the hardcover 1st edition 1992

Printed on acid-free paper.

Contents

Contributors

Melissa S. Anderson, Postdoctoral Fellow in Higher Education, University of Minnesota

William E. Becker, Professor of Economics, Indiana University

Mark C. Berger, Professor of Economics, University of Kentucky

Elchanan Cohn, Professor of Economics, College of Business Administration, University of South Carolina

Mark Drabenstott, Assistant Vice President and Economist, Federal Reserve Bank of Kansas City

Roger L. Geiger, Professor of Education, The Pennsylvania State University

Terry G. Geske, Professor and Chairperson, College of Education, Administrative and Foundational Services, Louisiana State University

Rebecca Dorsett Goodman, Senior Statistical Analyst, Bureau of Community Corrections, Hennepin County, Minnesota

James C. Hearn, Professor of Higher Education, Institute of Higher Education, University of Georgia

Larry L. Leslie, Director of the Center for the Study of Higher Education, and Professor of Higher Education, College of Education, University of Arizona

Darrell R. Lewis, Professor of Educational Policy, and Professor of Education, University of Minnesota

Kevin M. Murphy, Professor of Business Economics and Industrial Relations, Graduate School of Business, University of Chicago

Vernon W. Ruttan, Regents Professor of Agricultural and Applied Economics, University of Minnesota

G. Edward Schuh, Professor and Dean, Hubert H. Humphrey Institute of Public Affairs, University of Minnesota

Sheila A. Slaughter, Professor of Higher Education, University of Arizona
Tim R. Smith, Senior Economist, Federal Reserve Bank of Kansas City
William C. Weiler, Assistant Provost, Stanford University
Finis Welch, Professor of Economics, University of California at Los Angeles and Unicon Research Corporation

About the Editors

William E. Becker is a professor of economics at Indiana University. He is editor of the *Journal of Economic Education* and serves on the editorial board of the *Economics of Education Review*. His research appears in the *American Economic Review*, *American Journal of Agricultural Economics*, *Econometric Theory*, *Journal of Finance*, *Journal of Human Resources*, *Journal of Risk and Insurance*, *Monthly Labor Review*, *Review of Economics and Statistics*, and other journals. He is also the co-author of *Business and Economics Statistics* and co-editor of *Academic Rewards in Higher Education* and *Econometric Modeling in Economic Education Research*.

Darrell R. Lewis is professor of educational policy and higher education at the University of Minnesota. His research interests have been in the economics of education with a current focus on issues relating to educational efficiency and postschool outcomes. He is the author or co-author of numerous articles, monographs, and books. He has co-edited *Academic Rewards in Higher Education* and *Faculty Vitality and Institutional Productivity* and co-authored *And on the Seventh Day: Faculty Consulting and Other Supplemental Income Activities* and *Assessing Outcomes, Costs and Benefits of Special Education Programs*.

Preface

Postsecondary educational institutions in the United States are facing increasing financial stress and waning public support. Unless these trends can be changed, higher education can be expected to stagnate. What, if anything, can be done? As a starting point, advocates of higher education need to more fully recognize the issues associated with the economic mission of higher education and how this mission gets translated into individual student gains, regional growth, and social equity. This requires an understanding of the relationship between the outcomes of higher education and measures of economic productivity and well-being.

This volume addresses topics related to the role of postsecondary education in microeconomic development within the United States. Attention is given to the importance of colleges and universities in the enhancement of individual students and in the advancement of the communities and states within which they work. Although several of the chapters in this volume are aimed at research/teaching universities, much of what is presented throughout can be generalized to all of postsecondary education. Little attention, however, is given to the role of higher education in the macroeconomic development of the United States; this topic is covered in our related book, *American Higher Education and National Growth*.

The chapters in this book summarize the research literature and synthesize what economists and other social scientists have learned about the contribution of higher education to economic development within the American society. Many of the chapters were originally commissioned by the editors for a seminar on these topics at the University of Minnesota during the spring of 1989. The seminar was financed by grants from the Hubert H. Humphrey Institute and the College of Education at the

University of Minnesota. To the deans and faculty of both units, as well as David Berg and Stephen Hoenack (Management Planning and Information Services), we are indebted for institutional support and collegial interaction. Additional support for manuscript preparation was provided by the Joint Council on Economic Education, for which we are most grateful.

In *The Economics of American Higher Education* we have assembled a group of recognized scholars from economics and the other social sciences who have individually made significant contributions to the literature in higher education. The authors draw heavily from their own research in providing current evidence while focusing on their assigned chapter topics. To all of our 16 contributing authors we are thankful. Without their work this book would not have been possible.

Manuscript editing was done by Suzanne Becker as part of her duties as assistant editor of the *Journal of Economic Education*. As always her patience, eye for detail, and skill with the English language are acknowledged and appreciated. Together with the reference librarians at Indiana University, whose services are gratefully acknowledged, Sue did all the final reference work. Manuscript preparation was completed in the Department of Economics at Indiana University through the capable word processing skills of Elaine Yarde, to whom we are indebted.

William E. Becker
Darrell R. Lewis

1 PREVIEW OF THE ECONOMICS OF AMERICAN HIGHER EDUCATION

William E. Becker and Darrell R. Lewis

After decades of effortless growth and prosperity, America's postsecondary institutions have come under increasing financial stress and waning public support. During the first part of the 1980s, this stress largely resulted from a slowdown in the economy, with many state legislatures simply giving higher education lower priority and even some retrenchments. In 1989 and 1990 applications to institutions of higher education declined, after overall enrollments topped 13 million students in 1988 (as reported in the *Chronicle of Higher Education*, April 11, 1990, and June 20, 1990). The National Center for Educational Statistics (1989, pp. 17–28) projects enrollments falling to 12.4 million students by 2000 or, following a dip in the 1990s, possibly rising to 14.4 million students by 2000. Although most private institutions depend heavily on tuition and other student-related revenue and public institutions receive the largest portion of their funds from state appropriations, both are driven by student enrollments. Froomkin (1990) asserts that if revenues in higher education continue to depend mainly on the number of students, "a prolonged depression will be experienced by higher education, more serious than anything in the past fifty years" (p. 212). During this past decade budgets were balanced partly at the expense of faculty and staff compensation, thus creating additional internal stress within most institutions. Unlike expenditure cuts for the maintenance and repair of buildings, lack of growth in wage funds resulted in immediate cries of exploitation and despair.

With the increase in financial troubles and internal strife, higher education also faced increasing external demands for greater public accountability along with a general loss of public esteem. According to the *Chronicle of Higher Education* (September 14, 1988), "The spectacle of the two Presidential candidates at times trying to dissociate themselves from two of America's premier universities, and of pundits and politicians attacking those institutions, has raised the specter of anti-intellectualism in the campaign and prompted anxious questions of higher-education leaders" (p. 1). The basic causes of this dilemma are the rapid changes of demographic and technological change currently taking place in the United States and the inability of higher education to clearly articulate to students, local legislators, potential donors, and the general public the importance of its role in the context of these changes.

From the early work of Douglas (1948), Kendrick (1961), Schultz (1961), Denison (1967) to the more recent work of Maddison (1987) and Pencavel (1991), economists have studied the contribution of education to aggregate national economic growth. They used production functions in which the total economy's output of goods and services, O (e.g., measured by gross domestic product), is produced on a fixed amount of land by the inputs of augmented labor, L (e.g., measured by total person hours worked adjusted for years of schooling attained), and supplemented physical capital, K (e.g., measured by inventories of machines and equipment adjusted for its vintage). In functional notation,

$$O = f(L, K).$$

These aggregate production function studies, their results, and their implications for national policy are reviewed in detail by contributors to our book *American Higher Education and National Growth* (forthcoming). Although the results of these production function studies shed light on the relationship between aggregate national economic growth and human capital formation, they say nothing about the disaggregated effects enjoyed by individuals and the communities in which they live. It is these disaggregated effects, however, that will be appreciated by state legislators, potential donors, and community leaders. These individual and regional effects are the focus of this book.

Carnevale (1983) stated that "all signs point toward a shift in institutional authority away from public and nonprofit institutions toward the private sector" (p. 6). Postsecondary institutions, according to this view, are among those institutions that will be adversely affected. Unless current popular opinion is changed, state-supported and nonprofit private higher education institutions are presumed to face a slow but steady decline. What, if anything, should colleges and university officials do to respond to the attack?

As a minimum, the higher education community needs to more forcefully articulate and assert its role in contributing to the growth of individuals and regional economies and to the advancement of society in general. And the first step in making such a case for higher education requires an understanding of the linkages between the missions and outcomes of higher education and individual and regional economic development.

The Missions of American Higher Education

To more fully appreciate the unique contributions of higher education in the development of American society and its economy, an understanding of the historical missions of these institutions is helpful. The literature is rich in describing this evolution (e.g., Brubacher and Rudy 1976) and special character (e.g., Trow 1979, 1988) of American higher education. This literature indicates that American higher education exists to serve not a single purpose or mission, but several. It exists to instruct students, and it may strive simultaneously to offer instruction in the liberal arts and vocational training. It may offer advanced training in the core disciplines while providing continuing education for adults. It exists also to carry on research, both applied and basic. And it is often called on to provide a wide range of community services.

The history of American higher education gives vivid detail as to how the several thousands of such institutions in our society have responded to this multiplicity of purposes. The mission and goal statements of most institutions speak generally to these purposes of instruction, research, and service, often with varying degrees of priority and targeted constituents (Fenske 1980). The diversity of mission is reflected in the different types of institutions found within the United States. This institutional differentiation of higher education signals that we often deceive ourselves, and others, when we speak about the "role" of American higher education, somehow implying a homogeneous grouping of institutions with common purpose and mission. Institutional differentiation plays a very important role in understanding both the mission and outcomes of higher education.

The Carnegie Foundation for the Advancement of Teaching (1987) classified the 3400 accredited institutions in American higher education under 20 major categorical types that extend well beyond the research, teaching, and service missions that are usually referenced. This extensive differentiation places most faculty, students, and programs in settings other than that of the national research university, where only about one-third of all faculty and students currently are found. Another third of the higher education population can be found in regional public and private four-year colleges, which number about 1200; while another third are found in the nearly 1400 community colleges in larger cities throughout the nation. An extensive literature describes the many differences in these institutions (e.g., Peterson and Uhl 1977; Trivett 1973).

All postsecondary institutions purport to have some responsibility for transmitting existing knowledge to their students and, in various forms, to other constituents as well. Most also have service responsibilities of one form or another and many have an explicit research mission that calls for the creation of new knowledge. Among the academy of scholars and teachers, broadly identified, the creation of new knowledge through research is recognized as an important function of higher education even though it is not pursued by all. As documented in the *Chronicle of Higher Education* (July 5, 1990), even some private four-year liberal arts colleges, with their traditional teaching emphasis, are now expecting faculty members to produce research in order to receive promotions. At many state-supported universities greater emphasis is currently being placed on the creation of new knowledge than on the dissemination of existing knowledge even though their statements to legislators may say otherwise. Although all institutions of higher education feel they are contributing to the advancement of society, it is the articulation of how they contribute that is problematic.

Seldom does one find in a mission statement of an institution explicit reference to how it contributes to the economic well-being of the individual and his or her community or how its mission might serve the larger society through advancement of the infrastructure to accommodate economic development. With the possible exception of some community colleges and professional schools giving explicit attention to their vocational and career training or community service mission, most institutions continue to speak only in the broadest terms about knowledge creation and knowledge transmission. Coleman (1973) has argued that much of higher education, even today, has largely retained both its medieval body and purpose. This edited book is intended, in part, to address this often unspoken, if not overlooked, dimension of higher education's mission.

The cornerstone of popular support for American higher education has always been the image of our colleges and universities as engaged primarily in teaching young adults. On the other hand, the institutional and organizational reality of contemporary higher education may have begun to compromise both this image and its continuing support. Is the principle mission of American higher education to teach undergraduates? If so, how well are we doing? In the second chapter of this volume, "The Teaching Role of Contemporary American Higher Education: Popular Imagery and Organizational Reality," James Hearn examines this critical issue.

Focusing on "The Research and Service Missions of the University," Edward Schuh and Vernon Ruttan in the third chapter address the role of higher education in the creation and transfer of knowledge to others outside of the institution and specifically aim at the unique externalities of university research. They do this first by way of illustrating the contributions of university-based social science research to institutional change in society. They also examine the role of university service as it has contributed to extending technical knowledge to the private sector and to public policy makers.

Higher Education for Personal Investment and Advancement

The easiest motive for justifying investments in higher education is the increased financial returns that accrue to those who matriculate, as captured in the human capital literature advanced by Gary Becker (1964). During the 1970s, however, educators and legislators were shocked by the assertion that many Americans may have been "overeducated," at least when viewed from the relatively low financial returns for higher education reported by Freeman in his 1976 book *The Overeducated American*. More recent evidence indicates that the difference between the earnings of high school and college graduates increased rapidly during the 1980s. The returns to some occupations are now extremely impressive. In addition, the nonfinancial benefits of a college education may be greater today than ever before due to the requirements of living in a highly integrated and specialized society. These issues, along with the recent evidence, are presented and discussed in the second part of this volume.

In "Why Go to College?" (chapter 4), William Becker sets the stage for examining the personal advancement and investment effects from higher education. Several different ways of measuring the financial returns to higher education through the use of traditional human capital theory are introduced. Alternative theories, such as screening and the efficient wage hypothesis, are also examined as possible explanations for the relationship between the level of schooling and earnings. Special attention is given to recent evidence that shows the private returns to higher education rising rapidly in the 1980s. Kevin Murphy and Finis Welch, in "Wages of College Graduates," indicate that the difference between the earnings of college and high school graduates is now larger than it was 30 years ago. After 11 to 15 years of job experience a college graduate now earns some 60 percent more than a high school graduate. College graduates can expect to receive some $600,000 more than high school graduates over their lifetimes. Murphy and Welch show that potential college students have recognized fluctuations in this college premium in their desire to obtain college degrees.

Although the historical upward trend in the premium college graduates receive over high school graduates is not now in dispute, the cause of the fluctuations around this trend is not universally accepted and understood. The cause of the upturn in the 1980s is debated. For example, was it simply a by-product of holding the minimum wage artificially low? Or was it the result of a decrease in high-pay, low-skill jobs either together with or separate from an increase in high-pay, high-skill jobs (caused by the movement of manufacturing jobs overseas or technological change biased toward the skill jobs or shifts in final product demand)? Or was it caused by a change in the composition of the labor force, which might have been brought about by a change in an unobservable quality attribute of the different labor groups? Whatever the explanation, higher education still appears to be a good investment relative to alternatives. The competitive advantage held by college graduates likely will continue into the future.

In his chapter Becker argues that attempts to assess the contribution of institutions of higher education based solely on changes in student knowledge from the time of admission to graduation could be a misleading measure of the contribution of higher education to the individual because it ignores the financial returns that are associated with that knowledge. The chapter by Mark Berger, "Private Returns to Specific College Majors," gives detailed patterns and trends over the past three decades and shows the curious result that only in the male-dominated area of engineering do women's starting salaries surpass those of men.

Individuals, of course, enjoy more than increased salaries as a result of higher education. Indeed, Haveman and Wolfe (1984) have speculated that economic studies that have focused exclusively on increased earnings may have captured only 50 percent of the total value of an additional year of schooling. These other private benefits are identified and discussed by

Elchanan Cohn and Terry Geske in their chapter on the "Private Nonmonetary Returns to Investment in Higher Education." Through their examination of the literature dealing with the effects of education on family life, health, consumption behavior, asset management, migration behavior, increasing options, intergenerational effects, and other non market benefits, Cohn and Geske conclude that the nonmonetary and nonmarket private benefits of extended education are indeed real and considerable.

Higher Education and Regional Growth

Town and gown arguments are well documented in the literature and folklore of college towns. Within metropolitan areas enthusiasm for university links with industrial development is often cited as a reason for expansion and strengthening of higher education institutions. Often the strongest legislative arguments for the creation or expansion of such institutions have been those relating to community externalities. Witness, for example, the unusual coalitions of support for new community colleges. Colleges and universities, by their very existence, create jobs, add wealth, and enhance cultural activities within a community and contribute to economic growth in a region. As demonstrated by the uproar in Evanston, Illinois, over the taxing of student tuition, the production of college and university education also uses community resources. Higher education is provided through the inputs of labor, land, and capital that could have been used for other purposes elsewhere in the local community. In part III of this volume the issues and evidence associated with higher education and regional economic growth are considered.

Researchers have been attempting to establish a causal tie between higher education and regional or state economic growth. Several studies on the determinants of business location and regional growth contain some evidence that spending on higher education attracts new businesses that may lead to regional growth (e.g., Plaut and Pluta 1983; Wasylenko and McGuire 1985). Other studies (e.g., Jones and Vedlitz 1988; Helms 1985) have more directly examined the relationship between expenditures on higher education and regional economic growth and found strong and positive effects. Tim Smith and Mark Drabenstott review these and other studies in chapter 8, "The Role of Universities in Regional Economic Development." The land-grant system of universities is described as a clear example of how universities can contribute to regional rural economic growth through research, teaching, and service.

Universities also contribute to the economic development of their states by attracting funds from agencies outside the state, particularly the federal government. These federal funds are used to employ researchers and support university personnel. Further, the distribution of these funds for salaries and supply and equipment purchases produces a chain of subsequent spending that generates income and employment beyond the initial impact.

In their chapter on "Higher Education and Regional Development," Larry Leslie and Sheila Slaughter focus on the economic impact of specific higher education institutions on community growth. They review both the methodology and results of 74 different economic impact studies that have examined the economic effects on communities and regions of collegiate institutions housed within their borders. They note that there is considerable variability in economic effects according to institutional types and local conditions. They also state that there are important effects beyond those captured in most of the conventional impact studies. Most of the economic impact studies have focused primarily on single-year spending by an institution, employees, students, and visitors and have estimated multipliers in their growth projections. None of the studies looked closely at long-term university contributions to economic development, especially as they might relate to technology transfer.

The chapter by Rebecca Goodman and William Weiler on "Measuring the Regional Economic Effects of Federal Research Grants" is presented through the modeling of data from a large state university. Employing a two-region, input-output model, they estimate that important income and employment effects take place within the state and that the total employment increase in the state is at least 250 percent of the direct employment of research personnel at the university. The question that begs for an answer, however, is, How does this multiplier compare to those for other public funds that enter the state for roads, bridges, buildings, and other subsidies aimed at enhancing the infrastructure on which society also depends?

Although many institutional presidents and state governors, and even the National Science Foundation, are now extolling the virtues of technology transfer as an effective economic development strategy, there is surprisingly little research available as to the effects of such strategies. On the other hand, there is some developing literature as to how a university or college might collaborate with the private sector or use its own resources to more directly advance economic development through patents and the like. This literature and the historical patterns of university-industry relationships in the United States is reviewed by Roger Geiger in his chapter, "The Ambiguous Link: Private Industry and University Research." It is observed, for example, that since the mid-1980s the national share of research undertaken by higher education has increased spectacularly, surpassing historical norms. The most likely cause of this unusual development appears to be the proactive policies of universities, often assisted by government policies, for expanded efforts in dealing with technology transfer (e.g., industry–university relationships and university investment in patenting and in commercial development of high technology).

Geiger states that the case for an expanded role of universities in technology transfer and economic development rests on two important assumptions. The first is that industry has been underinvesting in generic research and could profitably utilize additional research from universities; the second is that discoveries of potential commercial value were being made in universities but were not reaching the market because of the absence of linking mechanisms in the commercial sector. Both appear to be true at the present time.

Higher Education as Social Investment for Equity

The American higher education industry differs from almost all others in the world in offering access to some part of the system to almost everyone who wants postsecondary education. As noted by Trow (1979) and others, public policy supporting this open access is largely driven by concerns for equity. Both private attitudes and public policy across the United States affirm that the more people who can be persuaded to enroll in a college or university, the better. With all of this attention to open access, little attention has focused on outcomes. The question of how well the outcomes of higher education are contributing to equality in society is critical. Accordingly, this question is examined in the fourth part of this volume.

In their chapter, "Equity Issues in Higher Education Outcomes," Melissa Anderson and James Hearn review evidence relating to this critical issue. They consider the extent to which the benefits of higher education are enjoyed by all members of society, regardless of socioeconomic background or ascriptive characteristics. It is important to note that they do not address issues of access (Who can attend?) or choice (Can an individual attend the institution of his or her choice?). These issues have been addressed by Manski and Wise (1983) and others.

Anderson and Hearn focus on equity of educational attainment as an outcome of the higher education system. They emphasize three different higher education outcomes (educational, occupational, and income attainment) and examine the three equity related factors of socioeconomic status, gender, and race (or ethnic background). The evidence suggests that those at the lower socioeconomic levels have most to gain from, but are least well served by, higher education. On the other hand, the effects of sex and race/ethnicity on college outcomes seem less deleterious and in some important ways appear to be positive. For women and minorities, the literature indicates that higher education has proven capable of appreciably improving their life chances.

Questions for Policy

The literature relating to the economic effects of higher education is broad and shows some disparate results. The chapters in this volume highlight perceived differences in the role of higher education in the economic development of individuals and the communities in which they live. More importantly, however, they focus attention on the generalizations that can be made for policy inference.

Numerous important policy questions naturally flow from the generalizations about the association of higher education with economic development. For example, if the private return to a college education is high, is it overly subsidized? Should the state employ tuition policies as cost subsidies to individuals to affect private rates of return? If so, which type of institution and individuals should receive the greatest subsidy? Should quality or quantity of research, service, or teaching within higher education be given priority for state funding? With the highest rates of return and growth effects coming mainly through the education of the "most able" in our population, should states give funding priorities to institutions with competitive admissions? Or should priority be given to those who may benefit most in terms of equity, namely: those of lower ability from lower socioeconomic backgrounds?

If research in higher education is an engine of regional growth, does this factor suggest differential treatment of research universities by states and the federal government? But which type of research university should receive the priority? Those that emphasize basic or those that emphasize applied research? On the other hand, if higher education provides the vehicle for the dissemination of knowledge, doesn't this suggest that institutions that emphasize teaching should receive priority in funding? But which type of teaching institutions? Those that emphasize a liberal arts education? Or those that emphasize new and highly specialized knowledge? Or those that emphasize training for existing jobs?

Is there a viable role for state leadership and funding in technology transfer between education and industry? If categorical funding is successful for knowledge creation and transfer in agriculture, would not this organizational and funding structure work in other fields as well? With so many of the major effects from higher education relating to social externalities, technology transfer, and economic growth, should states place greater pressure for funding on the federal government?

Should a community worry about being a net exporter of college graduates? Should the state use the location and placement of colleges as a major instrument for area development? Is it better to have many small, locally controlled institutions or to have fewer but higher quality institutions? If most benefits from community and technical colleges accrue largely to individuals and local communities, should the state have the major responsibility for funding them? Given that current tax policies discriminate against human capital formation through higher education as compared to private sector training, should states or the federal government change tax policies to influence participation in higher education?

These and many other questions concerning higher education and the economic development of the United States are addressed by the authors in this volume. We do not give prescriptions for answering these questions through specific policy recommendations. We leave that to the advocates. In this volume we only provide the data and related information for policy debate. We do expect, however, that as evidence of the connection between higher education and economic development continues to grow, state policy makers increasingly will look to their institutions of higher education.

The evidence presented in this volume suggests important dimensions through which higher education contributes to regional economic growth and social equity. The chapters also suggest several ways that the channels between institutions of higher education and other sectors of society can be enhanced. The dominant theme of this volume is that public policy can influence the long-term nature of the contributions that colleges and universities will make to individual and regional economic development.

References

Becker, G. S. (1964). *Human capital: A theoretical and empirical analysis with special reference to education*. New York: Columbia University Press.

Brubacher, J. S., & Rudy, W. (1976). *Higher education in transition.* New York: Harper & Row.
Carnegie Foundation for the Advancement of Teaching. (1987). *A classification of institutions of higher education.* Princeton, NJ: Author.
Carnevale, A. P. (1983). Higher education's role in the American economy. *Educational Record* (Fall), 6–16.
Coleman, J. S. (1973). The university and society's new demands upon it. In C. Kaysen (Ed.), *Content and context: Essays on college education.* New York: McGraw-Hill.
Denison, E. F. (1967). *Why growth rates differ: Postwar experiences in nine western countries.* Washington, D.C.: Brookings Institution.
Douglas, P. H. (1948). Are there laws of production? *The American Economic Review 38*(1), 1–41.
Fenske, R. H. (1980). Setting institutional goals and objectives. In P. Jedamus, M. W. Peterson, and Associates (Eds.), *Improving academic management: A handbook of planning and institutional research.* San Francisco: Jossey-Bass.
Freeman, R. (1976). *The overeducated American.* New York: Academic Press.
Froomkin, J. (1990). The impact of changing levels of financial resources on the structure of colleges and universities. In S. A. Hoenack and E. L. Collins (Eds.), *The economics of American universities* (pp. 189–214). Albany, NY: State University of New York Press.
Haveman, R. H., & Wolfe, B. L. (1984). Schooling and economic wellbeing: The role of nonmarket effects. *Journal of Human Resources 19*(3), 377–407.
Helms, L. J. (1985). The effect of state and local taxes on economic growth: A time series-cross section approach. *The Review of Economics and Statistics 67* November, 574–582.
Jones, B. D., & Vedlitz, A. (1988). Higher education policies and economic growth in the American states. *Economic Development Quarterly 2* February, 78–87.
Kendrick, J. W. (1961). *Productivity trends in the United States.* Princeton, NJ: Princeton University Press.
Maddison, A. (1987). Growth and slowdown in advanced capitalist economies: Techniques of quantitative assessment. *The Journal of Economic Literature 25*(2), 649–698.
Manski, C. F., & Wise, D. A. (1983). *College choice in America.* Cambridge, MA: Harvard University Press.
National Center for Educational Statistics. (1989). *Projections of education statistics to 2000.* Washington, D.C.: U.S. Department of Education Office of Educational Research and Improvement.
Pencavel, J. (1991). The contribution of higher education in economic growth and productivity: A review. *Journal of Economic Education 22* (Fall), 331–359.
Peterson, R. E., & Uhl, N. P. (1977). *Formulating college and university goals: A guide for using the IGI.* Princeton, NJ: Educational Testing Service.
Plaut, T. R., & Pluta, J. E. (1983). Business climate, taxes and expenditures, and

state industrial growth in the U.S. *Southern Economic Journal 50*, July, 99–119.

Schultz, T. W. (1961). Education and economic growth. In N. B. Henry (Ed.), *Social forces influencing American education*. Chicago: University of Chicago Press.

Trivett, D. A. (1973). *Goals for higher education: Definitions and directions*. Washington, D.C.: American Association for Higher Education.

Trow, M. (1979). Aspects of diversity in American higher education. In H. Gans (Ed.), *On the making of Americans: Essays in honor of David Riesman* (pp. 271–290). Philadelphia: University of Pennsylvania Press.

Trow, M. (1988). American higher education: Past, present, and future. *Educational Researcher 17*(3), 13–23.

Wasylenko, M., & McGuire, T. (1985). Jobs and taxes: The effect of business climate on states' employment growth rates. *National Tax Journal 38* December, 497–511.

I THE MISSIONS OF AMERICAN HIGHER EDUCATION

The two chapters of part I introduce the missions and differentiated roles of the 3400 different institutions in American higher education. Common ground is found in the popular image of undergraduate teaching. This image and its institutional reality is examined in chapter 2. Focusing on the research and service missions of higher education, chapter 3 addresses the role of higher education in the creation and transfer of knowledge to others outside the institution and specifically reviews the unique externalities of university research.

The two chapters of part I explore the meaning and [illegible] roles of the 3,400 different institutions in American higher education. [illegible] graduate is found in the [illegible] undergraduate education. This [illegible] chapter 2 focusing on the [illegible] and [illegible] higher education, chapter 3 addresses the role of graduate education and the [illegible] and specifically reviews the unique externalities of university research.

2 THE TEACHING ROLE OF CONTEMPORARY AMERICAN HIGHER EDUCATION: POPULAR IMAGERY AND ORGANIZATIONAL REALITY

James C. Hearn

A paradox is emerging in American higher education. On one hand, the popular image of colleges and universities portrays those institutions as engaged primarily in teaching the skills necessary for social and economic advancement in our society. That image has always been the cornerstone of popular support of American higher education, and it shows no sign of abating. Indeed, the nation's disadvantaged and minority populations, as well as its huge middle class, increasingly view a college education as the pathway to individual development, opportunity, and prosperity.[1] On the other hand, however, the evolving organizational reality of contemporary higher education may be compromising the traditional primacy of the teaching function. A variety of contemporary analysts suggest that such factors as economic constraints and competition for prestige are subverting the purposes of higher education as articulated in the popular image.[2] Therein lies the paradox: How can the widely held image of American colleges as places of student engagement and opportunity be reconciled with the reported reality of organizational life in those institutions?

To address this paradox we first should examine its factual underpinnings. One might hope to find the popular image true and the reported organizational reality false. From that perspective one would hope that the descendants of Mr. Chips are, in fact, not only alive but also flourishing and in control on the modern American campus, producing the competencies that individual students and society value and expect. There are indeed some indirect signs of support for this view. Evidence reviewed in other chapters in this volume suggests that college effects on individual and societal advancement do exist and are in predictably positive directions. Thus colleges are indeed providing enhanced opportunities for those who attend. Unfortunately, however, there is too much ambiguity regarding the actual role of teaching in these outcomes to allow us to accept the full popular image. This chapter asserts that high-quality teaching is clearly not a high priority on all of our campuses and therefore that the popular image of colleges as places dedicated to teaching undergraduates the skills necessary for social and economic opportunity is only partly true. Specifically, colleges may be falling short in their role as teachers but succeeding in their role as providers of opportunity.

This chapter develops and defends the argument that public perceptions of college teaching do not adequately portray the nature of undergraduate education in today's postsecondary institutions. Tempting though it may be, it is beyond the chapter's scope to investigate fully how it might be that the new and less educationally salutary organizational reality can still lead to the popularly expected outcomes.[3] Instead, the investigation here focuses on the components of the paradox, in turn and in some detail. The chapter begins by examining the origins and nature of popular imagery of higher education as teacher and provider of opportunity and then examines what is known about the realities of higher education organization. Discussion then portrays the difficulties institutions face in negotiating the conflict between imagery and reality. The chapter closes with a discussion of the implications of this analysis for research and organizational change.[4]

Popular Imagery of U.S. Higher Education—A Historical View

One may argue that the popular faith in higher education stems from a blend of meritocratic and egalitarian impulses in American life. The meritocratic impulse in higher education imagery has its roots in the philosophy of Thomas Jefferson (Brubacher and Rudy 1976). From this viewpoint college can be an avenue to productive citizenship, economic security, and higher social status for the very able from all social classes. Jefferson led two colleges in his life, the College of William and Mary and the University of Virginia, and he favored admitting to those schools the most talented students in his state, including some from the lower classes. In this way Jefferson hoped to create a true "aristocracy of intellect." In its time this Enlightenment-based view was something of a radical position. In all of his writings, however, Jefferson never envisioned a higher education system that was to serve more than a small number of Americans from any social class.

The egalitarian impulse in higher education imagery has its roots in the homespun philosophy of another early U.S. president, Andrew Jackson. Popular Jacksonian faith in education focused on its assumed capacity to reduce invidious class distinctions in the American social and economic system. From this viewpoint, one should distrust an elitist higher education based solely on either ability or social class, and one should also distrust established authority as gatekeepers (or definers of who is "able"). Instead, the doors of power should be opened to the masses, the nonelites. Jackson's views fit those of an emerging class of ambitious, independent strivers in the America of his era. At times, Jackson almost mocked the entrenched elites of the society and their claim on educational and occupational privilege.[5]

Both of these philosophical strands share a core concern with equity. Both directly or indirectly touch on college education as the passkey to the American dream. For example, Jacksonian democratic views were instrumental in the late nineteenth-century's Morrill Land Grant Acts, which broadened American colleges' clientele and educational missions and expanded the nation's supply of colleges. Both views continue to be influential well into the twentieth century. For example, it is no exaggeration to see Jacksonian thinking as influencing the founding of community colleges, or to see both Jacksonian and Jeffersonian thinking behind the explosive growth of federal and state student aid funding in the 1960s and early 1970s. Of course, support of both views ebbs and flows in the tides of public opinion.[6] But cyclical patterns such as these do not reflect variation in the belief in college attendance as a source of opportunity as much as they represent different views on the specific approach needed to attain that goal. The common logical appeal of the two views has fueled public support of the values of college attendance, encouraged growing government funding for college attendance, and spurred the growth of college attendance.

The conception of college-based learning as the great equalizer, and college teaching as the initiator of that learning, has come to have special relevance in the last one hundred years, as college attendance has become increasingly common and viewed as important. The late nineteenth century and the early twentieth century brought particular attention to the populist aspects of the vision of higher education as the great provider of opportunity. The wealthy founders of such institutions as Stanford and Cornell, noting the restrictive nature of higher education at the time, took special care to open their institutions to more diverse populations pursuing wider ranges of courses, as did Iowa and California in building their states' flagship institutions (Brubacher and Rudy 1976). The Wisconsin progressives made the provision of educational opportunity a major theme (Brubacher and Rudy 1976).

Universities, in particular, were increasingly seen at the turn of the century as the vehicles for the spread of knowledge and opportunity throughout the American population. Historian Laurence Veysey (1965) notes that, by 1910, the American university was essentially open to all those of northern European descent: "At this time, ... families who had begun to improve their circumstances were keenly interested in the tokens of reward which the established forms of opportunity ... provided. For its students, vicariously for their parents, and even for many of its faculty, the university offered a fairly easy means of 'advancement'" (1965, p. 440). Summarizing his investigation of the origins of the university sector, Veysey notes inherently democratic themes: equality of all fields, access to higher education, the institution as an agency for individual success, the diffusion of knowledge through society, and the input of common people into university activity. For the purposes of this chapter, it is most noteworthy that these popular ideals and images focused primarily on instruction, secondarily on service, and only lastly on research as a priority.

These dominant themes in the popular imagery of higher education continued into the middle years of this century and found further nurturance in the rhetoric of the 1950s, 1960s, and 1970s. In those years of growing social and political concern, it became increasingly clear that popular faith in the benefits of attending college rested most directly on college education's assumed benefits for students, but also, more indirectly, on the assumed efficiency and equity benefits for society. Extending college education to all who desired it was viewed as the key tactic in decreasing society's painfully obvious inequalities. In this spirit, Lyndon Johnson repeatedly argued for increased funding for college student aid on the grounds that "the answer for all our national problems, the answer for all the problems of the world, comes down, when you really analyze it, to one single word—education" (Gladieux and Wolanin 1976, p. 17). Later, these same themes found voice in the much-acclaimed reports on the state of the postsecondary enterprise by the Carnegie Commission on Higher Education.[7]

Now, as we enter the final years of the century, the general public's support of higher education attendance as a pathway to learning and opportunity seems largely unabated. Yankelovich (1987), for example, suggests that a growing majority of the public believe obtaining a college education is "very important," and Gallup (1985) reports that the percentage of adults believing that such education is "very" or "fairly" important rose to over 90 percent in the 1980s. According to the latter source, the percentage believing college education was "not too important" was only 7 percent. Not surprisingly, Elam (1983) notes that a belief in college education's importance is especially strong among those who have children in school. Importantly, faith in college education seems especially strong among those who come from disadvantaged or minority backgrounds. One national survey revealed that "lower-income [and] nonwhite ... respondents were more likely to view a college education as very important compared to others in [the] survey" (Dearman and Plisko 1979, p. 5). In summary, it seems that the general public, and especially the disadvantaged and minorities, place deep and abiding faith in both the experience and the longer-term value of a college education.[8]

Clearly, individual and societal faith in the benefits of college education accounts in large part for legislative, alumni, and charitable support of American higher education (see Hines 1988), as well as for the extraordinary willingness of ordinary Americans from a variety of backgrounds to sacrifice and save to provide sufficient funds for college attendance (e.g., see Miller 1985). Just as clearly, it is the instructional function of higher education, not the research and service functions, that most endears higher education to the public. There is no evidence that the public believes the benefits of college are independent of what is taught and learned there.

The Realities of Higher Education Organization

How is the ongoing faith of the American public in the nature and value of college attendance reflected, or not reflected, in the reality of institutional organization? To what extent are public ideals met through the delivery of a quality undergraduate educational product? The next section contrasts popular images regarding undergraduate education with organizational realities in American higher education, as depicted by a variety of organizational insiders and organizational theorists. On the basis of this review, it is argued that certain organizational realities thwart the education of virtually all U.S. undergraduates.[9] Prior to that discussion, however, it is important to acknowledge that the roots of this contemporary reality lie deep in the history of American higher education.

Historical Roots of the Current Organizational Reality

Many scholars (see especially Veysey 1965; Brubacher and Rudy 1976; Clark 1983) have chronicled the historical beginnings of the deemphasis of teaching and neglect of undergraduate education on campus. Initially, and to the present day, the primary cause of this trend has been the acceptance and encouragement of research as an alternative use of the professor's time. Nisbet (1967, p. 22) suggests that, in the nineteenth century, teaching was the academic's "first moral obligation, if not love, the invariable and unyielding pivot of one's contractual relation to the university and one's membership in the academic community." In the late 1800s, however, a number of American faculty members began to venture to Germany for graduate study. Because many of these faculty came back to their positions enamored of the German university ideal of research and graduate education, and because many of them had positions at the most influential universities in America, variations of the German model soon took firm root in the United States. High status was accorded those professors who had earned the doctoral degree and begun a program of research. Their research was necessarily specialized, so it tended to polarize formerly cohesive faculty communities. Faculty came to see themselves as members of distinct, discipline-based communities of scholars and reduced their participation in the common pursuits of the campus.

The initial intrusion of research into the ivied sanctum did not immediately end the dominance of professors' orientation to teaching, because research at that time "was small in scope, personal in character, finite in aspiration, and ... optional" (Nisbet 1967, p. 22). Not surprisingly, though, the basic organizational form of the postsecondary enterprise gradually adapted to fit the developing research ethos. For example, as Ben-David (1972) notes, the rise of the elective system and majors in undergraduate education was largely due to their fit with the emerging research orientation in higher education. Yes, undergraduate specialties gave students greater freedom to choose their academic subjects, but those specialties also supported and facilitated the development of the organizational forms required by the emerging realities of higher education: relatively autonomous departments and graduate schools. Kerr (1972, pp. 14–15) stresses the irony in all this:

> The elective system . . . came more to serve the professors than the students for whom it was first intended, for it meant that the curriculum was no longer controlled by educational policy. . . . [F]reedom for the student to choose became freedom for the professor to invent. . . . The modern university was born.

The emerging research imperative, and the development of departments and graduate schools, were fueled by more than philosophical devotion from certain worldly faculty members. Financial support for research, in the form of government grants and contracts with a variety of commercial enterprises, began in earnest around the turn of the century. Geiger (1986) suggests that this support began to divert colleges and universities from undergraduate teaching, which was traditionally their most important calling.[10] Departments, like graduate schools, were designed primarily to serve research. Fortunately, the department could also be employed as a less than optimal, but marginally acceptable, vehicle for delivering undergraduate education. As a consequence, faculty and administrators alike became attached to the academic department as the appropriate form for organizing all education in American universities. Eventually, the academic department's legitimation of, and emphasis on, research specialization made reduced teaching loads not only acceptable as a professorial goal but indeed a demarcator of status on campus (see Arrowsmith 1967). In this fashion, research specialization and faculty atomization led, perhaps inevitably, to a deemphasis of undergraduate education.

A number of anecdotes are told about the new fascination of American faculty with research. Veysey (1965, pp. 142–143) recounts the tale of a professor at Columbia in the late 1800s who had to decide between using five minutes to compute another coefficient of correlation or using the time to prepare for class—he computed the correlation. Similarly, the early twentieth-century educational theorist and philosopher Alfred North Whitehead was startled, on his arrival on the Harvard campus, by the novel attitude of his new faculty colleagues, who suggested, "Don't let the students interfere with your work! Ten or fifteen minutes is long enough for any conference with them."[11] Finally, Geiger (1985, p. 83) cites an anecdote about Henry A. Rowland, a late nineteenth-century physicist at Johns Hopkins: When asked what he intended to do with the students in his laboratory, Rowland sputtered with irritation, "Do with them? Do with them? . . . I shall neglect them!" Geiger emphasizes, quite correctly, that such stories are misleading as gross generalizations about universities, then or now. Still, as Geiger himself notes, the stories are evocative and resonate familiarly with many who work in higher education.

By the early 1900s research had clearly come to play a greater role, and teaching a lesser role, in the activities of universities.[12]

The nature of the balance between teaching and research, or between undergraduate and graduate education, continued to change in the years after World War II. Burton Clark discerns that teaching, once the primary activity of higher education, drifted after the end of the war toward the margins of both reward systems and interest; why else, Clark asks, would major universities "year in and year out send away brilliant young teachers rather than give them tenure?"[13] Ben-David (1972) notes economic reasons for this pattern: "Research, rather than being an overhead on teaching, became, in the most important universities, a main source of the finances of the university. The support of research at the universities became independent from teaching. And, while the rewards for research [grew] immensely, those for teaching remained stationary" (p. 88). These postwar changes in incentives were paralleled by the increasingly professionalized identities of many disciplines, both old and new. As Nisbet (1967) has observed, the years after World War II brought a shift in the ways faculty tended to think of themselves: One was no longer, for example, a faculty member who is incidentally a sociologist, but rather a sociologist who is incidentally a faculty member. Thus the rewards for research relative to teaching increased dramatically in the postwar years, and the typical professor's professional identity shifted from being primarily a member of a teaching faculty to being primarily a member of a research-oriented discipline. In concert with these trends, teaching loads began to decrease (see James 1990).

Beyond the emerging imperative for faculty to conduct research, the financial constraints of the last twenty years have added to institutions' difficulties in offering high-quality undergraduate education. Faculty's academic-year salaries have, on average, deteriorated somewhat since 1970, and recruitment into graduate programs and faculty positions has become more difficult (Bowen and Schuster 1986; Carnegie Foundation for the Advancement of Teaching 1989). It is not hard to imagine the organizational implications, in terms of loyalty and commitment to teaching responsibilities, such historical changes may entail.

"Insider" Perspectives on Contemporary Undergraduate Education

There are several ways to discern the conflicts inherent in the contemporary place of undergraduate education in today's universities and colleges.

Among the most valuable may be "insider" reports on the dilemmas of undergraduate life: reports in the professional press, policy-oriented studies of undergraduate education, fictional accounts by informed graduates and academics, and critical essays by academics. The following sections investigates the extent to which these sources suggest that the place of teaching, and undergraduate education in general, is threatened in American colleges and universities.

Media Covering Higher Education. First, consider the state of undergraduate education as portrayed in the media covering higher education. Often such sources as the *New York Times*, *Change Magazine*, and the *Chronicle of Higher Education* report on the conflicts inherent in contemporary academic life. For example, a report on two state legislatures' efforts to improve faculty attentiveness to undergraduate education appeared in the *Chronicle* of February 1, 1989 (see "The Work Schedules . . ."). One item in that column detailed an incident (this time in Alabama) of a perennial controversy in America's public higher education institutions—legislators' concerns about "slack" faculty work behaviors. The second item reported on an initiative by Texas legislators to provide financial rewards to state institutions whose tenured faculty regularly teach freshman and sophomore courses. It seems that the incentive system in those institutions was working to discourage senior faculty from taking substantial responsibility for undergraduate education.

Another issue of the same periodical reported on a dramatic refusal of a faculty honor ("'In' Box", May 10, 1989). Calvin B. Peters, a faculty member at the University of Rhode Island, turned down a university teaching award to "teach the university a lesson," arguing that publicly refusing the award would do more to promote the importance of good teaching than would accepting it. Several recent recipients of the award, he said, had been denied promotions, and although the award claimed to reward good teaching, it "doesn't reward it in any way. . . . Many of us believe that teaching is the practice of scholarship just as research is, and that the university needs to develop a less myopic view" (p. A11).

The question of the role of teaching in research universities received prominent treatment in an article by Lee Daniels in the *New York Times* of May 10, 1989. That article, based on interviews with a variety of university leaders, argues that top universities are having trouble sustaining both advanced research and strong undergraduate liberal arts programs. University authorities reported to Daniels that the tensions between research and teaching had sharpened in the 1980s, due to increasing parental and student resistance to large tuition increases, reductions in federal and state aid, restrictive corporate donations, and the growing expense of scholarly pursuits. Harold T. Shapiro, president of Princeton, remarked to Daniels that many faculty members "suggest that undergraduate teaching 'gets in the way' of frontline and increasingly complex research ... [and other faculty members] argue that blockbuster grants for research centers ... siphon internal funds away from teaching" (p. 23). In a similar tone, Evelyn Handler, president of Brandeis University, commented to Daniels that private institutions must sustain advanced research programs to attract the top faculty members, who are the best teachers of undergraduates: "How to finance these two expensive but vital commitments is the great dilemma. We do it with difficulty and under pressure." Handler concluded by noting that advanced scientific research, precisely because of its increasing expense and difficulty, might be leading the faculty further from interest in, or time for, undergraduates.

Sometimes, the media delve below familiar public images to consider conflicts associated with those images. For example, the popular press frequently presents college towns such as Bloomington, Princeton, and Charlottesville as simply places to visit for their beauty and charm. Describing such towns, *USA Today* (see "Campus Towns ...", 1989) was lyrical, "Listen carefully: You can almost hear the echoes of past glory and the footsteps of a new generation coming of age" (p. 7E). More informed and aggressive reporters may see the campus site as something of a battleground, however (see, for example, "Jefferson, Sadly for Monticello ...", a 1990 *Wall Street Journal* article about a fight between the University of Virginia and the residents of Charlottesville). A vigorous fight between town and gown, and image and reality, can be fueled by campus planners willing to sacrifice historical appeal to pursue revenues generated by the development of new buildings, modernized classrooms and labs, science centers, research parks, and the like.

Policy-Oriented Studies of Undergraduate Education. These media accounts of problems in undergraduate education are paralleled by a second source, policy-oriented studies of undergraduate education produced by higher education institutions, systems, associations, and task forces. Often, institutions and systems undertake efforts to address the organizational constraints on teaching themselves. Any number of reports on these efforts could be cited here as evidence for the view that undergraduate teaching is not highly valued. One report, a study for the Arizona Board of Regents by Davis (1988), seems especially thorough, however. Davis observes that both students and alumni tend to be frustrated by the constraints on teaching in research universities. He concludes:

> There comes a point where the research emphasis becomes so dominant that it obstructs the possibility of responsible, responsive instruction. ... What are the signs?: Too many absences at professional meetings; unavailability outside of the classroom; unpreparedness for lecture; the lack of extra effort that is revealed in old, tired examples instead of new lively contemporary illustrations; overspecialized content in comparison to what the course has advertised; very small teaching load semester after semester; and certain attitudinal characteristics, some none too subtle, such as direct statements in class saying "I don't really like to teach." [Pp. 853–854]

Davis notes these problems are all too present. His conclusions for Arizona are not unusual. Other states' policy analyses of undergraduate education report parallel conclusions. Similar themes were stressed by a recent foundation-supported panel of educational experts and leaders. That panel argued that higher education institutions must acknowledge "explicitly and forcefully" that teaching and learning are their chief occupation, that institutions must support steps to improve instruction on their campuses, and that "too seldom is collegiate teaching viewed for what it is: the business of the business—the activity that is central to all colleges and universities" (see Watkins 1989, p. A13).

Fictional Accounts. A third source, fictional accounts of undergraduate education, can also provide revealing details of the organizational tensions surrounding undergraduate education. Thelin and Townsend (1988), after studying a large sample of novels about undergraduate life, present a provocative discussion of the merits of using fictional sources to gain insight into empirical realities of that life. With all the appropriate caveats, and they are numerous, this author agrees that the use of such sources can be a significant aid to understanding the realities of contemporary higher education. Their ambitious effort reveals two consistent themes, both portraying undergraduate education in a less than favorable light, relevant to the current chapter. First, college classes are seen as largely irrelevant to real learning—such classes tend to be taught by pedantic, unworldly, or research-driven professors, and real learning takes place in extracurricular activities. Second, colleges are seen as preserves for the offspring of the rich—bright but poor youth always seem a little out of place.[14] Thelin and Townsend report that two popular images of college life only rarely appear in fictional accounts by college insiders: the image of faculty as beloved, talented, concerned mentors, and the image of college life as a time of engagement and opportunity for the poor.

A variety of acclaimed recent novels by college faculty members pay particular attention to the problems of academic life as it turns increasingly to research. In Alison Lurie's *Imaginary Friends* (1967), a group of faculty social scientists become extraordinarily embroiled in their "participant–observer" research on a cult. Their teaching, and other aspects of their professional and personal lives, begins to deteriorate. In DeLillo's *White Noise* (1985), a faculty member at a small, liberal arts college wins promotions and international renown by founding a pioneering "Department of Hitler Studies" and a parallel scholarly journal; his teaching goes largely unmentioned (see also Lodge 1989).

The fiction of Amanda Cross is of special interest on two counts. First, it explores the challenges of teaching undergraduates in greater detail than many other fictional sources. Second, the novelist's own background is relevant to the organizational realities discussed in this chapter. One of her novels, *Poetic Justice* (1972), is centered on a desperate battle for survival by an open admissions, teaching-oriented college clinging precariously to organizational life within a research-oriented university. The bitterness surrounding this controversy leads to the murder of a dean. The Cross novels are also of interest because of the author's identity. Cross is actually Columbia University English professor Carolyn Heilbrun. Heilbrun embarked on what she terms "a double life" in 1964, writing mysteries under the Cross pseudonym while writing scholarly pieces under her real name. Why? She feared that writing mysteries under her real name would reveal her "frivolous" crossover career and thus harm her chances of being viewed as a serious scholar and winning promotion and tenure in the research-dominated environment of Columbia. Subsequently, both her novels and her serious scholarship have won international awards and recognition (see "The Real Life . . .", April 10, 1989).

The Critical Essay. A fourth and final source of "insider" intelligence on the current state of teaching in academe is the critical essay, the most well known of which is *The Closing of the American Mind* (1987) by Professor Allan Bloom of the University of Chicago. Bloom states the case for an ineffective contemporary climate for undergraduate teaching in bald terms: "Those great universities—which can split the atom, find cures for the most terrible diseases, conduct surveys of whole populations and produce massive dictionaries of lost languages—cannot generate a modest program of general education for undergraduate students" (p. 340). Although such a polemic is exaggerated in many respects, as Sovern (1989) notes in his own argumentative essay, its congruence with the other sources presented here suggests that it contains at least a grain of truth.

Similar themes are raised in the critical essays of Sykes (1988) and

Smith (1989). These two books, by the journalist son of a veteran professor and by the former president of the University of California at Santa Cruz, respectively, have received widespread attention. Both, in essence, carry forth an agenda of debunking popular views of professors and academic institutions, both rely on a variety of insider reports, and both take on the tone of exposés.[15] Sykes is particularly taken by the contrasts between popular images and realities:

> Most parents, legislators, and perhaps even college trustees still have a mental picture of a university mainly as a place where young people go to be educated. The very phrase "higher education" encourages such speculation. Professors are still called college "teachers," as if their primary mission were the nurturing of young minds and the passing on of the accumulated wisdom of the academy to their students. And even though spending for instruction is less than one-third of university budgets . . . , the average American persists in thinking that the classroom is the center of activity of a university. . . . Because it makes for good relations with the public (as well as with the legislature), university administrators encourage such fanciful notions. But among themselves, they know how anachronistic and downright inaccurate they are. [P. 29]

Smith (1989) takes a slightly more scholarly approach than Sykes and has the advantage of many years as a professor and administrator within the system. Still, he reaches similar conclusions:

> [T]he so-called elite universities . . . set the tone and . . . poison the springs of academic life in the United States. . . . In many universities, faculty members make no bones about the fact that students are the enemy. It is students who threaten to take up precious time that might otherwise be devoted to research. I have heard colleagues boast of having infrequent office hours at awkward times to avoid contact with students outside the classroom; these same professors discharge their formal teaching obligations as cheaply and expediently as they can, usually by reading ancient notes to large classes of passive students two or three times a week, with "sections," if there are any, conducted by dedicated but inexperienced graduate assistants who also read and grade the students' papers and examinations. [Pp. 2, 6]

Thus, critical essays join the professional media, formal policy analyses, and academic novels in repeating the theme that a variety of constraints hamper undergraduate education, particularly in its formal aspects. The various sources reviewed here provide insight on the dilemmas posed by current organizational realities in higher education. Often noted are the strong pressures on faculty to accomplish more with fewer human or material resources, as well as the incentives given faculty to engage in noninstructional activities. Each of these sources draws troubling implications for the resulting quality of undergraduate education.

An Organizational Analysis of Undergraduate Education

Reports from organizational insiders, as just reviewed, tend to contradict popular imagery of the university as an organization in which undergraduate education is well supported and enduringly primary. Clearly, contrary images can exist somewhat independently of the organizational reality of contemporary undergraduate education. As Alpert (1985) has noted, however, far too little scholarly attention has been directed to the organizational mechanisms behind the ongoing problems of undergraduate education. This section employs organizational theory to explore more systematically institutional "reality": the postsecondary institution as a formal, complex organization. Discussion first focuses on the generality of the problem, then on the substantial organizational constraints on undergraduate education.

The Generality of the Problem. It would, of course, be fallacious to suggest that there is uniformity in undergraduate education in this country.[16] The most distinctive quality of U.S. higher education is its diversity (Ben-David 1972; Clark 1983), and good colleges for undergraduate education do exist. In particular, small, residential, teaching-oriented, single-sex, geographically isolated, selective liberal arts colleges offer, on average, quite favorable contexts for undergraduate education. The work of Feldman and Newcomb (1969), Astin (1977), and others suggests that attending such schools can have demonstrably positive effects on intellectual, social, and personal development. On those campuses, traditionally oriented to providing the best students with the best teachers and best material resources, current conditions for undergraduate education seem clearly favorable.

Unfortunately, only a small (and decreasing) minority of college students attend such institutions (U.S. Department of Education 1989). Instead, increasing numbers of students are attending large, research-oriented or service-oriented institutions, many of which serve commuters. Of all these other kinds of schools, organizational realities would seem most constraining of undergraduate education at the research universities. It was in those institutions that the increasingly pervasive dilemmas concerning the relative importance of research, service, and teaching first appeared earlier in this century. Not surprisingly, a national study by Baldridge and co-workers (1978) found dramatic differences (on the order of 2 to 1) between "quality" liberal arts colleges and research universities in (1) the time faculty spent on undergraduate teaching, (2) the proportional extent to which undergraduate teaching contributed to faculty's institutional rewards, and (3) the proportional extent to which faculty wished to have undergraduate teaching contribute to their institutional rewards (also see Dornbusch 1979; Hind, Dornbusch, and Scott 1974). More recently, analysts and administrators report that overcommitments made in the drive for increased prestige have brought educationally debilitating deficits to the elite private research universities (Daniels 1989). Clearly, the research university is the site of perhaps the most difficult conflicts between popular ideals and organizational realities.

Nevertheless, a variety of authors have suggested that sectors other than the research universities also deliver less than ideal undergraduate education for their students. For example, the Holmes Group (1986), a consortium oriented to improving the education of future teachers, found in its analyses that undergraduate education for education majors and other students is as full of bad teaching as American high schools. In the nonselective liberal arts colleges and the comprehensive private institutions, enrollment pressures driven by changing demographics and changing student curricular demands, coupled with the financial demands associated with maintaining up-to-date physical plants and competitive faculty salaries, have made for trying times and worries over the educational product as well as institutional viability (Schaw 1989; Pfnister 1985; Hearn 1988). At virtually all publicly supported institutions—including community colleges, four-year colleges, some land-grant institutions, and public research universities—financial pressures from weakened public funding, inflation, changing student demand, and unexpectedly high enrollments have created strains on the faculty's ability to attend closely to the quality of undergraduate instruction (Birnbaum 1985; Cohen 1985; Geiger 1985; Hines 1988). Finances are strained to the point that facilities have become antiquated and teacher salaries have lagged far behind inflation, or behind what seems educationally optimal (NIE 1984). Finally, the difficulties for undergraduate education in nonelite colleges also may include a growing emphasis on research. An apparently growing number of those schools are emulating the higher-prestige research institutions by downplaying the teaching function and providing new incentives for faculty research and service.[17]

The overall dilemma is reflected in the results of a recent Carnegie Foundation survey (1989) of a representative sample of all U.S. college faculty; in that survey 56 percent of full-time faculty rated their campuses' intellectual environment as "fair" or "poor" and two-thirds rated the sense of community on their campuses as "fair" or "poor." It seems fair to conclude, in concurrence with the well-known "Involvement in Learning" report of the National Institute of Education (1984), that a majority of

American college students are getting something other than a high-quality undergraduate education. Conditions on the campuses attended by most students tend to dictate that the delivery of high-quality undergraduate teaching is not always a high priority, or even a strong possibility.

Three Organizational Constraints on Undergraduate Education. To understand better the depth and persistence of the problem of inadequate undergraduate education, one should address those organizational factors that deflect and discourage attention to this facet of institutional operations. It would seem that at least three such factors constrain institutions in their delivery of quality undergraduate education: (1) the poorly understood "technology" of undergraduate education, including the difficulties of measuring teaching quality; (2) the existence of multiple resource dependencies, including an imperfect student enrollment market; and (3) the existence of countervailing incentives deterring faculty from attention to undergraduate education. Each will be discussed in turn.

Poorly Understood Technology. The first constraint is that the technology of undergraduate education is poorly understood (see Cohen and March 1974; Weick 1976; Baldridge et al. 1978). Who, after all, knows how to define the educated man or woman, much less how to specify the exact ingredients and processes necessary for shaping such a person? Are smaller classes always better? Is the lecture method the optimal classroom approach? How much faculty-student interaction is ideal? How are scarce funds best spent in undergraduate education? Under such conditions the provision of high-quality undergraduate education is highly problematic. Ambiguity is omnipresent.

That ambiguity is most constraining to assessment of quality in undergraduate education. The conclusion of the late Allan Cartter in 1967 still stands: There exist no truly effective and efficient measures for assessing the relative quality of undergraduate teaching. Measuring and rewarding faculty's performance in teaching is simply less straightforward than measuring and rewarding their performance in research. In the latter, reviews of quality tend to be consistent and accurate (Becker 1979*a*, 1979*b*; Tuckman 1976, 1979). In contrast, the difficulties of statistically defining and measuring teaching quality are great: Student reviews of teaching tend to be distrusted, peer reviews of teaching tend to be incomplete, and faculty members interact indeterminantly with students to produce teaching quality (see Doyle 1979; Feldman 1987; Hopkins 1990; James 1990). In such a context ascertaining teaching success is difficult and efforts to improve undergraduate education are hindered. Of course, a sizably increased investment in measuring teaching quality would have benefits in improved accuracy and consistency, but the funds for that investment are difficult to find in the current climate.

Multiple Resource Dependencies. A second organizational constraint to undergraduate education is the multiple resource dependencies that most colleges and universities face. In other words, undergraduate education is not their only business, and for many institutions it is not even their primary business. Under such conditions attention to undergraduate educational quality suffers. Resource dependency theory, as elaborated by Pfeffer and Salancik (1978) and others, suggests that organizations will attend most closely to protecting their primary sources of business, that is, their primary resource dependencies. Postsecondary institutions are in this sense economic entities with a wide variety of resource dependencies (trade arrangements) with other, external entities. These dependencies can involve not only state agencies and legislatures but also federal research agencies, federal student aid agencies, other colleges, professional organizations, corporations, foundations, accrediting agencies, students, donors, general publics, and so forth.

Obviously, for institutions with a heavy component of research or service business, students and the quality of their education are not the sole concern. As early as 1964 Kerr (1972) noted that grants from outside research-funding agencies were shifting universities' attention from undergraduate to graduate education. In more recent research Pfeffer and Salancik (1974) and Pfeffer and Moore (1980) found such grants increasingly critical to a department's influence in overall university funding flows. Louis (1989, p. 14) has observed that funding agencies can thereby exert an indirect influence over departmental expansion and thus over undergraduate education. They do so, however, in a largely unplanned way of undetermined consequences for that education. What is more, to the extent that slack resources are devoted to protecting and increasing an institution's research or service activities, those slack resources are not spent on undergraduate education. The latter will tend to suffer.[18]

That is not to say that the resources derived from undergraduate education are unimportant. Undergraduate course taking is a critical source of funds for virtually all institutions, even for those with heavy research funding. Indeed, undergraduate enrollment often subsidizes losses from graduate education (James 1978). Historical evidence suggests that grouping undergraduate education with graduate work and research makes good sense, in that undergraduates are valuable consumers for the excess instructional capacity on research-oriented campuses (Ben-David 1972,

p. 45). Recent work by Cohn, Rhine, and Santos (1989) tends to confirm that conclusion. They derive equations for costs incurred by higher education institutions, considering separate and interactive effects of three factors: undergraduate enrollments, graduate enrollments, and research. Their results suggest that institutions that specialize in one of the outputs appear to experience higher costs; the authors conclude that, on the whole, the three outputs are complementary. Thus undergraduate education enrollments undeniably comprise an important resource dependency.

Nevertheless, in the perspective of organizational theory, it is more the quantity than the quality of undergraduate education delivered that is involved in the resource dependency. As Coleman (1973) and Meyer (1977) note, attention to undergraduate education will tend to take the form of enrollment maintenance and efficient "processing," rather than aggressive internal quality assurance. The reason, in the vernacular, is that the undergraduate education wheel rarely squeaks. Universities, in particular, face imposing outside inspection and control in their research and service enterprises but relatively little such attention in their undergraduate educational offerings. In essence, faculty are expected to meet certain minimal responsibilities in the classroom but are free to pursue other, potentially more rewarding activities once that constraint is met (James and Neuberger 1981; also see Levin 1989).

The seeming weakness of the resource dependency created by undergraduate education therefore comes down to a problem of imperfection in the student enrollment market. Teaching is the most publicly manifest role of colleges and universities, in that it generally has more "constituents" than either the research or service roles. Most parents, students, and alumni attend more closely to an institution's efforts in undergraduate education than to its performance in other organizational roles. One might therefore imagine that marketplace pressures would ensure quality undergraduate education, that only those with a good educational product would survive. Nevertheless, and despite the high cost of undergraduate education to students and their families, classes proceed largely independently of market-driven assessments of their quality. Even though undergraduate education helps pay the bills and is in fact financially necessary to the operation of many universities, those organizations often are able to, and do, attend much more closely to the quality of their other activities. Colleges and universities are in the position of providing a highly demanded, lucrative product without having to attend closely to its ongoing quality.

How might this be so? Bok (1986) provides some initial understanding of this mystery. He agrees with many other observers that competition is a unique virtue of the American higher education system. Nevertheless, he reasons, competition is based in what can be measured and rewarded, and it therefore produces greater pressures for improving research than for improving teaching:

> In contrast to the problems encountered in evaluating the quality of education, the quality of research is evaluated much more credibly and the rewards for success are much greater and more visible. As a result, competition does not merely fail to stimulate serious effort to improve the effectiveness of educational programs; it may actually divert effort away from teaching toward research, since it is only natural to work hardest at activities that are most widely judged and rewarded. [P. 54]

Institutions thus are able to ignore the quality of undergraduate education in part because it is poorly understood and difficult to measure (the first organizational constraint on undergraduate education).

Bok's explanation, however, may go only part way to explaining the mystery. Colleges and universities have two great sources of support: support based on research and service and support based on enrollment. Foundations and governments support research and service enterprises, and projects funded by such organizations are tightly monitored, creating pressing resource dependencies. In contrast, the funds available for undergraduate education depend primarily on the enrollment marketplace. Because this support is quite substantial, measurement difficulties do not seem sufficient reason for higher education's stakeholders to avoid quality assessment efforts. We are still left with the original question: How are institutions able to ignore the quality of undergraduate education and consider it largely unmonitored by its consumers? The answer may lie in the willingness of student consumers and others to accept a highly questionable proxy measure for academic quality.

Let us explore this point in more detail. Available evidence suggests that undergraduate enrollments are driven not so much by the sale of a provably high-quality educational product as by factors like local employment conditions, price, an institution's location, program offerings, and, most intriguingly, prestige (see Hossler, Braxton, and Coopersmith 1989; Astin 1980). The latter finding is of particular interest. Students may tend to assume that high prestige translates directly into academic quality and so make their institutional choices on the basis of a prestigious reputation rather than on actual evidence regarding educational quality. By relying on prestige as a primary cue for their choices, students may be sacrificing their power as consumers in a competitive marketplace, because prestige seems to be generated primarily by institutional activities other than undergraduate education.

As Ben-David (1972) argues, institutional prestige is driven by history and research, and some schools have it and can charge more, but most only desire it. "If everything else were equal, then lower-cost institutions would be more attractive to students. The fact that some institutions can charge a great deal more than others and still attract students shows how unequal everything else is. ... Colleges with inherited prestige can 'sell' it for high fees and donations, then reinvest the resources in improvements which then generate further prestige" (pp. 38–39).

Because institutions seem to pay particular attention to those activities that generate prestige, it would not be too much of an exaggeration to argue that the resource dependencies to which institutions most closely attend are those that facilitate the pursuit and maintenance of institutional prestige. Students, funders of research, and legislators all are attuned to prestige. Of all the markets in which universities compete (markets for students, faculty, research dollars, and so forth), the market for prestige may be the most fundamental (Clark 1983). In many schools, and especially the research universities, the prestige, faculty, and research funding markets seem to build on each other in a kind of "Matthew effect": The rich get richer while the poor get poorer (see Merton 1968; Trow 1984). Greater prestige attracts more qualified faculty, who in turn attract greater research funding, which then strengthens prestige, and so on.[19]

James (1990) suggests that institutions do not reward quality of teaching because it is not a source of prestige:

> Research produces wide visibility while teaching is appreciated locally, at best. In addition, the ability to produce publishable research is a scarcer skill than the ability to teach, hence it is more highly rewarded, both in dollars and in prestige. ... In a society where half the secondary school graduates go on to higher education, there must be many acceptable professors. ... Moreover, research grants increase the institution's resources while there are no equivalent external teaching-quality grants. (Teaching quantity, on the other hand, is highly rewarded in the form of tuition fees or the equivalent from state legislatures.) [Pp. 84–85]

One might argue, therefore, that because it is mainly a function of factors other than educational quality, institutions' pursuit of prestige is a critical factor in the downgrading of the education function. Coleman (1973), for example, suggests that undergraduate education in universities is "to a great extent ... deprived of the discipline a market imposes; insofar as its graduates are in a job market, the quality of its product depends largely on the quality of its student input, which in turn depends largely on the university's reputation" (pp. 364–365). Coleman ignores the evidence that location and program also affect choices, but both are matters of noncompetitive markets as well. In effect, consumers can be rendered choiceless (held captive) by an institution's uniquely accessible location or targeted course offerings, or they can be attracted by an institution's prestige, a quality generated largely by its other, noneducational activities.

It should be noted that some authors have suggested that the pursuit of prestige is actually, in the long run, functional for improving undergraduate education. For example, Ben-David (1972) suggests that, because early public institutions could not buy prestige, they relied on service to "build up a 'capital' of prestige through their services" (p. 43). They did so by accepting poorly qualified students and responding to demands of local groups. "Their earliest successes in improving their bargaining power came through their professional schools and services in engineering, agriculture, and education. The superiority of training and research based on sound science and scholarship soon became evident in these fields. As a result, lay interference abated, and support became more regular" (p. 43). Thus prestige maximization can lead indirectly to benefits for undergraduate education over the longer term.[20] Allan Cartter (1967) pursued similar logic:

> In the absence of any technique for assessing the relative quality of undergraduate teaching, I would suggest the uncomfortable conclusion that a university which wishes to win national acclaim must do so first in its graduate and professional schools; if it wins a good reputation for Ph.D.'s, it will then attract the kind of undergraduates who will later justify its eminence as an undergraduate institution. As far as external reputation goes, good teaching in a university without an eminent graduate school earns its reward primarily in heaven. [P. 151]

The pursuit of prestige may therefore eventually provide benefits in admitting better qualified undergraduate students. Its benefits for the actual delivery of a solid educational product, however, are dubious.[21]

Countervailing Incentives to Faculty. A third factor limiting attention to undergraduate education is the fact that faculty face multiple, countervailing incentives. Whereas the preceding discussion addressed organization-level factors that direct colleges and universities to issues other than undergraduate education, this section considers similar factors at the individual level—that is, the factors that point faculty members toward attention to activities other than teaching undergraduates. Colleges and universities are, one must remember, not only agencies entrusted by society to carry out certain of its most highly valued activities. They are also workplaces. As such they provide their employees with incentives and disincentives for various kinds of behaviors. The mix of those incentives has been changing in recent years, and the shift has been generally away from incentives for teaching undergraduates often and well (Nisbet 1967).

Acting to counter this trend, many institutions have initiated teaching awards in the past few years. The initiation and presentation of these awards seems to do little to improve the state of teaching, however. Indeed, some institutions have moved to make these awards only to tenured faculty because institutional embarrassment so often ensues when recipients later are forced to leave the institution due to poor research productivity (Smith 1989). Classics scholar William Arrowsmith (1967) draws an interesting analogy regarding these awards: "At present the universities are as uncongenial to teaching as the Mojave Desert to a clutch of Druid priests. If you want to restore a Druid priesthood you cannot do it by offering prizes for Druid-of-the-year. If you want Druids, you must grow forests" (pp. 58–59).

Few such forests have yet been sighted on our university campuses. Numerous studies of faculty salary, promotion, and tenure systems show that research productivity is the prime determinant of individual rewards in universities and that teaching is clearly secondary (see Jencks and Riesman 1968; Katz 1973; Siegfried and White 1973; Tuckman 1976, 1979; Dornbusch 1979; James 1990). One might hope that research and teaching might in fact be complementary rather than zero-sum activities, in that attention to or skill in one might not imply less attention to or skill in the other. The results on this issue are quite mixed.[22] A number of studies have examined the question of how research performance is related to teaching effectiveness in universities and, as Finkelstein (1984), Feldman (1987), and Hopkins (1990) each note, some studies show a positive relationship, others a negative one, and others none at all. In reality, of course, faculty in research institutions simply cannot afford to be weak in research. According to Alpert (1985) the press for research in universities means that untenured faculty must strive to meet the single basic standard of performance in published research and that tenured faculty who do not succeed in that effort are not rewarded for success in other activities such as teaching (also see Bess 1982).

The academic departments and their associated disciplines lie at the organizational heart of the university and are critical to the dilemmas of undergraduate education. Loosely coupled to central administrations, they exist as semi-independent organizations in which most of the dramas of academic life are played out (Clark 1983; Weick 1976). In particular, the academic department is both the traditional setting for proving one's merits in research, teaching, and service and the agency sponsoring the eventual candidacy for tenure, so faculty members need to work hard to ensure they fit well with the cultural norms and values that are dominant therein (Balderston 1990). One might argue that the department is also the heart of the problem of undergraduate education, for it is there primarily that research is promoted, teaching denigrated, and the evaluation of teaching subverted (Arrowsmith 1967). Behind the academic departments lie the disciplines and fields, the seats of the core professional identities of many faculty (Clark 1983). Resistances to improved teaching quality lie at the discipline level as well as the departmental level, because seeking such improvements is not always congruent with the goals of faculty or with their interpretation of their professional role. An example may be telling: In an article on the problems in mathematics education, a professor of mathematics at a state university noted that "our primary responsibility as mathematicians is not to students but to mathematics: to preserve, create, and enhance good mathematics, and to protect the subject for future generations" (Turner 1990, p. A18).

The disincentives for spending much time on teaching are not accidents caused by administrative inattention. Departments, colleges, and institutions conduct their nonteaching activities in highly organized and purposeful ways, recruiting and rewarding their faculty in keeping with the increasingly salient nonteaching goals. The point most clearly applies to research institutions: "The big university does not whip or seduce an unwilling body of teachers into research and publication; it recruits research-minded men, and then rewards them for doing what it hired them to do, thus reinforcing their inclinations toward research" (Trow 1967, p. 168). The point is supported by the findings of a survey of the research-oriented Stanford faculty by Hind, Dornbusch, and Scott (1974; also see Dornbusch 1979). Those faculty members perceived evaluations of their teaching as much less influential in the university's reward system than evaluations of their research. Only 20 percent saw teaching as "very" or "extremely" influential in their rewards, compared to 78 percent for research.

As noted earlier in this chapter, it is not solely the research universities that have been increasingly pointing their faculty toward research. Burton Clark (1987) has discerned a more general tendency across the whole spectrum of institutions, including the ostensibly teaching-oriented campuses: "Most professors teach most of the time, but teaching is not the activity most rewarded by the academic profession" (pp. 98–99). That conclusion was upheld by a recent nationwide faculty survey by the Carnegie Foundation for the Advancement of Teaching (1989). The survey found that, although 71 percent of the faculty respondents said their interests lay primarily in teaching rather than research, a majority said it was difficult to get tenure if one did not publish. At the four-year institutions, 77 percent agreed with that statement. Carnegie Foundation President Ernest Boyer characterized the situation as one in which faculty "often felt trapped in a system where the work load and the reward system were disconnected" (Mooney 1990*a*, p. A16).[23]

Similar conclusions are reached in the analyses of Baldwin and Krotseng (1985), Wagener (1989), and Boyer (1986). Administrators and other leaders nonetheless downplay the average faculty member's views on research and structure reward systems toward research rather than away from it. These leaders seem to do so owing to their beliefs that (1) research is associated with prestige; (2) state governments often push for academic research that will aid economic development; (3) accrediting groups express expectations for research; (4) there is growing competition for federal money for research; and (5) a reputation for research will give them an edge as they compete more intensely for students (Peterson et al. 1986; Mooney 1990*b*). Despite the Carnegie results, it appears that many younger faculty on nonelite campuses willingly accept such efforts to deemphasize teaching in favor of research because it was at elite, research-oriented institutions that they themselves were educated (Dunham 1969; Mooney 1990*b*; Heller 1990).

An apparently growing number of nonelite schools are therefore emulating the higher-prestige research institutions by downplaying the teaching function and providing new incentives for faculty research and service (see Clark 1983, 1987; Trow 1984; Watkins 1989). Virtually all sectors are affected, especially the state universities and the four-year liberal arts colleges. Regarding the former, Burton Clark (quoted in Sykes 1988, pp. 60–61) said in 1985 that there are radical disincentives to teaching in virtually all state universities: "Rare is the material or symbolic reward that does not push or pull the professor toward research and graduate students. Something has to give and that something is the undergraduate program. Someone has to come up on the short-end, and that someone is the freshman-sophomore student." Regarding the small liberal arts colleges, Heller (1990) has noted that a number of such colleges are seeing faculty scholarship as a way to distinguish themselves among relatively similar – and expensive – colleges. Faculty teaching loads have been cut at Grinnell and Wellesley colleges, and similar proposals are being debated elsewhere. In some colleges, outside reviews of research performance are reducing the reward system's traditional weighting of internal reviews of teaching and service (Heller 1990).

What has emerged within institutions is not an outright, visible denigration of the teaching role, however. Instead, there has been an indirect devaluation of that role, via the development and elaboration of a rich set of alternative, organizationally legitimated activities for faculty members. New activities have crowded onto the university agenda, and faculty are now more involved with outside activities as well (Coleman 1973). Because those activities are highly rewarded, teaching has been placed in relatively lower priority. The demands of research contracts, conference presentations, and publications intrude. The status of undergraduate education is reflected in the language of the workplace. Alexander Astin (1980) has noted that it represents a "load" in the faculty vernacular (as in teaching load, advising load, and so on), whereas research is rarely spoken of so disparagingly. Faculty do not often receive direct, meaningful incentives from central administration to improve their teaching. The message they usually receive is that, yes, they must teach an established courseload, but no, their efforts are not best directed to doing so in better and better ways. Instead, they should pursue other activities with greater marginal returns.

To the extent that they can broaden their base of support, especially through obtaining external funding for their research and acquiring the prestige that comes with such funding, faculty can create power bases in the university that can reduce central administrative control, increase individual resources, improve working conditions, and buffer them from having to attend to teaching quality or even teaching quantity (Coleman 1973; Pfeffer and Salancik 1974; Pfeffer and Moore 1980; Manns and March 1978; James 1990).

Of particular relevance here are the several ways by which successful faculty, when threats are made to their working conditions, can act to buffer themselves from having to attend to offering quality education to undergraduates. Manns and March (1978) found that, if a department has high national prestige and research funding, it can decrease its vulnerability to efforts to improve its educational offerings. If not, it can work to increase undergraduate enrollments via changes in prerequisite requirements and other tactics, and thus to attend to the quantity, if not directly the quality, of undergraduate education. In this way, faculty may in effect be able to employ other mechanisms in the university incentive system to immunize themselves from having to pay attention to undergraduate education.

The leverage faculty can wield against institutional authority has been noted by other analysts as well. Anderson and Louis (forthcoming) note that the familiar image of college faculty as the somewhat unworldly denizens of a restful ivory tower is increasingly at odds with the reality of professors' everyday lives: As they consult with business and industry and report innovations and research findings of interest to wide-ranging external constituencies, faculty are more and more closely involved with people and organizations outside the university. Such involvements buy faculty important privileges, not only outside the institution but also within it.

Faculty can thus enjoy a level of independence from student consumers that is astonishing to those not familiar with academic life. At least in the research university, faculty can have virtually full control of their time. The one formal requirement imposed by the organization, teaching courses, is only a small part of one's work life (Coleman 1973). Accordingly, the faculty member is free to allocate time in directions that are rewarded. Levin (1989) has suggested that faculty members have de facto property rights to behave as they wish beyond their teaching role (also see James and Neuberger 1981). The notion of the professor as independent agent or entrepreneur, freely selling analytic talents in the open marketplace and little constrained by heavy teaching requirements, is supported by recent work on the faculty role (Louis et al. 1989). Coleman (1973), noting wryly that some of the university's constituents might question the compatibility of the new research, development, and consulting activities with teaching, suggests that the answer depends on exactly what is meant by compatibility: "If lions and zebras are compatible on the Serengeti Plain then these activities are compatible. But the lions eat the zebras, and the research or consulting time eats the teaching time" (p. 381).

The countervailing incentives discouraging faculty attention to teaching create curricular difficulties for undergraduates. The incentive system works to discourage professors from creating and teaching broadly focused courses. It instead favors the offering of courses that blend directly into professors' research projects. Perhaps the most perceptive organizational analysis of the fate of students in this context is contained in Clark Kerr's classic description (1972) of the research university. Kerr notes that students in such institutions can become prisoners of their professors' research focus: They are given an extraordinary range of class choices but often find few courses of real appeal. In place of a well-designed, coherent curriculum, the undergraduate faces an atomized array of courses having questionable relevance to his or her educational goals. Kerr concludes: "The professor's love of specialization has become the student's hate of fragmentation. A kind of bizarre version of academic laissez-faire has emerged. The student, unlike Adam Smith's idealized buyer, must consume—usually at the rate of fifteen hours a week" (pp. 14–15).

Given the increased generality of the research incentive in American higher education, it does not seem farfetched to argue that the conditions described by Kerr fit an increasing number of institutions, not solely the research universities.[24]

Negotiating the Conflict Between Image and Reality

Together, the aforementioned properties of poorly understood technology, multiple resource dependencies, and countervailing incentive systems comprise an organizational reality that contradicts public expectations of postsecondary institutions. Whereas external expectations demand that undergraduate education be offered at some minimal level of quality, organizational reality limits attention to undergraduate educational quality. The contemporary college or university thus faces a conundrum of conflicting demands. In this context undergraduate education becomes a negotiated activity. Its specific content and delivery derive from its mediating role between external views of appropriate institutional work and the realities of university organization as experienced by insiders.

The economics of universities are such that undergraduate education pays the bills for graduate education, and undergraduate education is supported because of public assumptions about the merits of universities as teaching enterprises. Still, it is an activity in disfavor on campuses. Alpert (1985, p. 249) notes that "the expectations of external stakeholders, to whom the university is presented as a single organization with clearly defined institutional structure and goals, are often at odds with the expectations of faculty members" that research will be valued over teaching. Thus,

> the problems facing the universities are exacerbated by the divergent goals of the disciplinary and campus communities. ... [T]he intellectual leaders are predominantly oriented to basic research and to the goals and directives of federal agencies that sponsor it; they properly justify their activities in terms of contributions to national welfare. ... The federal government allocates for academic research and development ... less than 20 percent of the operating costs of the overall system of research universities. ... [T]he major burden of financial support for research universities is assumed by stakeholders other than research agencies of the federal government, and much of the institutional support (including student tuition, state subsidies, and federal aid to students) is oriented to undergraduate education and public service rather than basic research. This offers a major dilemma that has not been confronted directly in the academic enterprise: science cannot be well served by inadequately funded

> universities but, given the current support mechanisms, universities will not be adequately funded if they default on their education and service missions. [Pp. 275–276]

From the perspective of the institution, therefore, something has to give. Given the organizational conditions described earlier, undergraduate education can be safely ignored as long as it remains within expected quality standards. Because outsiders apparently demand only minimal quality standards, as discussed earlier, there is little need for rigorous, expensive efforts at quality control. Nevertheless, once educational quality is perceived to venture into questionable territory (as defined by those externally imposed minimum standards), or once the standards rise or are perceived to rise, it will require increased attention. For example, if external authorities actually begin to evaluate teaching quality systematically, it will receive more attention. Similarly, if teaching quality becomes more central to maintaining undergraduate enrollment and the resources that enrollment provides, educators will begin to pay noticeably more attention to it. Put in the simplest terms of resource dependency, institutions will attend most closely to those issues most critical to their survival and prosperity, and undergraduate education will receive only the attention it deserves in relation to institutional survival and prosperity.

The problem of the role of teaching, and the place of undergraduate education, in the modern college or university is an example of a more generic problem in organization theory, that of coexisting goals or visions in organizations (e.g., see Allison 1971). Multipurpose organizations face problems in meshing their coexisting goals, determining their relative priorities, and assessing their relative salience when specific choice opportunities arise (e.g., see March and Simon 1958; Cohen and March 1974). Higher education institutions are generally perceived to maintain three simultaneous and familiar goals: teaching, research, and service. Of course, if one can assume a largely fixed total supply of "organizational attention" and little overlap among the three roles, to attend more closely to any of the three roles is to attend less closely to the other two (Coleman 1973).

In recent years attending more closely to research and service has apparently meant attending less closely to teaching. The work of Gross (1968) and Gross and Grambsch (1974), for example, suggests that the goals perceived as dominant by faculty, students, and administrators (at a variety of universities) were more oriented to research and other matters involving external constituencies than to the concerns of students.[25]

Negotiating differences in external image and internal reality poses special challenges for multipurpose organizations because they are capable of moving in several different directions. Although the public may rank certain of an institution's goals as primary among the variety of goals it pursues, the incentive systems within the institution may be ranking those goals very differently. What is more, because colleges and universities are evolving organizations that nonetheless educate successive generations of youth within given localities, they tend to confront unusual difficulties along these lines: Institutions' current external images may correspond to earlier, outdated institutional realities, due to the presence of alumni in the general public surrounding the institution. Clearly, an institution's activities can move out of synchrony with its external public's expectations.

Such differences between institutions and public perceptions of those institutions would be trivial were it not for the fact that the perceptions of "outsiders" are critical in several ways. For both private and public institutions, these publics are donors, they are political supporters of government subsidies for higher education, and, importantly, they are students and parents. As noted earlier, the flow of donations, subsidies, and undergraduate students into the university is vitally important for its economic health and survival. Postsecondary institutions face a pressing need to achieve at least a minimal match between the social values associated with their activities and the values of their larger social environment (Alfred and Weissman 1987, p. 6). Although the latent goal structure may favor research, it is in the interests of institutions to keep that priority as invisible as possible to external stakeholders favoring other priorities. To resolve the conflict institutions may need to downplay the ultimate incommensurability of the several goals they pursue. With goals often politically sensitive and often even actively contested (Cohen and March 1974), goal clarity tends to be kept as low as practicable. The manifest goal of offering quality undergraduate education is not simply abandoned or relegated to overtly second-class status, but rather left visible and as vague as possible. Undergraduate education is the goal most clearly central for public support so, given the internal dynamic at work, any other tactic would be counterproductive.

Perhaps only the most skillful institutional leaders can easily walk this public/private tightrope. Observing American higher education from abroad, Ben-David (1972) has noted:

> The need to obtain maximum support from as many sectors of the community as possible gave rise to a set of strategies which have been consistently followed (though rarely formulated) by American institutions of higher education. These strategies have been: (a) not to antagonize any significant part of the population or any significant local groups; (b) to actively solicit the goodwill of as many groups as possible; and (c) to preempt or monopolize the support of certain groups for the purpose of safeguarding the institution against possible changes in its competitive position. [P. 26]

Ben-David's analysis implies that it is in institutions' interest to work hard to maintain, or at least keep vague, their external *image* as providers of quality education for the masses, rather than attempt to change it radically to fit some contrary organizational vision, such as the ascension of research as a primary goal.

Often, this conflict avoidance is as much a matter of image management as of substantive decision making. Sultz (1989) notes that releasing incompetent teachers in colleges is difficult and that hiring on the basis of teaching rather than research skills is equally difficult, so he suggests that the academic administrator's role may consist mainly of managing organizational image. Skillful administrators can avoid crippling conflict over goal priorities by deft use of evocative analogies. For example, when a rural Wisconsin legislator showed signs of shock on hearing that University of Wisconsin faculty taught only nine hours a week, President Glenn Frank responded, "Sir, you are famous for your stud bulls. Would you judge their value by the number of hours a week they work?" (Bailey 1973, p. 9).

One aspect of image maintenance is astutely balancing and shaping the presentation of competing goals in negotiations with external publics. Multipurpose institutions may work to achieve a tenuous state of truce with their public supporters by seeming to serve several primary goals at once. Martin Trow (1983) has suggested that such principles may be in operation in California. Specifically, he notes that the state of California and the University of California, Berkeley have an unwritten compact: financial support for a world-class research university in exchange for instruction of the state's bright children. Perhaps only those public institutions with firmly negotiated standing in their home environments could make a statement as bold as the following, from Berkeley: "Notwithstanding the heavy and complex responsibilities in undergraduate education . . . continuing excellence in research and scholarship remains [Berkeley's] primary objective" (University of California 1986, p. 5).

Other public institutions develop relations with their home states that seem to ignore the research enterprise, however. In such states institutions are funded on the basis of their other activities, such as perceived academic quality and the success of athletic teams (Coughlin and Erekson 1986). Such funding patterns may persist even though research is most critical in internal organizational incentive systems. In this way, institutions may succeed in negotiating the image/reality conundrum by working to maintain one external image while pursuing divergent organizational goals as aggressively as external conditions allow. However the conflicts between undergraduate education and other roles are negotiated in higher education institutions, they do present a troubling state of affairs for those who attend college and for those who fund attendance, each buoyed by the optimism of popular expectations.

Implications for Further Research

The intent in this chapter has not been to debunk popular imagery of American higher education, but instead to describe ways in which it portrays a limited vision of the processes of college education. The focus has been largely organizational and macrolevel and, to the extent we have focused on the lives of individuals, it has been the lives of faculty that are of concern. Nevertheless, it is in the lives of individual students that the most interesting research implications may lie. Specifically, one cannot avoid concern over the fate of students in the environment described here. If one accepts the basic human capital principle that the individual returns to education are directly due to its contribution to improving individual productivity, how is it that the organizational reality described here can exist simultaneously with the undeniable positive returns to educational attendance? In particular, how is it that the worst organizational conflicts with popular images may well be found at the research university, which provides somewhat better individual returns to attendance than other kinds of institutions (see Tinto 1987; Useem and Karabel 1986)? How is it that such good things might come out of such bad educational contexts? Either the organizational analysis here is wrong, or important benefits are being provided independently of deficits in educational quality.

Earlier, two ideas were proposed to deal with this question. One, a weak human capital argument, suggests that students learn in spite of generally weak teaching. The other, not a human-capital argument, suggests that the nature of college teaching and the extent of student learning are largely incidental to student outcomes. These may be worth further study. The first possible answer, the weak human capital argument, is that significant knowledge transmission may occur on campus in spite of an organizational climate hostile to the teaching role. Many fictional and biographical accounts of the value of college recount the educational benefits of the extracurricular side of college life, such as athletic participation and all-night "bull sessions" (see Thelin and Townsend 1988), and some empirical evidence supports this perception (e.g., see Feldman and Newcomb 1969).

The second possible answer, the non-human-capital argument, suggests that positive college effects on individual development and advancement may take place independently of any aspects of the college experience. That is, significant knowledge transmission may not occur, and the specific qualities of colleges as organizations may be largely irrelevant, but a college education may still provide opportunities. It might do so via "screening," "sorting," or other purely allocative processes (see Arrow 1973; Mincer 1974; Winkler 1987), and it might also do so via other macrolevel processes unrelated to institutions' impacts on their students. Along the latter lines, sociologist John Meyer (1977) has argued that society expects college graduates to possess certain competencies and that such expectations lead not only to greater likelihood of valued employment (the purely allocative effect) but also to personal changes in the graduates themselves in line with those expected competencies. For Meyer, such a theory helps to explain how individual colleges seem to differ only slightly in their effects on students' personal characteristics and longer-term outcomes, despite widespread differences in the nature and quality of education provided at those colleges. In Meyer's view it is society's definition and legitimation of someone as a college graduate, rather than the actual educational experiences involved in obtaining that status, that have important personal effects.

Both sets of ideas have resonance and research support. Freeman's (1986) review of these two contrasting views, the human capital approach and the screening/sorting view, suggests that the human capital view seems clearly the more strongly supported in empirical work of impacts of education across its many levels. That is, although employers may indeed engage in some overestimation of the substantive (skill-based) impacts of education, those impacts are indeed significant and primary in determining observed incomes. Freeman's exhaustive review provides evidence of sufficient weight to force rejection of the cynical view that the quality of U.S. undergraduate education is so low as to be undetectable in econometric analyses of substantive educational impacts.

The question for further research is therefore not whether skill-based impacts are produced by the system, but rather how those impacts are produced in what is often an organizationally hostile context. Freeman's review includes studies of education at levels and sites other than post-secondary educational institutions and therefore is less targeted than optimal for our purposes. The present review is less econometric, more organizational, and more focused as to educational level. It seems to suggest a need for increased attention to the relative importance of the non-human-capital approaches to understanding the outcomes of post-secondary education. There is sufficient reason to suppose that a number of mechanisms may be actively at work in the returns to higher education.

Prospects for Change

The theme of this chapter has not been a particularly elevating one. A conflict exists between the public's fervently held images and the organizational realities of higher education. Undergraduate teaching is not as valued a part of the professorial role as it once was, and economic realities are constraining greater attention to its quality. What is more, the next few years bode poorly for improvements. As the demography of postsecondary faculty changes toward a younger overall mix (see Estrada 1988), the emphasis on research in American higher education is likely to increase rather than decline. Finkelstein (1984, p. 224) has suggested: "Age [is] the single most important source of individual change over the course of the academic career. ... Most notably, age is associated with increased conservatism, decreased research orientation, and a heightened orientation toward teaching, but without any perceptible change in publication rate or in teaching effectiveness" (also see Kelly and Hart 1971; Baldwin 1979). In sum, as Arrowsmith (1967, p. 64) observed in a provocative essay over two decades ago: "At every level the forces making for scholarly conformity are immense, and the rewards of conformity high. If these forces are not directly hostile to teaching, they are certainly profoundly indifferent."

Yet there may be reason to be hopeful. It was noted earlier that higher education will begin to attend seriously to the quality of undergraduate education when demonstrating that quality is seen as critical to institutional survival. Improving undergraduate educational quality does indeed seem to be attracting greater attention among both higher education authorities and outside observers. Several commission reports in the mid-1980s focused attention on the issue, including *Involvement in Learning* (a 1984 report of the NIE Commission on higher education quality), *Integrity in the College Curriculum* (a 1985 report of a committee of the Association of American Colleges), and *To Reclaim a Legacy* (a 1985 report, written by then soon-to-be U.S. Education Secretary William Bennett, from a study group of the National Endowment for the Humanities).

In 1989 yet another normatively focused commission effort was produced on the topic, this time through support of the Pew Charitable Trusts (see Watkins 1989). The group of experts convened for that effort was impressive for its knowledge of the subject with which it was to deal. It included William Massy and Henry Levin of Stanford, Robert Zemsky of Pennsylvania, Patricia Cross of Berkeley, Bruce Johnstone of the State University of New York, Lewis Solmon of UCLA, and Arthur Levine of Bradford College. The panel noted that it was imperative for faculty to be held more closely accountable for the quality of their teaching, just as they are held accountable for the quality of their research. The panel laid particular blame on contemporary incentive systems within universities: "It does little good to espouse teaching excellence if faculty consistently perceive that only research counts" (as quoted in Watkins 1989, p. A15). The panel suggested that faculty members must work to improve teaching and learning by engaging in assessment of their own and their students' efforts. Collective responsibility for teaching is critical, they added, and teaching quality should be a more explicit criterion for hiring, promotion, and tenure decisions. The panel asked that institutions, particularly universities, "face squarely" the conflict between their oft-stated commitment to good teaching and their actually more central emphasis on research (p. A15).

In 1990 the Carnegie Foundation for the Advancement of Teaching proposed a similar approach, focusing particularly on broadening the definition of scholarships to more fully recognize and reward teaching, service, textbook writing, and other faculty activities (Mooney 1990*a*). The foundation conceded that many institutions (including research universities and other universities seeking increased prestige), as well as many disciplinary associations and scholars, would resist the idea of a broadened definition of scholarship, but it persisted in its call for more serious attention to alternative approaches to faculty rewards. The foundation recommendations parallel the views of those who propose broad-based efforts of faculty development and faculty nurturance as the critical elements in improving undergraduate education. In that vein, Eble and McKeachie (1985) argue that we err when we ignore the fact that most faculty are not researchers and that we err when we train faculty in graduate school solely for research. Individual growth of faculty members, and institutional growth as well, is most enduring when institutions engage faculty collectively and attend to what interests them, such as teaching and other forms of scholarship, broadly defined.

After several years of widely publicized commission reports on the topic of undergraduate educational quality, one might have expected some ebbing in attention. Such has not been the case. The national attention to upgrading the academic quality of undergraduate education seems to have struck an increasingly responsive chord among postsecondary leaders and faculty, as well as government officials.[26] Chait (1990) has noted that "a tidal wave of rhetoric about the importance of undergraduate teaching has hit the shores of academe . . . [and] nearly every college, or so it seems, has a task force at work on the issue" (p. A36).

As might be expected, failures and successes have been recorded in those campus efforts. A recent survey of over 1000 top institutional administrators ("A Revolution in Higher Education Management?" 1990) revealed that those techniques used most frequently to improve teaching and learning are not necessarily perceived by their instigators as the most effective. The most frequently used management practices to improve teaching and learning were found to be faculty recruitment, selection, and promotion; educational technology and computers; academic planning; institutional emphasis on undergraduate education; and academic management information and analytic support systems. Of these, only the first two were reported by administrators as having high effectiveness. Interestingly, administrators reported that academic planning and management systems had low effectiveness. Three other techniques were only moderately used but are perceived as highly effective: admissions and enrollment management, assessing and rewarding teaching effectiveness, and student academic support services. The authors note that typical faculty development activities and efforts at instructional and teaching improvement are perceived as largely ineffective.

The initiation and occasional success of reform efforts thus far will likely not mark the end of concern over the topic. Surveys of college attenders are providing troubling signs for those who favor the status quo. Individuals who have attended college are more apt than others to question the quality of higher education; in fact, the more years of undergraduate education they have, the more doubts they express (survey by the Group Attitudes Corporation, cited by Alfred and Weissman, 1987, pp. 25–27). In a similar survey analysis, Dearman and Plisko (1979) found that the positiveness of national respondents' beliefs regarding the value of college for facilitating advancement was inversely related to their own levels of participation in college, a finding echoed by Bowen's examination (1977) of the results of a variety of surveys. The unavoidable conclusion is that exposure to college is associated with a tendency to criticize college, and colleges' greatest advocates are those who have never attended.

Local newspapers have also picked up the criticism of undergraduate education. The Minneapolis *Star Tribune* (1990) has written, "A nagging worry at the back of our mind has been catapulted rudely to the front. The nagging worry is whether a world-class university . . . for research and graduate study can do justice to teaching. In principle, we know, the answer must be yes: Good teaching rests on good learning, and what is world-class research if not good learning? But in practice, is a research emphasis likely to strengthen teaching? Or is there something about research and advanced-degree departments that leaves good teaching to chance?" (p. 28A). In a similar tone, the *Washington Post* printed an editorial applauding higher education's efforts to make a "long-desired shift" toward improving the status accorded teaching relative to research (Chait 1990).

Even some noted scholars have interrupted the flow of their objective analyses to question the normative implications of their findings on this topic. Bowen and Schuster (1986) ventured away from describing their empirical assessment of the modern professoriate into gently proffering their opinion:

> In the groves of academe, to question the importance of research approaches heresy. Still, we cannot help but wonder whether the stampede toward scholarship—or what passes for scholarship—serves the nation's needs or the longer-run interests of those campuses which historically have been strongly committed to excellent teaching. We fear that the essential balance between teaching and scholarship has been lost, that the scales are tipping too far toward [the latter] in many institutions. [P. 150]

Economist Estelle James (1990) is another accomplished scholar who has raised similar questions. Arguing that prestige maximization seems to be the dominant objective in universities, she focuses on the connections between what may be optimal for institutions and what is optimal for society. James concludes by asking, "Is prestige maximization a socially worthwhile goal and does it encourage higher education to concentrate on the most socially worthwhile activities?" (p. 105). Specifically, she asks whether "we have the right mix of teaching and research for the system as a whole" and expresses concern that, if the answer is no, the competition for prestige may lead us to "produce the wrong output mix, or to produce it inefficiently, in the long run" (p. 105).

The spread of attention to improving undergraduate education goes beyond the standard publication outlets of scholars, journals, and books. Essays on undergraduate educational quality are increasingly occupying space in professional periodicals. In a particularly evocative piece, Rosenzweig (1990) argued that public opinion is declining regarding the quality of American higher education, particularly its teaching, and it is cause for alarm. As a solution he advocates efforts to reintegrate teaching and research, arguing that "we are paying a heavy price for being insufficiently attentive to our largest body of constituents, our undergraduates" (p. A44).

In the midst of this extraordinary attention to improving undergraduate education, a number of quite specific suggestions have been made. Chait (1990) suggests that rhetoric regarding the woes of undergraduate education needs to be replaced by more effective approaches: "Right now pro-teaching advocates probably are investing too much in moral suasion and too little in economic pressures" (p. A36). Chait goes on to suggest (1) that undergraduate colleges unite to require their candidates for faculty positions to show evidence of their teaching preparation and skills and (2) that work be done to stimulate the market for effective teachers, through the award of master teacher (M.T.) credentials and the provision of arenas for the display of excellent teaching skills.

The theme of providing better financial rewards for teaching has been advocated by a number of authors. For example, Peterson and colleagues (1986, p. 55) have noted, "[F]ine words concerning a desire to improve attention to teaching will likely have less impact than fine words backed up by visible signs of reward and recognition." Visibly rewarding teaching is certainly a step in the right direction for institutions, but simply setting up such rewards may mark only a small improvement. Becker (1979*a*) constructs a mathematical model to understand better how faculty will respond to a change in the methods used for determining faculty rewards. His work suggests that increased attention to teaching quality will lead to better teaching only if better methods of screening for quality of teaching are devised. Becker (1979*a*, p. 1016) notes:

> Teaching, unlike research output, has no existing measure which is universally accepted as highly accurate. ... Unless accurate methods of screening are established, there may be no way other than stipulating minimal time commitment regulations to affect this output. Only if a university is able to adopt student evaluations, standardized student learning measures, or some other proxy index of teaching output can the reward structure be used to cause an increase in every faculty member's desire to increase productivity in teaching.

In the absence of a solution for that dilemma of measurement, we need to inquire whether there might be reward structures that could be perceived as consistent with the public's desire for teaching and the faculty's desire for knowledge. Proposals for "teaching tracks" to protect and honor teaching-oriented faculty inside research universities, like proposals for the Doctor of Arts degree, have largely gone nowhere (see Dressel and Thompson 1974; Mooney 1990*b*). Apropos of those failings, Louis (1989, p. 14) argues that, because each college or university is part of a larger, highly competitive system driven by research funding and research-oriented reward systems, "radical change in one institution (for example, changing the tenure system to give more weight to teaching) is difficult without concurrent changes in the larger context." Without such changes in the larger context, faculty with close ties to, and dependencies on, external agencies must choose between simply forfeiting parts of their funding or taking their resources to other, more congenial institutions. Pursuing the latter alternative could thwart efforts at structural reforms.

There may be "softer," nonstructural ways to recognize faculty who excel in areas other than research. Citing Kanter (1984), Louis stresses the need for developing a collective sense of reward and responsibility, and more provision of praise for all activities, not solely those related to research. This approach is echoed in that of the Pew commission (Watkins 1989).

In his own normative analysis of problems in the reward system for teaching and undergraduate education, Alpert (1985) lays blame at the feet of the research universities and calls on them to lead the system out of its problems. Specifically, he suggests that there is a pressing need to reconsider the current uniformities in the evaluation of institutional performance across the various sectors of the higher education system:

> Although inspired by the worthy motive of defining and achieving "excellence," the research universities of the nation have been led into a ratings game that places far greater rewards on conformity than diversity, measuring performance primarily in terms of original research published in scholarly journals. This situation has served to impose the values and mission of the outstanding research institutions on most of the other colleges and universities without providing, even in principle, for the justification or support of the overall research enterprise. ... In reconceiving measures of excellence [in higher education], a special responsibility falls on the leaders of the most prestigious universities, who educate the faculties and set the cultural climate for the enterprise as a whole. [Pp. 276–277]

It may be instructive to examine here in more detail what is arguably the most visible, if not the most popular, of the suggestions for the reform of undergraduate education: more systematic *assessment and evaluation of undergraduate educational outcomes.*[27] The paradox posed at the chapter's start probably persists at least in part because of faulty public information on the benefits and costs of higher education, and on the realities of attending college. To the extent that appropriate information dissemination is a goal of the many parties now working on assessing educational quality, one might expect the paradox to begin to disappear and market imperfections to be ameliorated.

It is far from certain that the higher education system, allowed for so long to operate under a "logic of good faith," will willingly and easily adapt to a regimen of greatly increased inspection and control, however.[28] Organizational habits die hard. In closing this chapter, it seems appropriate to consider ways in which the burgeoning assessment and evaluation movement will likely affect the "heart of the beast," the research university.

There, the sense of malaise regarding the maintenance of quality seems to have become pervasive in recent years. Troubled over the very themes that prompted the recent increase in national concern, a number of universities have begun to back away from 1970s experiments with open programs and decreased emphasis on grades and have begun to embrace instead more prescriptive, standards-oriented curricular structures at the undergraduate level. Yet such maneuvers may not in the end produce a fully satisfactory response to the recent calls for reform. There is a stubborn quality about the dominant organizational features of the research universities that thwarts even the most well intentioned and thoughtful reform efforts. Resistance to such efforts reflects *disciplinary and departmental divisions, research/teaching tradeoffs, and typical organizational adaptation patterns.*

First, the assessment and evaluation reform effort tends to be holistic (encompassing entire institutions) and therefore may founder on the thoroughgoing departmental and disciplinary base of American higher education at the university level.[29] Over time the increased disciplinary differentiation in U.S. higher education has led to decreased uniformity in the idea of an undergraduate education. The disciplinary base of university organization does not always serve undergraduate interests or the interests of the society in broadly educated college graduates.[30] Standards and processes in major programs vary significantly by department and, accordingly, "output" varies significantly. To the extent faculty are willing to think about undergraduate education, they are usually not too disturbed by this differentiation. Education is socialization as well as knowledge trasmission, and disciplines value their own distinctive norms of scholarship and styles of reasoning. Any attempt to define the appropriate outcomes of undergraduate education at the university level, much less implement an assessment program based in those definitions as desiderata, is apt to lead to controversy. To the extent universities encourage their faculty to turn their attention to undergraduate education writ large (i.e., the products of a university education), those institutions may also encourage their faculty to initiate or renew painful across-department conflicts.

Regarding departmental and disciplinary divisions, it is important to remember, as Tichy (1980) notes, that organizational problems such as deficiencies in undergraduate education are never by nature solely technical but are also political and cultural. In a study of an effort to improve undergraduate education at the University of Minnesota, Louis (1989) found both politics and culture involved in the interdepartmental controversies resulting from the change effort. Regarding politics, Louis (1989, p. 10) noted that significant efforts to improve undergraduate education have implications for both the distribution of resources among units and divisions and the overall patterns of influence within the university. Regarding culture, Louis (1989, p. 11) observed that value differences among faculty and between faculty and administrators regarding undergraduate education influenced faculty opinions on change efforts and that departmental culture was particularly influential.

Second, as noted earlier in some detail, there are trade-offs between teaching and other activities, such as research. If teaching already represents a "load," and if faculty incentives and working conditions remain as constricted as many claim (e.g., see Peterson et al. 1986), what are we to think of the prospects for significant additions to faculty responsibilities in the arena of teaching, learning, and assessment? Do institutions wish to invest more of their faculty time in such activities at the expense of noninstructional activities, including research? The benefits of such an investment are appreciable, but so too are the risks. Whatever their decision, institutions must be prepared to invest dollars as well as rhetoric in the effort to improve education.

The third and final area of research-university resistance regarding assessment and evaluation recommendations involves the possibly negative implications of those recommendations for the autonomy, heterogeneity, and innovativeness of American higher education. When accrediting agencies, states, and other outside organizations act to tighten the connections between their support of an institution and that institution's success in meeting certain preset educational criteria, *even if the criteria are those initiated and ratified by the institutional leadership itself*, concerns may be raised about the resulting effects on those parts of American higher education that are strengthened by current arrangements. One has to wonder if "one thousand flowers" can continue to bloom so freely as before on American campuses. Universities' adaptation to threats and opportunities in their external environments has been facilitated by their ability to make certain changes at the department or college level, without substantial top-down direction from university administrators (Weick 1976; Clark 1983). If reform recommendations lead to limitations on the ability of departments or colleges to sense the directions of change in their external environments and adapt their procedures accordingly and efficiently, universities are likely to resist.

In sum, three resistance points limit the prospects for change along the lines of recent reform recommendations for assessing and evaluating the quality of undergraduate education. First, disciplinary implications and conflict: Will attempts to define the optimal undergraduate outcomes lead to disabling interdisciplinary conflicts? Second, research/education trade-offs: Will the investment of additional faculty time in aspects of undergraduate education lead to decreased productivity in other activities? Third, organizational autonomy at the department or college level: Will the definition of optimal undergraduate outcomes, and the pursuit of those outcomes at the central level, lead to undesirably decreased adaptability at the departmental or collegiate level?

Ideally, presenting the resistance points in this fashion will lead to consideration of benefits and costs. The case for reform of undergraduate education along the lines currently suggested is appealing, but by no means closed. Certainly, the organizational resistance of colleges and universities to a reemphasis on teaching has its salutary as well as deleterious sides. For one thing, the precise nature of the new educational product to come after the suggested reforms remains to be seen. In addition, the research and service products currently produced by the higher education system are not at all without social value (a point stressed in several chapters in this volume). What is more, as Solmon and Fagnano (forthcoming) suggest, there is clear evidence that those who attend the most selective and wealthy institutions, including the most research-oriented universities, contribute somewhat more to national economic growth than students who attend other institutions, including the many nonelite liberal arts colleges focusing single mindedly on undergraduate education.

Most fundamentally, therefore, we should ask some questions rather out of keeping with the tone of much of the chapter. Why must we assume that the conflict between image and reality is not conducive to quality education? Is it possible that the teaching/research conundrum, the multiple constituencies, the poorly defined technology, and the problematic reward structures of American higher education may actually contribute to quality education? Would attending more closely to undergraduate education lead to less optimal use of precious scholarly resources? Intuition, and the analysis presented earlier in this chapter, suggest the answers to these questions must be no. Ultimately, though, there is no way to know. What is clear is that the conversion of postsecondary institutions to anything other than what they currently are will be difficult and will be resisted with some force by faculty and others benefiting from current arrangements.

Acknowledgments

The author very much appreciates the critical comments of Melissa Anderson and the editors of this volume. The author also appreciates the thoughtful questions and suggestions from students participating in the editors' spring 1989 graduate seminar at the University of Minnesota. Portions of this manuscript dealing with the potentials for reform in undergraduate education were presented in slightly different form in the author's 1985 talk at the National Institute of Education's Western Regional Conference on Quality in American Higher Education (see Hearn 1985).

Endnotes

1. See Dearman and Plisko (1979), Elam (1983), and Yankelovich (1987).

2. For example, see Carnegie Foundation (1989) and Watkins (1989).

3. Were that the purpose here, two ideas might be examined: one in which students learn in spite of generally weak teaching, and another in which the nature of college teaching and the extent of student learning are largely incidental to student outcomes. These possibilities will be discussed in more detail in the section of the chapter on research implications.

4. Two delimitations on the chapter's scope should be mentioned here. First, the focus here is mainly on higher education in the United States. The extraordinary and unique heterogeneity of the U.S. system, with its multiple purposes, its varied institutional forms, and its differentiated entry criteria, is an important part of what makes the focal concerns of the chapter significant. Namely, how are the varied, and potentially contradictory, faces of the system managed? To what extent are significant societal problems buried under the vague rhetoric and organizational diffuseness of the U.S. postsecondary enterprise? Second, this chapter examines all of U.S. higher education across its many forms. In a heterogeneous system, conflicts will inevitably arise between popular images and realities. The elite research institutions, despite their high levels of prestige with the general public, seem ironically to be the most out of touch with popular demands and images. Accordingly, special attention is paid to that setting here.

5. Remini (1966, p. 138) reports an evocative anecdote that makes this point nicely:

> [A]t Cambridge, Massachusetts, the President received an honorary degree of Doctor of Laws from Harvard—much to John Quincy Adams' intense disgust. Later, when Jackson addressed a small audience in another town someone called from the crowd, "You must give them a little Latin, Doctor." Whereupon, the President, his eyes twinkling, responded: "E pluribus unum, my friends, sine qua non!"

6. The periodic swings in the federal government's rationales for support for post-secondary student financial aid are an example: Hansen and Stampen (1987) note swings between a Jeffersonian, meritocratic, "excellence"-oriented definition of equity, based in equal treatment for those of equal talent, and a Jacksonian, egalitarian definition based in equal treatment for all.

7. See the review of those reports by Mayhew (1973).

8. There are, of course, some doubts associated with the public's general faith in the merits of higher education (see the review by Alfred and Weissman, 1987).

9. The generality of the problem across the many sectors of American higher education is discussed later in the chapter. Also see National Institute of Education (1984), Baldwin and Krotseng (1985), Birnbaum (1985), Cohen (1985), Geiger (1985), Pfnister (1985),

Peterson et al. (1986), Boyer (1986), Clark (1987), Wagener (1989), Kaiser (1989), Schaw (1989).

10. Thorsten Veblen (1957), as was usual for him, took a provocative stance on the emerging climate of the turn-of-the-century campus. Veblen proposed that undergraduate education, as well as professional education, be separated from the university. In his view, it was unlikely there would be any way of meshing the transcending beauty and purity of graduate education and research with the worldly difficulties inherent in the marketplace. For him, undergraduate and preprofessional education were too attached to self-interest for safe placement in the university. In this view, Veblen aligned himself with those who, with few regrets, would rather dispose of undergraduate education at the research universities than lament its uncertain fate therein.

11. Cited in Smith (1989, p. 217).

12. Also see Brubacher and Rudy (1976).

13. Clark's observations are obtained from Sykes (1988, pp. 60–61).

14. A well-known example is the movie *Breaking Away*, written by Steven Tesich as a reflection of his experiences as an Indiana University undergraduate (the movie was later adapted into a novel by Howard, 1979). The theme also is present in *Love Story*, the popular movie and book (1970) by former Harvard professor Erich Segal.

15. Both Sykes (1988) and Smith (1989) provide some useful anecdotes and references for this chapter. Both are colorful, and often persuasive, essays by insiders portraying serious deficiencies in the quality of undergraduate education in the United States. Nevertheless, both are nonscholarly works sacrificing precision and balance in favor of unstinting devotion to normative agendas. There are few grays in the work of either author, only blacks and whites. Their overall conclusions must therefore be accepted only with caution.

16. Finkelstein (1984), in his study of faculty in American higher education, found little uniformity among professors overall: "To attempt to generalize about faculty as a group except in the broadest possible way may be neither intellectually defensible nor operationally useful" (p. 226, italics removed).

17. This development is discussed at some length later in the chapter.

18. Balderston (1990, p. 33) has observed that the United States postsecondary education system uniquely favors the sacrifice of undergraduate education to research goals:

> Linking the conduct of large-scale research with graduate education, American universities differ from institutions in Europe and the Soviet Union, where a great deal of research is done in separate institutes and academies while instruction of students is the dominant function of universities. American analysts of higher education regard this multiplicity of functions in the U.S. universities as a strength. However, the research universities of the U.S. compete to some extent with other producers of research. Therefore, universities must demonstrate their effectiveness in the research enterprise if they are to retain their dominant role in basic research.

19. It is extremely difficult to untangle empirically institutions' pursuit of prestige (as denoted, for example, by reputational ratings, citation counts) from institutions' pursuit of performance (as denoted, for example, by starting salaries of graduates, the number of faculty articles). Those schools that are highest in prestige measures are also highest in performance measures. Obviously, performance and prestige feed on each other to create the Matthew effect. Those aspects of performance that enhance prestige are pursued ahead of those that do not. Still, an unexamined claim that one is somehow prior to the other is probably unwarranted.

20. A recent, highly publicized strategic change effort at the University of Minnesota,

entitled "Commitment to Focus," is intriguing because it reflected an implicit "trickle down" theory of this kind. Louis (1989) suggests that planning effort was based on an assumption that improved undergraduate education would result from the increased resources generated by the university's improving research reputation and thus its improved fortunes in grant seeking.

21. This argument is based on a notion that undergraduate education quality is more than the mere averaging of undergraduates' admissions test scores or high school grades. "Resource" or "input" measures of quality of this kind have been popular historically and have also taken the form of measures based in the number of volumes in campus libraries or the average educational level of an institution's faculty. Such measures ignore the interactive and "value-added" dimensions of education, and essentially define any other than a highly selective institution as being of lower quality. Such definitions lead to a hierarchy of institutional quality that merely parallels that of institutional prestige. As a consequence, such definitions beg the question of how best to educate undergraduates.

22. The connections between teaching and research talents may be more random than systematic. Employing both his experience and his review of empirical work on the topic, an educational psychologist who won a major teaching award at a research university recently expressed his views on the connections between teaching and research:

> A good teacher who does good research is rarer than common educational opinion would have. Seeking and guiding are very different activities. If a Nobel Prize winner in science is reputed to being a great teacher it is probably an incidental by-product. ... Great researchers love the truth; great teachers love students. In my experience, faculty members at a teaching and research university can be superb at one and mediocre at the other and still sleep well. Most universities accept this, but don't openly admit [it] because of their publicly stated mission. (Charlesworth 1990, p. 3)

23. The feeling of being uneasy with existing reward systems is not felt solely at the nonresearch institutions. The following minutes from the highest faculty governance committee at the University of Minnesota reflect parallel discomfort among a research-oriented faculty:

> Committee members discussed for some while the understanding among junior faculty that research and scholarship [are] primary and that everything else is secondary. [An associate vice president] acknowledged that department cultures tended in this direction; she was however, she said, surprised by the intensity of the emphasis on research. One Committee member made the point that it is contradictory to involve non-tenured faculty in undergraduate teaching; that is a recipe for failure because devoting effort to teaching would result in a denial of tenure. Junior faculty are told not to spend time on teaching—they have to do it, but not to spend time on it—and attempts to emphasize teaching [are] wrong so long as the tenure decision is based solely on research. [The associate vice president] agreed but expressed the hope that the situation would change. (University of Minnesota 1990, p. 5)

24. For support, see especially Birnbaum (1985) and Geiger (1985).

25. Nonuniversity settings were not studied, so the situation may be somewhat different there. Similarly, the Gross studies are dated, so changes may have occurred (although the evidence suggests the trend discovered in newer analyses would be further away from rather than toward goals related to undergraduate education.

26. See Alpert (1985) and Daniels (1989).

27. See Bok (1986), Peterson et al. (1986), and Chait (1990).

28. The "logic of good faith" is discussed at length by Meyer (1977).

29. Sociologist Burton Clark (1983) has commented that an indirect index of the cohesiveness of a campus community may be found in its number of coffee pots. As the disciplines have multiplied, the faculty commons or lounge has been gradually replaced by an assortment of departmental lounges, each with its own coffee pot.

30. The federation replaced the collegium as the dominant metaphor for campus governance. In a sense, the disciplinary base of organization at universities provides American universities with both their primary strength and their Achilles' heel. On the positive side, the innovativeness and productivity of the research enterprise are perhaps unparalleled worldwide, and the community service function is generally well served. Graduate education, while not without its difficulties, also seems profitably based at the department level. Less clearly on the positive side, however, are the implications of discipline-based organization for offering coherent, high-quality programs of undergraduate education.

References

Alfred, R. L., & Weissman, J. (1987). *Higher education and the public trust: Improving stature in colleges and universities.* ASHE-ERIC Higher Education Reports, Number 6. Washington, D.C.: Association for the Study of Higher Education.

Allison, G. (1971). *Essence of decision: Explaining the Cuban missile crisis.* Boston: Little, Brown and Company.

Alpert, D. (1985). Performance and paralysis: The organizational context of the American research university. *Journal of Higher Education 56*(3), 241–281.

Anderson, M. S., & Louis, K. S. (Forthcoming). The changing locus of control over faculty research: From self-regulation to dispersed influence. In John Smart (Ed.), *Higher education: Handbook of theory and research* (Vol. VII). New York: Agathon.

Arrow, K. J. (1973). Higher education as a filter. *Journal of Political Economy 2,* 193–216.

Arrowsmith, W. (1967). The future of teaching. In Calvin B. T. Lee (Ed.), *Improving college teaching.* Washington, D.C.: American Council on Education.

Association of American Colleges. (1985). *Integrity in the college curriculum.* Report of a Committee of the Association of American Colleges. Washington, D.C.: Association of American Colleges.

Astin, A. (1977). *Four critical years.* San Francisco: Jossey-Bass.

Astin, A. (1980). When does a college deserve to be called "high quality"? *Current Issues in Higher Education,* No. 1. Washington, D.C.: American Association for Higher Education.

Bailey, S. K. (1973). Combating the efficiency cultists. *Change,* June, pp. 8–9.

Balderston, F. E. (1990). Organization, funding, incentives, and initiatives for university research: A university management perspective. In Stephen A. Hoenack & Eileen L. Collins (Eds.), *The economics of American universities.* Albany, NY: SUNY Press.

Baldridge, J. V., Curtis, D. V., Ecker, G., & Riley, G. L. (1978). *Policy making and effective leadership*. San Francisco: Jossey-Bass.
Baldwin, R. G. (1979). Adult and career development: What are the implications for faculty? *Current Issues in Higher Education*, No. 2. Washington, D.C.: American Association for Higher Education.
Baldwin, R. G., & Krotseng, M. V. (1985). Incentives in the academy: Issues and options. *New Directions for Community Colleges 13*(3), 5–20.
Becker, W. E., Jr. (1979*a*). Professorial behavior given a stochastic reward structure. *American Economic Review 69*(5), 1010–1017.
Becker, W. E., Jr. (1979*b*). Perspectives from economics: The economic consequences of changing faculty reward structures. In D. R. Lewis & W. E. Becker, Jr. (Eds.), *Academic rewards in higher education*. Cambridge, MA: Ballinger.
Ben-David, J. (1972). *Trends in American higher education*. Chicago: University of Chicago Press.
Bennett, W. J. (1985). *To reclaim a legacy: A report on the humanities in higher education*. A report of the NEH Study Group on the State of Learning in the Humanities in Higher Education. Washington, D.C.: National Endowment for the Humanities.
Bess, J. L. (1982). *University organization: A matrix analysis of the academic profession*. New York: Human Sciences Press.
Birnbaum, R. (1985). State colleges: An unsettled quality. In National Institute of Education, *Contexts for learning: The major sectors of American higher education*. Washington, D.C.: National Institute of Education.
Bloom, A. (1987). *The closing of the American mind*. New York: Simon & Schuster.
Bok, D. (1986). Toward education of quality. *Harvard Magazine*, May–June, pp. 49–64.
Bowen, H. R. (1977). *Investment in learning*. San Francisco: Jossey-Bass.
Bowen, H. R. & Schuster, J. H. (1986). *American professors: A national resource imperiled*. New York: Oxford.
Boyer, E. (1986). *College*. Princeton: Carnegie Foundation for the Advancement of Teaching.
Brubacher, J. S., & Rudy, W. (1976). *Higher education in transition* (3rd ed.). New York: Harper & Row.
Campus towns: Scenic mind-set. (1990). *USA Today*, September 1, p. 7E.
Carnegie Foundation for the Advancement of Teaching. (1989). *The condition of the professoriate: Attitudes and trends*. Princeton, NJ: Author.
Cartter, A. M. (1967). University teaching and excellence. In Calvin B. T. Lee (Ed.), *Improving college teaching*. Washington, D.C.: American Council on Education.
Chait, R. (1990). The pro-teaching movement should try economic pressures. *Chronicle of Higher Education 36*(43), A36.
Charlesworth, W. R. (1990). *On teaching*. Unpublished manuscript, University of Minnesota, Minneapolis.
Clark, B. R. (1983). *The higher education system*. Berkeley: University of California Press.

Clark, B. R. (1987). *The academic life: Small worlds, different worlds*. Princeton, NJ: Carnegie Foundation for the Advancement of Teaching.
Cohen, A. (1985). The community college in the American educational system. In National Institute of Education, *Contexts for learning: The major sectors of American higher education*. Washington, D.C.: National Institute of Education.
Cohen, M., & March, J. (1974). *Leadership and ambiguity*. New York: McGraw-Hill.
Cohn, E., Rhine, S. L. W., & Santos, M. C. (1989). Institutions of higher education as multi-product firms: Economies of scale and scope. *Review of Economics and Statistics 71*(2), 284–290.
Coleman, J. S. (1973). The university and society's new demands upon it. In Carl Kaysen (Ed.), *Content and context: Essays on college education*. New York: McGraw-Hill.
Coughlin, C. C., & Erekson, O. H. (1986). Determinants of state aid and voluntary support of higher education. *Economics of Education Review 5*(2), 179–190.
Cross, A. (1972). *Poetic justice*. New York: Avon.
Daniels, L. A. (1989). Some top universities in squeeze between research and academics. *New York Times*, May 10, pp. 1, 23.
Davis, G. H. (1988). How should universities respond to the imperative, "Professors should spend more time teaching and less time on research!" *Arizona Board of Regents' Task Force on Excellence Efficiency and Competitiveness 2*, November, 849–858.
Dearman, N. B., & Plisko, V. W. (1979). Comparisons of public perceptions of education with the current status of education. Paper presented at the annual meeting of the American Educational Research Association, San Francisco, April.
DeLillo, D. (1985). *White noise*. New York: Viking Penguin.
Dornbusch, S. M. (1979). Perspectives from sociology: Organizational evaluation of faculty performances. In D. R. Lewis & W. E. Becker, Jr. (Eds.), *Academic rewards in higher education*. Cambridge, MA: Ballinger.
Doyle, K. O., Jr. (1979). Use of student evaluations in faculty personnel decisions. In D. R. Lewis & W. E. Becker, Jr. (Eds.), *Academic rewards in higher education*. Cambridge, MA: Ballinger.
Dressel, P. L., & Thompson, M. M. (1974). *College teaching: Improvement by degrees* (Monograph 13 of the American College Testing Program). Iowa City, IA: American College Testing Program.
Dunham, E. A. (1969). *Colleges of the forgotten Americans: A profile of state colleges and regional universities*. New York: McGraw-Hill.
Eble, K. E., & McKeachie, W. J. (1985). *Improving undergraduate teaching through faculty development*. San Francisco: Jossey-Bass.
Elam, S. M. (1983). The Gallup Education Surveys: Impressions of a poll watcher. *Phi Delta Kappan*, September, pp. 26–47.
Estrada, L. F. (1988). Anticipating the demographic future. *Change*, May/June, pp. 14–19.
Feldman, K. A. (1987). Research productivity and scholarly accomplishment of college teachers as related to their instructional effectiveness: A review and

exploration. *Research in Higher Education 26*(3), 227–298.

Feldman, K. A., & Newcomb, T. M. (1969). *The impact of college on students* (Vol. I). San Francisco: Jossey-Bass.

Finkelstein, M. J. (1984). *The American academic profession: A synthesis of social scientific inquiry since World War II*. Columbus: Ohio State University Press.

Freeman, R. B. (1986). Demand for education. In O. Ashenfelter & R. Layard (Eds.), *Handbook of labor economics* (Vol. I). Amsterdam: North-Holland.

Gallup Organization, The. (1985). *Public opinion survey: Attitudes toward higher education*. Princeton, NJ: Author.

Geiger, R. L. (1985). Research universities: Their role in undergraduate education. In National Institute of Education, *Contexts for learning: The major sectors of American higher education*. Washington, D.C.: National Institute of Education.

Geiger, R. L. (1986). *To advance knowledge: The growth of American research universities, 1900–1940*. New York: Oxford University Press.

Gladieux, L. E., & Wolanin, T. R. (1976). *Congress and the colleges: The national politics of higher education*. Lexington, MA: Lexington (Heath).

Gross, E. (1968). Universities as organizations: A study of goals. *American Sociological Review 33*(4), August, 518–544.

Gross, E., & Grambsch, P. V. (1974). *Changes in university organization, 1964–1971*. New York: McGraw-Hill.

Hansen, W. L., & Stampen, J. O. (1987). The economics and financing of higher education: The tension between quality and equity. In P. G. Altbach & R. O. Berdahl (Eds.), *Higher education in American society*. New York: Prometheus.

Hearn, J. C. (1985). The faculty role in assessment: Some reactions to recent national reports on quality in higher education. Invited paper presented at the National Institute of Education Western Regional Conference on Quality in American Higher Education, Los Angeles, May.

Hearn, J. C. (1988). Strategy and resources: Economic issues in strategic planning and management in higher education. In John Smart (Ed.), *Higher education: Handbook of theory and research* (Vol. IV). New York: Agathon.

Heller, S. (1990). Stronger push for research on liberal arts campuses brings fears that their culture is threatened. *Chronicle of Higher Education 36*(42), July 5, pp. A11, A14–15.

Hind, R. R., Dornbusch, S. M., & Scott, W. R. (1974). A theory of evaluation applied to a university faculty. *Sociology of Education 47*, 114–128.

Hines, E. R. (1988). *Higher education and state governments: Renewed partnership, cooperation, or competition*? (ASHE-ERIC Higher Education Report No. 5). Washington, D.C.: Association for the Study of Higher Education.

Holmes Group, The. (1986). *Tomorrow's teachers: A report of the Holmes Group*. East Lansing, MI: Author.

Hopkins, D. S. P. (1990). The higher education production function: Theoretical foundations and empirical findings. In Stephen A. Hoenack & Eileen L. Collins (Eds.), *The economics of American universities*. Albany, NY: SUNY Press.

Hossler, D., Braxton, J., & Coopersmith, G. (1989). Understanding student

college choice. In John Smart (Ed.), *Higher education: Handbook of theory and research* (Vol. V). New York: Agathon.
Howard, J. (1979). *Breaking away*. New York: Warner Books.
'In' box. (1989). *Chronicle of Higher Education 35*(35), May 10, p. A11.
James, E. (1978). Product mix and cost disaggregation: A reinterpretation of the economics of higher education. *Journal of Human Resources 13*(2), 157–186.
James, E. (1990). Decision processes and priorities in higher education. In Stephen A. Hoenack & Eileen L. Collins (Eds.), *The economics of American universities*. Albany, NY: SUNY Press.
James, E., & Neuberger, E. (1981). The university department as a non-profit labor collective. In M. J. Bowman (Ed.), *Collective choice in education*. Boston: Kluwer-Nijhoff Publishers.
Jefferson, sadly for Monticello, wouldn't need his telescope to watch his village grow. (1990). *Wall Street Journal*, January 3, p. A8.
Jencks, C., & Riesman, D. (1968). *The academic revolution*. New York: Doubleday.
Kanter, R. M. (1984). *The change masters*. New York: Simon & Schuster.
Kaiser, H. H. (1989). Rebuilding the campus. *Educational Record 70*(1), 4–7.
Katz, D. A. (1973). Faculty salaries, promotions, and productivity at a large research university. *American Economic Review 63*, June, 469–477.
Kelly, R., & Hart, B. D. (1971). The role preferences of faculty in different age groups and academic disciplines. *Sociology of Education 44*, 351–357.
Kerr, C. (1972). *The uses of the university, with a "Postscript-1972."* New York: Harper & Row.
Levin, H. M. (1989). *Raising productivity in higher education* (Report of the Pew Higher Education Research Program). Philadelphia: University of Pennsylvania.
Lodge, D. (1989). *Nice work*. New York: Viking Penguin.
Louis, K. S. (1989). Surviving institutional change: Reflections on curriculum reform in universities. *New directions for higher education: No. 66 (Improving undergraduate education in large universities)* 17(2) Summer, 9–25. San Francisco: Jossey-Bass.
Louis, K. S., Blumenthal, D., Gluck, M., & Stoto, M. (1989). Entrepreneurs in academe: An exploration of behaviors among life scientists. *Administrative Science Quarterly 34*(1), 110–131.
Lurie, A. (1967). *Imaginary friends*. New York: Coward-McCann.
Manns, C., & March, J. G. (1978). Financial adversity, internal competition, and curriculum change at a university. *Administrative Science Quarterly 23*, 541–552.
March, J. G., & Simon, H. A. (1958). *Organizations*. New York: Wiley.
Mayhew, L. B. (1973). *The Carnegie Commission on Higher Education*. San Francisco: Jossey-Bass.
Merton, R. K. (1968). The Matthew effect in science: The reward and communication systems of science. *Science 159*, 56–63.
Meyer, J. (1977). The effects of education as an institution. *American Journal of Sociology 83*, 55–77.
Miller, S. E. (1985). College costs: How do families pay? *Educational Record*

66(3), 40–43.

Mincer, J. (1974). *Schooling, experience and earnings*. New York: National Bureau of Economic Research.

Minneapolis Star Tribune. (1990). A world-class (and fun) proposal for the 'U.' March 25, p. 28A.

Mooney, C. J. (1990*a*). Higher education conferees applaud Carnegie plan to broaden the definition of faculty scholarship. *Chronicle of Higher Education 36*(30), April 11, pp. A1, A16.

Mooney, C. J. (1990*b*). Faculty generation gap brings campus tensions, debates over ratings of professors. *Chronicle of Higher Education*, 36(41), June 27, pp. A1, A8–9.

National Institute of Education, The [NIE]. (1984). *Involvement in learning: Report of the Commission on Quality in American Higher Education*. Washington, D.C.: U.S. Government Printing Office.

Nisbet, R.A. (1967). Conflicting academic loyalties. In Calvin B. T. Lee (Ed.), *Improving college teaching*. Washington, D.C.: American Council on Education.

Peterson, M. W., Cameron, K. S., Mets, L A., Jones, P., & Ettington, D. (1986). *The organizational context for teaching and learning*. Ann Arbor, MI: The National Center for Research to Improve Postsecondary Teaching and Learning.

Pfeffer, J., & Moore, W. (1980). Power in university budgeting: A replication and extension. *Administrative Science Quarterly 25*, 398–418.

Pfeffer, J., & Salancik, G. R. (1974). Organizational decision making as a political process: The case of a university budget. *Administrative Science Quarterly 19*, 135–151.

Pfeffer, J., & Salancik, G. R. (1978). *The external control of organizations: A resource dependency perspective*. New York: Harper & Row.

Pfnister, A. O. (1985). The American liberal arts college: Dinosaur or phoenix. In National Institute of Education, *Contexts for learning: The major sectors of American higher education*. Washington, D.C.: The National Institute of Education.

The real life of Amanda Cross. (1989). *Newsweek*, April 10, pp. 65A, 65B.

Remini, R. V. (1966). *Andrew Jackson*. New York: Twayne.

A revolution in higher education management? (1990). *NCRIPTAL Update 2*(2), 5–6. Ann Arbor: National Center for Research to Improve Postsecondary Teaching and Learning, University of Michigan.

Rosenzweig, R. M. (1990). Challenges to test the mettle of academe's best leaders. *Chronicle of Higher Education 36*(24), February 28, p. A44.

Schaw, W. A. (1989). The time bomb continues to tick. *Educational Record 70*(1), 8–11.

Segal, E. (1970). *Love story*. New York: Harper & Row.

Siegfried, J., & White, K. (1973). Teaching and publishing as determinants of academic salaries. *Journal of Economic Education 4*, Spring, 90–99.

Smith, P. (1989). *Killing the spirit*. New York: Viking.

Solmon, L. C., & Fagnano, C. L. (Forthcoming). Quality of higher education and economic growth in the United States. In W. E. Becker and D. R. Lewis

(Eds.) *American higher education and national growth*. Kluwer.

Sovern, M. (1989). Higher education: The real crisis. *New York Times Sunday Magazine*, January 22, pp. 24–25, 56.

Sultz, H. A. (1989). Had I the chance to be dean again, here's what my principles would be. *Chronicle of Higher Education 35*(38), May 31, p. B2.

Sykes, C. J. (1988). *Profscam*. New York: St. Martin's Press.

Thelin, J. R., & Townsend, B. K. (1988). Fiction to fact. In John Smart (Ed.), *Higher education: Handbook of theory and research* (Vol. IV). New York: Agathon.

Tichy, N. (1980). Problem cycles in organizations and the management of change. In J. R. Kimberly, R. H. Miles, & Associates, *The organizational life cycle: Issues in the creation, transformation, and decline of organizations*. San Francisco: Jossey-Bass.

Tinto, V. (1987). *Leaving college: Rethinking the causes and cures of student attrition*. Chicago: University of Chicago Press.

Trow, M. A. (1967). Undergraduate teaching at large state universities. In Calvin B. T. Lee (Ed.), *Improving college teaching*. Washington, D.C.: American Council on Education.

Trow, M. A. (1983). Organization and leadership in universities: The case of biology at Berkeley. Conference Paper, Swedish National Board of Colleges and Universities. Rosenon, Dalaro, Sweden.

Trow, M. A. (1984). The analysis of status. In Burton R. Clark (Ed.), *Perspectives on higher education: Eight disciplinary and comparative views*. Berkeley: University of California Press.

Tuckman, H. P. (1976). *Publication, teaching, and the academic reward structure*. Lexington, MA: D.C. Heath.

Tuckman, H. P. (1979). The academic reward structure in American higher education. In D. R. Lewis & W. E. Becker, Jr. (Eds.), *Academic rewards in higher education*. Cambridge, MA: Ballinger.

Turner, J. A. (1990). With number of Ph.D.'s down, mathematicians debate calculus reform and better teaching. *Chronicle of Higher Education 36*(20), January 31, pp. A15–A18.

U.S. Department of Education. (1989). *The condition of education* (Volume 2: Postsecondary Education). Washington, D.C.: U.S. Government Printing Office.

University of California. (1986). Report of the Committee on Academic Planning, University of California Academic Senate, June 17 (cited in Sykes, 1988, p. 157).

University of Minnesota. (1990). *Minutes of the meeting of the Faculty Consultative Committee*. Unpublished document, January 18: Author.

Useem, M., & Karabel, J. (1986). Pathways to top corporate management. *American Sociological Review 51*, April, 184–200.

Veblen, T. (1957). *The higher learning in America*. New York: Hill & Wang. (Originally published in 1918.)

Veysey, L. R. (1965). *The emergence of the American university*. Chicago:

University of Chicago Press.

Wagener, U. (1989). Affording quality teaching. Report of the Pew Higher Education Research Program. Philadelphia: University of Pennsylvania.

Watkins, B.T. (1989). Colleges urged to avow that teaching is central to their mission and to take steps to upgrade it. *Chronicle of Higher Education 35*(21), April 26, pp. A13, A15.

Weick, K. (1976). Educational organizations as loosely-coupled systems. *Administrative Science Quarterly 21*(1), 1–19.

Winkler, D.R. (1987). Screening models and education. In G. Psacharopoulos (Ed.), *Economics of education research and studies*. Oxford: Pergamon Press.

The work schedules of professors: Incentives for teaching new students. (1989). *Chronicle of Higher Education 35*(21), February 1, p. A18.

Yankelovich, D. (1987). Bridging the gap. *CASE Currents 13*(9), 25–27.

3 THE RESEARCH AND SERVICE MISSIONS OF THE UNIVERSITY

G. Edward Schuh and Vernon W. Ruttan

The skills of individuals and other forms of human capital have become increasingly important sources of economic growth and development in modern societies. Other forms of human capital include knowledge, the translation of that knowledge into instrumental forms—technology and social institutions—and good health and nutrition. Modern universities add to a society's stock of human capital by producing new knowledge through research, by applying that knowledge in the development of new technology and of new social institutions, by educating and training people, and by extending old and new knowledge to members of society generally, including those in the private and public sectors. Through these various activities, universities influence and shape the culture of the society, and this is an important form of human capital in its own right.

This chapter focuses on the research and service missions of the university. Although discussion does not deal explicitly with residential instruction, it does recognize the synergy between teaching and research. The chapter first addresses the research mission, before examining the service mission. The final section of the chapter discusses some issues modern universities face as they attempt to fulfill these missions.

The Research Mission

Perhaps the best way to understand the research mission of the university in the context of contributing to economic development is to consider the value of that research to society. We do this in two steps, first by considering the value of research in the natural sciences and in technology development, and then by considering the value of social science research and its role in the development of social institutions. Throughout this chapter *natural sciences* is used as a shorthand description for the biological and physical sciences, and for related areas such as engineering, medicine, and agronomy. The use of *social sciences* includes the related professionals such as law, business and management, public affairs, and social service.

The Value of Research in the Natural Sciences

If one starts with a societal rather than a parochial perspective of a university, two questions become important. First, what is or should be the relative role of the public and the private sectors in the advancement of knowledge and in technical, institutional, and cultural development and innovation? Second, what is the university's role within the public sector—that is, what research and development (R&D) should be conducted at universities rather than at national laboratories; what social science research should be done at the university rather than in the government that provides the institutional infrastructure?

Three criteria are employed in attempting to answer these questions:

- A primary rationale for public sector support for research has been that in many areas incentives for private sector research have not been adequate to induce an optimum level of research investment. The problem is that the social rate of return to such investments often exceeds the private rate of return. This can occur for two reasons. First, if the research results in an innovation that is easily copied, other firms will replicate it and thus reduce the return to the firm that produced the innovation. Second, if the innovation raises productivity in the sector or economy, prices will decline and the consumer will be the ultimate beneficiary.

  These results are referred to as *spillover* effects since the benefits are captured by groups other than those making the investment that generates the innovation. This spillover effect is relevant to university R&D as well as to private sector R&D. The spillovers (also referred to as externalities) tend to be largest for basic research and also may be larger in many areas of "generic" technology.

- A second reason for public sector support of university research is the complementarity between research and education. There is a strong synergistic interaction between research and education in the sciences and technology and between scholarship and education in the arts and humanities. This relationship is so strong that in many cases the productivity of research activities declines significantly when they are conducted apart from education. Similarly, graduate (and much undergraduate) education is less than fully productive when conducted apart from research.
- A third criterion is that public sector research contributes to the maintenance or enhancement of a more open or competitive economic and social structure even in those areas with substantial private sector incentives.

There is no reason to believe, however, that the optimum level of public sector research investment implied by each of the three criteria would be identical. For example, if firms sponsoring the research are able to capture the full benefits of that research, the incentives for private research investments will tend to be quite strong (the private rate of return to such investments will be quite high). In contrast, application of the education criterion in this same situation might imply a level of public sector research that is greater than that implied by the social rate of return criterion. Alternatively, where incentives for private research investment are weak the social rate of return criterion may exceed the level implied by the training criterion. Thus the allocation of resources to research primarily on the basis of student numbers may result in a substantial departure from the optimum level of support for university research and among the many disciplines and professions within the university.

The ability to measure the benefits from research has advanced very significantly over the last several decades. The most comprehensive set of studies has focused on estimates of the annual social rates of return to public investment in agricultural research. The returns to public sector agricultural research, much of it conducted at public universities, ranges well above the 15–20 percent return normally considered adequate to attract investment in the private sector. In fact, these rates of return range as high as 70 to over 100 percent per year. (See Ruttan 1982, and Thirtle and Bottombey 1988.)

The literature on rates of return to industrial research and development is less extensive than for the agricultural sector. The studies that are available, however, show social rates of return to private sector industrial research in roughly the same range as rates of return to agricultural research (Mansfield 1986). Private rates of return, however, average approximately half the social rates of return. Private returns are lower than social returns because the suppliers of new technology have to share the gains with users in order to achieve rapid adoption. One consequence is both public and private underinvestment in both agricultural and industrial research.

The Value of Social Science Research

The basic concept on which the evaluation of the returns to research and development in the natural sciences and technology is based is that the demand for knowledge is derived from the demand for technical change in the production of goods and services. (For more detail, see Ruttan, 1982, from which this section is drawn.) Once the output of research was clearly conceptualized as an input into the process of technical change in production, processing, and distribution, this link made it possible to develop models to measure the ex post returns to research. It then became possible to make ex ante estimates of the relative contribution of alternative uses of research resources and to specify rules that research managers might follow in the allocation of research resources.

Social scientists have only begun, perhaps somewhat reluctantly, to conceptualize adequately the contribution of knowledge in the social sciences. (For initial attempts, see Hayami and Peterson, 1972, and Norton and Schuh, 1981.) The first step in an attempt to value new knowledge in the social sciences is to specify the sources of demand for that knowledge. It is clear that the demand for knowledge in the social sciences is not derived primarily from either private or public demand for technical change. The demand for knowledge in these sciences—as well as in related professions such as law, business, and social service—is derived primarily from a demand for institutional change and improvements in institutional performance.

Conceptualizing the demand for institutional change in this manner opens up the possibility of a more precise identification of the link between the demand for institutional change and the demand for knowledge in the social sciences generally. Advances in knowledge in the social sciences offer an opportunity to reduce the costs of institutional innovation, just as advances in knowledge in the biological, physical, and natural sciences, and in the various fields of technology, have reduced the costs of technical innovation. The demand by policy makers for advances in knowledge about price and market relationships is, for example, appropriately viewed as derived from demand for improved performance on the part of market or nonmarket institutions.

What evidence supports the hypothesis that the demand for social science knowledge is derived from the demand for institutional innovation? Let us refer to three examples that tend to establish at least the plausibility of the hypothesis.

During the last one hundred years, the United States has experienced three major waves of institutional reform. The first was the Progressive Period that spanned the last decade of the nineteenth century and continued until the U.S. entry to World War I. The demands for reform were induced by the rapid technical and economic changes that had dramatically altered the conditions of American life since the Civil War. The unifying theme that underlay the reform proposals of the Progressive Era was a rejection of unregulated free enterprise capitalism. Reforms reflecting this perspective were initiated in the areas of income distribution, labor relations, social services, financial markets, transportation, industrial organization, and resource conservation. Popular demands for "direct democracy" were translated into expansion of women's suffrage, direct election of senators, and more active participation of voters in the legislative process through the initiative, referendum, and recall. A major consequence of these reforms was to widen substantially the participation of the federal government in economic affairs and in areas previously reserved to the states.

The second major wave of institutional innovation and reform was during the New Deal period in the 1930s. Political scientists and historians have debated the question of whether the New Deal reforms represented a drastic departure in American reformism or were primarily the realization of reforms proposed originally during the Progressive Era and incubated during the 1920s. But the New Deal reforms are not too difficult to characterize. They were in defense of security of property, of work, and of income—a reshuffle of the cards that had too long been stacked against the working man, the farmer, and the small businessperson. But federal government acceptance of responsibility for maintaining economic life represented a radical break with tradition. The result was a period of six years, 1933 to 1938, that represented the most rapid period of institutional change since the Civil War.

The third wave of institutional reform occurred during the Kennedy and Johnson administrations—the New Frontier and Great Society years of 1960–1968. These administrations sought to complete the liberal agenda.

They sought to eradicate racial discrimination in voting, housing, jobs, and schooling. And they sought to eliminate poverty—both black and white and urban and rural. These reforms were followed in the late 1960s and early 1970s by rapid innovation in new forms of property rights in natural resources induced by a rising concern about the impact of technology on both material resources and environmental amenities.

During each of these periods the demand for social science knowledge grew rapidly. The first period drew on a broad range of intellectual capacities and expertise in law, in economics, and in the newer social science disciplines—but there was relatively little theory and even less research on which to draw. During the second period economists played a much larger role in policy design. Unfortunately, lack of an adequate understanding of macroeconomic relationships and a pervasive pessimism about the prospects for growth led to a structuralist reform agenda. But the demands for institutional innovation did lead to substantial growth in the resources devoted to social science research and to strengthening the statistical services of the federal government.

By the late 1930s new theory and new information were being brought to bear on institutional innovation and reform. A new class of "service intellectuals" emerged in policy roles in the federal government. During the 1960s social science research played an even larger role in program design than in the two earlier periods. This was in part because of a greatly expanded body of social science knowledge, a larger social science research capacity, and improvements in capacity to generate, process, and analyze social science data. Attempts were made to introduce experimental design as a stage in program development. But in spite of the advances in theory and method, the policy-relevant social science knowledge on which the Kennedy and Johnson administrations were forced to draw in designing poverty programs of the 1960s was too weak to respond effectively to the demands placed on it.

If one accepts the notion that the demand for knowledge in the social sciences is derived from the demand for institutional change, one must consider the sources of supply of institutional change. The view that emerges from our work is that advances in social science knowledge act to increase the quantity of supplied institutional change at any given price. Throughout history improvements in institutional performance have occurred primarily through the slow accumulation of successful precedent or as a by-product of expertise and experience. Institutional change was traditionally generated through the process of trial and error much in the same manner that technical change was generated prior to the invention of the research university, the agricultural experiment station, or the industrial research laboratory. With the institutionalization of research in the social sciences, it is becoming increasingly possible to substitute social science knowledge and analytical skill for the more expensive process of learning by trial and error. This has resulted in a substantial appreciation in the value of university-based social science research.

The Service Mission of the University

The service mission of the university usually refers to its efforts to extend the talents of its faculty and staff beyond its resident instruction and research missions. This may be done in a variety of ways, including informal teaching, technical assistance, conferences and seminars for the general public, and interaction with policy makers in the design of new policies and institutional arrangements.

Higher education in the United States acquired a *formal* service mission with the establishment of the Land Grant universities in 1864. These universities were created as a reaction against the elitism of the liberal arts colleges in the East. In their original incarnation they were dedicated to teaching alone; later a research function was added, and still later an extension or outreach function.

The research function was designed to systematically apply the tools of science and technology — or better, knowledge — to the problems of society. The greatest fruition of this idea has been with agriculture, although nothing in the original mandate of the legislation limited the research to this subject matter. In fact, many of the land-grant universities early in their history had engineering experiment stations that paralleled their agricultural experiment stations.

It remains one of the great puzzles of institutional development in this country why engineering schools did not develop substantial state-supported research and extension programs directed toward state economic development. This failure caused this nation to lag behind Japan and Germany in the development of process technology for the nonfarm sector and in turn to experience increasing difficulty in competing in the international economy. It is precisely in developing process technology that there tends to be a disparity between private and social rates of returns.

The extension or outreach function was added to the land-grant universities when it became clear that merely creating new knowledge by means of research was not sufficient; there had to be a means of getting the new knowledge into the hands of those who would eventually use it.

Although this new system varied a great deal from one state to another, the basic idea was that it would be a cooperative system—shared among the federal government, the state government, and the country or local government. In general, the share of costs borne by each level of government has been approximately equal.

The close articulation among research, resident instruction, and extension in the land-grant universities is generally viewed as a uniquely American invention. Moreover, this perspective is widely emulated in other countries, in part because U.S. foreign economic assistance programs have often viewed extension as an institution worthy of export. In many cases, however, observers in other countries have viewed the land-grant universities as an agent of economic development, especially when agriculture is a principal part of their economy. Thus they have wanted these kinds of universities as a means to promote their own economic development.

Similarly, the concept of public service associated with the land grants is widely emulated in other universities within the United States. In fact, in today's world hardly any self-respecting university would consider itself worthy of the name without having an outreach program, even though it might not have, or have access to, the extensive statewide network of offices that the agricultural extension services have.

The service mission of modern universities is dispensed in a variety of forms, including extending technical knowledge to the private sector, extending technical knowledge to policy makers, providing public affairs education, verifying knowledge generated by the private sector, and providing feedback mechanisms. We discuss each of these briefly in the paragraphs that follow.

Extending Technical Knowledge to the Private Sector

Most universities believe they have a responsibility to provide or extend knowledge to the private sector. If an important share of university support comes from public sources, the university will "extend" itself as a quid pro quo and to show it is worthy of additional financial support. Private universities are similarly motivated and try to show their relevance to the problems of society as a means of encouraging private support of their programs.

Knowledge is extended to the private sector in a variety of forms. Probably the most well developed is through formal extension services set up in the name of the land-grant universities. Such programs are a mandated mission of these universities and are publicly supported. In addition to their extensive delivery systems nationwide, in most cases these programs have extension specialists from academic departments who assist the field staff by preparing extension material, helping to develop their programs, and helping them keep pace with the latest developments in their respective fields. These extension specialists also do a great deal of applied research that is extended through the field staff.

Such formal extension services are an important component of modern land-grant universities. In some states they still focus primarily on the agricultural sector, with a particular emphasis on the production side. In other states the mission of the extension service has been broadened to address the full breadth of the economy. The character of the programs delivered by such services also varies a great deal. In the early days of this system technical assistance to the individual farmer was emphasized, while in recent years less and less attention has been given to individual assistance and more and more knowledge has been extended through semiformal and formal course work. In some cases the material provided in adult education courses is little different than that provided through courses in resident instruction programs.

Knowledge is extended to the private sector in a variety of other forms. For example, conferences and seminars for specialized industrial groups are a popular means by which resident faculty interact with representatives from the private sector. Conferences may be complementary or have significant tuition fees, and they may be provided regularly, in some cases with sequencing, or be completely ad hoc in nature.

Some universities also develop regular channels of information to their alumni. In some cases alumni are advised of significant developments in the university; in other cases intensive training programs are made available. The level of instruction provided in such programs can also vary a great deal.

Universities can also extend knowledge to the private sector through patenting and joint venture activities. Faculty inventions are patented by the university and then released to the private sector on a royalty basis or by means of joint ventures. Faculty inventors may or may not participate in such joint activities and/or in the income from these enterprises, depending on the particular circumstances. In any case, this is an increasingly important means of extending technical knowledge generated in the university to the private sector.

Patenting, of course, gives rise to private returns and enables the patent holder to capture the returns from the innovation. Attempts by universities to obtain patents for innovations created by their faculty have on occasion created conflict between the right of privacy and the customary openness in the scientific community. An important recent example is the University of Utah's problems in patenting cold fusion (see McDonald 1990*a*, 1990*b*, 1990*c*).

Still another means of extending knowledge to the private sector is through specialized institutes and programs. They include institutes of public affairs and, in the case of the University of Minnesota, such units as the Center for Interfacial Engineering and the Gray Freshwater Biological Institute. These programs tend to be multidisciplinary units that integrate faculty from various academic units to focus on particular problems.

One significant issue in modern universities is the increasing number of individual faculty members who consider their private consulting as a form of outreach or extension. This raises serious ethical issues, especially since the knowledge extended is often generated with public resources and the consulting itself done at the expense of university-based outreach programs. We will return to this issue.

Extending Technical Knowledge to Policy Makers

Policy makers demand technical knowledge just as representatives from the private sector do. Universities and their individual faculty respond to this demand in a variety of ways and by providing a variety of services. For example, more than in perhaps any other country, individual faculty members in this country move back and forth between academia and government. A number of institutional arrangements facilitate this exchange at the federal level by allowing faculty to spend time in government without losing their tenure or tenure time. More generally, universities view such exchanges with favor because they give them visibility and because administrators generally view such experiences as a useful means of increasing the relevance of what is taught in the classroom and of broadening the perspectives of the faculty.

Universities also tend to develop particular academic units that specialize in developing and extending knowledge to the public sector. In the past one important means was through units of the university that provided analyses of business conditions in the state to the public and private sector. Bureaus of economic research in colleges of business are important examples. More recently, universities have created institutes of public affairs or of public policy that provide a more specialized form of knowledge to policy makers. The degree of involvement of such units with the public sector varies greatly from one university to another. Nevertheless, the goal of providing knowledge to the public sector, either in direct or indirect ways, is a common theme.

More generally, individual faculty consult with the public sector in the same way as they do with the private sector. In some cases this consultation is directly related to their professional activities, such as participating in various peer review groups to evaluate research and other kinds of proposals. In other cases the technical knowledge, insight, and wisdom is very similar to that provided by faculty to the private sector, with similar financial arrangements and often with similar conflicts of interest.

Providing Public Affairs Education

Democracy is predicated on an informed electorate. Citizens need to be well informed about public issues if they are to know how to elect their representatives. They also need to be well informed if they are to express their views to their representatives in a sensible way and if they are to evaluate those representing them.

Citizens generally need two kinds of information. First, they need to know how the political system works. Second, they need particular substantive or subject matter information on specific issues, together with a basis for interpreting that information. This represents information that they cannot easily buy from experts. It is information that is required in the voting booth, at the time of a decision, and in discussion with neighbors.

There is a growing demand and need for such information as the modern world becomes increasingly complex. This is reflected in the rapid spread of institutes of public affairs and public policy. It is also reflected in the growing disaffection with the political process among the body politic, as individual citizens feel themselves increasingly unable to make informed judgments, to articulate their views, and to evaluate those who represent them.

Another reason public affairs education is becoming increasingly important is that specialized firms in the private sector increasingly provide technical information to one and all, either as part of their general operations or on a fee basis. However, private sector firms are less able to provide public affairs information and education on a fee basis because they view such information as something that will not directly affect their income. Thus an important share of this information must come from the public sector.

Verifying Knowledge Generated by the Private Sector

Another important service provided by universities is verification of the knowledge and information generated and provided by the private sector. As long as such knowledge is proprietary and kept for proprietary purposes only, there is little or no need for verification; the owner of such information uses it at his or her own risk. However, once the knowledge and information is made available to the public, either freely or on a fee basis, it needs to be verified or at least evaluated by a public service.

The verification process can take a number of forms. If the knowledge is of a scientific nature, it may well be published in scientific journals. In that case, faculty may be chosen to serve as peer reviewers or to verify through replication the results in the course of their own research. This function is an important service that faculty provide in the regular course of their academic activities. As already noted, attempts by universities to patent the innovations of their faculty and staff conflict with this verification process.

An equally important service function is to verify and to serve as public critics of information extended to the private and public sector by private entities. This service may involve information disseminated in magazines, newsletters, bulletins and leaflets, newspapers, and electronic media. Information divulged in the context of promoting the use of a good or service sold by a company needs special verification in that the company's incentive to disseminate information favorable to that good or service will be strong. The recent discovery that vitamins and minerals taken by pregnant women add little to their general health status is a good example of such a service.

Evaluating the quality of such goods and services is another important service function of universities. Whether these goods or services actually include the operational agents that are claimed, such as in the case of fertilizers for agriculture and commonly used medicines for colds and other purposes, is another example. In both this and the case of information provided by the public sector, competitive pressures may eventually weed out those who provide misinformation. However, competitive pressures may not be sufficiently strong to compel this sorting out, or there may be sufficiently dangerous consequences from wrong information that there is a need for verification by the public sector.

Providing Feedback Mechanisms

Extending knowledge to the private and public sectors as discussed here provides another service in its own right. Providing a means of interacting with the users of such knowledge, and actually using the knowledge itself, affords an important feedback mechanism that can help redirect ongoing research programs. This may be in terms of evaluating the validity of the knowledge itself or in terms of identifying new problems that need to be solved. In either case, this new information or knowledge is a service in its own right, and often of considerable value both to the university and to society itself.

Some Issues in Managing University Research and Service Missions

Universities face a number of issues concerning their research and service missions. We address some of these issues in this section.

Managing R&D in the University

The problem of achieving the multiple objectives of intellectual development, knowledge generation, and innovation in technology, institutions, and culture poses difficult structural and managerial problems for university administrators. Knowledge workers do not work on an assembly line. One can command their time but not their creativity.

A great deal of concern has been expressed in the popular and professional literature about the appropriate relationships between the university and society. Much of this concern has been generated by the highly publicized entrepreneurial activities of university faculty in fields such as biotechnology and computer sciences.

The traditional model of university organization and behavior is what might be called the service model of the university. In this model generic knowledge is produced as a public good. A more realistic model views the university as a parastatal or semiprivate enterprise selling its services in several markets—to students, to alumni, to foundations, to state and federal governments, and to industry.

The senior human resources of the university—its faculty—can be viewed as subcontractors. They make their services available for the production of public goods within the university; they respond to public sector demand for generic and specific knowledge. If public sources of demand for their services weaken, they respond to private sector incentives for the production of proprietary knowledge.

By viewing the university as a parastatal enterprise and its faculty as independent contractors, it is possible to generate some rather interesting insights both into university behavior and into several management and policy issues that confront the university.

1. A decline in the quality of undergraduate education is a natural consequence of the fact that the consumers of undergraduate education are subsidized by the university—undergraduate education costs more than the revenue it generates. If the subsidies were paid directly to students—in the manner of the post-WWII GI Bill of Rights—behavior would change as a result of competitive pressure for improvement in the quality of undergraduate education.
2. The highest quality human resources at the university tend to respond to the demands of those buyers of university services that generate both direct and overhead costs. Faculty will thus draw more resources to themselves and their activities. They also receive high marks from their superiors. As a consequence, resources tend to be drawn from those parts of the university that supply intermediate inputs—such as English and mathematics—rather than from those that supply final products.
3. There are strong incentives by the subcontractors—the faculty—to divert the common resources of the university to private use. Faculty divert these resources from the production of public goods that are important for the production of internal services—teaching and governance—to the support of personal goals. This division of effort can be offset if departmental culture, governance, and resource use can be organized as a cooperative. With cooperation of governance and culture, it is possible to create behavioral incentives to achieve compatibility between the mission of the university and the personal objectives of the faculty.

   Fundamentally, this issue is one of incentives and rewards. The same incentives exist in a company to direct the resources of that company to private use. However, workers in a private company receive their rewards in the form of higher compensation and not in the mobilization of power, and private companies are also more tightly managed. It is the mores of low compensation and the loose management of faculty to engender creativity in the universities that create many of these problems.

The Shift to an International Economy

One of the outstanding developments in the U.S. economy in the post-World War II period is its significant expansion into the international economy, at the same time that the international economy itself has become increasingly well integrated. With the exception of five years, U.S. international trade has continuously grown faster than *global* GNP since the end of World War II, and those five exceptions have been years of significant economic recession. In a parallel fashion, a well-integrated capital market has emerged on the international scene, especially in the last thirty years. This international capital market links the economies of individual countries in ways every bit as important as international trade.

Because of these developments, citizens and companies of the United States are no longer just members of a nation-state. They are members of an international economy and society. Decisions they make in their every-day lives now must be informed with knowledge and information on the international economy and society. This places a significantly increased burden on universities to transmit new kinds of knowledge by means of resident instruction programs and to service the private and public sectors more generally. That in turn greatly expands the needed scope of research programs.

The failure to respond to this broadened demand for knowledge is one of the major failures of U.S. universities. It also poses one of the major challenges to our universities, since unless this demand is met, it will be increasingly difficult for our citizenry to vote intelligently and for the nation as a whole to compete in the international economy. To meet this challenge the universities face a major task in upgrading their own human capital. They also need to develop new institutional arrangements whereby they can collaborate with teaching and research institutions in other countries, whereby they can collaborate more effectively with one another in generating the new knowledge needed, and whereby they can share talent and output in fulfilling their various service missions.

A more serious challenge may underlie these issues. With a well-integrated international economy, the knowledge generated by U.S. universities may increasingly become a free good for the global economy. Thus the spillover effects from research will be larger in the future, thus increasing the case for publicly funded research. Moreover, the problem of the free-rider on the international scene will be increasingly important. New institutional arrangements may be needed internationally to assure that the burden of generating new knowledge is shared equitably. This could involve some system of international taxation or of mutual commitments of given expenditure levels. In any case, it seems unlikely that the body politic in the United States will want to continue to support knowledge-generating activities if a significant share of the benefits of that knowledge goes to strengthen the competitive advantage of other countries, as it now does.

Shifts in Where Policy Making Takes Place

A consequence of the growing internationalization of the global economy is that national economies become increasingly open. This means in turn that national economies become increasingly beyond the reach of national economic policies. When this occurs, there is a tendency for policy making and implementation to shift in two disparate directions. Some part of it shifts upward to the international level and becomes imbedded in the codes, rules, and disciplines of international institutions such as the General Agreement on Tariffs and Trade (GATT), the international monetary system, and the United Nations Environmental Protection Agency. Another part shifts downward to the state and local government level and changes in character, with more attention to local income and resource problems.

These shifts place new demands on both the research and service missions of the universities. More attention needs to be given to the international issues than has been the case in the past, which raises the same issue already discussed. At the same time, the demand for knowledge by policy makers at the state and local levels can be expected to grow significantly as their responsibility grows. Demands to extend knowledge to state and local governments will grow—and in fact have already grown significantly—as will demands for policy—relevant research useful at the state and local levels. Much of this new knowledge will be location-specific and will need to be produced by local universities.

Integrating the Social and Natural Sciences

Significant advances in knowledge have been made in this post–World War II period by the significant increase in disciplinary specialization. This specialization has probably also led to some efficiency in transmitting that knowledge. However, we may be at a point in the development of the sciences at which a greater integration of the disciplines is needed, if not for the generation of new knowledge, at least for its application in the production of new technologies and the design of new social institutions.

This can perhaps best be seen in the design of new social institutions and policy. There was a time when it was thought sufficient to bring the various social sciences together in institutes of public affairs or public policy to do policy-relevant research and to design new policies and social institutions. That is no longer adequate. Most policy issues and most institutional design questions require the input of the natural sciences as well as engineering and the social sciences. As examples, consider the cases of policies dealing with emerging health problems, the problems of biotechnology, and the increasingly acute problems of the environment. Few of these problems can be resolved by the social sciences alone; most need the combined inputs from the social sciences, engineering, and the natural sciences.

This is not just the case of having the natural sciences and engineering to inform the social sciences in devising new policies and designing new social institutions. Knowledge created by the natural sciences and engineering also needs to be informed by the social sciences and the humanities. Social and ethical problems arise as new technology is introduced into society, as illustrated by the serious environmental problems sometimes created by new technologies and by the growing ethical and social problems created by new medical technology.

Science and Technology Policy

Investments in science and technology account for an ever larger share of increases in per capita income as nation-states develop. Thus expenditures on these activities account for an ever larger share of public budgets, both at the national and state level. Moreover, the rational allocation of these resources involves increasingly difficult issues. Yet science and technology policy is an underdeveloped field among the various policy fields.

A number of examples will illustrate the magnitude of this problem. First, modern science increasingly involves large capital items, as in the case of the particle accelerators. Major commitments of resources are needed for these items, yet it is not at all clear how these items contribute to the advancement of commercially useful technology or whether they are congruent with the demands for such commercial technology. Similarly, some of the currently proposed research projects, such as the human genome project, involve large expenditures of money and the involvement of large numbers of scientists from a large number of research institutions. Is this a high-payoff investment to society? If so, over what time horizon?

Are there higher-payoff investments? These questions need to be addressed, but seldom are.

What should be the level of investment in the production of new knowledge, given the changes in the international economy? How can other countries be induced to share equitably in this burden? Who will receive the benefits of the new knowledge, and in what proportion? Answers to these questions are needed if a rational science and technology policy is to be developed. However, the questions are seldom asked, let alone attempts made to answer them.

New technology often creates environmental problems and generates social costs such as frictional unemployment. How can these externalities be internalized in a rational fashion? How can those imposing such costs on others be made to share in these costs? Similarly, how can the private sector be induced to make greater expenditures on science and technology when externalities are large?

Universities have the tools to begin to answer some of these questions. Finding adequate answers is critical to sustainable economic development. This gap needs to be filled.

Conclusion

It is useful to conclude this chapter by presenting a perspective on what society should expect from the modern research university and what the university should expect from society. To begin, we believe the primary objective of the university must be the intellectual development of its students (or in the crude phraseology of the economist—the creation of human capital). This means that the integrity of the university is threatened if it allows any of the other missions in which it is engaged to dominate the education mission. Let us illustrate.

- The university *is not primarily* an economic development institution. Its primary purpose is not to serve as a source of the new technology or as a training (as distinct from education) institution for the skills needed to sustain a dynamic economy.
- The university *is not primarily* a welfare institution—providing jobs, benefits, and prestige to its faculty and administrators.
- The university *does not exist primarily* to provide extended puberty rites, motivation training, and job placement for its students.
- The university *is not primarily* a screening agent for skill certification.
- The university *is not primarily* an entertainment institution providing

services in the form of sports and other cultural amenities for its community.

But all of these functions are legitimate. And if the university achieves its primary objective — if the undergraduates, the students in the professional schools, and the graduate students in the natural and social sciences and in the arts and humanities are provided with the opportunities for intellectual growth that they deserve — the other legitimate functions will also be served. But if the basic mission of the university is not served well, it is doubtful that the other missions can be sustained.

References

Hayami, Y., & Peterson, W. (1972). Social returns to public information services: Statistical reporting of U.S. farm commodities. *American Economic Review 62*(1), 119–130.

McDonald, K. A. (1990*a*). Chemists whose cold-fusion claims created furor ignite another controversy at the U. of Utah. *Chronicle of Higher Education*, June 6.

McDonald, K. A. (1990*b*). 'Anonymous' gift to Fusion Institute angers U. of Utah scientists. *Chronicle of Higher Education*, June 13.

McDonald, K. A. (1990*c*) U. of Utah president plans to retire, decision follows criticism of handling of cold-fusion controversy. *Chronicle of Higher Education*, June 20.

Mansfield, E. (1986). Microeconomics of technological innovation. In R. Landau & N. Rosenberg (Eds.), *The positive sum strategy: Harnessing technology for economic growth* (pp. 307–326). Washington, D.C.: National Academy Press.

Norton, G., & Schuh, G. E. (1981). Evaluating returns to social science research: Issues and possible methods. In G. W. Norton, W. L. Fiskel, A. A. Paulsen, & W. B. Sundquist (Eds.), *Evaluation of agricultural research* (pp. 247–261). St. Paul: University of Minnesota Agricultural Experiment Station Miscellaneous Publication 8–1981.

Ruttan, V. W. (1982). *Agricultural research policy* (pp. 242–246). Minneapolis: University of Minnesota Press.

Thirtle, C., & Bottombey, P. (1988). *The rate of return to public sector agricultural R&D in the United Kingdom: 1965–80* (pp. 5–6). Manchester: University of Manchester Working Papers in Agricultural Economics.

II HIGHER EDUCATION AS PERSONAL INVESTMENT AND ADVANCEMENT

The four chapters of part II focus on the private financial returns and nonmonetary benefits from higher education. Chapter 4 introduces the section through the use of traditional human capital theory in examining the question, "Why go to college?" Several alternative theories are also explored as possible explanations for the perceived relationship between schooling and earnings. Chapter 5 provides recent evidence that the private returns from higher education have dramatically improved over the past decade. Chapter 6 gives detailed patterns and trends in the private returns to specific college majors over the past three decades. Other nonmonetary private benefits are identified and examined in chapter 7.

4 WHY GO TO COLLEGE? THE VALUE OF AN INVESTMENT IN HIGHER EDUCATION

William E. Becker

In 1759 Adam Smith published his first book, *The Theory of Moral Sentiments*, in which he questioned the merits of higher education:

> The education of boys at distant great schools, of young men at distant colleges, of young ladies in distant nunneries and boarding-schools, seems in the higher ranks of life to have hurt most essentially the domestic morals, and consequently the domestic happiness, both of France and England. . . . Surely no acquirement which can possibly be derived from what is called a public education can make any sort of compensation for what is almost certainly and necessarily lost by it. [Pp. 363–364]

Two hundred years later, however, Schultz (1961), Mincer (1962), Becker (1964), and then many other economists, ignored this rhetoric and advanced the notion that the value of the knowledge and skills students acquire in school greatly exceeds it costs. According to this human capital theory of schooling, a student's decision to pursue education, as with a decision to acquire physical capital, is based on a comparison of the financial returns and costs of an investment in education. Gary Becker (1964) focused attention within economics on the rate of return in the college-going decision, although as he (1989) states, educators generally resisted the initial work on the economic effects of education: Focusing on jobs and earnings was viewed as being too narrow.

Debate on the merits of viewing college education as an investment expanded beyond economics in the 1970s with the publication of Richard Freeman's book *The Overeducated American*. As an alternative to the pecuniary return emphasized in human capital theory, education researchers and practitioners (as reviewed by Cohn and Geske in chapter 7 of this book) have emphasized the qualitative and intrinsic value of higher education, arguing that market forces cannot fully reflect human worth. Others, either knowingly or not, applied Spence's (1974) and Stiglitz's (1975) economic theories of signaling and screening as an explanation for the value of education in "certification." As part of the accountability craze, educators also adopted the economist's "value added" model while maintaining a belief that human knowledge need not have monetary value. These alternative views of why higher education is desired by individuals are discussed in this chapter.

The Return to Higher Education

What is meant by "a higher education" is not clearly defined in the education or economics literature. What types of schools (e.g., community colleges, vocational schools, trade schools, liberal arts colleges, universities) are included and what forms of training and skills acquisition are fostered are seldom addressed. Typically, years of schooling beyond twelfth grade is the quantitative measure used to define higher education. Economists (see for example, Behrman and Birdsall 1983; Hanushek 1986) recognize that years of schooling is a crude measure of the schooling experience. It ignores the influence of student–teacher ratios, teacher experience, peer grouping, curricula, and other factors that are believed to influence the amount of knowledge and skills embodied in individuals during the years of schooling.

Regardless of the type of schooling purchased, an expenditure for postsecondary schooling is an investment good if it generates additional income in the future; the skills acquired during these years of study are the human capital or asset created by the investment. If no additional income is created, however, then this education expenditure would be a pure consumption good, which implies no long-term benefit and only immediate satisfaction or utility.

Higher education is both a consumption good and an investment good. Students get immediate benefits from going to college, as they enjoy the college experience—learning for the sake of learning or partying until they drop may be goals of college-age students. Research by Leslie,

Johnson, and Carlson (1977) and Tannen (1978), however, suggests that the expectation of higher lifetime earnings is the primary reason for seeking a higher education. Astin and colleagues (1985, p. 47) report that 72 percent of the students in a national survey of college freshmen agreed that "the chief benefit of a college education is that it increases one's earning power"; 83 percent listed "get a better job" as a very important reason for attending college. Similarly, Willis and Rosen (1979) found the decision to go to college is highly sensitive to monetary considerations, with a 10 percent increase in starting salaries inducing almost a 20 percent increase in college enrollments. Clearly, the long-term pecuniary benefit of going to college has not been ignored by students.

Economists and educators do not agree on the best way to measure the return to higher education or on the reason for the return in the first place. They do agree that there are two returns that need to be identified.

First, the individual who attends an institution of higher education benefits personally from the higher lifetime earnings. At least conceptually a net measure of this private return to postsecondary education can be obtained by subtracting the cost of the education and taxes to be paid from the increased earnings that result from it. Alternative measures of this private return are considered in detail in this chapter.

Second, society may benefit from the increased productivity of a work force that is more highly educated. A social rate of return can be calculated by the difference between the value of this increased productivity and the cost to society of providing the education. This chapter deals primarily with the private return to higher education. Attention is given to the social return only to the extent that it relates to the private return.

Earnings Differential

The earnings differential approach to measuring the return on h years of school requires either (a) the calculation of the difference between the average sum of money that those with h years of schooling receive and the average sum received by those with only $h - 1$ years of schooling, or (b) the ratio of these two sums. In equation form these calculations are given as

$$\text{(a) DIFF} = \sum_{t=0}^{n} (W_{th} - W_{th-1}) \quad \text{or} \quad \text{(b) RATE} = \frac{\sum_{t=0}^{n} W_{th}}{\sum_{t=0}^{n} W_{th-1}}, \tag{4.1}$$

where W_{th} is average earnings, in year t, for persons with h years of schooling and n is worklife.

The earnings differential approach is usually used as a first method for approximating the value of h years of schooling. Typically the earnings of those with 16 or more years of schooling and the earnings of those with only 12 years of schooling are used to calculate the amount of money a college graduate makes over a high school graduate. Alternatively, instead of using only earnings, total person income can be used to capture the effect of education on all sources of income.

Calculations for the earnings (or income) differential approach are easy to understand and simple to perform. No attempt is made to control for student characteristics or schooling costs. The timing of those earnings, discounting, and the probability of receiving those earnings in any given year are ignored. Because of these shortcomings, the earnings differential approach is criticized as being "naive" and not "sophisticated" social science, as stated by Windham (1980) for example. As will be discussed, however, estimates of the return to schooling obtained from more complex methods are highly sensitive to changes in the assumptions. Estimates from the differential approach cannot be dismissed so easily; the simplicity in earnings and income differential calculation may be a virtue.

The ratios of median income for college and high school graduates are calculated for women and men in tables 4–1 and 4–2. The ratios of college to high school incomes for both women and men declined in the early 1970s but then resumed their ascent in the later 1970s, peaking in 1986. The assertion that "the premiums paid for a college education have declined for men but increased for women," made by Leslie and Brinkman (1988, p. 43) after a review of Rumberger's 1984 study of earnings, is not borne out by these data. Tables 4–3 and 4–4 also suggest that the fruits of higher education have not been restricted to whites; minorities may have benefited even more from higher education than their white counterparts.

Economists Murphy and Welch (1988) also reported earnings differentials that support the apparent upturn in returns to a college education. Their work, as reviewed by them in chapter 5 of this volume, shows that the difference between the earnings of college and high school graduates increased greatly after 1979 and is now larger than it was 30 years ago. Murphy and Welch assert that the gain enjoyed by college graduates is the result of a decrease in the rate at which college-age people enter the labor force and the decline in heavy industry, where high school graduates have done well, because of the shift from domestic to foreign produced final products. Similarly, Katz and Murphy (1990, p. 57) concluded that

Table 4–1. Median Income of 25- to 34-Year-Old Females with College Education or 4 Years of High School, with Income in Years 1963–1987

Years	*College (4+ years)*	*High School (4 years)*	*Ratios*
1963	3,275	2,170	1.51
1964	3,939	2,331	1.69
1965	4,568	2,483	1.84
1966	4,233	2,619	1.62
1967	4,812	2,776	1.73
1968	5,109	3,029	1.69
1969	5,393	3,023	1.78
1970	5,972	3,249	1.84
1971	6,615	3,519	1.88
1972	6,703	3,765	1.78
1973	7,107	3,945	1.80
1974	7,560	4,378	1.73
1975	8,332	4,825	1.73
1976	8,398	5,152	1.63
1977	8,836	5,554	1.59
1978	9,109	5,398	1.69
1979	10,283	5,583	1.84
1980	11,093	6,279	1.77
1981	12,177	6,703	1.82
1982	13,300	6,854	1.94
1983	14,422	7,203	2.00
1984	15,246	7,972	1.91
1985	16,550	8,302	1.99
1986	17,519	8,378	2.09
1987	18,792	9,444	1.99
1988	20,629	11,129	1.85
1989	22,033	11,270	1.96
1990	22,837	11,785	1.94

Source: U.S. Bureau of the Census, Current Population Reports, Series P-60, *Money Income of Households, Families, and Persons in the U.S.*, 1987, Table 35, and various prior years and tables.

"supply fluctuation (an acceleration in growth of the relative supply of college graduates in the 1970s and a deceleration in the 1980s) combined with stable trend demand growth do a good job of explaining overall movements in education differentials."

A popular explanation of why the college/high school earnings ratio

Table 4–2. Median Income of 25- to 34-Year-Old Males with College Education or 4 Years of High School; with Income in Years 1963–1987

Years	*College (4+ years)*	*High School (4 years)*	*Ratios*
1963	6,947	5,612	1.24
1964	7,397	5,933	1.25
1965	7,474	6,151	1.22
1966	8,373	6,600	1.27
1967	8,762	6,882	1.27
1968	9,264	7,402	1.25
1969	10,228	8,008	1.28
1970	10,661	8,217	1.30
1971	10,908	8,556	1.27
1972	11,751	9,316	1.26
1973	12,349	10,153	1.22
1974	12,637	10,701	1.18
1975	13,232	10,767	1.23
1976	13,965	11,416	1.22
1977	14,802	12,104	1.22
1978	15,783	13,129	1.20
1979	17,345	14,280	1.21
1980	18,773	15,181	1.24
1981	20,589	15,393	1.34
1982	21,149	15,298	1.38
1983	21,988	15,789	1.39
1984	23,687	17,030	1.39
1985	26,174	16,981	1.54
1986	27,141	17,551	1.55
1987	28,161	18,366	1.53
1988	28,288	19,650	1.44
1989	29,663	20,167	1.47
1990	29,568	20,051	1.47

Source: U.S. Bureau of the Census, Current Population Reports, Series P-60, *Money Income of Households, Families, and Persons in the U.S.*, various issues.

has risen over extended periods of time is that advances in physical capital displace unskilled workers more than skilled workers. In addition, technological change increases the demand for highly educated, specialized labor while it decreases the demand for less well educated individuals. Hamermesh (1986) claims that the evidence provides solid support for the idea that unskilled labor is a substitute for physical capital while skilled

Table 4–3. Median Income of Black Females with College Education or 4 Years of High School, 25 Years Old and over, with Income in Years 1967–1987

Years	*College (4+ years)*	*High School (4 years)*	*Ratios*
1967	5,823	2,712	2.15
1968	6,715	2,987	2.25
1969	6,747	3,257	2.07
1970	7,744	3,491	2.22
1971	7,805	3,583	2.18
1972	7,978	3,827	2.08
1973	7,987	4,092	1.95
1974	8,957	4,412	2.03
1975*	9,224	4,234	2.18
1976*	9,695	4,734	2.05
1977*	10,980	4,705	2.33
1978*	10,275	5,205	1.97
1979*	11,940	5,602	2.13
1980	13,767	6,856	2.01
1981	13,963	7,332	1.90
1982	15,337	7,671	2.00
1983	16,485	7,952	2.07
1984	18,401	8,381	2.20
1985	19,133	8,207	2.33
1986	20,711	8,244	2.51
1987	20,658	9,284	2.23
1988	22,721	11,509	1.97
1989	24,914	12,315	2.02
1990	25,874	12,675	2.04

Source: U.S. Bureau of the Census, Current Population Reports, Series P-60, *Money Income of Households, Families, and Persons in the U.S.*, various issues.

* Black females 18 years old and over.

labor is a complement of physical capital. Pencavel (1991), however, points to the work of Weiss (1977) and Denny and Fuss (1983) and concludes that the evidence on how human and physical capital combine in production is at best mixed. Bound and Johnson (1989) suggest that the major cause of the dramatic movement in the wage structure over the 1979–1987 period may have been some combination of changes in technology and changes in the relative nonobservable quality of different labor groups.

An alternative explanation for the rapid rise in the college/high school

Table 4–4. Median Income of Black Males with College Education or 4 Years of High School, 25 Years and over, with Income in Years 1967–1987

Years	*College (4+ years)*	*High School (4 years)*	*Ratios*
1967	7,246	5,340	1.36
1968	7,615	5,721	1.33
1969	8,567	6,144	1.39
1970	9,290	6,380	1.46
1971	10,448	6,579	1.59
1972	10,654	7,316	1.46
1973	11,294	8,284	1.36
1974	10,954	8,779	1.25
1975*	11,787	7,468	1.58
1976*	12,619	7,459	1.69
1977*	13,220	8,314	1.59
1978*	15,664	8,720	1.80
1979*	16,582	9,857	1.68
1980	16,811	12,074	1.39
1981	18,935	12,349	1.53
1982	18,908	12,498	1.51
1983	21,357	12,426	1.72
1984	21,908	12,949	1.69
1985	25,108	14,667	1.71
1986	24,747	14,465	1.71
1987	25,621	13,966	1.83
1988	27,932	16,751	1.67
1989	30,341	17,372	1.75
1990	30,282	17,181	1.76

Source: U.S. Bureau of the Census, Current Population Reports, Series P-60, *Money Income of Households, Families, and Persons in the U.S.*, various issues.
* Black males 18 years old and over.

earnings ratio in the 1980s is suggested by Becker (1990). He argues that the college–high school earnings differential narrowed because through the 1980s the minimum wage did not change with the rate of general price inflation while wages of college graduates did. Figure 4–1 shows that, at least since 1963, the ratio of college to high school income of males in the United States tends to be inversely related to the real value of the minimum wage. Although this negative relationship is far from perfect, it is significant, with a simple correlation coefficient of 0.77. A college

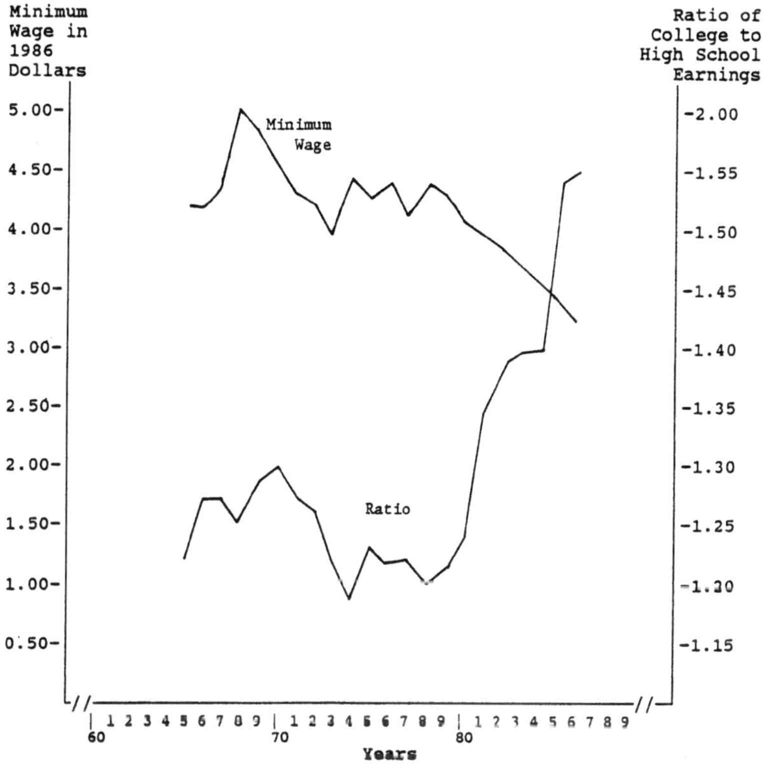

Figure 4–1. Minimum Wage and the Ratio of College to High School Male Earnings (*Sources*: Minimum wage data are from Smith & Vavrichek (1987). CPI data are from *Survey of Current Business*, various issues. CPI data for 1950–1977 are for urban wage earners and clerical workers; data post 1977 are for all urban consumers. Ratios of college to high school earnings are from table 4–2.)

education may not have become worth more; it may be that job prospects for those with only a high school education are now worse.

In the United States high school graduation does not qualify one for much more than low-paying service jobs. In Japan, on the other hand, high school performance and graduation can qualify recipients for lifelong jobs as an alternative to college admission, as emphasized by Bishop (1989). This point is also suggested by the work of Katz and Revenga (1989). Figure 4–2 shows the earnings of college graduates relative to

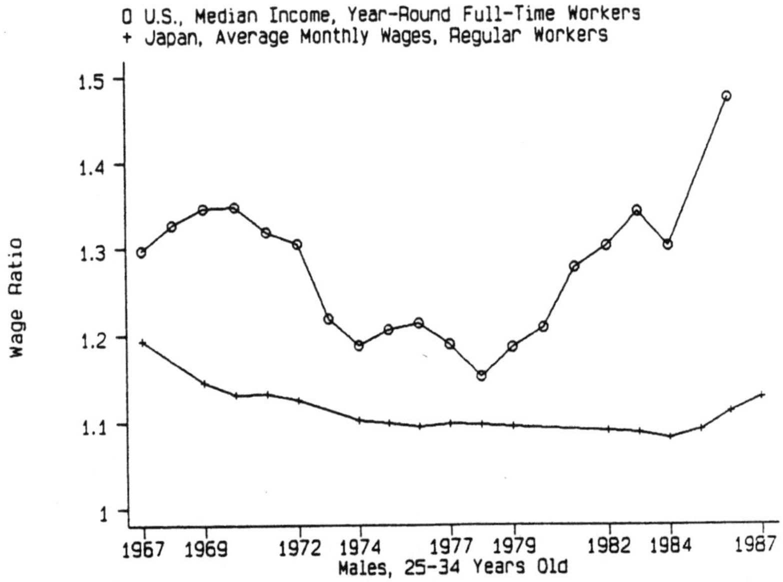

Figure 4–2. Earnings of Workers with College Relative to Earnings of Those with High School Backgrounds in the United States and Japan (*Source*: Katz and Revenga 1989.)

high school graduates to be much higher in the United States than in Japan. In addition, this college/high school earnings ratio for Japan did not rise rapidly in the 1980s as it did in the United States.

Regardless of the reason, the fact is that recent evidence on the earnings differential enjoyed by college graduates stands in direct contrast to that reported by educational writers of just a few years ago. As already stated, Freeman's (1976) book *The Overeducated American* was instrumental in convincing policy makers that the return to a college education was falling. Americans may have been overinvesting in education during the 1970s, when returns were relatively low, but after several years of work experience the average college graduate now earns some 50 to 70 percent more than a high school graduate. College graduates, on average, receive $500,000 to $1,000,000 more than high school graduates over their lifetimes.

The association of earnings with age and the differential for post-secondary and earlier years of schooling are shown in figure 4–3.[1] These age–earnings profiles give a cross-sectional view of men of different ages, earnings, and schooling as of a given date (March 1988), as opposed to a time-series view of the same individuals in succeeding years, and show

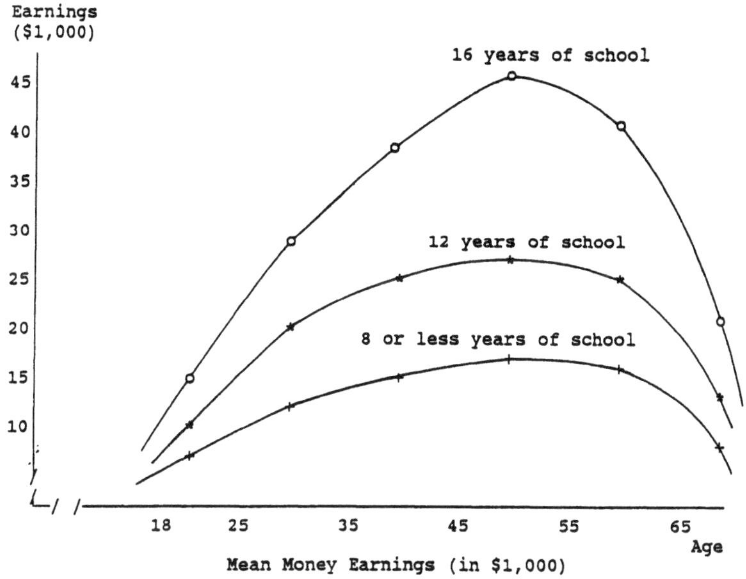

Years of School	Age 18-24	25-34	35-44	45-54	55-64	65 plus
8 or less	7.06	11.86	15.38	17.23	15.60	8.32
12	10.04	19.75	24.75	27.01	25.04	13.12
16	14.81	28.77	38.03	45.60	41.13	21.14
Relative Earnings of 16 to 12 years of school	1.48	1.46	1.54	1.69	1.64	1.61

Figure 4–3. Mean Money Earnings of Males in 1987 (*Source*: U.S. Bureau of the Census, Current Population Reports, Series P-60, *Money Income of Households, Families, and Persons in the U.S.*, Table 36, 1987.)

that earnings rise at a decreasing rate until they peak between ages 45 and 55. This rate of increase in earnings, however, increases with years of schooling. These profiles and the relative earnings ratios provided at the bottom of figure 4–3 suggest that the benefit of college is most noticeable later in life.[2] The occurrence of this benefit well after the completion of formal schooling raises an interesting question, however: Does schooling increase productivity or does it simply identify those who are most able to learn?

The relationship among age, earnings, and schooling may occur because those students who excel and persist in school also acquire skills and advance on the job faster than those who do not do well in school. After the basics of reading, writing, and arithmetic, the actual subject matter studied in school may be of secondary importance; it may be the process of learning to follow instructions and deal with unforeseen circumstances that leads to later success on the job.[3] Jamison and Lau (1982), for example, review evidence that suggests that the adoption of new technologies is directly related to the amount of formal education individuals possess. The work of Bartel and Lichtenberg (1988) and Dickens and Katz (1987) also suggests that the relative wage of more schooled individuals is greater in industries in which technological change is rapidly advancing. As presented by Berger in chapter 6 of this volume, certain areas of college study, such as majoring in the natural sciences or engineering (and sometimes business), result in an earnings premium. The type of college one attends may also influence earnings. For example, graduates of colleges whose entering freshmen have higher admission test scores seem to earn more than those from less select schools. As discussed later in this chapter, however, the question of whether it is the skills and knowledge acquired in schools or the selectivity of the schools that adds to an individual's earning power is an open question.

Net Present Value

A rule of thumb in finance is that an investment should be undertaken as long as the present value of expected future income exceeds the present value of any known or expected costs. To calculate present values, the investor must consider the premium he or she expects for accepting one dollar at a specified time in the future versus having it right now. This premium indicates the discount that the individual places on the future; it enables the investor (the student) to compare the current costs of an additional year of schooling with the discounted future value of the expected income. A comparison of simple differentials between high school and college earnings does not take account of this time value of money.

In the case of an investment in one more year of education beyond $h - 1$ years, the net present value (NPV) of this additional year of schooling is calculated by computing the following earnings differential:

$$\text{NPV} = \sum_{t=1}^{n} (W_{th} - W_{th-1})(1+d)^{-t} - \sum_{t=-s}^{0} (C_{th} + W_{th-1})(1+d)^{-t}, \qquad (4.2)$$

where: C_{th} is a measure of cost, in year t, for years of schooling h;
W_{th} is a measure of earnings, in year t, for a person with h years of schooling;
s is years of schooling considered;
n is a measure of working life; and
d is a rate of interest or discount.

The direct cost of the year h of schooling C_{th} includes such things as tuition, fees, additional living expenses, and travel to school. These direct costs would have to be calculated net of any grants or scholarships received in the year. During the s years of schooling earnings forgone in the hth year would be an added expense of schooling in that year. To the extent that the student works part time, this would be net earnings. After completing school the net benefit ($W_{th} - W_{th-1}$) is simply the difference between the earnings the student expects to receive after h years of schooling less the earnings he or she would have received with $h - 1$ years of schooling. Earnings here are net of taxes to be paid by the individual.

Although the direct costs of schooling are relatively easy to determine, expected earnings in each future time period are not. Age–earnings profiles are rarely available over time. Even if they were, the earnings observed would reflect actual or ex post earnings and not expected or ex ante earnings. Typically, cross-sectional data are used to approximate the required age–earnings profiles. As shown in figure 4–3, cross-sectional age–earnings profiles usually show earnings rising at declining rates. If pay raises are granted as a percentage of their previous level, however, one would expect age–earnings profiles specific to an individual to rise exponentially with age and time. Unlike panel data (observations on the same individuals over time), cross-sectional data do not show the possibility of this exponential growth.

The appropriate length of time over which earnings are to be projected is not obvious. The expected number of years of worklife reported in the Bureau of Labor Statistics worklife tables is not appropriate because this value is influenced by education. Even if this were not the case, Alter and Becker (1985, 1987) show that as long as discounted earnings in each future period differ the sum of earnings over expected worklife is not equal to the sum of expected yearly earnings over life.

As specified in equation (4.2) the calculation of NPV requires a single d value for discounting future earnings over n years. But what is d? Is it an ex post rate or ex ante rate? Real or nominal?

How individuals formulate expectations about the future becomes critical in the specification of *d*. The observed rate of interest at the time of a schooling decision need not be the rate used by the student or parents. They may use a rate that is expected in the future. That is, the observed ex post rate need not equal the ex ante rate used in the decision-making process.

Since the time of Irving Fisher (1930), economists have known how to control for the fact that lenders will want to be compensated for the effect of price inflation on the purchasing power of money. The real rate of interest is a measure of the rate lenders would desire if they did not expect inflation, whereas the observed or nominal interest rate has inflation expectations factored in. If *d* is a real rate, then *C* and *W* must be in real terms as well. Because real rates are not observed and must be calculated, several alternative methods are used for their determination. The method by which *d* is indexed must be the same as that for *C* or *W*. That is, if the real rate of interest is calculated on the basis of the Consumer Price Index, then *C* and *W* must also be based on this index of purchasing power. If calculated correctly, the net present value of an investment in college should not be affected by measurement in real or nominal terms. But if real values are based on different indexes, then the indices may produce different results.

Regardless of whether *d* is an ex ante or ex post rate or measured in real or nominal terms, small changes in the magnitude of *d* will produce large changes in the size of NPV, especially for a long working life. For example, an income stream of $1.00 to be received at the end of every year for the next 43 years has a present value of $9.83 at 10 percent discounting, $17.55 at 5 percent, and $43 only at a zero percent discount rate. To further appreciate the influence of small changes in *d* on the net present value of college, consider the work of Cohn and Geske (1986). Using 1979 Bureau of Census lifetime earnings data for men and women, they calculate NPV for college versus high school graduates for various discount rates and productivity growth rates. They report the following present value of earnings (ignoring cost):

	5% Discount, 0% Growth	*0% Discount, 0% Growth*
Men	$60,000	$329,000
Women	$44,000	$142,000

Note that as the discount rate rises, the present value of college falls.

For the lowest present value of earnings, Cohn and Geske subtract the present value of college costs and report an NPV of $23,000 for men and $7000 for women. These estimates are highly suspect, however, given the sensitivity of present value calculations to the discount factor and the time period over which and manner in which earnings are projected. Nonetheless, by the investment rule of thumb provided at the beginning of this section for the average male or female, college is a profitable investment because its net present value appears to be at least greater than zero.

Internal Rate of Return

Instead of prespecifying the value of the discount rate d, the critical value for which the net present value is zero can be determined as r in the equation

$$\sum_{t=-s}^{0} (C_{th} + W_{th-1})(1+r)^{-t} = \sum_{t=1}^{n} (W_{th} - W_{th-1})(1+r)^{-t}. \quad (4.3)$$

Solving for r in equation (4.3) is called the internal rate of return approach; r is the internal rate of return. It is the discount rate at which net present value in equation (4.2) is zero, as depicted in figure 4–4.

Knowledge of the internal rate of return can be useful in answering questions such as the following. How many years should I go to school? What school should I attend? In what should I major? In essence, one should pursue the investment with the highest rate of return. The net present value approach and internal rate of return approach need not lead to the same decision regarding schooling choice. For example, in figure 4–5, by the internal rate of return approach, schooling in hypothetical area e (e.g., economics) is preferred to a degree in hypothetical area f

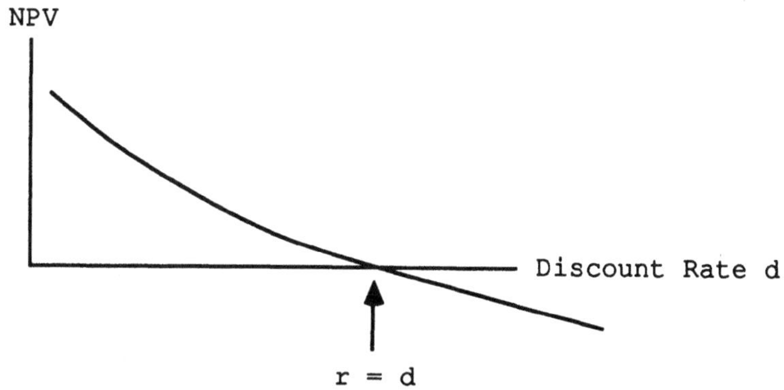

Figure 4–4. Internal Rate of Return

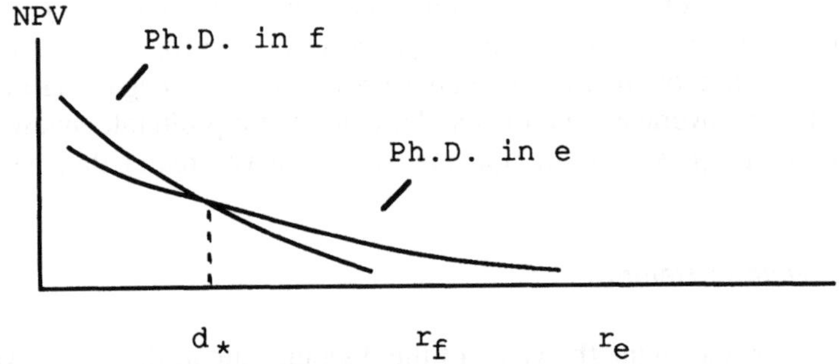

Figure 4–5. Net Present Value of Alternative Schooling

(e.g., finance) since $r_e > r_f$. For discount rates below d_*, however, f is preferred to e by the NPV criterion. Although the NPV would be preferred to the internal rate of return approach if the discount rate were known to be a specific value, most studies use the rate of return approach.

In addition to personal decisions, a rate of return can be calculated and used for decisions involving goals of society. Questions such as the following can be answered with knowledge of the "social rate of return." What is the optimum level of schooling for society? What kind of education (technical or general training, primary, secondary, or higher education) is conducive to economic growth? How large a subsidy should be provided by the state, and in what form? These are questions that require information on the social rate of return. To calculate r as a social rate of return, W must be measured as gross earnings (before taxes) and C as total schooling cost (regardless of who pays). For the private rate of return, W is net earnings and C is the cost incurred by the individual student.

Estimates of either the private or the social rate of return cannot be done without making adjustments to reflect the effects of noneducational factors. Factors such as the probabilities of survival and labor force participation already have been mentioned as affecting W. The earnings differential also is influenced by ability and socioeconomic background. The so-called "alpha coefficient" provides a rule of thumb for adjusting the earnings differential to remove the effects of noneducational factors. Research using earnings functions and regression analysis suggests a value of alpha in the 0.6–0.8 range (Psacharopoulos 1985). That is, 20 to 40 percent of the earnings differential may be due to factors other than education.

For the United States the private internal rate of return for a college education is currently thought to be a percentage in the low teens. Leslie and Brinkman's (1988) meta-analysis places it at 11.4 to 13.4 percent. Gary Becker (1988), using Murphy and Welch's (1988) data, places the rate of return on a college education at 10 percent, which is still competitive with returns on other investments. In the United States social rates of return are a couple of percentage points lower than private rates of return because of the manner in which higher education is subsidized. (Students typically pay only a fraction of the total costs while they enjoy most of the benefits.) Surprisingly, the social returns to vocational training designed to provide employers with a pool of workers who have immediate machine-ready skills is not generally thought to be high because of the tremendous cost of the training. It is the subsidy to this vocational training, which is provided by the state, that makes the private return high.

Over time very few investments have yielded 10 percent plus to the investor. Higher education in all its different forms has been a good personal investment even without bringing in the consumption benefits. This may explain why applications to colleges continued to rise until the latter part of the 1980s despite double digit yearly increases in tuition and fees and a shrinking pool of college-age people.

Regression Analysis

Most of the recent cost benefit analysis of higher education is based on the estimation of variation on Mincer's (1974, p. 83) earnings functions using individual earnings data (Y), years of schooling (S), years of labor market experience (X), and other attributes such as gender (G) or race (R). A typical "semilog" earnings regression equation is then of the form

$$\ln Y = b_0 + b_1S + b_2X + b_3X^2 + b_4G + b_5R + \ldots \qquad (4.4)$$

and the return to education is $\delta \ln Y/\delta S = \delta Y/Y\delta S = b_1$, while the return to experience is $\delta \ln Y/\delta X = b_2 + 2b_3X$, assuming Y, S, and X are continuous. Gender and race are clearly discrete, but S is also typically measured as discrete integer years of schooling.

According to Willis (1986, p. 526), "The Mincer earnings function has been one of the great success stories of modern labor economics. It has been used in hundreds of studies using data from virtually every historical period and country for which suitable data exist." Its use has been justified on theoretical grounds by assuming that earnings increase by compounding raises over time.[4] If starting earnings of the ith person in year 0 are Y_{i0}, then annual raises at a rate of c imply earnings in year t of

$$Y_{it} = (1 + c)^t Y_{i0}. \qquad (4.5)$$

With continuous compounding at rate c, earnings grow exponentially by

$$Y_{it} = e^{ct} Y_{i0}. \qquad (4.6)$$

In practice, the natural log transformation required to scale earnings has a greater effect at higher earnings, and a straight line sample relationship typically can be demonstrated between ln Y_i and any one of the explanatory variables. Logarithmic transformations also tend to reduce the level of heterogeneity (nonconstant variance) of the residuals in the sample regression.

For discrete changes in schooling, G. Psacharopoulos (1987) and most other economics of education researchers interpret the return to a year of schooling as

$$b_1 = \frac{\ln Y_h - \ln Y_{h-s}}{h - (h - s)} = \frac{1}{s}\left[\frac{Y_h - Y_{h-s}}{Y_{h-s}}\right]. \tag{4.7}$$

Thus the coefficient b_1 multiplied by 100 is said to be equal to the percentage change in Y for a small change in years of schooling from $h - s$ years to h years. But this is only an approximation. For a one-year change, where $s = 1$, we have

$$b_1 = \ln Y_h - \ln Y_{h-1} = \ln\left[\frac{Y_h}{Y_{h-1}}\right] \quad \text{and}$$

$$\exp(b) = \frac{Y_h}{Y_{h-1}} = 1 + c, \tag{4.8}$$

whereas in equation (4.5) c is defined by

$$Y_h = (1 + c)Y_{h-1}. \tag{4.9}$$

The exponent of b_1 is equal to $1 + c$ but c is only approximately equal to b_1 [i.e., $\ln(1 + c) \simeq c = b_1$] for small values of c. This is not always the case.[5] For instance, table 4–5 provides the means of the regression coefficients on years of schooling in a semilog earnings function in which the logarithm of earnings is a function of years of schooling, years of experience, and years of experience squared (Psacharopoulos 1985). The 9 percent figure for "advanced" countries such as the United States represents a 9.4 percent private rate of return to an additional year of education; the 14 percent figure for Latin American countries represents a 15 percent return. Unfortunately, these estimates do not control for interactions between the rate of return and the level of schooling represented. Psacharopoulos has shown that the rate of return to years of schooling declines as the level (primary, secondary, and higher education) increases.

Another often overlooked problem in the early fitting of earnings equations is sample selection bias. This bias arises because there are students who could enroll in college but do not. These students, for

Table 4–5. Semilogarithmic Regression Coefficient and Rate of Return to Years of Schooling by Country Type

County Type	*Average Coefficient on Years of School* (%)*	*Rate of Return for Year of School* (%)
Latin America: Brazil, Chile, Colombia, Costa Rica, El Salvador, Guatemala, Mexico, and Venezuela	14	15.0
Africa: Ethiopia, Kenya, Morocco, and Tanzania	13	13.9
Asia: Hong Kong, Malaysia, Pakistan, Singapore, South Korea, South Vietnam, Sri Lanka, Taiwan, and Thailand	11	11.6
Advanced: Australia, Canada, France, Germany, Japan, Sweden, United Kingdom, and United States	9	9.4
Intermediate: Cyprus, Greece, Iran, and Portugal	8	8.3

* As reported by Psacharopoulos (1985, p. 588).

whom there are no observations for years of college completed, are excluded from the analysis. This exclusion would not bias the coefficient estimators if the process that determined whether students enrolled in college was independent of the process that determines earnings. If, however, an unobserved factor influences both the selection process and the earnings process, least-squares regressions give biased estimates of the effects of schooling. Numerous researchers have used Heckman (1976, 1979) type adjustment techniques to correct for this bias, but the question continues to haunt education researchers: Is it the higher ability of those who go to college or the college education itself that causes the higher lifetime earnings?

Human Capital Versus Screening

As with most investments, the cost of a college education is incurred concurrently with participation while the benefits are received slowly over time. According to human capital theory, the education process instills skills and knowledge in the students that raise their productivity. The magnitude of the productivity increase, however, is never known beforehand. The value that prospective employers will place on the productivity is likewise unknown.

The receipt of benefits involves risk, but expenses occur with certainty. The work of Willis and Rosen (1979) suggests that students who terminate their schooling after high school recognize that their prospects as high school graduates are likely better than they would be as college students. Similarly, those who continue do so because their prospects are better as college graduates. Furthermore, although admission to some schools will reduce the risk of receiving future benefits, these elite schools tend to have high tuition costs and long application lists. As demonstrated by Manski and Wise (1983, pp. 7–9), prospective students know this and tend to apply to colleges for which they are suited (both financially and intellectually). Employers are aware of this sorting mechanism and thus tend to continue to use school identity and years of education or degrees completed as a screening device for potential hiring and job advancement.

The school one attends, the program completed, and grades received do signal performance and potential productivity to employers. The question to be asked, however, is, To what extent is the school screening for some innate attributes or for some ex post aptitude that reflects the productivity augmenting effect of the education and the training received while in school? From the standpoint of the employer, the answer to this question may be irrelevant. (Employers will offer the same salary for a given skill level regardless of whether it was developed by the schooling process or was an innate ability simply identified by schooling.) From the standpoint of the student and society in general, the answer to this question could make a difference in schooling decisions.

A world can be envisioned in which schools screen students and produce no change in the students' productivity as a result of the screening. Most of the early theoretical work on screening was based on this premise. For example, Arrow (1973) and Stiglitz (1975) present scenarios in which the education process is seen as simply ranking individuals in terms of their innate ability. To assess the consequence of this type of screening, consider a population in which individuals can be described by a single characteristic A. Let this characteristic be proportional to the individual's productivity. However, individuals of higher ability A_H can receive a higher salary W_H only if they can be identified as being more productive than the lower-ability A_L individuals.

While individuals may know their own abilities, in the absence of any information the market does not. The market treats all individuals the same. That is, in the absence of identification, individuals receive a salary equal to the mean value of the population. (Such would be the case, for instance, on an assembly line.) The mean income is given by

$$W = \frac{p(A_H H + A_L L)}{(H + L)}, \tag{4.10}$$

where H equals the number of high-ability individuals in the population, L equals the number of low-ability individuals, and p is the coefficient of proportional income-ability conversion. If the difference between W_H and W_L is greater than the cost of schooling (screening), then those knowing that they have higher ability would be willing to pay for schooling to signal their higher abilities to employers. Those schooled would receive the higher income W_H. Those not schooled get an income W_L, which is less than W. (This would be the equivalent of forming two assembly lines—one for the more able and one for the less able.) The gain to those schooled may exceed the loss to the nonschooled. Society as a whole, however, is made worse off by schooling.

For example, if H = 25 people, L = 75 people, A_H = 200 IQ points, A_L = 100 IQ points, W_H = \$200, W_L = \$100, and p = \$1.00, then W = \$125. If education costs \$60, then the individuals who know that they are of higher ability will pay for schooling. As a result of the school's screening function, the market identifies those who are more able. Each more able individual gains \$15 (\$200 − \$60 − \$125), for a total group gain of \$375 (25 × \$15). The private return to education for these individuals is clearly positive. Each lower-ability individual, however, has a loss of \$25 (\$125 − \$100) for a total group loss of \$1875 (75 × \$25). The social return to education is thus negative, as the population as a whole lost \$1500 (\$1875 − \$375). Tirole (1990, pp. 158–159) provides a discussion of the stability and social efficiency of alternative equilibria for signaling and screening models of education in which the educational attainment does not change student productivity.

W. Becker (1982) has demonstrated, within a formal mathematical model that builds on that of Stiglitz, that as long as the student gets some satisfaction out of learning and future consumption, a world in which productivity does not change as a result of education and screening is unlikely. His analysis shows that "an increase in the frequency, reliability, and validity of student assessment by any college will lead to an increase in student learning for all students above the modal knowledge level" (p. 236). The mere act of screening causes high-ability students to increase their learning; screening intensity cannot be changed without changing student learning. "If the distribution of student knowledge at the college is suspected to be right skewed, then an increase in screening of students should produce increased learning for the majority of students" (p. 236).

To see how learning may be motivated by screening, assume that a college could exist without giving any tests. Such a college has to conclude that all its students are equally knowledgeable. It can give students any letter grade but it must give them all the same letter. If an employer were to hire all the college's students, it would pay each student the average value of this cohort's actual knowledge. With the exception of the truly average student, no students would be labeled correctly by the college or paid correctly by the employer. On the other hand, if the college does test and assigns three grades, then a low-, medium-, and high-achievement labeling is possible. A potential employer can now pay a graduate the mean product (knowledge) value for a grade. However, all of the students receiving one of these labels need not be equally knowledgeable (for example, all test scores between 100 and 90 equal an A grade). Those at the high and low ends of each grade are mislabeled and incorrectly paid, but not as badly as without assessment. Through yet more intensive screening, the college could continue to reduce the measurement error and conceptually get to the point of perfect labeling of all students. But as the college increases its screening intensity, the knowledge base of the students would not remain fixed.

Prior to screening a bright student could only get the average grade (salary) for the entire student body regardless of his or her knowledge — little incentive to learn more. After the three-grade achievement scale is implemented, bright and high-performing students could get the average of the top achievers with whom they are grouped (for example, those who scored between 90 and 100 on the test) — an incentive to acquire knowledge sufficient to get into this group. To the extent that these students would not have striven for and acquired this high level of mastery prior to the screening, this educational assessment has produced learning and there is a social benefit that is measured by the value of the increased student learning.

In addition to motivating student achievement, educational screening also may assist students in finding their most valued activity. Walstad and Becker's (1990) review of the literature on high school student preparation and post–high school plans suggests that high school achievement affects the decision to attend college and the type of course taken in high school affects the selection of a major. As already noted, Willis and Rosen (1979) found that those who elect to go on to college tend to be those who were likely to benefit from it, as reflected in high school performance.

They state, for example, that "plumbers (who do not have to excel in academics) may have limited potential as highly schooled lawyers, but by the same token lawyers may have much lower potential as plumbers than those who actually end up choosing that kind of work" (p. 11). In other words, school may be helping students find their comparative advantages.

If higher education is inexpensively screening individuals by providing them with credentials for a given type of job for which they are relatively best suited, then education is serving a productive function to the student and society as well. It is providing a positive kind of "externality" in the form of information. For example, assume that there are two types of output produced by society, each valued at $100 per unit, and two kinds of individuals. Individuals of characteristic A_x (plumbers, for example) can produce 100 units of output X and zero units of output Y. Individuals of characteristic A_Y (lawyers, for example) can produce 100 units of output Y and zero units of output X. If the size of the population is 100, with 50 of each type of individual, then random assignments of jobs would imply an output for society (GNP) of $5000. On the average, half of society would be in the wrong occupation. With equal income distribution, however, all individuals share in the output, with each individual receiving $50.

If higher education can assist individuals by assigning them to (or by helping them identify and select) their most productive jobs at a cost of less than $5000, then society and individuals can gain from screening. At an educational cost of $1000, for instance, society's net GNP would be $9000. All individuals would be in their most productive occupation. With the cost of education paid equally and with equal income distribution, each individual would receive $90. The private and social return to education is clearly positive for this type of educational assessment even though there is no change in a person's abilities produced by the screening.

Unfortunately, the mathematical models of screening provide few testable hypotheses, not because of lack of clarity in the theory but because of lack of uniqueness in the predictions and lack of data to identify subtleties. For instance, the observation that salaries and productivity increase with academic credentials is consistent with both the human capital and the screening theories of schooling. Nonetheless, there is a history of empirical research that has tried to settle the debate—Taubman and Wales (1973), Layard and Psacharopoulos (1974), Wolpin (1977), and Riley (1979), to name a few. This empirical evidence neither confirms nor rejects the screening model. Thus theoretical screening models continue to pose a challenge to the human capital theory of schooling, productivity, and salary determination.

Education Value Added

The preceding discussion of human capital and screening theories is based on the presumption that college graduates are more productive on average than nongraduates at certain tasks desired by employers. The value added by college is measured in dollars (for example, $W_{th} - W_{th-1}$ in equation 4.1); thus it is the market that is giving worth to the college experience.

Former U.S. Commissioner of Education Francis Keppel may have been the first major political figure to propose that the benefit of college be assessed by comparisons (over time and across schools) of nationally normed test results.[6] ACT and ETS now sell such tests for assessment of general education foundational skills typically attained in the first two years of college. Along with other nonmarket measures, offices of student affairs at many colleges are using differences in these test scores as proxies for the "value added" by their institutions.[7]

As modeled by W. Becker (1982), students do get satisfaction out of certain forms of learning, as defined by the differences between pre- and posttest knowledge in a specific discipline. If one could measure individual utility or social welfare on a ratio-preserving scale, the nonpecuniary value of this learning would be known. Individual utility and social welfare do not lend themselves to such measures, however. Knowing the difference between test scores is of little help to a student or to society without knowing the value of the difference.[8]

The market for new college graduates does not place a value on student learning in college. Employers are interested in skill levels and knowledge at the time of employment; they are buying terminal college aptitudes. What the student knew four or five years ago in the first semester of the freshman year is irrelevant to employers, except insofar as it affects or indicates the rate of learning.[9] Starting salaries reflect the pecuniary value an employer puts on a new graduate's human capital at the time of hiring.

For the individual student the financial information needed for an investment decision is the cost of college, the expected salary improvement, and a rate of discount; for society the relevant information is similar, but an adjustment for subsidies paid and taxes received is required. Differences between college and high school earnings measure the market exchange value of human capital. Changes in test scores or any other nonpecuniary measure of effectiveness have no such interpretation and are thus worthless in an investment decision about the value of higher education.

Changes in test scores may have administrative or production value to a department chair or classroom teacher, but these scores may have little or no relationship to the economic concept of value.[10] The value added as reflected in differences in test scores is not an appropriate measure of economic value when used in cross-course, cross-department or cross-school comparisons. For example, Harvard might produce very little value added as measured by an average change score (e.g., because students are close to the ceiling on the pretest or because the test is set to become progressively harder), whereas a local community college may produce big change scores but still have average postscores well below those of Harvard. The marketplace, however, is not going to reward the community college education above that of Harvard.

Just as water has a high "value in use" but a low "value in exchange" (because of its abundance) while diamonds have high value in exchange (because of their scarcity), some basic skills such as an ability to reconcile a checkbook may have high value in use but low value in exchange. Other skills may have a high value at one point in time and little value at another; for example, the ability to manipulate a slide rule or do arithmetic quickly in one's head has fallen in value with the availability of the inexpensive hand calculator. Although some skills may be viewed as essential for education, their market value is determined by demand and supply. The beliefs of an officer of student affairs, business executives, the state legislature, or a faculty about the importance of intellectual skills are elusive without reference to what employers are paying for the bundle of skills embodied in a college graduate.

Concluding Comments

Higher education is an investment that yields a financial return to both society and the individual. While individuals typically enjoy their college experience, it is the potential future benefits that drive the decision to attend college. The financial benefit to a college education has risen dramatically in the last ten years. This increase, however, may be more a function of lower pay to high school graduates than of great increases in the actual returns to a college education in the United States. Regardless, compared to alternatives a college education continues to be a good investment.

To the extent that students are aware of and respond to earnings differentials (and there is considerable evidence that they do), they will demand the type of education that is most conducive to economic growth. In a market economy technological change provides signals of where specific skills are needed through earnings differentials. Federal, state, and even employer policies that distort earnings differentials (such as minimum wage legislation) have the potential to interfere with the flow of resources. School policies that ignore the market value of certain forms of knowledge and skills may also, at least temporarily, obstruct the efficient allocation of resources if emphasis is placed on worthless skills. Enlightened educational policies are those that recognize the role of earnings differentials in the allocation of resources in a market economy.

Acknowledgments

Colleen Davidson's assistance in preparing tables 4–1 through 4–4 and figure 4–1 is gratefully acknowledged. The constructive criticism provided by Mario Aedo, Suzanne Becker, and Michael Watts on earlier drafts is likewise most appreciated.

Endnotes

1. Because one more year of job experience is typically associated with one more year of life, the independent influences of age and experience on earnings have been difficult to discern even in multivariate studies.

2. More detailed data would show the actual peak in earnings appearing at a more advanced age for college graduates than for those with only a high school education.

3. There is little research that indicates which school subjects contribute most to worker productivity and wages, although Bishop (1988) suggests that skill in mathematics may be critical in problem-solving situations. The NSF literature review of Walstad and Becker (1990) also suggests that the number of mathematics courses taken in high school may be the single most important contributor to career choices in the natural sciences and engineering.

4. An alternative to a compensation scheme based on percentage increases would be one based on fixed dollar additions. For example, all those of a certain level of merit get the same dollar pay raise regardless of their salary levels.

5. The effect of this approximation was first noted by Halvorsen and Palmquist (1980) who found that Hanushek and Quigley's (1978) regression showing that a postgraduate degree increased the wages of black workers by 64 percent, based on the approximation $b = c$, was actually 90 percent after using the exact relationship $b = \ln(1 + c)$.

6. See Jack Magarrel (1980) for a discussion of Keppel's proposal.

7. Hanushek (1986) reports that test scores are typically unrelated to the control variables (teacher–student ratios, teacher education, and the like), leading many educators and policy makers to conclude that expenditures to improve education by these variables is a waste. On the other hand, the work of Card and Krueger (1990) suggests that these variables are related to the financial returns to an additional year of schooling. They report, for example, that a decrease in the pupil–teacher ratio from 30 to 25 is associated with a 0.4 percentage point increase in the rate of return to education. As argued by Becker, Rosen,

and Greene (1990), and discussed further here, whether one looks at test scores or financial returns obviously makes a difference for policy.

8. In addition to this fundamental problem of valuation, there is also a practical problem of measuring change. Because students "drop out" between the pre- and the posttest, and because the process that determines who drops out is likely related to the process of determining scores, as demonstrated by Becker and Walstad (1990) there is a sample selection problem inherent in pre–post assessment that has been ignored by evaluators.

9. This is not to say that the rate at which a student learns is not of interest. A potential employer may be interested in the rate at which the student learns at the time of graduation and hiring, but the rate at which a student learned in his or her freshman year is immaterial.

10. Burt Weisbrod (1979) has made this point in his discussion of research in economic education where investigators typically use a change score to assess interventions in classroom teaching.

References

Alter, G., & Becker, W. (1985). Estimating lost future earnings using the new worklife tables. *Monthly Labor Review*, February, pp. 39–42.

Arrow, K. (1973). Higher education as a filter. *Journal of Public Economics 2*, 193–216.

Astin, A. W., Green, K. C., Korn, W. S., & Schalit, M. (1985). *The American freshman: National norms for fall 1985*. Los Angeles: Higher Education Research Institute, University of California at Los Angeles.

Bartel, A. P., & Lichtenberg, F. R. (1988). Technical change, learning, and wages (Working Paper No. 2732, October). National Bureau of Economic Research.

Becker, G. S. (1964). *Human capital: A theoretical and empirical analysis, with special reference to education*. New York: Columbia University Press.

Becker, G. S. (1988). Contrary to popular belief, the economic boom did trickle down. *Business Week*, September 29, p. 20.

Becker, G. S. (1989). A note on this issue. *Educational Researcher 18*, 4.

Becker, W. E. (1982). The educational process and student achievement given uncertainty in measurement. *American Economic Review 72*(1), 229–236.

Becker, W. E. (1990). The demand for higher education. In S. A. Hoenack & E. L. Collins (Eds.), *The economics of American universities* (pp. 155–188). Albany: State University of New York Press.

Becker, W. E., & Alter, G. (1987). The probability of life and work force status in the calculation of expected earnings. *Journal of Risk and Insurance*, June, 364–375.

Becker, W., Rosen, S., & Greene, W. (1990). Research on high school economic education. *American Economic Review 80*(2), 14–23, and an expanded version reprinted in *Journal of Economic Education* (Summer 1990), 231–253.

Becker, W. E., & Walstad, W. B. (1990). Data loss from pretest to posttest as a

sample selection problem. *Review of Economics and Statistics 72*, 184–188.
Behrman, J. R., & Birdsall, N. (1983). The quality of schooling: Quantity alone is misleading. *American Economic Review 73*(5), 928–946.
Bishop, J. (1988). Why high school students learn so little and what can be done about it (Working Paper No. 88–01). Center for Advanced Human Resource Studies, New York State School of Industrial and Labor Relations, Cornell University.
Bishop, J. (1989). Is the test score decline responsible for the productivity growth decline? *American Economic Review 79*(1), 178–197.
Bound, J., & Johnson, G. (1989). Changes in the structure of wages during the 1980s: An evaluation of alternative explanations. NBER handout, May.
Card, D., & Krueger, A. (1990). Does school quality matter? Returns to education and the characteristics of public schools in the United States. National Bureau of Economic Research, Working Paper No. 3358.
Cohn, E., & Geske, T. G. (1986). Benefit-cost analysis of investment in higher education. Paper prepared for the Seventh Annual Yearbook of the American Education Finance Association.
Denny, M., & Fuss, M. (1983). The effect of factor prices and technological change on the occupational demand for labor: Evidence from Canadian telecommunications. *Journal of Human Resources 18*(2), 161–76.
Dickens, W. T., & Katz, L. F. (1987). Interindustry wage differences and industry characteristics. In K. Lang & J. S. Leonard (Eds.), *Unemployment and the structure of labor markets* (pp. 48–89). New York: Basil Blackwell.
Fisher, I. (1930). *The theory of interest*. New York: Macmillan.
Freeman, R. B. (1976). *The overeducated American*. New York: Academic Press.
Halvorsen, R., & Palmquist, R. (1980). The interpretation of dummy variables in semilogarithmic equations. *American Economic Review 70*, 474–475.
Hamermesh, D. S. (1986). The demand for labor in the long run. In O. Ashenfelter & R. Layard (Eds.), *Handbook of labor economics volume 1* (pp. 429–71). Amsterdam: North-Holland.
Hanushek, E. A. (1986). The economics of schooling: Production and efficiency in the public schools. *Journal of Economic Literature 24*(3), 1141–1177.
Hanushek, E. A., & Quigley, J. M. (1978). Implicit investment profiles and intertemporal adjustments of relative wages. *American Economic Review 68*, 67–79.
Heckman, J. J. (1976). The common structure of statistical models of truncation, sample selection and limited dependent variables and a simple estimator for such models. *Annals of Economic and Social Measurement 5*, 475–492.
Heckman, J. J. (1979). Sample selection bias as a specification bias. *Econometrica 47*, 153–61.
Jamison, D. T., & Lau, L. J. (1982). *Farmer education and farm efficiency*. The World Bank, Johns Hopkins University Press.
Katz, L., & Revenga, A. L. (1989). Tables and figures from Changes in the structure of wages: The U.S. vs. Japan. NBER handout.
Katz, L. F., & Murphy, K. M. (1990). Changes in relative wages, 1963–87: Supply and demand factors, NBER Preliminary mimeograph, April.

Layard, R., & Psacharopoulos, G. (1974). The screening hypothesis and the returns to education. *Journal of Political Economy 82*, 985–998.

Leslie, L. L., & Brinkman, P. (1988). *The economic value of higher education.* New York: Macmillan.

Leslie, L. L., Johnson, G. P., & Carlson, J. (1977). The impact of need-based student aid upon the college attendance decision. *Journal of Education Finance 2*, 269–285.

Magarrel, J. (1980). Use tests of students to judge performance of colleges, ex-education commissioner urges. *Chronicle of Higher Education*, March 10, p. 8.

Manski, C. F., & Wise, D. A. (1983). *College choice in America.* Cambridge, MA: Harvard University Press.

Mincer, J. (1962). On the job training: Costs, returns, and some implications. *Journal of Political Economy 70*, 50–79.

Mincer, J. (1974). *Schooling, experience, and earnings.* National Bureau of Economic Research, Columbia University Press.

Murphy, K., & Welch, F. (1988). Wage differentials in the 1980s: The role of international trade. Paper presented at the Mont Pelerin Society General Meeting, September 9.

Pencavel, J. (1991). The contribution of higher education in economic growth and productivity: A review. *Journal of Economic Education 22* (Fall), 331–359.

Psacharopoulos, G. (1985). Returns to education: A further international update and implications. *Journal of Human Resources 20*(4): 583–604.

Psacharopoulos, G. (1987). The cost-benefit model. In G. Psacharopoulos (Ed.), *Economics of education research and studies* (pp. 342–347). Oxford: Pergamon Press.

Riley, J. G. (1979). Testing the educational screening hypothesis. *Journal of Political Economy 87*, 227–252.

Rumberger, R. W. (1984). The job market for college graduates, 1960–90. *Journal of Higher Education 55*(5), 433–454.

Schultz, T. W. (1961). Education and economic growth. In N. B. Henry (Ed.), *Social forces influencing American education.* Chicago: National Society for the Study of Education.

Smith, A. (1976). *The theory of moral sentiments.* (Originally published 1759.) Indianapolis: Liberty Classics.

Smith, R. E., & Vavrichek, B. (1987). The minimum wage: Its relation to incomes and poverty. *Monthly Labor Review*, June, pp. 24–30.

Spence, M. (1974). *Market signalling.* Cambridge: Harvard University Press.

Stiglitz, J. E. (1975). The theory of "screening," education, and the distribution of income. *American Economic Review 65*, 283–300.

Tannen, M. B. (1978). The investment motive for attending college. *Industrial and Labor Relations Review 31*, 489–497.

Taubman, P. J., & Wales, T. J. (1973). Higher education, mental ability and screening. *Journal of Political Economy 81*, 28–55.

Tirole, J. (1990). In honor of David Kreps, winner of the John Bates Clark Medal. *Journal of Economic Perspectives 4*(3), 149–170.

U.S. Bureau of the Census. *Money income of households, families, and persons in the U.S.*. Series P-60, annual.

Walstad, W. B., & Becker, W. E. (1990). A literature search and data base analysis of high school student preparation and post high school plans. NSF literature review.

Weisbrod, B. A. (1979). Research on economic education: Is it asking the right questions? *American Economic Review 69*(2), 14–21.

Weiss, R. D. (1977). Elasticities of substitution among capital and occupations in U.S. manufacturing. *Journal of the American Statistical Association* 72(360), 764–771.

Willis, R. J. (1986). Wage determinants: A survey and reinterpretation of human capital earnings functions. In O. Ashenfelter & R. Layard (Eds.), *Handbook of labor economics volume 1*. Amsterdam: North-Holland.

Willis, R. J., & Rosen, S. (1979). Education and self-selection. *Journal of Political Economy*, Supplement 87(5), Part 2, 65–97.

Windham, D. M. (1980). *The benefits and financing of American higher education: Theory, research and policy* (Project Report No. 80–A19). The Institute for Research on Educational Finance and Governance, a Research and Development Center of the National Institute of Education. Stanford, CA: Stanford University.

Wolpin, K. I. (1977). Education and screening. *American Economic Review 67*, 949–958.

5 WAGES OF COLLEGE GRADUATES

Kevin M. Murphy and Finis Welch

The wage earned by college graduates over that earned by high school graduates is often described as perhaps the major incentive to get a college education. Although wages of college and high school graduates vary widely, when using large nationally based surveys to compare people who finished school at the same time, we find on average college graduates earn more than high school graduates. There are, of course, many exceptions where individual high school graduates earn more than college graduates, but, as a rough approximation, it has been true for men that the college wage premium averages 50 percent of the high school graduate wage.[1] The premium typically increases over the career so that when we restrict calculations to recent graduates, we find smaller college–high school graduate differentials than those found when we compare men at midcareer. The premium also varies through time.

In 1970 young college graduate men earned 46 percent more per week than young high school graduate men. By 1979 the difference in earnings had fallen to what appears to be an all-time low of 32 percent. Richard Freeman (1976) and others have attributed the decline to crowding caused by the large influx of baby boom cohorts and the rise in college continuation and completion rates that occurred in the 1960s and early 1970s. The declining college wage premium led Freeman to speculate that the U.S.

labor force had become overeducated. Much less well known, but equally dramatic, is the rapid rise in the returns to education that began around 1979. From 1979 to 1986 the earnings differential expanded from 32 percent to about 70 percent, so that by 1986 college–high school earnings differentials were larger than ever.

In this chapter we describe these and other changes in the economic returns to education over the last 25 years and discuss their relationship to the work force arrival of the baby boom cohorts, the changing patterns of college completion, and the changing demand for educated workers. Our framework for interpreting and understanding these changes is the human capital model introduced by Gary Becker (1964) and Jacob Mincer (1962).

The human capital approach views education as an investment. Individuals give up current earnings and incur tuition and other direct expenses while attending school in exchange for the prospect of higher future earnings associated with a higher level of education. Although monetary benefits and costs are not the only ones associated with added schooling, few would argue that they are not of primary importance. In fact, the evidence for a positive association between schooling and earnings is so strong that it is impossible to ignore the role of education in systematic studies of individual earnings. A point that we hope to document is that it would be equally impossible to study changes in average levels of schooling without reference to wage premiums that result from increased education.

Early estimates of the payoff to schooling relied on the 1960 census. These studies suggested that an additional year of schooling was associated with 7–10 percent higher earnings or, equivalently, that college graduates earn about 50 percent more than high school graduates.[2] One who continues in school an additional year postpones entry into the job market and incurs direct expenses. The investment in schooling will be financially profitable only if future earnings are increased by enough to offset the time and money costs of the additional schooling. An alternative to investing in education would be to invest the same amount (the earnings that would be given up by going to school and the tuition and other expenses) in other assets such as stocks or bonds. If the investment in education is profitable, the increased earnings from the added year of school must be greater than or equal to the returns to a similar amount invested in other assets. The early studies showed that education provides monetary returns roughly in line with what would be expected elsewhere.

For a long time the benchmark studies from the 1960 census established the stylized fact that schooling pays, and as evidence from later periods arrived, differences between the estimates reported and the baseline studies were dismissed as minor perturbations. Returns were viewed as either static or perhaps increasing slightly, and the possibility of a truly dynamic process was not seriously considered. The more-education-is-better ethic was deeply seated, and economists had reinforced the view by showing that, as an investment, expenditures on schooling carried their own weight. This in part explains the consternation surrounding Freeman's mid-1970s pronouncement that the U.S. population was overeducated.

The focus of the human capital approach extends beyond comparisons of returns on educational investments with returns on other assets. A key element is that returns to schooling are determined by the interaction of supply and demand. Greater returns to education induce greater numbers to obtain higher levels of education (the supply response), while greater numbers of educated workers reduce returns as job competition increases. The framework provides a natural basis for interpreting fluctuations through time. As the size of the college graduate population grows, the returns to education will fall unless the growth in supply is offset by growing demand. In contrast, growing demand will lead to greater returns to education unless the demand growth is swamped by growth in supply. The point of Freeman's argument was that the demand for college graduates was growing slowly if at all, while, especially in the early 1970s, the supply was increasing rapidly. The decline in the college wage premium was increasing rapidly. The decline in the college wage premium was a predictable result of supply growth outstripping growth in demand.

We now know that the economic returns to schooling have varied hugely in the past three decades. Our purpose here is to document the dramatic increases of the 1980s. Education has usually paid, and the current dividends exceed anything documented in earlier studies. If Americans were overeducated in the 1970s, they were undereducated in the 1980s in the sense that continuation rates appear to have been lower than the optimal investment view predicts. More generally, we explore the demand and supply evidence to argue that our economy is changing in ways that appear to continue to support rising average education levels. From a broader perspective, the erosion in the economic incentives to attend college that was experienced in the 1970s seems to have been the predictable consequence of a phenomenal increase in numbers of college graduates that coincided with the entry of the baby boomers into the job market. The subsequent erosion in returns to schooling appears in retrospect to have been temporary against a general pattern of increasing returns.

We describe the data used to measure the returns to education as well as the educational composition of the work force. We then trace the returns to education over the past 25 years for young workers and the labor force as a whole. Next we provide preliminary explanations of these changes in light of the changing supply of educated workers and the changing patterns of demand. Finally we summarize the main findings.

The Data

Data on annual earnings and weeks worked in the previous year are collected by the Census Bureau as part of the March Demographic Supplement to the Current Population Survey. The Current Population Survey forms the basis of published unemployment statistics and represents the largest source of data on individual earnings available on an annual basis. The numbers reported in this chapter are based on more than one million individuals found in the 24 surveys between 1964 and 1987, although most of the calculations are restricted to college and high school graduates. The data on annual earnings and weeks worked refer to the year preceding the survey, so the earnings measures include calendar years 1963 through 1986. The population is aggregated into several groups to simplify the analysis. First, there is school completion, defined as 0–7 years of schooling, 8–11 years of schooling, high school graduates (12 years of schooling), those with some college (13–15 years of schooling), college graduates (16 years of schooling), and those with graduate training (17 or more years of schooling). Next, we group the sample by race (white/black), sex, and single years of age for those ages 16 to 65. This classification gives a total of 1200 ($6 \times 2 \times 2 \times 50$) categories. For each of the 24 years we then calculated average annual earnings and average weeks worked for those with valid wage and weeks worked data.[3] In addition to earnings we also calculate the number of individuals in each category in each year.[4] The raw data are summarized by the average weekly wage (computed as average annual earnings divided by average weeks worked) and population counts for the 1200 groups for each of the 24 years of the survey.

In spite of the large number of observations, the average weekly wages for individual cells are imprecisely measured (particularly for blacks, for whom sample sizes are only about 1)10 as large as for whites). To solve this problem and fill in missing observations, we fitted independent wage equations by education, sex, race, and year classes where the (logarithm of the average) weekly wage is taken as a quartic (fourth-order polynomial) in age. Predicted values from these regressions generated the results in this chapter. As we show in another article (Murphy and Welch 1990), this specification provides sufficient flexibility to fit the wage data and still reduces noise associated with sampling variation.

Finally, we use the measure of potential experience suggested by Mincer (1974), rather than age. This amounts to identifying approximate thresholds of labor market entry for the different schooling levels and using them to calculate years of potential experience (time since leaving school). For high school graduates we define experience as age minus 19, and for college graduates (those with 16 years of schooling) we define experience as age minus 23. Since we use experience levels 1 through 40, we include those aged 20 to 59 for high school graduates and those aged 24 through 64 for college graduates.[5] Hence, when we compare young college graduates (those with 1–5 years of experience) with young high school graduates, we are comparing the earnings of 24- to 28-year-old college graduates with earnings of 20- to 24-year-old high school graduates. Restricting the analysis to 40 years of experience within each group reduces the number of cells from 1200 to 960 each year.

All earnings data are presented as fixed weight averages of the weekly wages to reduce the 960 cells to manageable numbers. Weights are the sample representations (i.e., counts) of the number of individuals in each group over the full 24 years of the sample. Hence, we compute the average wage of high school graduates in a year by averaging over all age, sex, and race groups using the counts in the full 24-year sample as weights. Fixed weight indices avoid confounding changes caused by the shifting age, race, and sex composition of the population.[6] Calculations for college graduates are performed in the same way and typically include those with graduate education using the same type of fixed weight index. This method avoids changes in the wage of college graduates generated by the changing fraction of college graduates with graduate training.

Trends in the Returns to Education

Figure 5–1 graphs the wage premium earned by college graduates between 1963 and 1986. It is calculated as the percentage earnings differential between those who have graduated from college (including those with graduate training) and those with 12 years of schooling (high school graduates). The figure gives two indices, one for all levels of experience (1–40 years) and another for young workers (1–5 years of experience).

In 1963 college graduates earned 47 percent more than high school graduates, while young college graduates earned 41 percent more than young high school graduates. These differentials are similar to those calculated from the 1960 census and show that the college premium has historically been lower for new entrants than it is at higher levels of experience. Put differently, earnings rise more rapidly over the career for

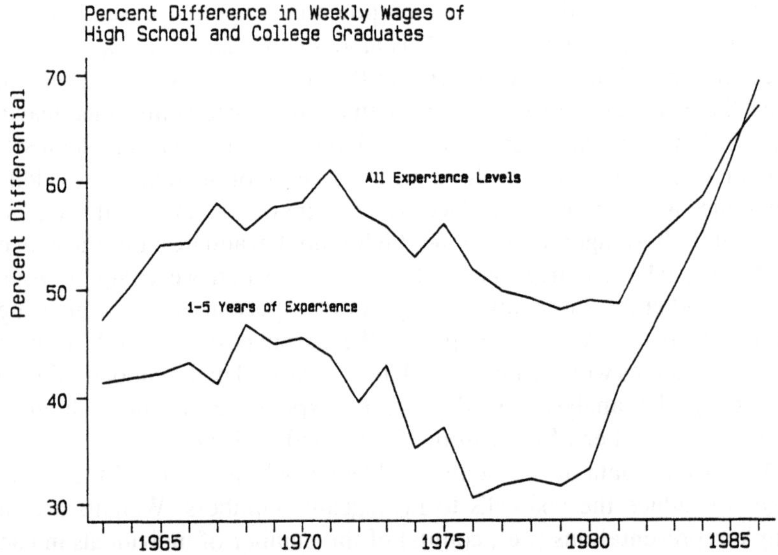

Figure 5–1. Trends in College Wage Premium

college than for high school graduates. As an example, the college premium for those with 26–35 years of experience was 53 percent in 1963 although, as noted, it was 41 percent for new entrants.

We see in figure 5–1 that the wage premium for young workers increases slightly from 1963 to 1970, when it reached 46 percent. When all ages are considered, the trend is more obvious and the 1970 premium is 58 percent (up from 47 percent in 1963). The first eight years (one-third of the span of our data) are characterized by rising returns to education. Since the return increased by 11 percent overall and only by 5 percent for those with 1–5 years of experience, the tendency for the college premium to rise with years of experience was more pronounced in 1970 than in 1963. Our other research (Murphy and Welch forthcoming *a*) shows this to be a result of the increasing differentials between old and young college graduates.

The next eight to ten years, from 1970 or 1971 until about 1979 or 1980, are characterized by a decline in the wage premium earned by college graduates. Over all experience levels, the estimated premium declines from a peak of 61 percent in 1971 to a trough of 48 percent in 1979. Even so, the earnings premium in 1979 slightly exceeds its 1963 level. The decline in the college premium for young workers (1–5 years of experience) is more pronounced and is concentrated in the period from 1971 to 1976. The earnings premium for them was approximately constant between 1976 and 1979. The decline from 46 percent to 31 percent implies that the earnings advantage of a young college graduate was about 1/3 smaller in the late 1970s than it was only a decade before. While the 1979 earnings premium for college graduates averaged over all ages was above its 1963 value, the premium at young ages was lower in 1979 than in 1963. Based on these numbers, Freeman's speculation that Americans were becoming overeducated is not surprising. In retrospect, as is clear from figure 5–1, his view that changes experienced by young workers are leading indicators of what is to follow for older workers seems to be wide of the mark.

As figure 5–1 shows, the decline during the 1970s is not the end of the story. Since 1979 the returns to education have risen enormously. Over all ages the college premium increased from 48 percent in 1979 to 67 percent in 1986; the earnings advantage of college graduates increased by almost 20 percent in only seven years. The increase more than offset the decline during the 1970s and put the college earnings premium at a level that exceeds anything found for earlier periods.

The increase in the college premium for young workers is more dramatic. From 1979 to 1986 the earnings premium for college graduates among workers with 1–5 years of experience grew from 32 percent to almost 70 percent; that is, the earnings advantage of young college graduates more than doubled in only seven years. As a result, by 1986 the college premium was about 28 percent above its 1963 value and about 23 percent above its level at the beginning of the 1970s.

In comparison to the rise in the 1980s, the decline in the college premium during the 1970s is actually quite small. Given the attention received by what now appears as a relatively modest decline, it is surprising that the numbers for the 1980s have received so little attention. The rapid rise in the college premium at low experience levels from 1979 to 1986 is so dramatic that for the first time the college premium is higher at low experience levels than is the average over all ages.

The results in figure 5–1 appear to answer the contemporaneous question about the profitability of attending college, but to those who wonder "why," these results raise other questions. Some that we consider briefly are (1) Has the rising college premium in recent years been generated by rising wages for college graduates or falling wages for high school graduates? (2) Have changes in wages been due to the declining quality of college graduates in 1970s and declining quality of high school graduates in the 1980s? and (3) How have the changes in school-related wage differentials differed by race and sex? We briefly address each of these questions before turning to causes and consequences of fluctuations in returns.

First, determining whether the rising wage premium for college graduates in the 1980s has been caused by falling wages for high school graduates or rising wages for college graduates necessitates comparisons of the level of wages over time instead of wage ratios. This requires the choice of a price deflator to translate observed nominal wages into units that are comparable in purchasing power. For the overall calculations in figure 5–1, deflating by the Consumer Price Index implies that real wages for high school graduates fell by 6.5 percent from 1979 to 1986 while real wages for college graduates increased by 5.6 percent. These calculations imply that when real wages are defined in terms of the CPI, the rise in college returns is due to percentage gains for college graduates that equal the percentage losses for high school graduates. These results are sensitive to the choice of a deflator, however, since when real wages are defined in terms of the GNP price deflator, college graduate wages rise by 12.6 percent while high school wages are essentially constant (in real terms).

Deflating by the CPI, we find that the rise in the college premium for less experienced workers was generated by a decline in the real wage for high school graduates of 15.7 percent and a rise in the real wage of young college graduates of 8.5 percent. When wages are deflated by the GNP price deflator instead of the CPI, the changes are a decrease in real wages of 9.6 percent for young high school graduates and an increase in real wages of 14.6 percent for young college graduates. Hence, using either the CPI or GNP deflator, both falling real wages for young high school graduates and rising real wages for young college graduates have contributed to the rising college wage premium.

One explanation for fluctuations in the returns to education (particularly at young ages) is changes in the quality of college and high school graduates. While such changes have undoubtedly occurred, it does not appear that they have been the primary cause of the observed fluctuations in earnings. First, as we have shown elsewhere (Murphy and Welch forthcoming *a*), the rise in earnings differentials is approximately as large within cohorts as between cohorts. For example, looking across cohorts within white men we find that the earnings differential for those with 1–5 years of experience rose from 27 percent in 1980 to 55 percent in 1985. Looking within cohorts generates strikingly similar results, since the college premium for those with 6–10 years of experience in 1985 (the same cohort used to measure the 27 percent differential in 1980) was 55 percent as well. Similarly, the college premium for those with 6–10 years of experience in 1980 was 29 percent compared with a differential of 58 percent for those with 11–15 years of experience in 1985. Since both of these comparisons look at the same groups of college and high school graduates at different periods in time (which holds quality constant), it seems clear that changing quality is not the primary story behind the observed fluctuations.

Table 5–1 addresses the question of whether the increase in the college premium has been broadly based or is limited to a particular subset of the population. The table gives the college premiums separately for men and women and for blacks and whites measured both overall and for those with 1 to 5 years of experience. For simplicity, the time period is divided into four six-year intervals: 1963–1968, 1969–1974, 1975–1980, and 1981–1986. In the top panel the overall college premium (calculated as in figure 5–1) is given for the full sample of men, women, whites, and blacks. As was illustrated in figure 5–1, the overall earnings premium was lowest in the 1975–1980 interval (50.4 percent) and highest in the final period, with an average of 58.4 percent. The same basic pattern shows up for each subgroup as well. For example, the premium for all men was 44.4 percent in the 1975–1980 period and increased to 53.8 percent in the 1981–1986 period. The only exception to the rule that returns were lowest in the third interval and highest in the final interval is that the education premium for all women is smaller in the final interval than in the 1963–1974 interval. (However, in examining the data for

Table 5–1. Trends in Returns to College

Years	*All*	*Men*	*Women*	*Blacks*	*Whites*
			Panel A: All Experience Groups		
1963–1968	53.6	46.0	53.9	50.9	52.2
1969–1974	57.0	50.0	54.1	51.0	56.1
1975–1980	50.4	44.4	46.3	47.1	49.6
1981–1986	58.4	53.8	51.3	54.3	57.5
			Panel B: 1–5 Years of Experience		
1963–1968	42.9	40.7	48.0	40.5	42.2
1969–1974	41.8	37.7	50.1	56.6	40.5
1975–1980	32.7	28.3	41.4	42.1	31.8
1981–1986	54.2	53.2	57.2	59.8	53.2

Note: Returns to obtaining a college degree are measured as the average wages of those with 16 years of schooling relative to the average wages of those with 12 years of schooling, in percentage terms.

individual years, we find that the premium for women in 1986 is the highest observed by significant margin.) The basic pattern of the returns to college being higher in the second subperiod than in the first subperiod, lower in the third subperiod than in the second subperiod, and higher again in the final subperiod holds uniformly for all race and sex groups.

The bottom panel looks at the college premium for workers with 1–5 years of experience. The calculations for all groups shown in the first column and the returns for each of the race and sex categories shown in the other columns reflect what is shown in figure 5–1. Without exception, the college premium is lowest from 1975–1980 and highest in the final period. Interestingly, the largest fluctuations are for white men, so that the decline and subsequent rise in the returns to college are most pronounced for the classifications whites and men. The increase in returns between the third interval and the final interval is 22.5 percent for all groups. It is 24.9, 15.8, 17.7, and 21.4 percent for men, women, blacks, and whites, respectively. In all cases, returns increased dramatically from the late 1970s to the 1980s. In sum, the calculations for younger workers shown in the bottom panel, together with the results for all experience levels shown in the top panel, imply that the changes in educational returns shown in figure 5–1 have been broadly based across sex and race groups with similar timing and magnitudes.

Understanding Changes in the Returns to Schooling

Observed changes in the returns to education have a natural interpretation in terms of changes in the demand for educated workers and changes in the available supply. When the demand for educated workers grows faster than the available supply, the earnings premium for educated workers will rise. When growth in supply exceeds growth in demand, the wage premium for educated workers will decline. Although the growth in the available supply of educated workers can easily be measured from our data, the growth in the demand for educated workers can only be inferred. Since demand growth is more difficult to measure, we discuss it first.

Growth in demand can be divided into changes between and changes within industries. Industries that experience greater increases in output expand their demand for workers (holding output per worker fixed), whereas industries that experience labor-saving technical change tend to reduce employment for a fixed level of output. In contrast, changes in demand within an industry are more typically associated with changes in the methods of production, such as switching from a manual filing system to an automated computer accounting system. Changes in the demand for educated workers can be generated by either type of change.

A shifting industrial composition of employment will increase demand for education if the industries whose share of employment is increasing are also the ones with the most highly educated workers. As an example, workers in the financial, real estate, and insurance industries are more likely to be college graduates than are workers in manufacturing. The shift toward services, especially in the business, financial, and health-related areas, and away from traditional manufacturing industries has no doubt provided support for rising average levels of education, but the picture on this score is mixed. Employment shares are increasing in wholesale and retail trade, for example, where average levels of education are not as high as in schools and universities, where shares of aggregate employment are falling. The national average level of education of employed people is the average within industries weighted by each industry's share of total employment. A simple way to estimate the effect of changing industrial employment on the demand for education is to assume that average levels of education are constant within industries and compute what happens to the overall average when industrial shares shift at observed rates. Our calculations show that roughly 10 to 20 percent of the observed change in the fraction of workers who are college graduates can be attributed to growth in employment in educationally intensive industries. The remaining 80 to 90 percent of the growth has been within industries where proportions of college graduates have grown. Since the supply of college graduates has increased, it must be that demand has also increased. Our examination of changes in the industrial structure of employment (Murphy and Welch forthcoming *b*) shows that shifts in employment patterns have contributed to the increase in demand and, moreover, that the pattern of change is driven, at least in part, by changing patterns of international trade. Although industrial shifts in employment may be a contributing factor, it is clear that the bulk of demand growth has occurred within industries through changing techniques of production. Whatever the reason, firms rely increasingly on college graduates.

The fraction of the population with a college degree increased from 8.3 percent in 1963 to 17.7 percent in 1986. If demand were constant, growth in the proportion of workers with college degrees would have led to a decline in the college wage premium. However, from the numbers presented in the previous section, we see that educational returns have increased despite the observed growth in supply. There seems little doubt that the demand for educated workers has grown substantially. While the coincident increase in the supply of college graduates and the increase in their relative wage implies that the demand must have grown, we cannot identify the timing of demand growth from observations at two points in time. One simple hypothesis is that demand grew at a constant rate over this period. In this case, the growth in the college wage premium (presented in figure 5–1) should vary inversely with the growth in the fraction of the population with a college degree. When the number of college graduates grows faster than demand, the college wage premium should fall; when supply grows slower than demand, the college premium should rise.

The growth rate of the fraction of the population with a college degree (i.e., the percentage change in the fraction of the population with 16 or more years of schooling) is presented in figure 5–2. The horizontal line gives the average annual growth rate of 2.4 percent for the period as a whole. As is clear from the figure, the fraction of the population with a college degree grew slower than average for the period 1963 to 1970, faster than average from 1970 to about 1977, and slower than average again from 1978 through the end of the data. These periods line up closely with the increase in the college premium observed from 1963 to 1970, the decline in the college premium from 1970 through 1977, and the subsequent rise in the college premium from 1979 through the end of the data. However, though the timing coincides, the magnitudes of change do

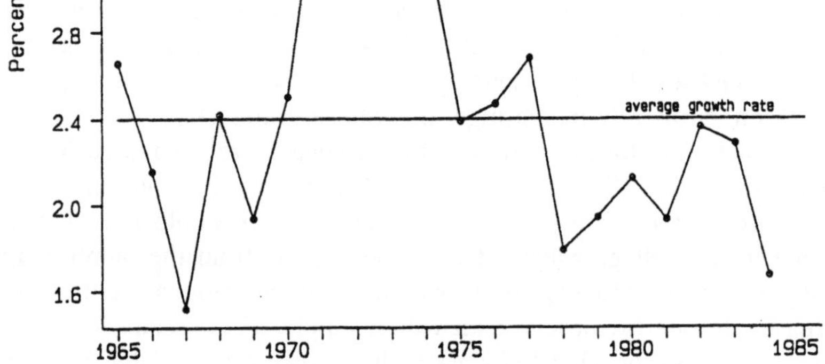

Figure 5–2. Growth in Numbers of College Graduates

not agree exactly. During the 1963–1970 period the college premium grew only slightly for inexperienced workers, whereas from 1979 the college premium grew enormously for this same group. At the same time the growth rates of the college graduate population were only slightly lower in the final period than in the early period. Because the college wage premium increased more rapidly in the 1980s than in the 1960s, it appears that demand growth must have been faster in the 1980s.

Table 5–2 summarizes these comparisons by averaging annual growth rates over the same six-year periods used to summarize returns in the previous section. The first column gives the years; the next column gives the average annual growth rate by period in the fraction of the working population with 16 or more years of schooling, and the final two columns give the average annual growth rates of the college premium for all experience levels and those with 1–5 years of experience. As is clear from a comparison of the three rate columns, the periods of most rapid growth in the fraction of the population with college degrees (the two middle periods) are associated with the declines in the college wage premium. The figures presented in table 5–2 and some of our other research (Murphy and Welch forthcoming *a*) indicate that much of the decline in the college premium can be attributed to the rapid growth in the number of college graduates in the early and mid-1970s shown in the table and illustrated in figure 5–3. This rapid increase in the number of college graduates appears in turn to have been generated by the arrival of the baby boom cohorts into the labor market and the rapid rise in college completion rates over the previous decade.

Further evidence for the effect of rising numbers of college graduates on the college wage premium can be gained by looking at changes in the relative numbers and wages of young and old college graduates. Figure 5–3(b) shows how the fraction of college graduates with 1–5 years of

Table 5–2. Annual Growth Rates of College Graduates and Returns to Obtaining a College Degree

Years	*Growth Rate of College Degrees*	*Growth Rate of Returns for all*	*Growth Rate of Returns for Those with 1–5 Years of Experience*
1963–1968	2.70	1.65	1.07
1969–1974	3.37	−0.42	−1.91
1975–1980	3.23	−0.67	−0.33
1981–1986	2.17	3.02	6.03

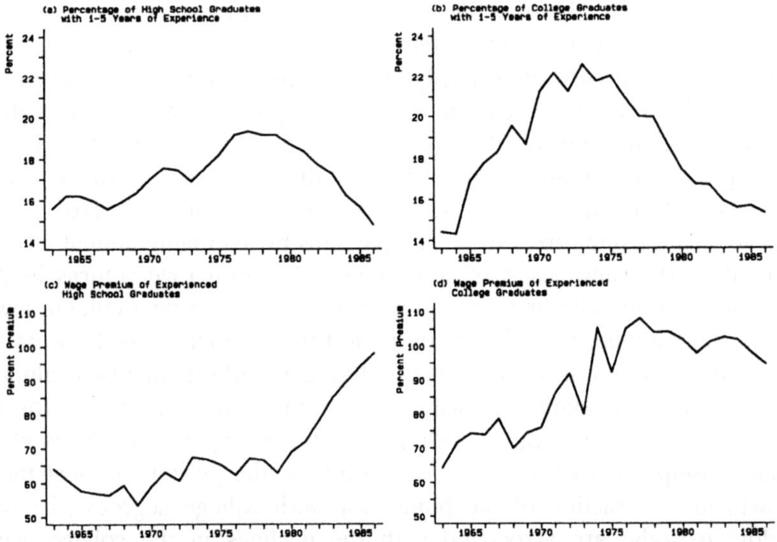

Figure 5–3. Proportions of new entrants and wages of experienced workers

experience changes over the sample period. The college work force became progressively younger from 1963 until the early 1970s as the rapid entry of young college graduates increased the fraction of college graduates in their first 5 years since leaving school. From 1975 though 1986 this fraction then declined steadily as the entry rate of college graduates leveled off and began to decline and the previous cohorts of entrants moved into the older experience categories. As figure 5–3(d) illustrates, the wages of experienced college graduates increased relative to the wages of young college graduates from 1963 through 1975 and then leveled off over the latter period of the data. The evidence in these figures seems consistent with the view that the large influx of college graduates in the 1970s depressed the college wage premium (particularly for younger workers), since we would expect to see the largest effect of such growth to be for those with the least experience.

Figure 5–3(a) and (c) provide the same information for high school graduates. As shown in figure 5–3(a), the decreasing age of the labor force was less pronounced for high school graduates than for college graduates over the early 1970s, and the crest of the baby boom did not occur for high school graduates until the late 1970s. However, unlike the data for college graduates, the relative wage movements for high school graduates are perverse. From 1980 to 1986 the fraction of high school graduates with 1–5 years of experience declined, whereas the wages of older high school graduates rose relative to the wages of younger high school graduates. As suggested by figure 5–3 and the results in table 5–2, it appears that the shifts in demand have been strongly against young high school graduates in the 1980s and have tended to increase the college wage premium at all experience levels.

Our interpretation is that the demand for college-educated workers has been increasing throughout the past 25 years (and perhaps significantly longer) and has tended to exceed the rate of growth in the supply of college graduates. The temporary decline in the wage premium over the 1970s seems to be due largely to the greater than average rate of growth of college graduates, and the particularly strong decline for inexperienced workers appears to be a natural consequence of the influx of inexperienced workers associated with the rapid growth in the college graduate population. Finally, the dramatic growth in the college premium in the 1980s is due to both a decline in the rate of growth of the college graduate population (as a share of the work force) and abnormally rapid growth in demand.

A final question is whether people respond by adjusting their school completion levels to changes in college wage premiums. Figure 5–4 takes us full circle by plotting the college wage premium for men at all levels of

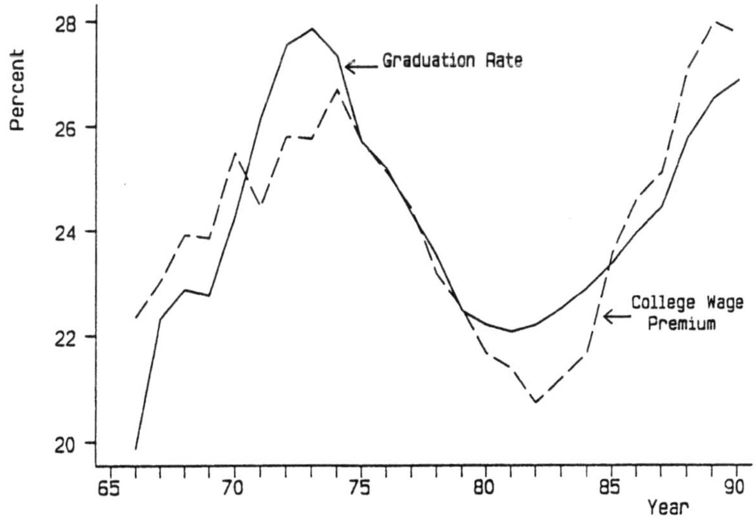

Figure 5–4. Graduation rates and college wage premiums

experience against the ratio of the number of bachelor degrees awarded to men to one-half the combined population of men ages 22 and 23. The data for bachelor degrees are from the *Educational Digest*, Earned Degrees Conferred series. The data are converted to a graduation rate using the data for live births of boys from Vital Statistics between 1943 and 1968. Numbers of live births are converted to survivals for ages 22 and 23 using 1985 mortality tables from Vital Statistic to form estimates of populations of men ages 22 and 23 for each year from 1966 through 1990.

Beginning at 18.4 percent, the graduation rate increased smoothly to 27.9 percent in 1973. It fell to 22.1 percent in 1981 and increased to 24.0 percent in 1986 and, according to degree conferrals projected by the National Center for Educational Statistics, it will reach 26.9 percent in 1990.

The wage series is shifted three years to the right so that wage ratios observed in 1963 are graphed against the 1966 graduation rate, the 1964 wage ratio is graphed against the graduation rate for 1967, and so forth. Finally, the wage ratios are transformed to have the same average and standard deviation as the graduation rates. The reason for the shift in timing is that a changed wage, as an approximation to incentives to complete college, requires time before graduation rates can respond.

Although the wage series is somewhat rough, perhaps due to sampling variation, its agreement with the graduation rate series is striking. It is hard to view these data and not believe that the patterns are more than coincidence. It appears that there is a more or less straighforward dynamic.

First, there is a general tendency for wages of college graduates to increase relative to wages of high school graduates and this tendency may have accelerated in the 1980s. Next, in periods like the 1970s when proportions of the working population who are college graduates grow exceptionally fast, the relative wage of college graduates declines under pressure from the supply growth. Finally, fluctuations in relative wages, with a lag of perhaps three years, induce parallel fluctuations in graduation rates. The story is that wages appear to be determined in a straightforward demand–supply manner and that wages affect behavior.

The supply response graphed in figure 5–4 does not hold for women and for blacks, however, where patterns are more complex. Until recently, women were much less likely than men to graduate from college. For example, in 1964 women received only one-third of the bachelors degrees awarded. Since there are approximately equal numbers of women and men of college age, we infer that in the early 1960s men were twice as likely as women to graduate from college. In the most recent data, women receive the majority of bachelors degrees! Close inspection of the data suggests that men are still a little more likely to graduate from college and that many recent recipients of degrees for women refer to people in their late 20s to early 30s who have returned to school after lengthy interruptions. Whatever the fine points, it is clear that the gap between the sexes has narrowed very sharply. We did not observe the falling college graduation rates for women during the 1970s, although the college graduate wage premium followed a pattern parallel to that for men.

For blacks, the story is the opposite. Similar to the college wage premium, college graduation rates increased sharply during the 1960s and early 1970s and then fell during the mid- to late 1970s. Even though the college wage premium grew in the 1980s for blacks as it did for whites, graduation rates have not returned to the peaks of the 1970s and college enrollment rates have only recently begun to respond.

Conclusion

This chapter has documented changes in the economic return to college observed over the past 25 years. Measured by wage differences between workers with a college and with a high school education, returns increased between 1963 and 1971 (from 47 percent to 61 percent overall and from 41 percent to 44 percent for young workers). Returns to college declined from 1971 until 1979 (from 61 percent to 48 percent overall and from 44 percent to 32 percent for young workers). The most dramatic change is the increase that followed from 1979 through 1986, when returns rose from 48 percent to 67 percent overall and from 32 percent to 69 percent for young workers.

Our analysis gives a detailed picture of how college wage premiums have changed over the past twenty-five years but provides only limited insight into the question of why these fluctuations have occurred. The evidence that we provide here and elsewhere (Murphy and Welch 1990; forthcoming *a*) suggests that the erosion in college returns during the 1970s resulted from greater than average growth in the college population during the early and mid-1970s. This greater than average growth in supply exceeded the rate of growth in the demand for college-trained workers and depressed the wage premium of college graduates in general and young college graduates in particular. In contrast, the rapid growth in the college wage premium in recent years seems to be a result of a slowdown in growth of the college population and greater than average growth in the demand for college-educated workers.

Unfortunately, the explanations for the erosion in returns during the 1970s and the rapid rise in returns in 1980s are incomplete. Our analysis has not established why the college population grew so rapidly during the 1970s (though the arrival of the baby boom cohorts into the educational system seems to have been a factor, and increasing rates of continuation to college during the Vietnam war probably played a role as well). We believe, however, that it helps to explain why the college graduation rate stopped increasing in the 1970s after several decades of growth: Historic wage premiums were quickly eroded. Even so, additional research into the contribution of the baby boom cohort bulge and changes in continuation rates is required to help us understand the observed fluctuations in supply.

Our explanations on the demand side are even less complete. Although the data suggest a rapid rise in demand for educated workers in the 1980s, we have yet to identify its precise cause or causes. Possible explanations include changing patterns of international trade and international competition (see Murphy and Welch forthcoming *a*, *b*), structural changes in the domestic economy (such as the shift in employment from manufacturing to the services), and changes in production technologies within industries (such as the shift to flexible production and the increased use of computer-aided technologies). Our analysis simply establishes that demand for college-trained workers has increased, especially during the 1980s. Future research will have to document the source of the increase.

In a similar vein, we have observed parallel movements in the college wage premium and in the college graduation rate, but further research is required for explicit determination of the way that individuals vary their school continuation decisions in response to changes in the monetary rewards to attending college. Clearly, tuition rates and interest rates must play a role and to our knowledge these relations have not been explored. Finally, only by knowing the source of the demand increase will we be able to know whether the increase in college returns is a temporary phenomenon that will be eliminated as conditions return to normal or whether it represents a permanent change.

Acknowledgments

The research reported in this chapter was funded by a grant from NICHD to the Unicon Research Corporation. In addition to their university appointments, the authors are members of Unicon's research staff. With minor revisions, and some updates, this chapter is taken from Murphy and Welch (1989).

Endnotes

1. Individual wages vary widely, and wages of college graduates tend to be more dispersed that wages of high school graduates. If we select high school and college graduates who finished school at about the same time and compare wages over their subsequent careers, the patterns that emerge have several features worth noting. To compare wages over the full range rather than at the average only, think of wage rankings with percentile scores like the percentile scores used for standardized tests. Think specifically of three wage levels separately for high school and college graduates. The first-quartile, or 25th percentile, wage is the wage such that 25 percent earn less (and therefore 75 percent earn more); the median, or 50th, percentile wage is one where 50 percent earn less (and 50 percent earn more); and, the third-quartile, or 75th, percentile wage is one where 75 percent earn less (and 25 percent earn more). When comparing college and high school graduates at the 50th percentiles on average over a long period of time using replications at several career points, we find that college graduates earn roughly 50 percent more than high school graduates. When the comparison is at the 25th percentile, the differential is smaller than 50 percent and typically exceeds 50 percent when the comparison uses 75th percentile wages.

Conversely, if we compare above-average high school graduates, those at the 75th percentile, to below-average college graduates, those at the 25 percentile, we find that wages cross and that the high school graduates earn roughly 20 percent more than the college graduates. This is an observation worth keeping in mind because it is often treated as axiomatic that college graduates earn more than high school graduates and therefore that a college degree ensures a higher wage. It does not.

2. The exact magnitude of the differential depends on the age at which the comparison is made and which other characteristics (sex, race) are held constant, but a wage differential of about 50 percent is typical of the early studies.

3. The conditions for being in the wage sample were (1) civilian; (2) not self-employed; (3) worked 40 or more weeks last year; (4) did not live in group quarters; (5) not working without pay; (6) school not the major activity; (7) did not work part year due to school, retirement, or armed forces; (8) earned at least $10 per week; (9) earnings not imputed.

4. These counts were based on all individuals in the CPS whether or not they had valid wage information.

5. For those with 8–11 years of schooling, experience is defined as age minus 18. For those with 13–15 years of schooling, experience is age minus 20, and for those with graduate training, experience is age minus 23.

6. Our measures contain another form of composition bias in that wages differ by race, sex, and age and average education levels are not the same for all race, sex, and age groups. In this case, the bias would be caused by changes in relative wages across age, race, and sex group over time rather than changes in the weights associated with individual groups. Based on our other work, we feel that this bias is not large and hence avoid the problems associated with correcting for these other sources of change in this chapter.

References

Becker, G. S. (1964). *Human capital: A theoretical and empirical analysis with special reference to education*. New York: National Bureau of Economic Research.

Freeman, R. B. (1976). *The overeducated American*. New York: Academic Press.

Mincer, J. (1962). On-the-job training: Costs, returns, and some implications. *Journal of Political Economy 70*(5), 250–279.

Mincer, J. (1974). *Schooling, experience, and earnings*. New York: National Bureau of Economic Research.

Murphy, K., & Welch, F. (1989). Wage premiums for college graduates: Recent growth and possible explanations. *Educational Researcher 18*(4), 17–26.

Murphy, K., & Welch, F. (1990). Empirical age-earnings profiles. *Journal of Labor Economics 8*(2), April, 202–229.

Murphy, K., & Welch, F. (Forthcoming *a*). The structure of wages. *Quarterly Journal of Economics*.

Murphy, K., & Welch, F. (Forthcoming *b*). Wage differentials in the 1980s: The role of international trade. In M. Kosters (Ed.), *AEI Conference Edition*.

6 PRIVATE RETURNS TO SPECIFIC COLLEGE MAJORS

Mark C. Berger

This chapter examines patterns and trends in the private returns to specific college majors. The returns to investment in college may vary both across majors and over time for a number of reasons. The individuals in different fields may have different abilities and skills so that they are paid different amounts in the labor market. Changes in the structure of the economy or business cycle influences may cause the demand by employers for different fields to vary over time, leading to changes in wage differences between fields. Discrimination may lead to female–male differences in the returns to specific majors. Supply side factors may also be at work. There may be changes in the number of individuals choosing to attend college, leading to wage changes over time. The relative wages of college graduates will be affected by these supply side changes depending on their complementarity with other types of workers. And the private monetary returns to specific majors may vary because of differences in fringe benefits or nonpecuniary returns. Some majors may qualify individuals for jobs with attractive fringe benefits or pleasant working conditions. These jobs will tend to pay less, other things equal, than jobs with less attractive fringe benefit packages or less pleasant working conditions.

The private monetary returns to an investment in college are a large part of the total return. Differences in the these returns serve as signals to individuals, employers, and educators making decisions about private investments, hiring, and fields of study to offer. The private returns to college have varied remarkably over time. Freeman (1977, 1980, 1981*b*) and others pointed to a decline in the value of college in the 1970s. Murphy and Welch (1987) report that in the 1980s the trend has been reversed, with a marked increase in the wages of college graduates. Although there is some evidence suggesting which fields were hit hardest by the decline in the returns to college in the 1970s, little if anything is known about the experiences of specific fields during the recovery of college wages in the 1980s.

This chapter presents data on private monetary returns to various college majors from 1960 to 1988. Starting salaries of male and female college graduates from the College Placement Council *Salary Survey* (CPC) are examined along with data from the National Longitudinal Survey of Young Men (NLS). The results provide a comprehensive picture of differences in the private monetary returns to specific college majors over the last three decades.

Background

Differences in the returns to specific majors have received limited attention in the literature. Freeman (1971, 1975*a*, 1975*b*, 1976) presents models of the markets for various fields. His "cobweb models" hypothesized that markets for highly trained individuals are cyclical in nature due to swings in the number of individuals entering the various fields. Individuals choose a major based on the returns at the time of the choice, typically in the sophomore year. When the returns are high, many individuals enter the field, which depresses the returns two years later. At that time the number of individuals entering the field is lower, starting the cycle all over again. Others, such as Hoffman and Low (1983), Siow (1984), Zarkin (1985), and Berger (1988*a*) have improved on Freeman's framework by assuming that individuals choose their field of study in a more forward-looking manner, based on what they expect the return will be when they are working, not on what the return is when they make their choice. In fact, McMahon and Wagner (1981, 1982) find that college students can predict accurately relative differences in earnings across fields.

Comparisons of the returns to various fields at the bachelor's degree level can be found in just a few studies. Freeman (1981*a*) presents evidence on the changes in real starting salaries in various fields from 1970 to 1981. McMahon and Wagner (1982) give differences in real starting salaries for several fields from 1960 to 1980. Rumberger (1984) reports differences in the returns to technical and nontechnical degrees between 1971 and 1976. The National Science Foundation (e.g., 1985) periodically publishes data on the enrollments, degrees, and the returns to investments in science and engineering fields. Berger (1988*a*) compares the returns to graduates with bachelor's degrees in business, liberal arts, engineering, science, and education, using data from the National Longitudinal Survey of Young Men. Berger (1988*b*) looks at variation in starting salaries from 1960 to 1981 for males with bachelor's degrees in business, liberal arts, engineering, and science.

Some studies have explicitly examined the market for and the returns to graduate and professional education. In addition to considering the markets for bachelor's degree graduates, Freeman (1971) also modeled the MBA and doctorate markets. Alexander and Frey (1984) modeled the demand for MBA enrollment. Freeman (1981*a*) and McMahon and Wagner (1982) examined changes in starting salaries in various fields for master's and Ph.D. graduates. Scott (1979) and Hansen and colleagues (1980) consider the market for Ph.D. economists. The market for and the returns to a law degree also have received substantial attention; Freeman (1975*a*), Pashigan (1977), Sio (1984), and Goddeeris (1988) all consider some aspect of the market for lawyers.

It is useful to examine whether any common findings emerge from these previous studies examining differences in the returns across various majors. McMahon and Wagner (1981, 1982) find that those in health, science, and technical fields expected the highest starting salaries in 1972 and received the highest salaries in 1974–1975. Those in humanities, liberal arts, and education expected and received the lowest starting salaries. McMahon and Wagner (1982) report that from 1960 to 1980, while real starting salaries for Ph.D. mechanical engineers in general dropped, they still exceeded salaries of master's degree graduates in chemistry and bachelor's degree graduates in numerous fields. Among bachelor's degree graduates, the real starting salaries of mechanical engineers exceeded those of accountants and math majors, with humanities and social science majors earning less than the other three groups. The real starting salaries of all fields dropped in the early 1970s, with some evidence of an upturn in the late 1970s among bachelor's degree graduates in mechanical engineering and mathematics and master's degree graduates in chemistry.

A similar pattern is found by Freeman (1981*a*). He finds real starting salaries in all fields and degree levels declined from 1970 to 1975, with the smallest declines being among engineering bachelor's degree graduates.

Consistent with Freeman's evidence for 1970–1975, Rumberger (1984) found using National Longitudinal Survey data that the declines in the returns to college from 1971 to 1976 were less for technical degree holders than for nontechnical degree holders. For 1975 to 1981 Freeman (1981*a*) found only small changes in real salaries occurred for most fields. The biggest increase was found for master's degree graduates in chemistry. Smaller increases occurred for doctorates in engineering and bachelor's degree graduates in math and computer science. The largest decreases from 1975 to 1981 were for MBA's and bachelor's degree graduates in accounting and humanities and social sciences.

Berger (1988*a*) also uses National Longitudinal Survey data and concludes that earnings growth over the early career slowed down for bachelor's degree graduates in the 1970s in business, liberal arts, and education when compared to graduates in the 1960s. His evidence suggests that the greater declines in starting salaries in these fields found in the early 1970s were accompanied by flatter earnings profiles as well. Berger (1988*b*) examines trends in starting salaries for male graduates with bachelor's degrees in business, liberal arts, engineering, and science from 1960 to 1981. Similar to other studies, he finds declines in real starting salaries across all fields in the early 1970s, with an increase in real salaries in engineering and science in the late 1970s.

These previous studies give some idea of differences in private monetary returns across specific majors and their movements over time. However, they do not provide a complete picture. For instance, the evidence stops with starting salaries in 1981. Also there are no results on differences in returns by field for men and women or on how much of the differences across majors or over time is attributable to variation in the usual determinants of earnings. In this chapter, a comprehensive examination of the private monetary returns to college for men and women, both across fields of study and over time, is undertaken. Trends, patterns, and models explaining variation in the private monetary returns to specific college majors are presented, updating previously available evidence through the late 1980s.[1]

Starting Salary Trends by College Major

Probably the best source of consistent time series evidence on earnings across majors is the College Placement Council *Salary Survey*. The *Salary Survey* contains starting salary offers for a number of fields at the bachelor's, master's, and doctorate level. The data are available for 1960 through

1988 for men and from 1974 through 1988 for women. Evidence on starting salary trends is presented in this section. To emphasize differences across fields and not differences due to the amount of schooling, the focus here is on the bachelor's degree data. For simplicity and to construct consistent series over time, the fields are aggregated into four groups: business, liberal arts (humanities and social sciences), engineering, and science. The exact majors included in each group are given in the appendix to this chapter.

For each of the four college major groups, average salaries are constructed and converted to 1988 dollars using the Consumer Price Index. These average salaries are presented in table 6–1 for males and in table 6–2 for females. Also shown in these tables are the percentage deviations from the average salary of the four groups; these deviations sum to zero each year. The tables show differences in salary levels across major groups in any given year and how salaries have moved relative to one another over time.

Male starting salaries rose in real terms throughout the 1960s, peaking in 1969 and 1970. Consistent with Freeman's work, salaries in all fields dropped in the early 1970s. In business and liberal arts the decline continued throughout the decade, but for science and engineering there was a mild upturn in the late 1970s. Real starting salaries have generally increased in the 1980s except in engineering, where they have been fairly constant.

From 1960 to 1970 all fields gained in real terms, but business showed the biggest gain (32 percent). Liberal arts and engineering gained 24 percent and 26 percent, while science gained 16 percent. From 1970 to 1980, the pattern was almost reversed. Business starting salaries dropped 23 percent, liberal arts fell 20 percent, and science and engineering fell 10 percent and 8 percent, respectively. Apparently, the decline in the value of college hit business and liberal arts graduates most severely. From 1980 to 1988 the biggest real increase in starting salary was observed for liberal arts (13 percent), while business salaries rose 7 percent, science increased 4 percent, and engineering stayed almost constant. In 1988 starting salaries were at the same level in real terms as in the early to mid-1960s and 1970s, somewhat lower than the peak salaries reached in 1969 and 1970. In general, business and liberal arts salaries appeared to have fluctuated the most over the last three decades.

With few exceptions, engineering salaries have been the highest, followed by those in science, business, and liberal arts. Engineers have been paid the most throughout the entire period, ranging from 10 percent above the average of the four fields in 1960 and 1969 to 21.8 percent

Table 6–1. Monthly Starting Salaries of Male Bachelor's Degree Candidates

Year	Salaries[a]				Percent Difference from Average[b]			
	Business	*Lib. Arts*	*Engineering*	*Sci.*	*Business*	*Lib. Arts*	*Engineering*	*Sci.*
1960	$1,786	$1,719	$2,106	$2,042	−6.6	−10.2	10.0	6.8
1961	1,797	1,741	2,166	2,125	−8.2	−11.0	10.7	8.5
1962	1,874	1,818	2,238	2,182	−7.6	−10.4	10.4	7.6
1963	1,937	1,852	2,307	2,208	−6.7	−10.8	11.1	6.4
1964	1,966	1,893	2,352	2,244	−7.0	−10.4	11.3	6.1
1965	2,016	1,923	2,390	2,287	−6.4	−10.7	10.9	6.2
1966	2,097	1,997	2,459	2,344	−5.7	−10.2	10.5	5.4
1967	2,191	2,086	2,559	2,447	−5.6	−10.1	10.2	5.5
1968	2,254	2,128	2,617	2,475	−4.8	−10.2	10.5	4.5
1969	2,311	2,150	2,650	2,527	−4.1	−10.8	10.0	4.9
1970	2,353	2,134	2,646	2,359	−.8	−10.1	11.5	−.6
1971	2,246	2,042	2,568	2,178	−.5	−9.6	13.7	−3.6
1972	2,239	1,987	2,524	2,136	.8	−10.6	13.6	−3.8
1973	2,184	1,913	2,470	2,199	−.4	−12.7	12.7	.4
1974	2,085	1,808	2,387	2,070	−.1	−13.4	14.4	−.9
1975	2,028	1,731	2,436	1,975	−.7	−15.2	19.2	−3.3
1976	1,983	1,768	2,467	1,988	−3.4	−13.8	20.3	−3.1
1977	1,956	1,761	2,498	2,048	−5.3	−14.8	20.9	−.8
1978	1,937	1,758	2,527	2,150	−7.4	−16.0	20.7	2.7
1979	1,888	1,737	2,488	2,157	−8.7	−16.0	20.4	4.3
1980	1,806	1,704	2,432	2,131	−10.5	−15.5	20.5	5.5
1981	1,808	1,713	2,483	2,179	−11.6	−16.3	21.4	6.5
1982	1,855	1,772	2,569	2,241	−12.0	−16.0	21.8	6.2
1983	1,813	1,774	2,503	2,203	−12.5	−14.4	20.7	6.2
1984	1,814	1,828	2,491	2,250	−13.4	−12.8	18.9	7.3

1985	1,839	1,834	2,481	2,243	−12.4	−12.6	18.2	6.8
1986	1,880	1,976	2,502	2,323	−13.4	−8.9	15.3	7.0
1987	1,866	1,992	2,454	2,258	−12.9	−7.0	14.5	5.4
1988	1,937	1,919	2,427	2,221	−8.9	−9.7	14.1	4.5

[a] Expressed in 1988 dollars (CPI) as calculated from the College Placement Council, *Salary Survey*.
[b] ((Salary$_i$ − Avg. Salary)/Avg. Salary) × 100.

Table 6–2. Monthly Starting Salaries of Female Bachelor's Degree Candidates

	Salaries[a]				*Percent Difference from Average*[b]			
Year	*Business*	*Lib. Arts*	*Engineering*	*Sci.*	*Business*	*Lib. Arts*	*Engineering*	*Sci.*
1974	$2,025	$1,629	$2,408	$1,960	1.0	−18.7	20.0	−2.3
1975	2,008	1,558	2,505	1,889	.9	−21.7	25.9	−5.1
1976	1,954	1,579	2,552	1,941	−2.6	−21.3	27.2	−3.3
1977	1,916	1,541	2,592	1,982	−4.6	−23.2	29.1	−1.3
1978	1,900	1,566	2,597	1,994	−5.7	−22.2	28.9	−1.0
1979	1,857	1,561	2,545	2,056	−7.4	−22.1	26.9	2.6
1980	1,772	1,521	2,474	2,032	−9.1	−22.0	26.9	4.2
1981	1,773	1,513	2,505	2,058	−9.7	−22.9	27.7	4.9
1982	1,822	1,560	2,605	2,155	−10.5	−23.4	28.0	5.9
1983	1,788	1,591	2,522	2,097	−10.6	−20.4	26.1	4.9
1984	1,787	1,634	2,508	2,138	−11.3	−19.0	24.3	6.0
1985	1,796	1,632	2,504	2,160	−11.2	−19.3	23.8	6.7
1986	1,843	1,725	2,527	2,267	−11.8	−17.5	20.9	8.4
1987	1,836	1,794	2,470	2,200	−11.5	−13.5	19.0	6.0
1988	1,914	1,751	2,452	2,160	−7.5	−15.4	18.5	4.4

[a] Expressed in 1988 dollars (CPI) as calculated from the College Placement Council, *Salary Survey*.
[b] ((Salary$_i$ − Avg. Salary)/Avg. Salary) × 100.

above the average in 1982. The only time that science salaries fell below second highest was in the early 1970s, when business salaries fell more slowly than science salaries. In the late 1970s business salaries returned to third in the ranking. Liberal arts salaries were the lowest except in 1984 and 1986–1988, when they passed up business salaries. The variation across fields was the narrowest at the beginning of the sample period, with a 20 percent gap between liberal arts and engineering. The gap stayed around 20 percent throughout the 1960s and then began to widen, reaching a peak in 1982 at 38 percent. The gap has started to narrow in the 1980s, with engineering salaries staying constant and salaries in other fields increasing.

Table 6–2 presents evidence on starting salaries by college major group for females beginning in 1974. Real starting salaries declined for business and liberal arts graduates during the late 1970s and increased somewhat for engineering and science graduates, similar to the pattern for males. During the 1980s all fields except engineering experienced real increases in starting salaries. From 1974 to 1980 starting salaries dropped 12 percent and 7 percent for business and liberal arts graduates, respectively, while they increased 3 percent and 4 percent for engineering and science graduates, respectively. From 1980 to 1988 liberal arts salaries rose the most (15 percent), while business and science salaries rose 8 percent and 6 percent, respectively. Engineering salaries have actually declined by 1 percent over the 1980s.

As with males, engineers received the highest starting salaries, followed by science, business, and liberal arts graduates. The only exception to this pattern occurred in the mid-1970s when business graduates earned more than science graduates. The spread between the highest- and lowest-paid fields has been somewhat wider than for males. It ranged from 32.5 percent in 1987 to 51.4 percent in 1982. This disparity occurs because female liberal arts graduates earn about 10 percent less than male liberal arts graduates and male and female engineers receive similar starting salaries.

Explicit female–male comparisons of starting salaries in each field are given in table 6–3. The ratios of female starting salaries to male starting salaries for each of the four major groups from 1974 to 1988 are shown. Although there are some year-to-year movements in the female–male salary ratios, there are no clear long-term trends. From 1974 to 1988 the biggest change occurred among science graduates, with the female–male salary ratio increasing by 2.6 percent. However, the female–male ratios do differ across fields. In engineering female salaries actually exceed those of males. In the other fields females make somewhat less, ranging

Table 6–3. Female/Male Monthly Starting Salary Ratios for Bachelor's Degree Candidates

Year	*Business*	*Liberal Arts*	*Engineering*	*Science*
1974	.971	.901	1.009	.947
1975	.990	.900	1.028	.956
1976	.986	.893	1.035	.976
1977	.980	.875	1.037	.968
1978	.981	.891	1.028	.928
1979	.984	.899	1.023	.954
1980	.981	.893	1.017	.954
1981	.980	.883	1.009	.944
1982	.982	.880	1.014	.962
1983	.986	.897	1.007	.952
1984	.985	.894	1.007	.950
1985	.976	.890	1.009	.963
1986	.980	.873	1.010	.976
1987	.984	.901	1.006	.974
1988	.988	.912	1.010	.972

Note: Table calculated from the College Placement Council, *Salary Survey*.

from 87 to 91 percent of male salaries in liberal arts, from 93 to 97 percent in sciences, and from 97 to 99 percent in business. The reason for these differences is not clear. There may be differences in the exact fields chosen by males and females within the four broader groupings. Or there may be differences in the characteristics of men and women choosing the various fields. It should be noted, however, that these ratios are much higher than female–male earnings ratios reported for the labor force as a whole (e.g., O'Neill 1985; Blau and Beller 1988; Carlson and Swartz 1988). This is in part because the data hold constant the amount of schooling, college major category, and level of experience. There also may be less discrimination at the beginning of the career. Discrimination may show up primarily in promotions and growth in earnings over the career (e.g., Olson and Becker 1983).

Earnings Profiles by College Major

The previous section considered only starting salaries and not earnings profiles over the entire career. This limitation may result in misleading conclusions about the attractiveness of one field relative to another if earnings profiles differ across fields. To provide some evidence on earnings over the career, this section presents regression estimates explaining hourly rates of pay for individuals with different levels of experience, using data from the National Longitudinal Survey of Young Men (NLS). The results allow an assessment of the potential problems involved in using starting salaries, as well as examination of variation in the characteristics of individuals choosing alternative fields. The NLS results can be used to determine the amounts of the observed wage differences across majors that are due to differences in the characteristics of individuals choosing the various majors.

The NLS data allow individual choices of major to be observed along with subsequent experiences in the labor market. The survey began by interviewing approximately 5000 males in 1966 aged 14 to 24. Data from interviews taken in 1967–1971, 1973, 1975–1976, and 1978 are also used here, representing males who obtained their bachelor's degree and entered the labor market from 1962 to 1977. Thus the data include both new entrants and individuals who have been in the labor market several years. Several observations for each individual are potentially included in the data. Only those who had obtained a bachelor's degree by 1978 are included in the sample, and anyone obtaining an advanced degree by 1978 is excluded.

Although 40 distinct fields of study are identified in the NLS data, the categories are grouped to match the College Placement Council data as closely as possible. The four major categories used in the CPC data are used along with education, a category not available in the CPC data. The exact fields of study in each major category for both the CPC and NLS data are given in the chapter appendix.

The dependent variable used in the regression analysis is the log of the hourly rate of pay, deflated by the Consumer Price Index. Position in the career is given by the log of the number of years of experience, measured by the number of years since graduation. This variable allows for the concavity of the log wage profiles without resorting to the usual quadratic specification of experience. Because the sample of workers is relatively young, it is not necessary to allow for the downturn that typically occurs later in life, which is what the quadratic specification accomplishes. The log of experience specification is also simpler and easier to interpret than the quadratic one.

The other explanatory variables in the log wage equations are two ability measures available in the NLS, IQ and KWW (Knowledge of the World of Work) test scores, and the dummy variables RACE (nonwhite = 1), HLIM (health limits work = 1), MARRIED (married, spouse present = 1), SMSA (residence in a metropolitan area = 1), SOUTH (residence in the South = 1), and ENROLLED (individual enrolled in school = 1). Also included are nine sample year dummies to control for year-to-year variation in the wage profiles due to secular effects (e.g., economywide productivity changes) or business cycle effects not otherwise controlled for in the model.

Also included in the wage equations is a variable controlling for self-selection bias (LAMBDA). This variable is constructed along the lines of Heckman (1979) and Lee (1982, 1983). It controls for the fact that individuals are only observed choosing majors that are best for them. Thus it is difficult to predict what a random individual would earn in a particular major from the experiences of those who have self-selected into a major. By including LAMBDA, consistent population estimates of the parameters of the wage equation are obtained. LAMBDA is constructed by first estimating a multinomial logit college major choice equation. The choice is estimated as a function of individual and family background variables, controlling for differences in tastes and investment costs. LAMBDA is then a transformation of the predicted probability of choosing the major the individual actually selected. The variable is derived by Lee (1982, 1983) and was also used by Berger (1988*a*).

The means of the variables by field of study (aside from the sample year dummies) are shown in table 6–4. The ordering of wages across fields is very similar to that observed in the CPC data. The highest wage, expressed in 1988 dollars, is for engineers ($16.80). Business majors receive $15.27, science majors get $13.56, liberal arts majors receive $13.30, and education majors earn $11.66. One of the reasons observed wages differ across majors is that the characteristics of those choosing the various majors differ. For instance, those choosing different majors may have different levels of ability or different amounts of labor market experience. Engineers have the most experience on average in the sample and education majors have the least, but the differences are not large. The greatest concentration of nonwhites is among education majors, the largest proportion of those having health limitations is among liberal arts majors, engineers are the most likely to be married, business majors are most likely to live in a metropolitan area, science majors are most likely to live in the South, and education majors are most likely to be currently enrolled in school. Science majors have the highest average IQ test scores, and education majors have the lowest. Business majors scored highest on the Knowledge of the World of Work test, and education majors scored the lowest. As can be seen, there are in some cases rather sizable differences in the average characteristics of the individuals choosing various majors.

The wage equation results are shown in table 6–5.[2] Recall that liberal

Table 6–4. Variable Means, NLS Young Men

Variables	*Business*	*Liberal Arts*	*Engineering*	*Science*	*Education*
WAGE[a]	15.27	13.30	16.80	13.56	11.66
EXP[b]	4.67	4.64	4.81	4.57	4.43
RACE[c]	.035	.117	.041	.068	.237
HLIM[d]	.049	.073	.025	.031	.047
MARRIED[e]	.716	.672	.759	.702	.722
SMSA[f]	.843	.790	.842	.663	.592
SOUTH[g]	.336	.253	.361	.346	.344
ENROLLED[h]	.060	.098	.104	.131	.134
IQ[i]	110.4	111.0	112.4	113.2	104.6
KWW[j]	39.8	39.3	39.7	39.0	36.0
LAMBDA[k]	−.336	−.207	−3.14	−1.30	−2.49
n	651	743	241	413	299

[a] Hourly rate of pay, 1988 dollars.
[b] Years since receiving bachelor's degree.
[c] = 1 if nonwhite, = 0 otherwise.
[d] = 1 if health limits work, = 0 otherwise.
[e] = 1 if married, = 0 otherwise.
[f] = 1 if residing in an SMSA, = 0 otherwise.
[g] = 1 if residing in the South Census region, = 0 otherwise.
[h] = 1 if enrolled in school, = 0 otherwise.
[i] IQ test score.
[j] Knowledge of the World of Work test score.
[k] Self-selection correction variable.

arts graduates had the lowest starting salaries in the College Placement Council data. Aside from education majors, liberal arts majors receive the lowest wages in the NLS data. The regression results for the LNEXP variable (the logarithm of years since receiving bachelor's degree) indicate that they also have the fastest wage growth. Next is business, followed by education, science, and finally, engineering. So while engineers have the highest starting salaries, they have the slowest wage growth or the flattest wage profiles. An important question is whether the slower wage growth means that engineering is a less attractive career from a lifetime perspective. This would occur if engineering graduates earned sufficiently less later in the career to outweigh their higher earnings early in the career. A partial answer to this question will be obtained by calculating predicted earnings at different stages of the career in each major.

Most of the control variables have estimated effects that are consistent with prior expectation or previous studies. For example, those living in

Table 6–5. Log Hourly Wage Equation Regression Estimates NLS Young Men (*t*-statistics in parentheses)

Explanatory Variables[a]	*Business*	*Liberal Arts*	*Engineering*	*Science*	*Education*
LNEXP[b]	.199	.212	.147	.170	.176
	(9.38)	(8.36)	(5.09)	(5.24)	(5.87)
RACE[c]	−.069	−.024	−.064	.129	.021
	(.659)	(.449)	(.760)	(1.65)	(.329)
HLIM[d]	−.180	.028	.081	.144	−.035
	(3.07)	(.466)	(.750)	(1.37)	(.365)
MARRIED[e]	.134	.089	.183	.143	−.081
	(4.58)	(2.66)	(4.53)	(3.49)	(1.75)
SMSA[f]	.097	.099	−.045	.174	.117
	(2.71)	(2.64)	(.997)	(4.35)	(2.80)
SOUTH[g]	−.068	−.046	.019	−.137	−.058
	(2.45)	(1.24)	(.564)	(3.56)	(1.00)
ENROLLED[h]	−.087	−.233	.081	−.082	−.071
	(1.62)	(4.51)	(1.44)	(1.50)	(1.21)
IQ[i]	−.000	−.006	.001	.004	−.004
	(.005)	(4.70)	(.476)	(2.02)	(2.24)
KWW[j]	.005	.005	.009	.007	−.001
	(2.21)	(1.98)	(2.88)	(2.22)	(.377)
LAMBDA[k]	.057	−.080	−.002	.005	−.018
	(1.49)	(2.64)	(.291)	(.473)	(3.32)
Intercept	5.27	5.90	5.14	4.72	6.15
	(24.9)	(27.1)	(18.5)	(17.6)	(20.2)
R^2	.289	.240	.358	.297	.245
n	651	743	241	413	299

[a] Nine sample year dummy variables are also included.
[b] Log (years since receiving bachelor's degree).
[c] = 1 if nonwhite, = 0 otherwise.
[d] = 1 if health limits work, = 0 otherwise.
[e] = 1 if married, = 0 otherwise.
[f] = 1 if residing in an SMSA, = 0 otherwise.
[g] = 1 if residing in the South Census region, = 0 otherwise.
[h] = 1 if enrolled in school, = 0 otherwise.
[i] IQ test score.
[j] Knowledge of the World of Work test score.
[k] Self-selection correction variable.

metropolitan areas earn significantly more in four of the five fields, those living in the South earn significantly less in business and science, and married men earn significantly more in everything but education. In fact, married men earn less in education. Health limitations negatively affect earnings significantly only among business majors, while enrollment in school negatively affects earnings significantly for liberal arts majors. For the most part, race differences are insignificant. There is some evidence that nonwhites actually earn more than whites, other things equal, in science. Those with higher KWW test scores earn more in every field except education. The results for IQ scores are perhaps unexpected. While those with higher IQs in science earn more, those with higher IQs in liberal arts and education earn less. This may be explained by the fact that those with higher IQs in liberal arts and science are more apt to choose greater amounts of nonpecuniary compensation relative to money earnings.

The LAMBDA variable controls for self-selection bias. Overall, the evidence for self-selection bias is not overwhelming. The LAMBDA coefficient is negative in liberal arts and education, the two cases where it is significant. Since the LAMBDA variable is also negative, it follows that the wages of those choosing liberal arts and education are greater than the wages in these fields would be for a random individual. This is consistent with the Willis and Rosen (1979) evidence of sorting according to comparative advantage when deciding whether to attend college.

Some idea of how much of the differences in wages across fields is due to differences in the observable characteristics of the individuals in the various fields can be obtained by using a variant of the Blinder (1973) and Oaxaca (1973) wage decomposition. The proportion of the difference between each major's average wage and the overall average wage that can be attributed to differences between the characteristics of those in that major and the average characteristics across all majors can be computed. This is simply the log wage difference predicted using the estimated coefficients in table 6–5 and differences in characteristics divided by the actual difference in the log wages.[3] The amount of the wage difference from the average that can be explained by differences in characteristics varies markedly across fields. In liberal arts 90 percent of the difference is due to differences between the observed characteristics of the sample of liberal arts graduates and the full sample of college graduates. In science 72 percent can be explained by differences in observed characteristics and in business 65 percent can be explained in this way, while in engineering only 9 percent is due to differences in observed characteristics.

To obtain more evidence on differences in wage profiles by college major, the predicted wages for each of the five fields in 1988 dollars at 1, 5, 10, and 15 years of experience were calculated, as shown in table 6–6. These predicted wages are calculated using the parameter estimates in table 6–5, letting experience vary, and using the overall sample mean values of the remaining variables.[4] Thus these predicted values hold constant observable characteristics across the different majors. For the first year of experience the pattern of predicted wages is similar to the College Placement Council data. Engineers have the highest wages, followed by business, science, liberal arts, and education. The only difference is that typically in the CPC data science majors receive the second highest salary behind engineers. The wage regressions showed that liberal arts graduates have the fastest wage growth and engineers the slowest, suggesting that the wage difference between the two groups narrows as they age. The differences between the various fields do narrow, but after 15 years of experience the rank ordering of the wages by field is the same as at entry into the labor market. In other words, even after 15 years of experience, liberal arts majors do not catch up to the wages of engineers.[5] This evidence suggests that using starting salaries as measures of the relative attractiveness of majors from a lifetime perspective does introduce some error because of the differences in growth rates over the career. However, the error is fairly small since wage patterns that are observed at the start of the career are not disrupted through the early stages of the career.

The results shown in table 6–6 provide summaries of differences in earnings profiles across disciplines throughout the 1960s and 1970s. They do not address the question of whether the earnings profiles have different

Table 6–6. Predicted Wages by Years of Experience, NLS Young Men

	Years of Experience			
Area	*1*	*5*	*10*	*15*
Business	$10.97	$15.11	$17.35	$18.80
Liberal arts	8.99	12.64	14.63	15.94
Engineering	13.08	16.56	18.33	19.45
Science	10.35	13.60	15.29	16.38
Education	8.34	11.06	12.49	13.42

Note: Figures expressed in 1988 dollars using the Consumer Price Index. Calculated using the parameter estimates reported in table 6–5 (except LAMBDA), the overall sample means of the variables in the equation, and letting the level of experience vary.

shapes for graduates entering the labor market in different years. Berger (1988*a*) uses the same data to examine whether the earnings profiles vary for different vintages of college graduates. He finds that earnings profiles in business, liberal arts, and education were flatter for graduates in the 1970s than in the 1960s. This is another reason for exercising caution when using starting salaries as indicators of differences in the returns to various majors over time.

Relative Earnings Trends by College Major

Up to now the analysis has been of the real earnings of college graduates in various fields. Tables 6–1 and 6–2 presented evidence from the College Placement Council *Salary Survey*, while tables 6–4 through 6–6 provided results from the National Longitudinal Survey of Young Men. To examine the returns to investments in various majors, the earnings in the various majors must be compared to earnings in alternative careers. If a lifetime stream of earnings were available in the various majors and in alternative careers, a rate of return to the investments in the various careers could be calculated. Since these data are not available, a measure of the starting salaries relative to a measure of alternative earnings by year and major is constructed. Specifically, the monthly starting salaries in each major are divided by the average weekly earnings of production and nonsupervisory workers in the private nonagricultural sector of the economy multiplied by 4.33. Scaling the weekly earnings measures up by a factor of 4.33 converts them into estimates of monthly earnings. The average earnings of production and nonsupervisory workers is intended to be an approximation of what the individual might earn without a college education.[6]

Table 6–7 shows the relative earnings of male bachelor's degree candidates from 1960 to 1988 and for female bachelor's degree candidates from 1974 to 1988. Among males in 1960 engineering majors earned 51 percent more than the average production or nonsupervisory worker, while the earnings premium in science was 46 percent, in business 28 percent, and in liberal arts 23 percent. These premiums rose steadily throughout the 1960s and reached their peaks at the end of the decade. In 1969 the premium for science majors was 58 percent, while in 1970 it was 67 percent for engineering majors, 49 percent for business majors, and 35 percent for liberal arts majors. Consistent with the Freeman (1977, 1980) work showing a decline in the return to a college education, the relative earnings series shown in table 6–7 began to fall in the 1970s. The

Table 6–7. Starting Salaries of Bachelor's Degree Candidates Relative to Earnings of Production or Nonsupervisory Workers

	Males				Females			
Year	*Business*	*Lib. Arts*	*Engineering*	*Sci.*	*Business*	*Lib. Arts*	*Engineering*	*Sci.*
1960	1.28	1.23	1.51	1.46				
1961	1.27	1.23	1.53	1.50				
1962	1.28	1.25	1.53	1.50				
1963	1.31	1.25	1.56	1.49				
1964	1.30	1.25	1.56	1.48				
1965	1.30	1.24	1.54	1.47				
1966	1.34	1.28	1.57	1.50				
1967	1.40	1.33	1.64	1.56				
1968	1.42	1.34	1.65	1.56				
1969	1.44	1.34	1.66	1.58				
1970	1.49	1.35	1.67	1.49				
1971	1.39	1.27	1.59	1.35				
1972	1.33	1.18	1.50	1.27				
1973	1.30	1.14	1.47	1.31				
1974	1.30	1.12	1.48	1.29	1.26	1.01	1.50	1.22
1975	1.30	1.11	1.56	1.27	1.29	1.00	1.61	1.21
1976	1.25	1.12	1.56	1.26	1.24	1.00	1.61	1.23
1977	1.22	1.10	1.56	1.28	1.20	.96	1.62	1.24
1978	1.21	1.10	1.58	1.34	1.19	.98	1.62	1.25
1979	1.22	1.12	1.60	1.39	1.20	1.01	1.64	1.32
1980	1.23	1.17	1.66	1.46	1.21	1.04	1.69	1.39
1981	1.26	1.19	1.73	1.51	1.23	1.05	1.74	1.43
1982	1.31	1.25	1.81	1.58	1.28	1.10	1.83	1.52
1983	1.25	1.23	1.73	1.52	1.24	1.10	1.75	1.45
1984	1.25	1.26	1.72	1.56	1.24	1.13	1.74	1.48
1985	1.29	1.29	1.74	1.57	1.26	1.14	1.76	1.52
1986	1.32	1.39	1.75	1.63	1.29	1.21	1.77	1.59
1987	1.32	1.41	1.74	1.60	1.30	1.27	1.75	1.56
1988	1.39	1.37	1.74	1.59	1.37	1.25	1.75	1.55

Note: Monthly starting salary/(Avg. weekly earnings of private nonagricultural production and nonsupervisory workers × 4.33).

trough is reached earliest for engineering majors in 1973, when they received 47 percent more than the average production or nonsupervisory worker. The low point in science was reached in 1976, when the premium had fallen to 26 percent. Among business and liberal arts majors, the nadir came in 1978, when the premium in business was 21 percent and only 10 percent in liberal arts.

Earnings premiums began to rise in the 1980s, consistent with the findings of Murphy and Welch (1987). By 1986 beginning engineers were receiving 75 percent more than the average production or nonsupervisory worker, while science majors were receiving a 63 percent premium. In 1987 liberal arts majors were receiving a 41 percent premium, while in 1988 business majors were receiving a 39 percent premium. For every field except business, the premiums reached in the 1980s were higher than at any other time since 1960. However, given the evidence presented in tables 6–1 and 6–2, these high premiums were not reached because real starting salaries were higher than at any other time since the 1960s, but rather because the earnings of production and nonsupervisory workers stagnated in the 1980s.

For women, the beginning of the sample period is 1974. At that time, beginning female engineers received 50 percent more than the average production or nonsupervisory worker, business majors received a 26 percent premium, science majors earned 22 percent more, and liberal arts majors received only 1 percent more. These premiums were fairly constant throughout the late 1970s for business and liberal arts majors and increased for engineering and science majors. By 1986 female engineers were receiving starting salaries 77 percent higher than the average production or nonsupervisory worker, and science majors were receiving a 59 percent premium. In 1987 liberal arts majors received a 27 percent premium, and in 1988 business majors received a 37 percent premium. The relative earnings trends for female graduates in the 1980s have been very similar to those for male graduates.

Explaining Variations in Relative Earnings

Table 6–7 shows the relative earnings of the four major categories by year and sex. A more difficult task is to explain the variation in these relative earnings series over time. Relative earnings will change over time if supply or demand conditions for one group relative to the other change or if the characteristics of one or both of the groups change. The effects of variables measuring these influences are investigated in tables 6–8

Table 6–8. Male Relative Earnings Regression Estimates, 1960–1988 (*t*-statistics in parentheses)

Explanatory Variable (Mean)	Dependent Variable: EARN[a]							
	Business		Liberal Arts		Engineering		Science	
SAT[b] (938)		2.92		2.52		−.202		.230
		(6.36)		(3.37)		(.360)		(.363)
UNEMP[c] (4.83)		−.078		−.082		−.036		−.063
		(4.08)		(2.63)		(1.55)		(2.39)
PCTMANU[d] (.237)		−4.91		−.637		−.086		−.182
		(3.36)		(2.69)		(.480)		(.905)
YR70[e] (.345)	−.026	.011	−.095	−.094	−.010	−.020	−.132	−.137
	(1.14)	(.426)	(3.56)	(2.28)	(.658)	(.649)	(7.46)	(3.92)
YR80[f] (.310)	−.032	.100	.006	.058	.099	.077	.031	.030
	(1.36)	(2.04)	(.227)	(.728)	(6.60)	(1.28)	(1.68)	(.447)
Intercept	.288	−20.4	.242	−17.3	.453	1.78	.412	−1.33
	(17.6)	(6.25)	(12.8)	(3.36)	(44.0)	(.446)	(32.8)	(.295)
R^2	.075	.784	.406	.724	.709	.743	.781	.836
n	29	29	29	29	29	29	29	29

[a] log (male monthly starting salary/avg. weekly earnings of private nonagricultural production and nonsupervisory workers × 4.33). Means—Business: 1.310; Liberal Arts: 1.238; Engineering: 1.619; Science: 1.461. All means are presented in linear rather than logged form.
[b] log (average SAT math score + average SAT verbal score).
[c] log (unemployment rate, males aged 20 and over).
[d] log (GNP produced in manufacturing/GNP).
[e] = 1 if year > 1969 and < 1980, = 0 otherwise.
[f] = 1 if year > 1979, = 0 otherwise.

Table 6–9. Female Relative Earnings Regression Estimates, 1974–1988 (*t*-statistics in parentheses)

Explanatory Variable (Mean)	Dependent Variable: *EARN*[a]							
	Business		*Liberal Arts*		*Engineering*		*Science*	
SAT[b] (908)		1.80 (8.24)		−.019 (.025)		−1.68 (3.92)		−1.88 (2.77)
UNEMP[c] (6.61)		.028 (1.80)		−.064 (1.12)		.119 (3.83)		−.006 (.117)
PCTMANU[d] (.210)		−.706 (13.2)		−.968 (5.04)		−.300 (2.86)		−.530 (3.19)
YR80[e] (.600)	.034 (1.78)	−.001 (.045)	.140 (4.58)	−.001 (.016)	.092 (6.56)	−.014 (.610)	.185 (8.79)	.038 (1.02)
Intercept	.204 (13.9)	−13.2 (8.84)	−.007 (.299)	−1.18 (.220)	.470 (43.3)	11.3 (3.85)	.218 (13.4)	12.3 (2.65)
R^2	.196	.970	.617	.930	.768	.939	.856	.958
n	15	15	15	15	15	15	15	15

[a] log (female monthly starting salary/avg. weekly earnings of private nonagricultural production and nonsupervisory workers × 4.33). Mean—Business: 1.253; Liberal Arts: 1.084; Engineering: 1.692; Science: 1.397. All means are presented in linear rather than logged form.

[b] log (average SAT math score + average SAT verbal score).

[c] log (unemployment rate, females aged 20 and older).

[d] log (GNP produced in manufacturing/GNP).

[e] = 1 if year > 1979, = 0 otherwise.

through 6–11. Tables 6–8 and 6–9 report regressions explaining relative earnings by major for men from 1960 to 1988 and for women from 1974 to 1988. Table 6–10 does the same for all college graduates, and table 6–11 decomposes movements in relative earnings for all college graduates into effects due to each of the variables in the models.

The first regressions reported for each major in tables 6–8 and 6–9 are intended to summarize the movements in the natural log of relative earnings over time. Included in the regressions are dummy variables indicating the decade of the 1970s and 1980s for males and the decade of the 1980s for females. The coefficients on these variables show how much higher or lower relative earnings were in the 1970s and 1980s compared to the 1960s for males, and in the 1980s compared to the 1970s for females. Consistent with previous research and the pattern found in table 6–7, relative earnings were lower in the 1970s than in the 1960s, and then increased in the 1980s. For males, in liberal arts and in sciences relative earnings were significantly lower in the 1970s than in the 1960s, and in engineering they were significantly higher in the 1980s than in the 1960s. For females, earnings of beginning graduates were uniformly higher in the 1980s than in the 1970s.

Do these patterns remain after holding constant other factors affecting relative earnings? The second set of regressions in tables 6–8 and 6–9 includes one variable to control for the overall quality of college graduates, the average SAT math and verbal score four years earlier, and two demand side variables, the percentage of GNP produced in manufacturing (PCTMANU) and the male or female unemployment rate of those aged 20 and older (UNEMP).[7] Each of these variables is expressed in natural logs.[8] The SAT variable has a positive and significant effect on the relative earnings of male business and liberal arts majors and on female business majors. Somewhat puzzling, however, is the negative and significant effect on the relative earnings of female engineering and science majors.[9]

The effect of the UNEMP variable is negative in six of the eight regressions shown in tables 6–8 and 6–9. Thus increases in the overall unemployment rate lower the earnings of beginning college graduates relative to the average production worker. This result can be explained by the fact that new college graduates have no specific human capital so that their salaries are more sensitive to cyclical conditions than are the earnings of the average production worker. Some production workers are unionized and hold multiyear contracts, which further cushions their earnings to the business cycle.

The PCTMANU variable has a negative effect on the relative earnings of new college graduates in every field for both men and women. The bigger the share of total production devoted to manufacturing, the greater the demand for production and nonsupervisory workers. The net result is a decline in the starting salaries in all college majors relative to average production and nonsupervisory earnings.

While in most cases significance levels are reduced, the only case for men in which the decade dummy variables change sign is for business majors. After controlling for SAT, UNEMP, and PCTMANU, relative earnings for business majors were higher in both the 1970s and 1980s than in the 1960s, and significantly higher in the 1980s. Relative earnings were also significantly higher in the 1980s for engineers, and significantly lower in the 1970s in liberal arts and science. Among women, the signs on the YR80 variable change in three out of four cases and in each case the YR80 variable is insignificant. In other words, after controlling for SAT, UNEMP, and PCTMANU, there are no significant differences in the relative earnings of new female college graduates between the 1970s and 1980s.

What explains the differences across the three decades for males, even after controlling for SAT, UNEMP, and PCTMANU? Obvious candidates are supply side factors, and chief among them is the relative size of the group of new college graduates. Cohort size has been shown to be an important determinant of earnings in several previous studies (Freeman 1979; Welch 1979; Berger 1985, 1988*b*). The general finding is that larger cohorts lead to lower levels of earnings, although the effect on the shape of the earnings profile is less certain. A cohort size variable is constructed here for all college graduates. For males it is the natural log of the number of male graduates in a given year relative to the population aged 20 and older in that year. For females it is the natural log of the number of female graduates in a given year relative to the population aged 20 and older. The number of graduates and the population are used instead of the number of workers and working graduates to avoid the problem of the endogeneity of the participation decision. The test of the cohort size variable is done for all college graduates instead of field by field because there may also be an endogeneity problem with the choice of field. Choice of field and relative earnings in each field may be simultaneously determined within the framework used here. Thus the focus is on the relative earnings of all college graduates.[10]

Table 6–10 reports male and female regressions that replace the decade dummies with the cohort size variable (COHORT). The earnings variable is now the weighted average of earnings across all four fields relative to the average wage of production and nonsupervisory workers. In the male

Table 6–10. Relative Earnings Regression Estimates, All Fields of Study (*t*-statistics in parentheses)

	Dependent Variable: EARN[a]			
	Means		*Estimates*	
Explanatory Variable	*Males 1960–1988*	*Females 1974–1988*	*Males 1960–1988*	*Females 1974–1988*
COHORT[b]	.00323	.00304	−.110 (2.49)	−.140 (.381)
SAT[c]	938	908	−.602 (.902)	−2.16 (4.82)
UNEMP[d]	4.83	6.61	−.058 (1.95)	.049 (1.12)
PCTMANU[e]	.237	.210	−.141 (.831)	−.245 (2.00)
Intercept			3.78 (.780)	13.8 (3.61)
R^2			.406	.923
n			29	15

[a] log (monthly starting salary/average weekly earnings of private nonagricultural production and nonsupervisory workers × 4.33). Means—Males: 1.5166; Females: 1.374. All means are presented in linear rather than logged form.
[b] Males: log (number of male bachelor's degrees granted/population aged 20 and older). Females: log (number of female bachelor's degrees granted/population aged 20 and older).
[c] log (average SAT math score + average SAT verbal score).
[d] Males: log (unemployment rate, males aged 20 and older.
Females: log (unemployment rate, females aged 20 and older.
[e] log (GNP produced in manufacturing/GNP).

regression the COHORT variable is negative, as expected, and significant. In other words, larger cohorts of graduates lead to lower relative starting salaries. For females, cohort size is negative but insignificant.

Table 6–11 accounts for changes over time using changes in the values of the variables in the model and the parameter estimates reported in table 6–10. For males, 1973–1974 was both the trough in weighted average relative earnings across fields and the peak in cohort size over the entire sample period of 1960–1988. Therefore, table 6–11 accounts separately for changes in earnings from 1960 to 1973 and from 1974 to 1988 for

Table 6–11. Predicted Changes in Relative Earnings over Time Due to Changes in Explanatory Variables

	Actual Changes			*Predicted EARN Changes**		
	Males 1960–1973	*Males 1974–1988*	*Females 1974–1988*	*Males 1960–1973*	*Males 1974–1988*	*Females 1974–1988*
EARN	−.042	.124	.258	–	–	–
COHORT	.602	−.442	−.058	−.066	.049	.008
SAT	−.028	−.055	−.055	.017	.033	.119
UNEMP	−.354	.213	−.116	.020	−.012	−.006
PCTMANU	.154	−.271	−.271	−.022	.038	.066
Total Predicted Change	–	–	–	−.051	.108	.187

* Calculated from the actual changes in the variables and the parameter estimates reported in table 6–9.

males. For females, changes over the entire 1974–1988 sample period are used.

Table 6–11 first shows the actual changes in each of the variables in the model, followed by the predicted changes due to each variable, obtained by multiplying the actual change by the corresponding regression coefficient in table 6–10. As can be seen, for males the log of relative earnings dropped .042 from 1960 to 1973 but rose .124 from 1974 to 1988. For females, the log of relative earnings rose .258 from 1974 to 1988. The increase in COHORT by itself accounted for more than all of the decrease in EARN from 1960 to 1973 for males. The increase in the size of the manufacturing sector alone accounted for 43 percent of the predicted decline in log relative earnings (–.051). These two negative changes in relative earnings were partially offset by drops in unemployment and SAT scores from 1960 to 1973. From 1974 to 1988 the relative earnings of college graduates rose. In this case, however, the drop in COHORT explained only 45 percent of the predicted increase over the period, while the portion explained by the reduction in the size of the manufacturing sector was 35 percent of the predicted change in earnings. The increased contribution of demand side factors to changes in the relative earnings of college graduates, especially in the 1980s, is consistent with Murphy and Welch (1987). However, in the analysis here, decreases in cohort size still play an important, though smaller role in the increase in the relative earnings of college graduates in the 1980s.[11] For females, almost all of the relative earnings change is accounted for by changes in the average SAT score and the size of the manufacturing sector. Little if any is accounted for by the decrease in cohort size during the period.

Conclusions

This chapter has examined differences in the private returns to specific college majors. The focus is on the earnings of bachelor's degree graduates in business, liberal arts (humanities and social sciences), engineering, and science. Time series data on starting salaries are obtained from the College Placement Council *Salary Survey*, and data over the early portion of the career are obtained from the National Longitudinal Survey of Young Men.

Engineering graduates have the highest starting salaries, but the NLS data indicate that they have the slowest earnings growth over the early part of the career. Aside from education, liberal arts graduates typically have the lowest entry level salaries but the steepest wage profiles. Business and science graduates are in the middle, both in terms of starting salaries and growth in wages over the early career. The NLS data indicate that the observable characteristics of individuals choosing different majors varies, and this explains some but not all of the differences in wages across fields. Regression estimates of hourly rates of pay from the NLS indicate that liberal arts graduates do not catch up to engineering graduates after 15 years in the labor market. However, wage differences across fields do in general decline as workers gain more experience. The pattern of starting salaries across fields of study is similar for males and females.

The returns to the various majors have varied substantially over time. Male starting salaries in real terms peaked in 1969–1970, as did starting salaries relative to average production or nonsupervisory earnings. Real starting salaries and relative earnings fell throughout most of the 1970s for business and liberal arts majors and during the early 1970s for engineering and science graduates. During the 1980s male real and relative earnings rose in all fields except engineering. The patterns for females since 1974, the first year data were available, are similar to those observed for males.

Across all male college graduates, starting salaries relative to average production or nonsupervisory earnings rose throughout the 1960s, then fell, reaching a trough in 1973–1974 before rising throughout the late 1970s and the 1980s. The increase in the relative cohort size of the new groups of graduates played a large part in the decline in their relative earnings in the 1970s. The change in the structure of the economy, as measured by the fraction of GNP produced in manufacturing, also contributed to a lesser extent. However, the effect of decreases in cohort size has had a smaller impact on the increase in the relative earnings of college graduates since 1973–1974 than did increases in cohort size during the 1960s and early 1970s. At the same time, the impact of changes in the size of the manufacturing sector made bigger contributions to the relative earnings change since 1974 than before that time. Among females since 1974, changes in cohort size have had no impact on the increase in the relative earnings of beginning college graduates, while the decrease in the size of the manufacturing sector has had an important impact. It will be interesting to see whether the trends observed in the 1980s continue, especially if there are further declines in the relative size of entry cohorts of college graduates and in the relative size of the manufacturing sector of the economy.

Although this chapter has presented a fairly comprehensive view of starting salaries of males since 1960, the analysis for females has been hampered by the shorter time-series beginning in 1974. Clearly, more work examining the relative earnings of females is warranted, especially as longer time-series become available. Also wage differences other than starting salaries have been presented only for males early in the career, using the National Longitudinal Survey of Young Men. More evidence is needed on differences in the shapes of earnings profiles and differences in lifetime earnings for both men and women across fields of study. Perhaps other data sets such as the NLS Youth or Women or the NLS High School Class of 1972, which cover longer or different time periods than those used here, can be employed.

Appendix: Specific Majors Included in Each Area of Study

Area	*Data Source*	*Specific Majors*
Business	CPC Salary Survey	Accounting, banking and finance, business administration, human resources, institutional management, management information systems, marketing and distribution
	NLS Young Men	Business and management, business technology
Liberal arts	CPC Salary Survey	Economics, letters, humanities, criminal justice, history, psychology, social sciences
	NLS Young Men	Area studies, communications, fine and applied arts, foreign languages, letters, psychology, public affairs and services, social sciences, theology, interdisciplinary studies
Engineering	CPC Salary Survey	Aerospace and aeronautical, agricultural, biomedical and biochemical, civil, electrical, geological, industrial, mechanical, metallurgical, mining and mineral, nuclear, and petroleum engineering, engineering technology
	NLS Young Men	Engineering
Science	CPC Salary Survey	Agricultural sciences, architectural and environmental design, biological, chemistry, computer science, mathematics, allied health professions, nursing, pharmacy, physics, physical and earth sciences, renewable natural resources
	NLS Young Men	Agriculture and natural resources, architecture and environmental design, biological sciences, computer and information sciences, library science, mathematics, military science, physical science
Education	CPC Salary Survey	N/A
	NLS Young Men	Education

Acknowledgments

This research was supported in part with funds from the National Science Foundation (grant no. RII-8610671) and the Commonwealth of Kentucky through the Kentucky EPSCoR Program.

Endnotes

1. There are some potential drawbacks to examining only private monetary returns. Analysis of private monetary returns does not provide evidence on fringe or nonpecuniary benefit differences across majors. While anecdotal evidence of nonpecuniary benefit differences across majors may be available, consistent measurements of differences in these benefits or even fringe benefits would be difficult if not impossible to obtain. Similarly, differences in social benefits across majors would be hard to obtain. Therefore, in this chapter, the emphasis is on private pecuniary differences.

2. Separate wage regressions were estimated for each of the five fields of study. An F-test rejects the hypothesis of equal coefficient vectors across the five fields at better than a .99 level of significance. The calculated $F(80, 2327) = 3.57$.

3. The fraction of the actual wage difference between field i and the overall average wage accounted for by differences between the characteristics of individuals choosing i and the average individual can be expressed as $((X_i - X_A)b_i)/(\text{WAGE}_i - \text{WAGE}_A)$, where X_i is the vector of mean characteristics of individuals choosing major i, X_A is the vector of mean characteristics across all majors, b_i is the vector of estimated coefficients for the wage equation for major i, WAGE_i is the average log wage in major i, and WAGE_A is the average log wage across all majors.

4. LAMBDA and its estimated coefficient are excluded from the calculations presented in table 6–6 because, after including LAMBDA in the regressions, the remaining parameters are consistent estimates of their population values.

5. Predictions of earnings later in the career are not given because the earnings equations by major are estimated with a relatively young sample, which may produce unreliable estimates of earnings later in the career. Errors are likely to increase when predicting outside the bounds of the sample and no one in the sample has more than 16 years of experience, and very few have that many. The LNEXP specification further compounds the problem. Although it may be fine for a relatively young sample, using it to predict earnings throughout the career will produce errors in the later years.

6. The relative earnings measure used is probably biased downward as a measure of relative lifetime earnings since starting salaries understate the average earnings of college graduates over the career. Also, a further complication is that the average earnings over the career for a particular cohort may not be very well approximated by earnings at a point in time, especially if earnings profiles for that cohort are different from cross-sectional earnings profiles.

7. Earnings equations estimated with microdata, such as those reported in table 6–5 using the NLS Young Men data, typically include several control variables besides those that are used here to explain time series variation in relative earnings. These variables are either unavailable or unnecessary in the time series models estimated here. For example, the average characteristics of entry level college graduates by field of study are not contained in

the CPC data. In any case many of these characteristics do not vary a great deal over time for this group.

8. The regression estimates reported in tables 6–8 through 6–10 are obtained using ordinary least squares with no correction for serial correlation. All four Durbin-Watson statistics for the full male models in table 6–8 are in the uncertain range, and all four for the full female models in table 6–9 exceed the upper bound at the 5 percent level.

9. The same result is obtained when the regressions are estimated using the average female SAT scores instead of the overall average SAT scores. Average scores by gender are available only back to 1967, so the average male scores cannot be used to estimate the male model over the full 1960–1988 sample period.

10. Of course, the decision to attend college may still be endogenous but should be less of a problem than the choice of field. Berger (1988*b*) uses a cohort size variable based entirely on population and obtains results similar to those reported in table 6–10. He also estimates cohort size effects within each field, using both a population-based variable and one based on number of degrees in each field, ignoring any simultaneity problems. He estimates these effects for males and finds the biggest negative effects for liberal arts and then science graduates and smaller effects for business and engineering graduates.

11. Berger (1983) predicted increases in the earnings of young college graduates relative to other workers based solely on changes in the composition of the labor force, which are essentially cohort size effects. The results here of a continued role for demographic factors are consistent with those earlier predictions.

References

Alexander, E. R., & Frey, D. E. (1984). An econometric estimate of the demand for MBA enrollment. *Economics of Education Review 3*, 97–103.

Berger, M. C. (1983). Changes in labor force composition and male earnings: A production approach. *Journal of Human Resources 18*, 177–196.

Berger, M. C. (1985). The effect of cohort size on earnings growth: A reexamination of the evidence. *Journal of Political Economy 93*, 561–573.

Berger, M. C. (1988*a*). Predicted future earnings and choice of college major. *Industrial and Labor Relations Review 41*, 418–429.

Berger, M. C. (1988*b*). Cohort size effects on earnings: Differences by college major. *Economics of Education Review 7*, 375–383.

Blau, F., & Beller, A. (1988). Trends in earnings differentials by gender, 1971–1981. *Industrial and Labor Relations Review 41*, 513–529.

Blinder, A. (1973). Wage discrimination: Reduced form and structural estimates. *Journal of Human Resources 8*, 436–455.

Carlson, L., & Swartz, C. (1988). The earnings of women and ethnic minorities, 1959–1979. *Industrial and Labor Relations Review 41*, 530–546.

Freeman, R. B. (1971). *The market for college-trained manpower*. Cambridge: Harvard University Press.

Freeman, R. B. (1975*a*). Legal cobwebs: A recursive model of the labor market for new lawyers. *Review of Economics and Statistics 58*, 171–179.

Freeman, R. B. (1975*b*). Supply and salary adjustments in the changing science manpower market. *American Economic Review 65*, 27–39.

Freeman, R. B. (1976). A cobweb model of the supply and starting salary of new engineers. *Industrial and Labor Relations Review 30*, 236–248.

Freeman, R. B. (1977). The decline in the economic rewards to college education. *Review of Economics and Statistics 59*, 18–29.

Freeman, R. B. (1979). The effect of demographic factors on the age-earnings profile in the U. S. *Journal of Human Resources 14*, 289–318.

Freeman, R. B. (1980). The facts about the declining economic value of college. *Journal of Human Resources 15*, 124–142.

Freeman, R. B. (1981*a*). *Implications of the changing U. S. labor market for higher education* (Working Paper No. 697). National Bureau of Economic Research.

Freeman, R. B. (1981*b*). *Career patterns of college graduates in a declining job market* (Working Paper No. 750). National Bureau of Economic Research.

Goddeeris, J. H. (1988). Compensating differentials and self-selection: An application to lawyers. *Journal of Political Economy 96*, 411–428.

Hansen, W. L., Newburger, H. B., Schroeder, F. J., & Youngday, D. J. (1980). Forecasting the market for new Ph.D. economists. *American Economic Review 70*, 49–63.

Heckman, J. J. (1979). Sample selection bias as a specification error. *Econometrica 47*, 153–161.

Hoffman, D. L., & Low, S. A. (1983). Rationality and the decision to invest in economics. *Journal of Human Resources 18*, 455–479.

Lee, L-F. (1982). Some approaches to the correction of selectivity bias. *Review of Economic Studies 49*, 355–372.

Lee, L-F. (1983). Generalized economic models with selectivity. *Econometrica 51*, 507–512.

McMahon, W. W., & Wagner, A. P. (1981). Expected returns to investment in higher education. *Journal of Human Resources 16*, 274–285.

McMahon, W. W., & Wagner, A. P. (1982). The monetary returns to education as partial social efficiency criteria. In W. W. McMahon and T. G. Geske (Eds.), *Financing education* (pp. 150–192). Urbana: University of Illinois Press.

Murphy, K. M., & Welch, F. (1987). *The structure of wages*. Unpublished paper, University of Chicago.

National Science Foundation. (1985). *Science and engineering personnel: A national overview* (NSF Surveys of Science Resource Series, No. 85–302). Washington, D.C.

Oaxaca, R. (1973). Male-female wage differentials in urban labor markets. *International Economic Review 14*, 693–709.

Olson, C. A., & Becker, B. E. (1983). Sex discrimination in the promotion process. *Industrial and Labor Relations Review 36*, 624–641.

O'Neill, J. (1985). The trend in the male-female wage gap in the United States. *Journal of Labor Economics 3*, S91–S116.

Pashigan, P. B. (1977). The market for lawyers: The determinants of the demand

for and the supply of lawyers. *Journal of Law and Economics 20*, 53–85.
Rumberger, R. W. (1984). The changing economic benefits of college graduates. *Economics of Education Review 3*, 3–11.
Scott, C. E. (1979). The market for Ph.D. economists: The academic sector. *American Economic Review 69*, 137–142.
Siow, A. (1984). Occupational choice under uncertainty. *Econometrica 52*, 631–645.
Welch, F. (1979). Effects of cohort size on earnings: The baby boom babies' financial bust. *Journal of Political Economy 87*, S65–S98.
Willis, R. J., & Rosen, S. (1979). Education and self-selection. *Journal of Political Economy 87*, S7–S36.
Zarkin, G. A. (1985). Occupational choice: An application to the market for public school teachers. *Quarterly Journal of Economics*, May, 409–446.

7 PRIVATE NONMONETARY RETURNS TO INVESTMENT IN HIGHER EDUCATION

Elchanan Cohn and Terry G. Geske

Numerous recent studies have provided estimates of the rate of return to higher education. A survey by the authors (Cohn and Geske 1986) indicates that estimates of the private internal rates of return (IROR) to four years of college education in the United States ranged from about 10 to 21 percent during the past 50 years, while the social IROR ranged from 9 to 14 percent. Despite fluctuations in the returns over time, the IROR have remained remarkably stable, especially over the long run. Results for other countries, summarized in Psacharopoulos (1989) and Cohn and Geske (1990, pp. 129–32), suggest that social IROR to higher education are generally higher in less developed countries and are lower in more highly developed economies. Social rates range from as low as 5 percent in Greece to as high as 23 percent in Mexico; private rates range from as low as 6 percent in Cyprus and Greece to as high as 47 percent in Malawi.

The IROR to graduate education are typically much smaller. Estimates in the United States range from negative to 23.6, with the bulk of estimates under 10 percent. Similarly, low returns to graduate education have also been observed for Canada (Dodge and Stager 1972) and Australia (Selby-Smith 1975). Moreover, substantial subsidization of students enrolled in graduate programs has resulted in private IROR that are substantially higher than their social counterpart. Although some of the very low estimates might be questioned (see, e.g., Tomaske 1974), and although some graduate programs (e.g., law, dentistry, and medicine) appear to be quite profitable, it appears that on the whole graduate programs do not appear to be highly profitable either to the individual or to society.

The conclusion of the low returns has raised an obvious question. If certain college and university programs are not profitable to the individual, why is that the people continue to enroll in such programs? Morever, if these programs are also not socially profitable, why do nations and states continue to subsidize them?

One answer to these questions it that college education (and education in general) bestows not only labor market benefits that are measurable in terms of earnings differentials, but also various types of nonmarket (including nonmonetary) benefits. These benefits might be sufficiently high to justify both private and social investment in college and university education.[1] Indeed, Haveman and Wolfe (1984) speculate that benefit–cost studies that have focused exclusively on increased earnings may have captured only 50 percent of the total value of an additional year of schooling.

The purpose of this chapter is to provide a survey of studies on the nonmarket effects of education. Although quantitative estimates are provided in some cases, the emphasis is on the type and nature of such effects. It should be pointed out at the outset that this survey is not exhaustive. Some selectivity was exercised due to time and space constraints.

Family Life

Considerable empirical work has focused on the effects of education on family life, including marriage, family planning, and the rearing of children (Schultz 1974; Becker 1981). With regard to marriage, it goes without saying that an individual's opportunities for selecting or attracting a desirable mate (one with a higher earnings capacity) are much improved by going to college. Michael (1982) develops the argument that education appears to facilitate a more productive sorting of men and women in the marriage market by pointing out that there is a positive correlation of at least 0.4 between spouses in their education levels. In turn, this marital sorting may lead to subsequent benefits such as more stable marriages (Becker, Landes, and Michael 1977) and also positive assortative mating by intelligence, which increases the probability of parenting "bright" children. The methodological problems in examining the notion of marital sorting are formidable, and "the measurement of non-monetary benefits of schooling here are not easily calculable, but they may be substantial both privately and socially if schooling facilitates positive assortative mating by intelligence" (Michael 1982, p. 137).

Family Planning

Economists have increasingly applied the new theory of consumer behavior to the household production of children since the early 1970s (Michael 1973, 1975*a*; Michael and Willis 1976). Studies by Michael and Willis examine the effects of education on the demand for children. The basic research strategy has been to analyze the choices and decisions made jointly by husband and wife with regard to the quantity and quality of children desired. The household production model specifies that children provide a flow of services to parents and that parents attempt to maximize the satisfaction derived from these services. Thus parents exercise control over fertility behavior—the prevention or spacing of births—in order to optimize utility (satisfaction), given the cost and time constraints within the household. The decisions that couples make reflect the real costs of fertility control, which include not only the direct expenditures of time and money but also considerations such as foregone sexual pleasure, increased health risk, or conflict with religious principles.

Michael (1975*b*) examines the effects of education on fertility behavior with particular regard to the efficiency with which contraceptive techniques are used to regulate family size. Michael extends those studies that document the indirect effects of education on family size through family income and the price of parental time. In addition to these indirect effects, he argues that education may also have a direct effect on family size through the efficiency with which parents process information about contraceptive products and techniques. Michael hypothesizes that more-educated couples should be more proficient in fertility control, thus lowering both the money and psychic costs related to contraceptive use. His analysis discloses that more-educated couples tend to adopt contraceptive practices more readily and at an earlier stage in marriage, are better informed about and more receptive to new techniques, and thus engage in more effective fertility control than do less-educated couples. Using regression analysis to isolate the effects of education, he found that the education level of the husband, as well as the education level of the wife relative to that of her husband, had a significant negative association with the number of children.

Using data from the Panel Study of Income Dynamics, Calhoun (1989) shows that other things equal, the number of children born to white women decreases as mother's education increases. The results are consistent for two different versions of his model. On the other hand, education does not appear to be related (in a statistically significant manner) to desired family size.

Time Allocation Patterns

Another important line of inquiry investigates the effects of education on the time parents spend with their children. Hill and Stafford (1974) found that women of high socioeconomic status (SES) spend substantially more time with preschool children than do women of low SES—between two to three and one-half times as much on a per-child basis. Benson (1982; see also Benson, Medrich, and Buckley 1980), on the other hand, using a sample of sixth graders and their parents, found that both high- and low-SES parents appeared to devote equal amounts of time in exercising control over their children and in helping them with homework, but the high-SES parents may have been using their time to better effect. Nevertheless, Benson's study did not disclose any definite relationships across SES levels between time use and student achievement.

Hill and Stafford (1980) provide a more extensive and detailed analysis on how parents spend time with their children. They use data from the Michigan Time Use Survey to analyze parental time inputs to their children, particularly in their preschool years. Their analysis disclosed that more-educated women spent more time with their children, including both more play time and teaching time. The most pronounced difference across educational levels, however, is related to mothers' time spent in child-related travel. "College-educated women spend about 30–40 minutes per week in child-related travel, high school–educated women spend about 20 minutes, and women who went to grade school spend almost no time in child-related travel" (p. 236). One explanation for this particular finding, consistent with Benson's findings, is that the child-related travel of the more-educated mothers is associated with the provision of appropriate child development experiences. The finding may also reflect suburban dwelling, which simply involves longer driving distances to the children's various activities.

Leibowitz (1975) examines the effects of education on the allocation of women's time between labor market and home production activities. She also focuses on the use of women's time in the home devoted to the care and training of preschool and school-aged children. As expected, she found that more-educated women are more likely to spend more time in the Labor market than other women. At the same time, however, more-educated women are less likely to work when they have preschool or school-aged children in the home. In addition, although aggregate time devoted to home production is about the same for the different education levels, women with more education spend less time in home maintenance activities and considerably more time in child care activities. In short, college-educated women, as well as their husbands, spend more time with their children than do other parents.

Leibowitz (1974*a*; see also 1974*b* and 1974*c*) uses Ben-Porath's life cycle model to demonstrate that home production, primarily parental time inputs, serves to increase preschool and childhood stocks of human capital. She uses the 1921 Terman sample consisting of gifted children to investigate the relationship between home investments and the subsequent schooling level achieved by the now adult participants. Leibowitz found that mother's education was significantly related to child's IQ, and that preschool home investments strengthened this relationship beyond the genetic endowment factor. Furthermore, the study, after controlling for income, revealed that parental schooling levels were positively related to the schooling levels attained by their offspring. Thus Leibowitz provides evidence of a nonmonetary benefit of schooling, that is, the effect of parental education on their children's education, resulting in children's future higher earnings.

In a much more focused study, Murnane (1981) replicates a dimension of Leibowitz's work, using a very different sample consisting of low-income black families. Confirming Leibowitz's earlier observation, Murnane also documents a significant relationship between mother's education and children's cognitive skills. Similarly, he also concludes that this relationship reflects, at least in part, the positive influence of home environment, including the quality of child care.

Health

Research has documented the positive correlation between increased schooling and good health. Studies by Grossman (1972*a*, 1972*b*, 1976, 1982) provide solid evidence of education's contribution to better health. Grossman (1976) uses a recursive system of equations to formulate and estimate health-schooling relationships. To test his model, Grossman uses data contained in the NBER-Thorndike-Hagen sample of Army Air Corps cadets of 1943. Thorndike and Hagen collected data for a civilian sample of these in 1955, and the NBER conducted subsequent surveys of this civilian sample in 1969 and 1971. Grossman points out that his sample represents an atypical group of white males who exhibited good health in 1943 and were characterized by above average scholastic ability, schooling, and earnings. Grossman found that schooling has a positive effect on health, and since past health is controlled for in his model, he argues that the evidence supports a causal relationship that runs from schooling to current health.

Grossman's findings indicate that a one-year increase in schooling is associated with a 3.5 percent increase in health capital when only age is held constant. This increase in health capital declines to 1.2 percent when all relevant variables are held constant (e.g., age, background characteristics, ability levels, wage rates, job satisfaction). Given an assumed demand function for health, Grossman suggests that "schooling raises productivity in the production of health by 2.4 percent at a minimum" (1976, p. 179). Grossman compares this nonmarket productivity effect of schooling on health to the market productivity effect of 5.5 percent in the hourly wage rate for his sample. "Although the nonmarket productivity effect of schooling may appear to be small in an absolute sense, it is approximately 40 percent [2.4 ÷ 5.5] as large as the market productivity effect" (1976, p. 179).

Grossman also found that a wife's schooling had a strong positive effect on husband's health. "The effect of wives' schooling is striking, because the coefficient of this variable [wive's schooling] exceeds the coefficient of [husbands'] own schooling" (p. 180). Grossman argues that this finding does not simply reflect selective mating because the research controlled "for important correlates of selective mating, such as general intelligence, parents' schooling, and past health" (p. 181). Finally, Grossman examines the mortality experience of the NBER-Thorndike-Hagen sample between 1955 and 1969. As the sample members aged from approximately 32 to 46 years of age during this time interval, their mortality rate (2.8 percent) was less than the mortality rate for the general population (4.3 percent). Schooling had a positive effect on the probability of survival: A one-year increase in schooling lowered the probability of death by 0.4 percent.

Other researchers have also provided solid evidence documenting the relationship between schooling and health. Lefocowitz (1973) argues that there is a causal relationship between levels of education and individual health status and that the observed correlation between income and medical deprivation appears to be a consequence of education's relationship with both variables. Similarly, studies have shown that parental schooling levels (after controlling for differences in earnings) are positively correlated with the health status of their children (Edwards and Grossman 1981). Finally, Orcutt and colleagues (1977) disclose that increased schooling (and higher relative income) are correlated with lower mortality rates for given age brackets.

Likewise, Lando (1975) shows that increased levels of education, while holding age constant, are associated with reduced rates of work disability and that about four-fifths of racial differences in work disability can be related to educational differences between the races. Lando concedes that this relationship may be due in part to the relationship between education and occupational choice, as well as to possible discrimination against persons with disability. On the other hand, as Becker (1964) points out, much of the educational effect is through occupation, so that there is no reason to be too agnostic about the empirical relationship found between education and health.

A more sophisticated study of the relation between education and health was conducted by Berger and Leigh (1989). Using data from the Health and Nutrition Examination Survey and the National Longitudinal Survey of Young Men, and employing Garen's (1984) technique for self-selection correction, the authors find a direct causation between increased education and improved health (measured by blood pressure). "Taken together, the results ... strongly suggest that the observed schooling–health correlation ... is due primarily to the direct effect of schooling on the production of health rather than due to the effect of unobservables such as differences in the rate of time discount" (Berger and Leigh 1989, p. 447).

Behrman and Wolfe (1989) employ data from Nicaragua and conclude that estimates from both random and fixed-effects models "reinforce the relationships found in standard estimates—that women's schooling affects their health and nutrient intakes; the latter result is particularly robust" (pp. 644–645). They concur with Berger and Leigh that "the estimated positive health impact of the women's schooling is largely representing schooling per se rather than unobserved fixed endowments" (p. 660). In addition, their "results provide strong support for the proposition that women's schooling increases nutrient intakes" (p. 661).

Regression analysis performed by Ng (1989), using data from the National Medical Care Expenditure Survey, indicates that increased education is a statistically significant predictor of expenditures on physician care—but not of days spent in a hospital—for both men and women. The regressions include a large number of other variables, such as age and its square, race, wage rate, family size, number of young children, marital status, health condition, location of residence, type of insurance coverage, and a risk factor.

Of related interest is the study on Haiti by Easton and Fass (1989). They list a number of nonmarket benefits of schooling, including employment from emigration and "social insurance services and feeding programs provided by foster child sponsorship schemes" (p. 188). Evidently, in Haiti and in other countries enrolling a child in school entitles the family to various health and nutritional benefits that might be worth a great deal to the student and the family. In regard to primary schooling in Haiti, Easton and Fass calculate that "by paying 7.2 percent of income (about $0.35 per adult) for tuition each month, [the families] were not only able to raise income by a net value of $0.50, or 12.5 percent more than the sums received from all other sources, but also to obtain insurance for risk at the same time" (p. 189). To the extent that enrollment in higher education provides students and their families free or reduced-cost meals, insurance, and other amenities, such benefits would also constitute nonmarket benefits of education. Indeed, subsidized food and medical services in colleges and universities are quite common in many countries. Moreover, since subsidized meals, medical services, housing, and other amenities provided by colleges and universities enter into the calculus of the social *costs* of education—but not the *benefits*—the tendency is then to underestimate the social rate of return to schooling.

Consumption Behavior

Michael (1972, 1975*a*) compares the effect of education on consumer behavior in the home or nonmarket sector with the effect of education on earnings in the labor market. He uses a household production model to examine how education affects or alters consumer expenditure patterns. Viewing the household unit as a small multiproduct firm, Michael points out that members of each household combine purchased market goods (capital) with their own time (labor) to produce those commodities desired. Thus Michael postulates that education may enhance the efficiency with which households convert these goods and time into commodities. He argues that if education raises the productivity of time used in one activity (labor market activities), it should also have a similar effect on the productivity of time in other activities (household and nonlabor market activities). In addition, households with more education "have relatively more access to knowledge, concepts, facts, and ideas that may enable the household to arrange nonmarket production more efficiently" (1975*a*, p. 239).

If more-educated persons are more productive in nonmarket activities, families with more education should produce a higher level of output (commodities) for a given quantity of inputs (time and money). Accordingly, Michael reasons that more-educated households will have more real wealth (in terms of commodities) and that these households will, in effect, behave as if they have more real income (the equivalent of greater money income). Michael labels this effect of schooling on real income through nonmarket productivity the "consumption income effect." To verify and estimate this consumption income effect, Michael structures an empirical test to determine if differences in education levels influence consumer behavior in the same manner that they influence money income. Michael tests this hypothesis by correlating educational elasticities with income elasticities based on data drawn from the Consumer Expenditure Surveys of 1950 and 1960–1961 by the Bureau of Labor Statistics. Michael found a positive association between the two elasticities, indicating that increases in education resulted in consumption patterns similar to those produced by increases in money income. Michael concludes that education produces a positive effect on the efficiency of consumption, and he estimates that the effect of schooling is approximately 60 percent as great in nonmarket activities as in the labor market.

In addition to Michael's work, several other studies have focused on the effect of schooling on specific consumption activities. There is substantial evidence, for example, that individuals with more education seek out, and are better informed, about consumer goods markets. Thus these consumers are more likely than others to adopt new products more quickly (Stigler 1961). Similarly, individuals with more education are more likely than others to use credit cards. Mandell (1972) found that credit card use increased steadily with level of schooling, from 28 percent for those with a grade school education to 81 percent for those with a college degree. Finally, Hettich (1972) conducted an empirical exercise to illustrate the potential savings attributable to education that could be realized by the "informed" consumer. His estimates suggest that the potential savings generated through more efficient purchasing behavior increase rates of return to college education from 14.5 percent to about 16.0 percent.

Asset Management

Solmon (1975) analyzes the relationship between education and savings behavior and hypothesizes that more-educated individuals will save a higher proportion of income and will also tend to exercise different savings alternatives. To examine savings behavior, Solmon first employs a conventional definition of savings concerned with the change in financial and nonhousing property assets minus the change in nonhousing debt. His second definition of "full savings" includes net additions to business assets (of proprietors and independent professionals), postschool investment in human capital (on-the-job training), and the value of consumer durable goods purchased. Solmon conducts a number of empirical tests using data from a 1959 Consumers Union survey, a sample of over 3300 families that was composed of a relatively high-income, highly educated subgroup of the population as a whole. Overall, his various analyses supported the basic proposition that more-educated individuals have a higher propensity to save and that they are also more efficient at managing their savings portfolios.

Based on responses to a series of questions in the Consumers Union survey with regard to different aspects of savings, Solmon was also able to examine relationships between schooling and individuals' attitudes with respect to portfolio management, savings objectives, and risk preference. The respondents, for example, were asked a question that could be used to assess their knowledge about protecting themselves against the effects of inflation. Solmon concludes that "at least with respect to inflation, the more educated are more sophisticated (or efficient) investors" (pp. 279–280). While controlling for income and age, Solmon found that the most popular hedges against inflation for the more-educated respondents included common stock, real estate, and mutual fund investments. Respondents with less education, on the other hand, were much more likely to invest in fixed-income securities such as savings accounts and savings bonds. "In an economy with a continually changing price level, the more educated are better able to cope with these fluctuations; that is, they are more likely to minimize the costs associated with changes in the price level" (p. 283).

With regard to families' objectives for savings, respondents were asked, "In planning to save, what are your goals in building up your savings?" Solmon found, after controlling for other relevant variables, that families with more education were more likely to indicate that the primary purpose of savings was to provide children with education and to help children establish households. At the same time, there was a highly significant negative relationship between educational attainment and stated savings objectives such as building up a business or providing for emergencies. One interpretation of these results is that the more educated are more prone to invest in their children's future and that the more educated possess a longer time horizon. Solmon infers from these findings that the more highly educated are more likely to accept risk, to be more informed and rational in investment decision making, and to plan ahead with a longer time horizon.

Michael (1982) points out that it is difficult to isolate the effects of education or document a real productivity effect in this research area. With regard to the effect of schooling on investment knowledge in the capital market, "one has the impression that a rather low burden of proof is imposed on the evidence" (p. 131). For the most part, the assessed effects of education do not operate directly from schooling to savings, but rather indirectly from educational differences to savings through other important determinants such as household level of income and individual time preferences.

Migration

Several studies have examined the effects of education on migration behavior. Research on the determinants of migration has documented that more-educated persons are much more likely to be involved in long-distance moves than are less-educated persons (Schwartz 1971; Greenwood 1975). A few explanations have been offered for this observed phenomenon, including both the search efficiency hypothesis and the psychic costs hypothesis. The efficiency hypothesis suggests that schooling serves to reduce the costs associated with job searching or job switching. The argument asserts that the more educated are better skilled at gathering needed information about employment opportunities, the economic attractiveness of new locations, and the moving process itself. The latter hypothesis suggests that there are psychic costs associated with migration, e.g., uncertainties inherent in change, regional cultural differences, or impact on family unit, that increase with distance moved. Nonetheless, education permits individuals to identify and address these costs and consequently serves to diminish the influence of these costs.

Schwartz (1976) uses net and gross migration flows from the 1960 census to investigate the interrelationships between migration, age, and education. To conduct his analysis, Schwartz develops a model based on the tenets of human capital theory, particularly with regard to what is known about the earnings function. Schwartz contends that "the shape of the earnings-age function and the way education affects it can explain all the empirically observed relations of migration measures ... and education" (p. 718). Schwartz points out that human capital arguments essentially explain his findings and that while alternative explanations about the relationship between migration and education — for example, job search efficiency or reduction of psychic costs—may not be wrong, they do not contribute to an understanding of his results.

In a more recent study Da Vanzo (1983; also Da Vanzo 1976, Da Vanzo and Morrison 1981, 1982) argues that analyses of migration behavior based on overall migration flows suffer from considerable aggregation bias. She investigates repeat migration by using an eight-year panel (1968–1975) from the Panel Study of Income Dynamics. DaVanzo distinguishes among those migrants who, after an initial move, relocate to a new location, return to a previous location, or remain at the existing location. To test several hypotheses about repeat migration, DaVanzo uses a polytomous model that holds constant a number of key variables—unemployment, house ownership, and distance of initial move.

DaVanzo reports that educational attainment is a critical variable for repeat migrants who move after a brief one-year interval, stating that "the more educated the migrant, the less likely he is to return, compared with both the alternative of not moving again and that of moving onward" (p. 556). She concludes that "the less educated are the likeliest to return quickly," whereas "the most highly educated are the likeliest to move quickly onward" (p. 558). In an attempt to interpret this education effect, DaVanzo speculates that "the less educated may base their initial moves on more limited information, lowering the success rate of their moves and hence increasing the likelihood of 'corrective' return moves" (p. 556). In contrast, for those migrants who sustained a longer tenure in their new residence after the initial move, that is, from two to six years, there was no significant education effect on future migration alternatives.

Option Values

Weisbrod (1962) points out that there is a financial option open to students. This option refers to the fact that the completion of one level of schooling (e.g., level *a*) enables one to pursue additional levels of schooling ($a + 1$, $a + 2$, . . .). The returns that one might expect to receive for a higher educational investment (say, $a + 1$) might induce him or her to invest in a lower educational level (e.g., *a*), even if the expected return on the latter (*a*) would not be sufficient to justify the necessary expenditure. (According to Mincer, 1962, increased amount of schooling is also associated with the option of securing increasing amounts of on-the-job training).

Weisbrod (1962) goes further, arguing that the returns to elementary education are actually higher than customarily estimated because a portion of the returns to higher levels of schooling are due to the completion of primary schooling. This notion is worthy of consideration, especially in cases where a consideration of two or more consecutive educational levels is at stake. For example, a study by Hu, Lee and Stromsdorfer (1969, 1971) shows much higher returns to students completing a vocational rather than a comprehensive secondary program. The results are intuitively sound for those secondary students who do not contemplate going on to college. On the other hand, if a student has an aptitude for occupations for which a college diploma is required, a choice of a secondary academic or secondary comprehensive program might be more profitable, taking into account both the private returns to the high school program and the expected returns to college (adjusted by the probability that the student will be accepted by a college).

An empirical study of the returns to education, using Canadian data, by Comay, Melnik, and Pollatschek (1976) is a case in point. They show that when option values are explicitly considered, the profitabilities of various early educational investments are strongly affected by the probability of completion of higher educational levels, so that one's decision regarding an educational investment is critically affected by the option value.

A second class of options is Weisbrod's nonfinancial options. For instance, college professors have some nonfinancial advantages associated with their position. These include not only the degree of freedom and flexibility in work but also the daily contact with students and the joy of teaching and research. It is not surprising that a large number of individuals who have the capacity for both teaching and industrial work (research, management) choose teaching in a college or university despite its generally lower salaries (i.e., financial return). The monetary value of these non-financial options could conceptually be measured by the difference between the wage that the individual could have earned and the actual wage earned.

Other nonfinancial options include the "hedging option" (i.e., the flexibility of educated individuals in adapting to new job opportunities) and the "nonmarket option" (i.e., the fact that with education an individual can perform a variety of activities that could not be done without it). Cipriani (1967) and Melnik (1969) provide a further discussion of hedging. Cipriani argues that the principal benefit of the hedging option is to reduce risk from job obsolescence, and that primary benefits would arise for individuals with relatively low educational backgrounds. He does argue, however, that a general education is likely to provide workers with increased flexibility in handling changes in the requirement for jobs. Melnik extends Cipriani's work for the case in which job obsolescence occurs gradually rather than suddenly. He concludes that the need for labor market hedging is lessened when obsolescence occurs gradually.

Weisbrod's example of the nonmarket option is the filing of income tax returns, for which sufficient competence in arithmetic and other skills is required. Weisbrod (1962, p. 114) performed some interesting calculations indicating that the savings to the total population in the United States realized in this manner amounted to at least $250 million in 1956, suggesting "a current year return of 3.2 percent of current investment" in elementary school. Other activities falling within the nonmarket category include typewriting and driving.

Intergenerational Effects

In addition to the previous nonmonetary benefits described, one must also consider possible educational benefits that won't accrue until a generation later. The alleged intergenerational effects of education stem mainly from studies showing that persons are more likely to complete a given level of education if their parents are (or were) more highly educated. The intergenerational effect is the increment in a person's education that can be ascribed to the incremental education of the parent. Hence, we could trace some of the higher expected earnings of the children back to their origin in the increased educational investment by the parents. Therefore, if we confine our investigation of the benefits of education to the parents only, some (perhaps serious) underestimation of benefits would result. One needs to guard, however, against the possibility that double counting of a person's educational benefits will take place—once in the calculation of one's own educational investment and then once more in calculating intergenerational benefits.

A study by Swift and Weisbrod (1965) shows that the returns to elementary and secondary education would be increased substantially when intergenerational benefits are taken into account. On the other hand, they did not find positive intergenerational benefits to college education of the parent. Some methodological refinements of the Swift and Weisbrod method are discussed by Ribich (1968), who provides additional data on the returns to compensatory education.

Another study in which the intergenerational effect was estimated was Spiegelman (1968). He considered two types of benefits: (1) the social benefits of increased income and productivity in the future and (2) the private benefits—namely, the satisfaction that the first generation obtains from knowing that the second generation will be better educated. The intergenerational effects in the Spiegelman study appear to be a great deal stronger than those suggested either by Swift and Weisbrod or by Ribich. For example, the sum of social and private intergenerational benefits amounts to more than one-half of the direct benefits estimated for the Title I program of the Elementary and Secondary Education Act in California.

Other Nonmarket Benefits

A number of additional nonmonetary and nonmarket benefits have been indentified in the literature, including the effect of education on culture and values, job amenities and fringe benefits, and adoption of new technologies. We will discuss these in turn.

Culture and Values

Feldman and Newcomb (1969) offer a comprehensive analysis of the impact of college on student behavior and beliefs. Their summary of various studies suggests "that students going through college increase their interest in aesthetic and cultural values, decrease their adherence to traditional religion and other traditional values, [and] become more realistic and less moralistic in their ethical judgments. They also take an increasingly liberal rather than conservative position on political and socioeconomic issues and become more open minded as measured by scales on authoritarianism, dogmatism, ethnocentrism, and prejudice" (Gurin 1971, pp. 27–28). Work by Trent and Medsker (1968), moreover, suggests that whereas both college students and those of similar age who were employed during the four years showed improvement in social maturity, "the increase was much greater for the college group" (Gurin, p. 35).

Strumpel (1971) reports that college graduates appear to have a more optimistic view of their past and future personal progress and are more likely to agree that it is a good idea that their wives would obtain a paying job. College graduates also appear to be more risk averse, one aspect of which is the greater likelihood of using seatbelts.

Finally, Withey (1971) discusses results of "a study of 87 cities around San Francisco" (p. 83). Although the most highly educated persons in these cities were not represented on city councils, college education is highly related to the probability of being represented on a council: "In the population of these cities, 57 percent have more than a high school diploma, but 95 percent of councilmen are educated above that level" (p. 83).

Job Amenities and Fringe Benefits

Strumpel (1971) utilized a variety of studies to describe the effect of higher education on economic behavior. He shows that more-educated persons are much less likely to be unemployed or to be on strike and to lose work time due to illness, unemployment, or strike. Individuals with higher education are less likely to have many different jobs and occupations, but they are more likely to have few jobs in the same occupations. They are much more likely to receive a vacation, especially vacations of three weeks or more, and are much more likely to assign a high rank to their chance for promotion. College graduates are far more likely than others to find their job enjoyable and to believe that automation is a good thing.

Kiker and Rhine (1987) use the National Medical Care Expenditure Survey to study the impact of fringe benefits on the returns to schooling. Their results indicate that, for males, earnings "are statistically significantly higher [for college graduates] in the presence of fringe benefits . . . , albeit the magnitude is small" (p. 134). For females, they find that "the return to college graduation . . . is biased downward by about 20 percent in the absence of fringe benefits" (p. 134).

In a recent study Mathios (1989) provides evidence that nonmonetary benefits are especially important for more-educated individuals. Using the NAS-NRC Twin Offspring sample, Mathios measured nonmonetary benefits "from answers given to a group of questions introduced with 'As best as you can remember, was the following a reason for your entering the present occupation?'" (p. 459). Respondents were asked questions concerning "(1) pay offered including fringes, (2) prospects for eventual financial success, (3) chance to help others, (4) represented a challenge, (5) job security, (6) provided much free time, (7) liked that kind of work, (8) status, (9) convenient hours, (10) convenient location" (p. 459). Other factors included "interesting work, . . . person to person contact, . . . and chance for independent work" (pp. 459–460). Mathios estimated earnings equations for low- and high-education groups, alternatively excluding and including the above-listed "compensation factors." He concludes that "the inclusion of the occupational factor variables explains an additional 9 percent of the earnings variation in [the high education] group . . . but only an additional 2 percent of the earnings variation in the [low education] group" (p. 464). Moreover, the results show that people are willing to substitute certain nonmonetary benefits for a pay increase. For example, individuals who indicate that leisure time is the most important occupational factor are estimated to earn (in 1980) $2800 less than those for whom leisure time is not important. Similar findings (in qualitative terms) are reported for 15 out of 18 factors studied. The author concludes that issues such as sex discrimination in employment must consider nonmonetary benefits because "estimated earnings differences may overstate the magnitude of discrimination if nonmonetary rewards are a more important part of total compensation for female workers" (p. 457). Similarly, rates of return to college education may be understated, or differences in rates of return by race and sex that rely exclusively on earnings might mask differences in nonmonetary benefits.

Adoption of New Technologies

Several studies provide some evidence that education is related to improvement in research and development (e.g., Nelson 1973; Mansfield 1982). Other studies have shown that educated farmers are more productive and are more likely to adopt new technologies. Early work on the latter subject was completed by Huffman (1974, 1977). Moock (1981) and Phillips and Marble (1986) also have shown that education is related to farmer productivity. More recently, Wozniak (1987) concludes "that education and information reduce adoption costs and uncertainty, and thereby raise the probability of early adoption" (p. 101). He explains that farmers tend to resist early adoption because of "uncertainty and fixed costs of adoption" (p. 104) but that education helps overcome this resistance by providing information as well as the ability to process that information. Using data from the Iowa Family Farm Research Project Survey, and employing probit and logit models, Wozniak obtained results indicating that "increases in education enhance the innovative ability and increase the probability of early adoption, and that the positive marginal effect is diminishing" (p. 107).

Concluding Comments

The foregoing survey leaves us convinced that nonmonetary and nonmarket benefits of education are considerable. Whether the IROR to college education is underestimated by more or less than 50 percent is not clear;

what is clear is that attention must be paid to benefits of this type. Indeed, in many instances investment in higher education is justified almost exclusively in terms of expected nonmarket benefits, rather than increased income for graduates. The difficult task is to provide a comprehensive list of nonmarket and nonmonetary benefits and to estimate the magnitude and distribution of such benefits.

On the other hand, West (1988) is quite leery about the policy implications of consumption benefits:

> The subject is more complex than appears at first sight. As Blaug (1970) observes, since tastes are directly affected by schooling, assertions about consumption benefits from education involve the use of a yardstick that is itself constantly changing. "It is perfectly true that there is an extraordinary consensus in most societies on the positive psychic benefits of education but, of course, it is a consensus of educated people whose taste for learning has been affected by the learning process itself" (p. 21). For policy purposes, moreover, it is important to know whether the electorate wants more education for consumption or investment purposes, or, if both, in what particular proportions. Without such quantitative information economists must either make and state an arbitrary estimate of the size of the consumption benefits, or simply announce that their calculated rates are under-estimates because they are based on monetary earnings exclusively. [P. 61].

Acknowledgment

The authors thank B. F. Kiker for valuable comments on an earlier draft of this chapter.

Endnote

1. The existence of external benefits such as the effect of education on crime prevention (see e.g., Ehrlich 1975 and Webb 1977), or the effect of education on political participation (see, e.g., Taylor and Wolfe 1971 or Stapleton 1976), might further justify social investment; external benefits will be ignored in this chapter.

References

Becker, G. S. (1964). *Human capital*. New York: Columbia University Press (for NBER).

Becker, G. S. (1981). *A treatise on the family*. Cambridge, MA: Harvard University Press.

Becker, G. S., Landes, E. M., & Michael, R. T. (1977). Economics of marital instability. *Journal of Political Economy 86*(6), 1141–1187.

Behrman, J. R., & Wolfe, B. L. (1989). Does more schooling make women better nourished and healthier? Adult sibling random and fixed effects estimates for Nicaragua. *Journal of Human Resources 24*(4), 644–663.

Benson, C. S. (1982). Household production of human capital: Time uses of parents and children as inputs. In W. W. McMahon & T. G. Geske (Eds.), *Financing education: Overcoming inefficiency and inequity* (pp. 52–77). Urbana: University of Illinois Press.

Benson, C. S., Medrich, E. A., & Buckley, S. (1980). A new view of school efficiency: Household time contributions to school achievement. In J. W. Guthrie (ed.), *School finance policies and practices* (pp. 169–204). Cambridge, MA: Ballinger.

Berger, M. C., & Leigh, J. P. (1989). Schooling, self-selection, and health. *Journal of Human Resources 24*(3), 433–455.

Blaug, M. (1970). *An introduction to the economics of education.* London: Penguin Press.

Calhoun, C. A. (1989). Estimating the distribution of desired family size and excess fertility. *Journal of Human Resources 24*(4), 709–724.

Cipriani, C. J. (1967). Hedging in the labor market. *Southern Economic Journal 34*(2), 286–292.

Cohn, E., & Geske, T. G. (1986). Benefit-cost analysis of investment in higher education. In M. P. McKeown & K. Alexander (Eds.), *Values in conflict: Funding priorities for higher education* (pp. 183–215). Seventh Annual Yearbook of the American Education Finance Association; Cambridge, MA: Ballinger.

Cohn, E., & Geske, T. G. (1990). *The economics of education* (3rd ed.). Oxford: Pergamon.

Comay, Y., Melnik, A., & Pollatschek, M. A. (1976). Dropout risks, option values, and returns to investment in schooling. *Canadian Journal of Economics 9*, February, 45–56.

DaVanzo, J. (1976). Differences between return and nonreturn migration: An econometric analysis. *International Migration Review 10*, 13–27.

DaVanzo, J. (1983). Repeat migration in the United States: Who moves back and who moves on? *Review of Economics and Statistics 65*(4), 552–559.

DaVanzo, J., & Morrison, P. A. (1981). Return and other sequences of migration in the U.S. *Demography 18*, 85–101.

DaVanzo, J., & Morrison, P. A. (1982). *Migration sequences: Who moves back and who moves on?* R-2548-NICHD. Santa Monica, CA: The Rand Corporation.

Dodge, D. A., & Stager, D. A. A. (1972). Economic returns to graduate study in science, engineering and business. *Canadian Journal of Economics 5*, May, 182–198.

Easton, P. A., & Fass, S. M. (1989). Monetary consumption benefits and the demand for primary schooling in Haiti. *Comparative Education Review 33*(2), 176–193.

Edwards, L. N., & Grossman, M. (1981). Children's health and the family. In

R. M. Scheffler (Ed.) *Advances in health economics and health services research* (Vol. 2). Greenwich, CT: JAI Press.

Ehrlich, I. (1975). On the relation between education and crime. In F. T. Juster (Ed.), *Education, income and human behavior* (pp. 313–338). New York: McGraw-Hill.

Feldman, K. A., & Newcomb, T. M. (1969). *The impact of college on students.* San Francisco: Jossey-Bass.

Garen, J. (1984). The return to schooling: A selectivity bias approach with a continuous choice variable. *Econometrica 52*(5), 1199–1218.

Greenwood, M. J. (1975). Research on internal migration in the United States: A survey. *Journal of Economic Literature 13*(2), 397–433.

Grossman, M. (1972*a*). On the concept of health capital and the demand for health. *Journal of Political Economy 80*, March–April, 223–255.

Grossman, M. (1972*b*). *The demand for health: A theoretical and empirical investigation.* New York: Columbia University Press (for NBER).

Grossman, M. (1976). The correlation between health and schooling. In N. E. Terleckyj (Ed.), *Household production and consumption* (pp. 147–211). New York: Columbia University Press.

Grossman, M. (1982). *Determinants of children's health.* National Center for Health Services Research Report PHS 81–3309 and NTIS P380–163603.

Gurin, G. (1971). The impact of the college experience. In S. B. Withey (Ed.), *A degree and what else? Correlates and consequences of a college education* (pp. 25–54). New York: McGraw-Hill.

Haveman, R. H., & Wolfe, B. L. (1984). Schooling and economic well-being: The role of nonmarket effects. *Journal of Human Resources 19*(3), 377–407.

Hettich, W. (1972). Consumption benefits from education. In S. Ostrey (Ed.), *Canadian higher education in the seventies.* Ottawa Economic Council of Canada.

Hill, C. R., & Stafford, F. P. (1974). Allocation of time to preschool children and educational opportunity. *Journal of Human Resources 9* (Summer), 323–341.

Hill, C. R., & Stafford, F. P. (1980). Parental care of children: Time diary estimates of quantity, predictability, and variety. *Journal of Human Resources 15*(2), 219–239.

Hu, T-W., Lee, M. L., & Stromsdorfer, E. W. (1969). *A cost-effectiveness study of vocational education.* University Park, PA: Institute for Research on Human Resources, Pennsylvania State University.

Hu, T-W., Lee, M. L., & Stromsdorfer, E. W. (1971). Economic returns to vocational and comprehensive high school graduates. *Journal of Human Resources 6* (Winter), 25–50.

Huffman, W. E. (1974). Decision-making: The role of education. *American Journal of Agricultural Economics 56*, 85–97.

Huffman, W. E. (1977). Allocative efficiency: The role of human capital. *Quarterly Journal of Economics 91*, February, 59–80.

Kiker, B. F., & Rhine, S. L. W. (1987). Fringe benefits and the earnings equation: A test of the consistency hypothesis. *Journal of Human Resources 22*(1), 126–137.

Lando, M. E. (1975). The interaction between health and education. *Social Security Bulletin 38*, December, 16–22.
Lefocowitz, M. J. (1973). Poverty and health: A reexamination. *Inquiry*, March, pp. 3–13.
Leibowitz, A. (1974*a*). Education and home production. *American Economic Review 64*, May, 243–250.
Leibowitz, A. (1974*b*). Home investments in children. *Journal of Political Economy 82*, March–April (pt. 2), S111–131.
Leibowitz, A. (1974*c*). Home investments in children. In T. W. Schultz (Ed.), *Economics of the family: Marriage, children and human capital* (pp. 432–452). Chicago: University of Chicago Press.
Leibowitz, A. (1975). Education and the allocation of women's time. In F. T. Juster (Ed.), *Education, income and human behavior* (pp. 171–198). New York: McGraw-Hill.
Leibowitz, A. (1977). Parental inputs and children's achievement. *Journal of Human Resources 12* (Spring), 242–251.
Mandell, L. (1972). *Credit card use in the United States*. Ann Arbor: Institute for Social Research, University of Michigan.
Mansfield, E. (1982). Education, R and D, and productivity growth. National Institute of Education Special Report, Washington.
Mathios, A. D. (1989). Education, variation in earnings, and nonmonetary compensation. *Journal of Human Resources 24*(3), 456–468.
Melnik, A. R. (1969). Hedging in the labor market. *Southern Economic Journal 35*(3), 270–272.
Michael, R. T. (1972). *The effect of education on efficiency in consumption*. New York: Columbia University Press (for National Bureau of Economic Research).
Michael, R. T. (1973). Education and the derived demand for children. *Journal of Political Economy 81*, March–April (pt. 2), S128–164.
Michael, R. T. (1975*a*). Education and consumption. In F. T. Juster (Ed.), *Education, income and human behavior* (pp. 235–252). New York: McGraw-Hill.
Michael, R. T. (1975*b*). Education and fertility. In F. T. Juster (Ed.), *Education, income and human behavior* (pp. 339–364). New York: McGraw-Hill.
Michael, R. T. (1982). Measuring non-monetary benefits of education: A survey. In W. W. McMahon & T. G. Geske (Eds.), *Financing education: Overcoming inefficiency and inequity* (pp. 119–149). Urbana: University of Illinois Press.
Michael, R. T., & Willis, R. J. (1976). Contraception and fertility: Household production under uncertainty. In N. E. Terleckyj (Ed.), *Household production and consumption* (pp. 27–93). New York: Columbia University Press.
Mincer, J. (1962). On-the-job training: Costs, returns and some implications. *Journal of Political Economy 70* (October, Supplement), 50–79.
Moock, P. R. (1981). Education and technical efficiency in small farm production. *Economic Development and Cultural Change 30*, 723–739.
Murnane, R. J. (1981). New evidence on the relationship between mother's education and children's cognitive skills. *Economics of Education Review 1*(2), 245–252.

Nelson, R. R. (1973). Recent exercises in growth accounting: New understanding or dead end. *American Economic Review 63*, June, 462–468.

Ng, Y. C. (1989). The demand for medical care by gender: Additional evidence. Columbia: Department of Economics, University of South Carolina, mimeo.

Orcutt, G. H., Franklin, S. D., Mendelsohn, R., & Smith, J. D. (1977). Does your probability of death depend on your environment? A microanalytic study. *American Economic Review 67* February, 260–264.

Phillips, J. M., & Marble, R. P. (1986). Farmer education and efficiency: A frontier production function approach. *Economics of Education Review 5*(3), 257–64.

Psacharopoulos, G. (1989). Time trends in the returns to education: Cross-national evidence. *Economics of Education Review 8*(3), 225–231.

Ribich, T. I. (1968). *Education and poverty*. Washington, D.C.: Brookings Institution.

Schultz, T. W. (Ed.). (1974). *Economics of the family: Marriage, children and human capital*. Chicago: University of Chicago Press (for NBER).

Schwartz, A. (1971). On efficiency of migration. *Journal of Human Resources 6*(2), 193–205.

Schwartz, A. (1976). Migration, age, and education. *Journal of Political Economy 84*(4, pt. 1), 701–719.

Selby-Smith, C. (1975). Rates of return to post-secondary education in Australia. *Economic Record 51*, December, 455–485.

Solmon, L. C. (1975). The relation between schooling and savings behavior: An example of the indirect effects of education. In F. T. Juster (Ed.), *Education, income and human behavior* (pp. 253–294). New York: McGraw-Hill.

Spiegelman, R. G. (1968). A benefit/cost model to evaluate educational programs. *Socio-Economic Planning Sciences 1*, 443–460.

Stapleton, D. C. (1976). Social benefits of education: An assessment of the effect of education on political participation (Workshop Paper 7606). Social Systems Research Institute, University of Wisconsin, Madison.

Stigler, G. J. (1961). The economics of information. *Journal of Political Economy 69*(3), 213–225.

Strumpel, B. (1971). Higher education and economic behavior. In S. B. Withey (Ed.), *A degree and what else? Correlates and consequences of a college education* (pp. 55–79). New York: McGraw-Hill.

Swift, W. J., & Weisbrod, B. A. (1965). On the monetary value of education's intergeneration effects. *Journal of Political Economy 73*, December, 643–649.

Taylor, E. K., & Wolfe, A. C. (1971). Political behavior. In S. B. Withey (Ed.), *A degree and what else? Correlates and consequences of a college education* (pp. 111–126). New York: McGraw-Hill.

Tomaske, J. A. (1974). Private and social rates of return to education of academicians: Note. *American Economic Review 64*, March, 220–224.

Trent, J. W., & Medsker, L. L. (1968). *Beyond high school*. San Francisco: Jossey-Bass.

Webb, L. D. (1977). Savings to society by investing in adult education. In

Economic and Social Perspectives on Adult Illiteracy: A Conference Report (pp. 52–73). Tallahassee, FL: Florida Dept. of Education.
Weisbrod, B. A. (1962). Education and investment in human capital. *Journal of Political Economy 70*, October (Supplement), 106–123.
West, E. G. (1988). *Higher education in Canada: An analysis*. Vancouver: The Fraser Institute.
Withey, S. B. (1971). Some effects on life-style. In S. B. Withey (Ed.), *A degree and what else? Correlates and consequences of a college education* (pp. 81–93). New York: McGraw-Hill.
Wozniak, G. D. (1987). Human capital, information, and the early adoption of new technology. *Journal of Human Resources 22*(1), 101–112.

III HIGHER EDUCATION AND REGIONAL GROWTH

Part III considers the issues and evidence associated with higher education and regional economic growth. Chapter 8 reviews the relationship between expenditures on higher education and regional development and finds strong and positive effects. Chapter 9 discusses the methodology and provides the results of 74 different economic impact studies of the economic effects on communities by collegiate institutions within their borders. The income and employment effects resulting from federal research grants are examined in chapter 10. The literature and historical patterns of university–industry linkage and specific dimensions of technology transfer are reviewed in chapter 11.

8 THE ROLE OF UNIVERSITIES IN REGIONAL ECONOMIC DEVELOPMENT

Tim R. Smith and Mark Drabenstott

The 1980s have been a decade of great regional variation in economic growth. Some regions—the Northwest, the Southeast, and the Pacific coast—have enjoyed vigorous expansion. Other regions—the Great Plains and the Southwest—have trailed far behind the fast-growing regions and the nation as a whole. Although many economic factors may explain the variation in growth, some analysts are looking at variation in university spending as one possible explanation.

Publicly supported colleges and universities play a critical role in economic development, but that role is neither well defined nor easily understood. States seeking to improve their economic fortunes are turning to these postsecondary institutions to participate more fully in economic development. For their part, universities are promoting new economic development agendas while trying to increase state support. A few studies have found education generally to be an important business location factor, but little attention has been directed at understanding how universities stimulate economic development.

Understanding the role of universities in economic development is difficult because the key linkages between universities and economic growth are complex, hard to quantify, and subject to change over time. Nevertheless, a detailed comparison of university programs and economic growth in various states does begin to illuminate a connection between university spending and economic growth. The precise nature of the link is more difficult to determine, but the success of the land-grant university system in promoting economic development in rural states over the past century provides some concrete clues to the link between university programs and economic development.

This chapter concludes that there is a connection between universities and economic growth and that states can adjust their policies to make universities more effective as tools of economic development in the 1990s. The first section of this chapter describes the channels through which universities can affect economic growth and discusses how universities are changing the emphasis of individual programs across these various channels. The second section describes regional differences in support for higher education. The third section examines evidence of the influence of higher education on regional economic growth and discusses the key problems in quantifying that influence. The fourth section recalls the experience of the land-grant university system to show how universities can be viewed as instruments of basic research, technology, and job training. The chapter concludes with some policy implications that follow from an improved understanding of the connection between universities and economic development.

Changing University Channels to the Economy

Universities have numerous opportunities to enhance the economic future of their states. Some of these opportunities were seized long ago, while others have only recently been recognized. Although some universities have long viewed their traditional research and teaching functions as major contributors to economic growth, their overall posture in the past can be described as passive. Except for the extension service at land-grant institutions, few resources were directed to specific economic development objectives. Now universities are generally becoming more active.

Economic development activities at universities can be placed on a continuum from "passive" to "active" (see figure 8–1). For example, the de facto provision of jobs and the direct economic stimulus that a university campus brings to its local community are passive. On the other hand, technical assistance to businesses and technology transfer are examples of active economic development initiatives. Somewhere in between the active and passive extremes are the fundamental university functions of basic research and human resource development, which lie at the heart of the role of universities in economic growth.

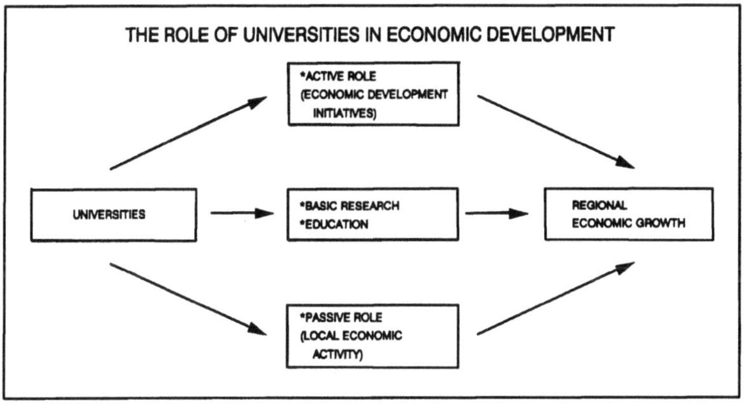

Figure 8–1. The Role of Universities in Economic Development

A recent survey of state-supported universities by the Federal Reserve Bank of Kansas City discovered universities moving in a more active direction (Smith, Drabenstott, and Gibson 1987).[1] This change stems from two sources. First, universities are reevaluating their traditional roles and focusing attention on the contribution of basic research and teaching to economic growth. Second, universities are starting to engage in new activities that directly contribute to economic development by fostering a stronger relationship between the universities' traditional functions and the business sector.

The emphasis on traditional research and teaching functions reflects the long-term nature of regional economic development. Once entirely passive, universities are now incorporating strong research and human resource development programs into their overall economic development plans. For example, research centers in fields such as biotechnology, automation design for manufacturing, optical communications, and robotics have been established to enhance technology transfer to the private sector.[2] Universities are also reevaluating educational curriculums with a goal of providing students with diverse and more flexible skills. Some universities are emphasizing liberal arts courses and communications skills, claiming that graduates are likely to make an average of six or seven job changes in their careers.

Universities are increasingly incorporating development considerations into their strategic planning. For example, land-grant extension services have served agriculture well, but universities are beginning to consider where these programs fit into the economic environment of the 1990s. Can agricultural extension be successfully transformed into industrial extension? Overall, universities see themselves as leading agents of economic growth, not just passive educators.

Regional Variation in University Spending and Economic Growth

Renewed attention toward university links to the economy comes at a time when the differences in regional growth are wide. Public financial support for higher education also ranges widely across the United States. Some observers argue that differences in the levels of funding for higher education among states and regions may have important implications for potential involvement of universities in economic development.

A cross-sectional review of recent state appropriations to higher education provides a picture of interstate variations in support for higher education. Table 8–1 groups states into eight regions and then compares the per-student level of state and local appropriations to higher education in 1986.[3] The table also presents indexes for each state's tax capacity, tax effort, and the percentage of state tax revenues allocated to higher education. Tax capacity is a measure of a state's potential to raise revenues, while tax effort is a measure of a state's actual revenues as a proportion of potential revenues.[4] Together, these three figures provide proxy measures of a state's potential fiscal condition, the willingness of a state to raise public funds through taxation, and the relative importance a state places on higher education.

Fiscal condition and willingness to tax apparently have some effect on a state's disposition toward higher education funding. Alaska, California, and Hawaii in the West, and New York and New Jersey in the Mid-Atlantic region, were among the states with the highest appropriations relative to the national average. All of these states also have relatively high measures of tax capacity and tax effort. Appropriations in New Hampshire and Vermont in New England and in several states in the Plains and Southeast fall substantially below the national average. These states generally have lower measures of tax capacity and tax effort.

Although some states lack the potential to raise revenue or the willingness to use the capacity they have, many of these states devote a relatively large share of their tax revenues to higher education. For example, most of the Plains states ranks below average in appropriations, tax capacity, and tax effort, yet appropriations in these states generally exceed the average proportion of tax revenues.[5] On the other hand, New Jersey ranks far above average in appropriations, tax capacity, and tax effort but

Table 8–1. State and Local Fiscal Condition and Support for Higher Education in the 50 States, 1986

State	*Appropriations for Higher Education per Student (index)*	*Tax Capacity (index)*	*Tax Effort (index)*	*Higher Education as a Percentage of Tax Revenues*
U.S. Average	100	100.0	100.0	8.1
Great Lakes				
Illinois	92	95.9	106.0	7.5
Indiana	93	86.9	94.3	8.5
Michigan	94	96.2	118.2	8.1
Ohio	83	90.8	103.0	7.1
Wisconsin	93	85.8	133.5	8.9
Mid-Atlantic				
Delaware	111	121.4	81.0	10.7
Maryland	90	107.6	98.9	7.7
New Jersey	133	120.5	102.7	5.8
New York	151	106.8	151.5	6.3
Pennsylvania	99	89.7	101.4	6.3
New England				
Connecticut	133	135.2	94.1	5.4
Maine	116	94.5	98.8	7.8
Massachusetts	111	123.5	103.4	5.5
New Hampshire	64	119.4	61.6	5.1
Rhode Island	101	91.9	111.0	7.5
Vermont	53	99.4	91.4	4.2
Plains				
Iowa	92	83.7	112.9	8.9
Kansas	84	95.7	96.4	9.2
Minnesota	100	102.4	107.8	8.7
Missouri	87	92.7	81.6	8.1
Nebraska	68	91.2	96.2	7.7
North Dakota	81	93.9	88.6	10.6
South Dakota	67	77.8	95.0	6.5
Rocky Mountain				
Colorado	69	116.8	83.4	6.7
Idaho	103	76.9	89.7	12.3
Montana	86	88.0	103.2	7.9
Utah	100	80.4	106.5	10.5
Wyoming	176	150.7	116.5	8.8

Table 8–1. (cont.)

State	*Appropriations for Higher Education per Student (index)*	*Tax Capacity (index)*	*Tax Effort (index)*	*Higher Education as a Percentage of Tax Revenues*
Southeast				
Alabama	78	74.3	86.4	11.2
Arkansas	89	73.3	90.7	8.7
Florida	81	105.1	76.5	6.6
Georgia	113	94.0	88.6	8.2
Kentucky	93	76.4	89.3	9.2
Louisiana	76	90.1	90.8	6.2
Mississippi	69	65.3	96.7	9.6
North Carolina	99	88.3	91.5	13.1
South Carolina	116	78.6	93.5	10.5
Tennessee	115	83.5	83.7	11.1
Virginia	95	100.7	85.1	9.9
West Virginia	76	76.4	98.0	7.1
Southwest				
Arizona	94	98.7	98.5	10.1
New Mexico	107	91.3	87.8	11.4
Oklahoma	67	98.1	84.7	7.3
Texas	78	103.5	79.1	8.1
West				
Alaska	252	176.9	168.4	6.0
California	121	117.8	95.3	10.9
Hawaii	203	113.3	105.0	12.9
Nevada	106	146.8	65.2	7.1
Oregon	91	93.3	98.3	9.1
Washington	92	97.8	102.7	9.0

Sources: Halstead (1987) and Advisory Commission on Intergovernmental Relations (1986).

devotes only 5.8 percent of tax revenues to higher education, compared with the national average of 8.1 percent.

Although no clear regional patterns emerge from the information in table 8–1, a state's ability and willingness to tax its residents appears to have some positive effect on spending for higher education. However, high tax capacity and effort does not guarantee that a state will be inclined to spend a high proportion of tax revenues on higher education.

Recognizing this fact, many universities have begun to emphasize their economic development function as a way to increase their share of the state fiscal pie.

Is there a correspondence between regional economic growth and spending on higher education? Most economists and educators would agree that, in principle, the answer is yes. Yet the evidence of such a relationship is sorely lacking.

One difficulty in establishing a relationship between economic growth and higher education in a state is in the measure of the two concepts. Economic growth can be measured in many ways. Growth in income, employment, or gross state product all can serve as proxies for state economic growth. Moreover, using spending on higher education to measure a state's higher education input often clouds the direction of causality. The condition of a state's economy directly affects the state's fiscal condition, which in turn influences how much it can spend on higher education. And the time horizon over which a relationship between economic growth and higher education spending might develop is unknown.[6]

Indeed, a comparison of states and regions reveals that economic growth (measured by growth in real per capita personal income) does not appear to correspond directly to spending on higher education (measured by real per capita current spending by state governments on higher education). Table 8–2 lists growth in personal income and current per capita spending on higher education over several periods for eight regions of the United States. Although rapid income growth in the late 1960s corresponds with rapid growth in education expenditures and slower income growth in the 1970s and 1980s corresponds with slow growth in education expenditures, there is no apparent relationship across regions.[7]

Thus casual observation does not reveal a strong link between university spending and economic growth. Certainly, no linkage emerges that could explain the wide range of economic growth rates. But as the next section shows, a link between universities and the economy, though difficult to define, does appear to exist.

Linking Higher Education and Economic Growth

The lack of a clear correlation between growth in income and growth in higher education spending does not mean there is no connection between the two. On the contrary, limited evidence linking higher education to economic growth is emerging from the literature on public policy and

Table 8–2. Real Personal Income and Real Current Spending by State Governments on Higher Education, per Capita (average annual growth rates)

	1965–1969		1970–1979		1980–1987		1965–1987	
Years	*Personal Income*	*Current Spending*	*Personal Income*	*Current Spending*	*Personal Income*	*Current Spending*	*Personal Income*	*Current Spending*
Region								
Great Lakes	3.83	10.53	2.10	2.22	0.72	1.20	1.99	3.61
Mid-Atlantic	3.99	10.55	1.56	4.50	2.33	2.74	2.35	5.17
New England	4.24	15.46	1.62	4.67	3.31	1.72	2.77	5.87
Plains	4.20	10.07	2.82	2.44	0.89	0.88	2.44	3.50
Rocky Mountain	3.32	9.73	2.95	1.78	0.33	−0.71	2.11	2.57
Southeast	5.19	11.76	2.82	4.54	1.77	−0.06	2.96	4.42
Southwest	4.72	9.34	3.15	2.85	0.40	0.37	2.52	3.35
West*	3.50	1.86	2.20	1.16	1.01	1.42	2.07	1.40
United States	4.16	9.12	2.21	3.10	1.40	0.99	2.35	3.63

Sources: Data Resources Incorporated, and *Government Finances*, U.S. Bureau of the Census, and *Higher Education Price Indexes, 1989 Update*, Research Associates of Washington.

* Excluding Hawaii.

business location. Increasingly, the education–economic growth connection is examined in the context of more fully specified economic models with improved measures of the complex attributes of higher education.

A broad understanding of the linkage between higher education and economic growth can be gained in two steps. The first step is to place higher education in the context of more general models linking public policy to regional economic growth and to review empirical evidence of the connection between higher education and economic development. The second step is to identify the important problems associated with measuring regional characteristics of higher education. Together, these two steps reveal both the complexities and the important role of higher education in regional economic development.

The Role of Public Policy in Business Location

State policy toward higher education is one part of a broader set of public policies that can influence regional economic growth. State policy makers interested in spurring economic development in their states have been guided in the past by studies of business location. Based on the assumption that a business will choose a location that will enhance revenues and lower costs, these studies have identified several factors that appear to be important to the location of a new business and branch facilities or to the decision to expand an existing production or office facility.[8]

Location factors pertaining to a state's overall economic environment, such as labor market conditions, access to markets, transportation, tax structure, weather, quality of life, and education, have generally been found to be the most important influences on business location. Most of these business environment factors can be enhanced by long-range economic development programs, but policy makers have little control over these environmental factors in the short run. Public policy cannot influence weather and certain quality-of-life factors, and changes in other broad business environment factors can be accomplished only over a long period of time. Roads and airports can be built to improve a state's transportation infrastructure, and university curriculums and research programs can be altered to improve a state's educational environment. But changes like these cannot be made overnight.

The relatively short tenure of state policy makers has led to economic development efforts that generally rely on short-run discretionary policies. States use direct financial and tax incentives to attract businesses instead of focusing on the overall business environment. But the short-run focus of state policy makers is in direct contradiction to the evidence on the importance of long-run environmental factors to business location. Nowhere is this more evident than in education, where the dividends to current policies may not accrue for a decade or more.

The mounting evidence that the overall business environment in a state may be an important influence on the state's economic future has caused education and infrastructure issues to gain favor in governors' offices and state legislatures across the country. The marked differences in regional economic performance during the 1980s have underscored this progression in state policy on economic development.

Evidence Supporting the Higher Education–Economic Development Connection

Evidence linking higher education to regional economic growth is not extensive. But a body of economics literature on the linkage has begun to emerge. Recent studies on the determinants of business location and regional growth contain limited evidence that spending on higher education attracts businesses and leads to regional growth.

Although not overwhelmingly abundant, specific evidence linking education (broadly defined to include primary, secondary, and postsecondary education) to regional economic growth can be found among the studies linking business environment factors to firm location and economic growth. Plaut and Pluta (1983) find a positive relationship between state industrial growth and total education expenditures after controlling for the effects of other relevant market, labor, land, tax, and expenditure variables. Wasylenko and McGuire (1985) find a statistically significant, positive relationship between total employment growth and state spending on education. Helms (1985) presents convincing evidence that the disincentive effects of state and local taxes on business location may be overcome when tax revenue is used to finance improved public services such as education, highways, and public health and safety.

In addition to the findings that link broadly defined education to regional economic growth, additional evidence supports the view that higher education, in particular, is positively related to regional growth. Helms (1985) shows that state spending on higher education has a positive and significant effect on a state's personal income. Moreover, this effect outweighs the negative effect on growth of the taxes used to finance the expenditures. Jones and Vedlitz (1988) conclude that the levels of state spending for higher education and the level of educational quality are positively related to state economic growth.[9]

Problems in Measuring the Contribution of Universities to Regional Growth

Most of the problems in fully specifying the connection between higher education and regional economic growth involve the measure of education input. The level of spending on higher education is the most readily available and widely used measure of state-to-state variations in education input. But this measure fails to capture a number of important dimensions of the role played by higher education. These dimensions include the consistency of higher education funding over time, the types of postsecondary institutions comprising a state's system of higher education, the mix of effort between the teaching and research functions at universities, and the spillover effects of education policy in neighboring states.

Variation in Spending over Time. The variation of higher education spending across states is documented in table 8–1. However, the level of spending on higher education at a point in time does not reflect the consistency of that spending over a longer period. Consistency is critical in developing excellence in teaching and research at universities. Table 8–2 shows that growth in state spending for higher education also differs from state to state, but average annual growth rates obscure the year-to-year variability in funding levels. Table 8–3 shows the average level of state spending for higher education and a measure of variability (the standard deviation) in the level over the period from 1964 to 1987. Some states have maintained relatively stable support for higher education, and other states have not. For example, higher education spending in Colorado and Delaware averaged about the same amount over the 24-year period, but the annual spending levels were far more widely dispersed in Delaware than in Colorado.

Types of Institutions. Public postsecondary institutions range from major research universities with average enrollments exceeding 30,000 and extensive research programs to two-year academic and occupational schools and other specialized institutions such as art, music, engineering, and law schools. Halstead (1987) reports significant differences among states in the kinds of institutions of higher education. Moreover, the distribution of enrollments and appropriations differs across states. Some states concentrate their higher education efforts on a few large institutions, whereas others spread their resources across many different types of institutions.[10] Depending on the economic makeup of a particular state, the types of institutions and the distribution of funding to them could affect the quality of the higher education input in economic development.

Table 8–3. Real Current Spending on Higher Education per Capita, Average and Standard Deviation in the United States, 1964–1987

State	*Dollar Average Current Spending per Capita*	*Standard Deviation*
U.S. Average	116.73	24.88
Great Lakes		
Illinois	97.14	16.89
Indiana	156.99	21.17
Michigan	155.33	18.64
Ohio	108.68	33.23
Wisconsin	169.49	32.59
Mid-Atlantic		
Delaware	203.19	64.61
Maryland	108.61	27.63
New Jersey	73.15	21.74
New York	71.61	23.29
Pennsylvania	60.30	14.14
New England		
Connecticut	88.16	25.28
Maine	110.97	27.48
Massachusetts	73.90	26.60
New Hampshire	119.83	25.47
Rhode Island	132.00	37.22
Vermont	199.93	41.54
Plains		
Iowa	154.69	27.49
Kansas	151.58	23.02
Minnesota	173.73	31.51
Missouri	94.42	20.82
Nebraska	142.67	33.89
North Dakota	205.54	46.52
South Dakota	165.80	26.67
Rocky Mountain		
Colorado	201.33	31.03
Idaho	129.87	28.34
Montana	145.93	20.11
Utah	233.83	32.46
Wyoming	180.78	20.95

State	*Dollar Average Current Spending per Capita*	*Standard Deviation*
Southeast		
Alabama	137.39	42.32
Arkansas	105.40	25.40
Florida	66.74	11.01
Georgia	105.90	28.60
Kentucky	123.78	37.96
Louisiana	123.52	25.24
Mississippi	109.33	24.45
North Carolina	123.29	29.59
South Carolina	122.82	48.41
Tennessee	109.66	32.10
Virginia	130.63	44.41
West Virginia	115.77	23.86
Southwest		
Arizona	162.49	22.48
New Mexico	208.81	29.01
Oklahoma	159.84	28.18
Texas	116.79	30.70
West		
Alaska	276.63	100.62
California	126.16	24.22
Nevada	122.36	22.34
Oregon	154.47	13.77
Washington	198.27	36.59

Source: *Government Finances*, U.S. Bureau of the Census, and *Higher Education Price Indexes, 1989 Update*, Research Associates of Washington.

Mix of Effort. Within a single institution the emphasis on basic functions such as teaching and research can vary. Therefore, economic growth in states with similar types of institutions could be affected differently depending on the teaching–research mix at those institutions. Of course, the differences in economic impact will depend on the economic makeup of each state. Some industries may require a trained labor force to prosper, and others may thrive on commercial applications of university research.

Regional Spillover Effects. Even when measured accurately, the quantity and quality of higher education in a state may not reflect the true contribution of that education to regional economic growth. The contribution will be overstated if the state receives economic benefits from universities in neighboring states and that contribution is not counted in a measure of the individual state's higher education. The contribution will be understated if the regional economy surrounding a state benefits from the state's universities and those benefits are not reflected in a measure of the individual state's growth.

Universities and Economic Development: The Case of Agriculture

The connection between universities and economic development is, as shown in the last section, an important but ill-defined relationship. Lacking more rigorous quantitative analysis, the link may best be seen in an historical example. One of the richest examples in the United States is the land-grant university system.[11] It is also a relevant example because land-grant universities are major public institutions in many states whose economies have been trailing the national economy. Thus they may be at the center of public efforts to stimulate economic development.

In the 1980s many of the states that have trailed the national economy have been predominantly rural and located in the heartland. Ironically, all of these states have a strong history of economic development success through universities but have found it difficult to develop a strategy for the 1990s that capitalizes on that past success. For more than a century rural states have been highly successful in developing their agricultural resources through the land-grant university system, and it is this case history that offers some insights into how universities can be viewed as instruments in basic research, technology transfer, and job retraining.

Universities and Agricultural Development

Land-grant universities were created in the 1860s and charged with a very pragmatic mission: to apply an expanding frontier of knowledge to the real problems of society. To carry out that mission three basic components were created within land-grant universities: teaching, research, and extension. Created with agriculture in mind, the land-grant system was also launched with a vague hope that it would evolve to address other economic problems as well. At the outset, agriculture, production agriculture in particular, was put at the heart of the land-grant triad of teaching, research, and extension.[12]

Land-grant universities have met their mission of agricultural development with great success. Public investment in agricultural development institutions has paid big social dividends (Huffman and Evenson 1987). U.S. agriculture is highly competitive in world markets due to its agricultural technology, in contrast with many other industries where U.S. competitiveness has deteriorated. As a result the United States controls a significant share of world food markets and makes sizeable contributions to U. S. balance of payments. Rural poverty levels have declined significantly as agricultural productivity has increased the returns to farm labor. Consumers have enjoyed steadily declining real food prices as farm productivity has advanced. And agricultural development has underwritten a relatively smooth movement of rural labor to urban jobs.

How have land-grant universities been so successful in agriculture? The reason is quite simple: The tripartite organization of the land-grant university—teaching, research, and extension—has proven a very effective strategy. The process begins with basic research, one founded on problem solving. The process proceeds with technology transfer—first the application of basic research to commercial use and then the transfer of technology to private businesses. The private sector has played a key role in finding commercial applications for public research breakthroughs, but the extension service has been the critical link in educating farmers about new technologies, what might be called the education aspect of technology transfer. Finally, the teaching of the university underpins all phases of the process: improving the skills of farmers, training new scientists, and generally raising the human capital skills of the state's citizens.

Replicating the Agricultural Development Model

While the land-grant model has worked exceptionally well in agriculture, its success in other economic development arenas is more mixed. Land-grant universities have clearly developed teaching curriculums that emphasize numerous disciplines. And research programs are as diverse at land-grant universities as at other universities. Engineering research has been especially strong. But what has been lacking in these broad endeavors is the same sense of mission that led to singular achievement in agriculture.

In short, the diverse activities of land-grant universities have not been coordinated with new economic development problems in mind. To the contrary, many observers suggest that the universities have become more fragmented, as professors focus more attention strictly on pursuing their disciplines. In the words of one observer, "A strong bent to a disciplinary orientation seems to be eroding allegiance to the land-grant [mission]. For large parts of the university the land-grant [mission] is completely alien" (Schuh 1986, p. 6).

One leg of the land-grant triad that has remained almost completely tied to agriculture is extension. The Cooperative Extension Service continues its extensive network of county agents that are linked to universities and the USDA. Although that network has been successful in encouraging rapid adoption of new agricultural technology, declining numbers of farms have raised new questions about what role the extension service should play. Those questions remain largely unanswered.

Examples of major extension efforts in industries other than agriculture remain limited. Ohio State University has developed the Ohio Technology Transfer Organization (OTTO). That effort has received widespread recognition for taking new technology to small businesses. But in the main, extension remains an agricultural effort.

The question is, Can this agricultural development model be replicated to address the economic development challenges of heartland states? The socioeconomic problem that the land-grant institutions were created to address has largely been solved—the agricultural development cycle appears largely complete. The challenge, therefore, is for states to be innovative in considering ways that teaching, research, and extension can be combined to address a new mission. Moreover, the agricultural development model may provide valuable clues about the role universities can play in economic development generally.

In sum, a history of land-grant success in agriculture offers a rich example of universities' setting an economic development mission and then completing the mission through all components of the institution—teaching, research, and extension. Many of the pieces needed to redirect the universities to the economic development challenges of the 1990s are already in place. A wide array of teaching and research excellence can be found at most land-grant universities. What is lacking is a new mission that would forge these pieces together to meet the economic development problems at hand.

Universities and Economic Development Policy

Though many questions remain unanswered about the precise connection between universities and economic development, the general conclusions reached thus far do offer some clear implications for policy makers. And with many universities and states considering major shifts in university programs, sound guidelines appear especially timely. This section discusses two types of policy implications that derive from the analysis. General implications are discussed first, followed by implications for heartland states facing rural economic challenges.

General Policy Implications

The general evidence linking universities and economic development points to two general guidelines for policy makers. First, consistent support for higher education appears critical. Nearly all states exhibit strong support for university spending at one time or another. But, due to the long-term nature of the university link to economic growth, those states that consistently invest in their universities during both good times and bad may reap the greatest economic rewards. Excellence in research and teaching takes time to develop, and the results of that excellence also take time to filter into the economy. Once developed, however, such inputs provide ongoing, consistent benefits in the economy.

The long-term nature of this connection complicates economic development decisions. Frequently policy makers have a bias for policy choices that offer a quick effect on the economy. Universities do not fit that profile. Rather, they represent a more plodding approach to development. Thus policy makers must be willing to make steady commitment to a university approach, recognizing that dividends will flow but only through the course of time.

A second implication is that university efforts need to be concentrated. At a purely educational level, universities are by definition multifaceted. But from an economic development point of view, excellence in key areas becomes more important. That is, most states have a unique base of resources that defines a state's economic development potential. The university can best contribute to successful economic development strategies by developing new and better uses of those resources. University commitment to research and teaching in these key areas will, by necessity, require a diminution of resources to some of the broader programs of the university.

Thus positioning universities to play key roles in economic development necessitates a careful balancing of university programs. The more general programs may have to be curtailed somewhat in the interests of developing excellence in research and teaching programs that fit with sound economic development strategies for the state. Such balancing requires careful planning by both university leaders and state policy makers.

On strategy to minimize the trade-off between general programs and concentrated excellence is for states to pool their efforts. Few states have the resources to become excellent in all fields of enquiry. Resource limitations are especially pronounced in heartland states, where economic growth has trailed the nation in the 1980s. States need to expore new multistate agreements that would enable universities to naturally pursue areas of excellence while drawing on the efforts of other universities. Unfortunately, such cooperation is rarely seen within states, let alone across state lines.

Heartland Policy Implications

Confronted with difficult challenges for rural economic development, the policy implications in heartland states can be identified somewhat more specifically. Heartland states might consider four steps as part of an overall strategy to utilize universities to encourage rural economic development.

Policy Changes at Land-Grant Universities. The first step is to identify a new mission at land-grant universities. These universities have great resources; the challenge is to mobilize the resources toward a common goal. The first step, therefore, must be a clear mission statement that identifies the economic challenge facing a state and the role universities will play in meeting that challenge.

Once a development policy is established, a second step probably would be to deemphasize production agriculture in teaching and extension programs. The structure of U.S. agriculture has changed so dramatically that there is little justification for strong emphasis on educating commercial farmers. The largest 300,000 farmers in the United States now control roughly three-fourths of U.S. farm production. These sophisticated small businesses do not require the major curriculum emphasis of the past. Most would be quite willing to pay for extension services, for example. The question of research is more open to question. With the tremendous quantity of farm resources in heartland states, basic research to make these resources more productive will pay social dividends. Nevertheless, more research probably can and will be undertaken by the private sector.

The problems created by overemphasizing production agriculture are illustrated by an example from a survey of universities by the Federal Reserve Bank of Kansas City. An engineering dean at a land-grant university in the region was intent on developing more fully an industrial extension program. But his efforts were hamstrung by the extension budget's being earmarked almost exclusively for farmers. Of late, the extension service is doing some considerable soul searching, but the evidence of change is very slow in emerging. The great success of the extension service in providing information to solve real economic problems ought to be a rich resource to address the rural economic problems of the 1990s. A highly effective economic development tool will be lost if institutional rigidity keeps the extension service wedded only to agriculture.

A third step states can take is to encourage new areas of research with rural business and industry in mind. The agricultural technology developments of the past century emerged because scientific skill was married to a pragmatic approach to solving a problem. No doubt, many technologies today would lend themselves to rural application, but the pragmatic dimension has not been brought to bear.

A fourth step states can take is to coordinate university efforts in rural job retraining. The land-grant universities and extension service have a long history of adult education, but again most of the efforts have been aimed at agriculture. With a diversity of rural economic problems, a multifaceted rural training program is needed. States are in a unique position to coordinate the resources of universities, the extension service, and local and community colleges. Such pooling of educational resources has been sorely lacking at a time when the need has been great and state budgets tight.

Constraints to Land-Grant Change. The past successes of land-grant universities can point the way to effective solutions of current rural economic problems. But the institutional changes necessary to mobilize university resources will not come easily due to two principal constraints. One is a perceived abandoning of agriculture and the other is the emergence of new support for university programs.

Because production agriculture has been at the heart of the land-grant mission for more than a century, it is not surprising that agricultural groups have been some of the strongest public supporters of university programs—research, teaching, and extension. It is also not surprising that these same groups oppose any diminution in agricultural programs. University officials indicated in the Federal Reserve Bank survey that opposition from traditional support groups was a factor in slowing the university's shift to new economic problems.

One factor will tend to moderate such opposition: Nonfarm rural jobs will be necessary to preserve many small communities in farm-dependent areas. Some farm organization are beginning to understand this more fully, and, as a result, a new base of support for rural economic programs is beginning to emerge in the traditional land-grant support base.

The other constraint to change is the emergence of a new client base for the land-grant university. Some observers argue that the economic problems of the 1980s will eventually force land-grant universities to renegotiate their social contract (McDowell 1988). That is, the university will forge a new mission to address the economic challenges of the 1990s. That will necessitate a working relationship between the university and a new coalition of economic groups. The problem is that no coalition of economic development target groups exists. Thus universities tend to be more sensitive to clearly identified traditional groups, whose needs have largely been met, and pay less attention to a loose amalgamation of economic development groups, whose needs are growing.

Summary

The linkage between universities and regional economic growth is difficult to document, but few analysts doubt that it exists. The best evidence currently available linking university programs and economic growth can be drawn from the literature on public policy and business location and from historical examples. One such example, the land-grant system of universities, demonstrates a clear contribution of universities to rural economic growth through research, teaching, and extension.

As evidence of the university–economic growth connection emerges, state policy makers will increasingly look toward their institutions of higher education to play an enhanced role in economic development. The evidence presented in this chapter suggests several ways that the channels between universities and regional economic growth can be enhanced. The dominant theme of these policy implications is the recognition of the long-term nature of the relationship between universities and economic growth.

Acknowledgments

The authors thank Michael Morgan and Julie Stanley for research assistance. The views expressed herein are solely those of the authors and do not necessarily reflect the views of the Federal Reserve Bank of Kansas City or the Federal Reserve System.

Endnotes

1. Although the generalizations in this section are based on a survey of universities in only seven states, a 1985 survey of 300 universities across the United States by the American Association of State Colleges and Universities found that 97 percent had plans to increase their efforts in economic developments. For additional examples of individual university efforts, see American Association of State Colleges and Universities (1986).

2. In addition to the technology transfer efforts identified in the survey by the Federal Reserve Bank of Kansas City (Smith, Drabenstott, and Gibson 1987), the Government-University-Industry Research Roundtable, the National Governors' Association, and the National Research Council (1987) describe the general characteristics of science and technology programs to encourage economic growth in many states.

3. State and local appropriations per student do not represent total funding for higher education. Some state universities depend heavily on tuition and fees to supplement their budgets. It also should be noted that state ranking by per-student appropriations does not account for the costs each state faces for higher education. States supporting one or more medical schools, for example, will have higher education costs than states with no medical school facility.

4. Tax capacity, as developed by the Advisory Commission on Intergovernmental Relations (1986), is "the revenue that each state and its local governments would raise if it applied a nationally uniform set of tax rates to a commonly used set of tax bases. ... Because the same tax rates are used for every state, estimated revenue yields vary only because of differences in the underlying bases" (p. 2). A tax capacity of more than 100 indicates the state has more fiscal capacity than average for the 50 states. Similarly, tax effort measures a state's total tax collection relative to its total capacity.

5. Using similar data from 1984, Smith, Drabenstott, and Gibson (1987) found the Tenth Federal Reserve District states (Colorado, Kansas, Missouri, Nebraska, New Mexico, Oklahoma, and Wyoming) to be" relatively generous toward higher education—willing to give higher education a respectable slice of the revenue pie—but unwilling to increase the size of the pie through taxation" (p. 9).

6. The example of high-technology manufacturing suggests that higher education stimulates economic growth with a considerable lag. Parsons (1988) proposes that the relocation of high technology industry is encouraged by an innovation process that takes seven to ten years to complete. Measurable improvement in economic growth, therefore, would occur over a longer time period.

7. A Spearman rank correlation of 0.36 between growth in per capita real personal income and higher education spending for 49 states from 1964 to 1987 supports this conclusion.

8. A thorough review of the business location literature and a summary of its findings can be found in Wasylenko (1985) and in Wasylenko and McGuire (1985).

9. This finding emerges from a disequilibrium-adjustment model in which the change in economic growth over a five-year period from 1979–1984 is assumed to be related to the levels of education spending and quality at the beginning of the period. Quality is measured by federal research and development funds awarded to institutions of higher education in each state.

10. California and New York are examples of states where public enrollments in 1983 were spread over a wide range of institutions. Hawaii and Iowa are examples of states where enrollments were concentrated in fewer types of institutions. See Halstead (1987, p. 27). Note that this information only describes the types of institutions in each state; it does not

convey how many institutions of each type are supported in each state.

11. The land-grant university system is a set of colleges and universities with roots in the study of agriculture and the mechanical arts. The universities were created by the Morrill Act of 1862. Under the act federally owned land was granted to the states for the establishment of the universities, hence the term *land-grant*.

12. To enhance public investment in agricultural research, the states established the state agricultural experiment stations from 1874 to 1887. And to improve the transfer of agricultural knowledge to farmers, the Cooperative Extension Service was launched in 1914, establishing county agents in all 3000 plus counties in the nation. The extension service also became a bridge between the land-grant system and the USDA, hence the term *cooperative*.

References

Advisory Commission on Intergovernmental Relations. (1986). *State fiscal capacity and effort*. Washington, D.C.: Author.

American Association of State Colleges and Universities. (1986). *The higher education economic development connection: Emerging roles for public colleges and universities in a changing economy*. Washington, D.C.: Author.

Government-University-Industry Research Roundtable, National Governors' Association, and National Research Council. (1987). *State government strategies for self-assessment of science and technology programs for economic development*. Washington, D.C.: National Academy Press.

Halstead, K. (1987). *State profiles: Financing public higher education, 1978 to 1987*. Washington, D.C.: Research Associates of Washington.

Helms, L. J. (1985). The effect of state and local taxes on economic growth: A time series-cross section approach. *The Review of Economics and Statistics 67*, 574–582.

Huffman, W., & Evenson, R. (1987). *The development of U.S. agricultural research and education: An economic perspective* (Staff Paper No. 168). Iowa State University.

Jones, B. D., & Vedlitz, A. (1988). Higher education policies and economic growth in the American states. *Economic Development Quarterly* 2, 78–87.

McDowell, G. R. (1988). Land-grant colleges of agriculture: Renegotiating or abandoning a social contract. *Choices* (Second Quarter), 18–21.

Parsons, M. H. (1988). *The integration of economic development and education: Making high technology work*. Washington, D.C.: U.S. Department of Education, Office of Educational Research and Improvement.

Plaut, T. R., & Pluta, J. E. (1983). Business climate, taxes and expenditures, and state industrial growth in the U.S. *Southern Economic Journal 50*, 99–119.

Research Associates of Washington. (1989). *Higher education price indexes: 1989 update*. Washington, D.C.: Author.

Schuh, G. E. (1986). Revitalizing land grant universities: It's time to regain relevance. *Choices* (Second Quarter), 6–10.

Smith, T. R., Drabenstott, M., & Gibson, L. (1987). The role of universities in economic development. Federal Reserve Bank of Kansas City, *Economic Review*, November, 3–21.

Wasylenko, M. (1985). Business climate, industry and employment growth: A review of the evidence (Occasional Paper No. 98, October). Syracuse University, Metropolitan Studies Program.

Wasylenko, M., & McGuire, T. (1985). Jobs and taxes: The effect of business climate on states' employment growth rates. *National Tax Journal 38*, 497–511.

9 HIGHER EDUCATION AND REGIONAL DEVELOPMENT

Larry L. Leslie and Sheila A. Slaughter

At the outset it is necessary to clarify what is meant by economic development as it relates to higher education. Currently, when community leaders speak of economic development in relation to higher education, they seem to have a fairly limited, investment as opposed to consumption, benefit in mind.[1] Their attention appears drawn exclusively, or nearly so, to how higher education research can be translated into community jobs and related economic gains over the long term. There is an implied focus on indirect benefits—investment benefits—as opposed to direct benefits normally associated with consumption spending. Phrases such as "technology transfer" and "university—business partnerships" capture the essence of what seems intended or hoped for.

Yet these gains may be the most difficult of all higher education benefits to identify and quantify. Further, preoccupation with these benefits may lead to omissions of other, perhaps larger benefits and in turn to erroneous higher education policy decisions. Thus we begin with an itemizing and cataloging of higher education—related benefits, not only to reduce the risk of invalid policy making through benefits omission, but also to reduce double counting as well. What then are the economic benefits of higher education and how can and have they been measured?[2]

An Organization and Taxonomy

Like any benefit or utility, higher education-related spending may be viewed either as consumption or as investment. When a college business office places an order for paper clips with a local vendor, from the vendor's viewpoint—and from that of the business officer as well—the college merely has purchased some consumable paper clips. It is the use to which the paper clips are put that determines whether the expenditure is consumption or investment.

However, it seems clear that colleges and universities are about investment far more than they are about consumption. Collegiate institutions largely are intended to "add value" rather than to consume resources. From a policy perspective, the assumption is that the teaching, research, and service functions of higher education are worthy of private and public investment because they enhance private abilities to realize economic gain, similar state and regional potentials for gain, and the nation's ability to compete internationally. As such, spending on higher education properly is viewed largely as an investment, even though many students and the public at large may gain certain consumption benefits as well.

For students, consumption examples are the satisfaction gained from attendance at college events, from the joys of learning, and simply from the intrinsic value of college life. In similar consumption terms, the public gains not only from attendance at collegiate cultural and sporting events but from numerous services, such as educational television, university hospital care, and speech and hearing clinics.

But higher education is mostly about investment. It is about the individual's ability to build his or her private stock of human capital, thereby commanding a higher labor market wage through enhanced labor productivity and, when viewed in toto, similarly building state and national human capital stock and enhancing labor force productivity. It is about the provision of consultative advice in the selection and application of fertilizers, in the improved management of small businesses, and in better classroom teaching practices in the schools. And it is about economic gain through research, through the effective application of research findings to products and practices. In other words, the implicit aim of higher education, the raison d'être for public support of higher education, is, in a word, investment. There is a strong belief that higher education spending will result in significant economic gains for individuals and for society.

How, then, can and have these gains been measured, particularly those benefits associated with community economic development? The answer is that certain benefits have been measured often and with relative care and that others have been most elusive in concept and identity. Put more succinctly, we can get some grasp of the economic gains from higher education, but most approaches are problematic and measurement of the so-called economic development benefits currently of such great interest is most difficult of all.

In a word, the approach to measurement taken herein is to "surround" the problem, stating what we presently know, adding what we can, and identifying what remains unmeasured. As will be seen, the "new ground" in economic development—the stuff of technology transfer and university—business partnerships—is poorly defined, but the traditionally recognized benefits probably are larger and more precisely known, or at least more frequently measured. One way or another, a fair amount already can be said about higher education's contributions to the economy. Our surrounding of the problem begins.

First of all, we know that individuals benefit from their investment in higher education, and because college graduates as a whole are a component part of society, society benefits as well. From a synthesis of essentially all such studies completed prior to the mid-1980s—some 43 studies (Leslie and Brinkman 1988)—a good estimate of individuals' (pecuniary) rate of return on their (and their families') investment in undergraduate education, as measured by earnings marginal to high school education, is about 12 percent for college graduates. Rates for the master's and doctoral degrees, as conventionally measured, are roughly 8 and 7 percent, respectively. If only the student's personal investment were considered, the average rate would be considerably higher, and if nonpecuniary benefits were added, the returns would be much higher still. Of course, returns vary with personal circumstances—with course of study, with student aid, with time taken to earn the degree, and with much more—but the 12 percent undergraduate rate is a good, conservative estimate that exceeds the 10 percent rate received historically from benchmark investments. (In Leslie and Brinkman, 1988 these so-called rate of return studies, along with the many companion issues, have been discussed in great detail.)

Measurement of society's rate of return in this regard is more problematic. Although social return rates typically are estimated to be a few tenths of a percentage point less than private rates, this is only because the conventional estimation method limits social benefits to the pretax earnings of the *individuals* educated—a peculiar formulation that is more a data convenience than anything else. The assumption that all social benefits are captured in the earnings of college attendees, of course, points up the incompleteness of this measure. For example, the notion that the only benefits of research are the marginal wages of college-educated researchers is obviously invalid. Indeed, the very idea of community economic development is based on the assumption that university research benefits others in the community.

In any case, this first category of studies includes only the marginal (to high school) earnings of college attendees and graduates. Even the social benefits included are limited to the earnings of the former students themselves. No consideration is given to spillovers, either of a pecuniary or nonpecuniary sort. Methodologically, the assumption is that all the benefits are captured by the college attendees/graduates. All else is left to some other type of study. The error of these studies in measuring economic impacts is largely an error of omission.

The second group of studies takes the opposite tack. The so-called growth accounting studies begin with all economic benefits gains, as measured by aggregate national income growth, and partitions out explanations of that growth among the three classic factors of production: land, labor, and capital. Education is viewed as "improvement in labor," that is, qualitative growth in stocks of human capital in the work force. Because the related input data in growth accounting studies are rate-of-return-based information, the education component (variable) is limited in the same way as in the rate of return studies—to earnings directly related to education, at the margin. Any contributions by education to the earnings of others, independent of land and physical capital, must accrue in the residual term of the analysis. Identification of the residual is a matter of central importance to the question addressed in the present chapter and is a matter of much controversy in the growth accounting literature.

The growth accounting studies compose a literature that is difficult to summarize. Beginning with the least debatable it appears that education, as a "pure" effect, probably accounts for 11 to 34 percent, and more likely from 15 to 20 percent of national income growth. Higher education's share of this pure effect of education probably is about one-fourth—or about 4 or 5 percent (Leslie and Brinkman 1988, pp. 80–86). But this is the simple part; this is the part we already knew indirectly from the rate of return studies, which employed the same earnings data.

The far more difficult term to identify in the growth accounting analyses is the residual: that which remains unexplained after the identified components of land, labor, and capital are removed. We lean in the direction of Denison's (1962, 1964, 1984) interpretation, that the residual reflects "improvements (or advancements) in knowledge application and miscellaneous," which accounts for 20 percent of income growth between 1929 and 1957 and 40 percent between 1948 and 1973, according to Denison.

Although we agree with Sheehan (1973, pp. 65–66), that much (probably most) knowledge application occurs in business and industry, and not in colleges and universities, we suspect that those who render the applications in the former are in large part products of the latter and that their capabilities are, at the least, enhanced by their collegiate experiences.

This raises a similar question regarding the national income growth contribution of physical capital—the remaining major factor in explaining economic development (since land is a relatively fixed commodity). The question is, Is education a cause of income growth or does income growth lead to greater consumption of education?[3] This question concerns not only the matter of which way the (equation) arrow points but also the matter of the interaction between human and physical capital. In concept the two are one and the same.

To illustrate the issue, one may conceive of two countries of very different circumstances: one rich in physical wealth but with very little skilled manpower, the other blessed with a highly trained work force but deprived of working capital, of hard currency or the means to obtain it. In neither case is the nation likely to experience significant income growth until conditions change. Clearly, economic development requires physical *and* human capital, complementarily.

In these extreme examples, the necessity of both physical and human capital to economic growth and development is evident. In the United States today, relative needs are far less clear; yet the necessity of an educated and skilled work force appears critical. Although labor shortages of highly educated people presently exist in only a few fields (e.g., nursing and math/science teachers), continued economic development surely rests on maintenance of a steady flow of highly skilled personnel.

In sum, the growth accounting studies seek to capture all economic growth, at least as measured by national income. Although higher education can be shown to connect directly to only 4 or 5 percent of national income growth, it is probably connected indirectly to another 20 to 40 percent and perhaps the entire amount is dependent in some part upon higher education. This is not to mention the fact that maintenance of the economic "base" to which growth is added annually depends on maintenance of past labor and capital capabilities as well.

This gives us two bodies of research that are pertinent to assessing economic development and its connection to higher education, one that is limited to the wage gains of college-educated individuals and one that is quite unlimited in scope but is much more difficult to specify quantitatively. The third and remaining set of relevant studies, the economic impact studies (EIS), is the primary focus of this chapter, which focuses on regional growth. EIS are studies of "community" economic impact, community being variously defined by EIS researchers but usually involving metropolitan areas, if urban, or a single or several counties, if rural. EIS are not mutually exclusive of either of the first two study sets. Whereas rate of return studies are considered investment assessments and growth accounting studies ostensibly capture both investment and consumption components, from the community perspective EIS typically are viewed as consumption studies because they measure the current year effects of college and college-related spending. In this view, EIS yield the most direct measurements of community and regional economic development, even though they seem to ignore the long-term, investment benefits.

Economic development is about bringing wealth into a community. Mostly, that means creating jobs,[4] but it also means adding to the wealth of those who already possess jobs or other forms of livelihood. These additions are what EIS seek to measure.

Colleges and universities, by their very existence, add jobs and wealth to a community. From the community perspective these additions are the two major, direct, economic gains from higher education.[5] That is, EIS measure the financial additions colleges and universities make to communities by their very being: by employing their workers, otherwise spending their budgets, attracting (consuming) students to the community or effectively dissuading students from leaving to study elsewhere, and serving as an attraction for outside visitors. Research universities *may* be the exception to this consumption emphasis in that they may contribute large investment benefits as well. It is worth reemphasizing here that what individuals and society are all about in this higher education spending is primarily investment and that in the end the consumption/investment distinction is artificial.

To summarize, three kinds of "economic development" studies commonly are found in the literature. Rate of return (ROR) studies, which are not geographically focused, relate private and public spending to the earnings of college attendees/graduates, marginal to high school graduates. ROR studies are investment studies. Growth accounting studies (GAS), which are nationally focused, partition all national income growth among land, labor, and capital, again with marginal college-related earnings being used to estimate effects of higher education. Thus the higher education effect directly measured in GAS is seen again to be the (pecuniary) investment effect; however, since all national income growth is represented, consumption gains are captured too. (Of course, GAS do not capture changing stocks of human or physical capital.) The residual term in GAS almost certainly contains additional, large effects of higher education as well. Economic impact studies (EIS) are local or regional in orientation (occasionally they may be state based). In their exclusive attention to current year spending, EIS typically are seen as consumption studies; of course, most of this spending has an investment purpose, but the benefit measured in EIS is only the direct benefit of that spending.

The relationship among the three kinds of studies is seen best through a cost-benefit accounting approach. The generic term, economic development, conveys a notion of expenditures followed by financial gain. What is required in estimating these gains is identification of expenditures and careful expenditure tracking. If this is achieved, we should be able to specify the gains accurately in a common metric.

Economic Impact Studies

From the accounting perspective EIS are the easiest studies to comprehend because expenditures are relatively easy to understand and track. Economic base theory holds that economic gain is achieved by the community or region only when resources are brought into the community (or region) from outside. All else is merely resource *transfer*. Thus the accounting task is to identify nonlocal funds expended locally due to the existence of the collegiate institution and then to track those funds until they leave the area. Major expenditure accounts will be those of the institution, employees, students, and visitors. We should include all area spending that occurs due to the presence of the institution, being careful not to omit such consideration as extra-institutional earnings (and subsequent spending) of employees, of employee spouses and children, and of retirees and alumni who reside locally due to the presence of the institution. Once local spending patterns are known for employees, students, and visitors, the second round and subsequent spending rounds can be estimated. Gravity theory and local economic multipliers can contribute greatly to simplifying the accounting process.[6]

EIS fall short in accounting for local and regional economic growth only in their incompleteness, not in their concept. If all spending were tracked fully, we would capture all impacts, including all investment earnings. We have noted already that perhaps the major (pecuniary) economic gain from higher education is in the earnings (and spending) of college graduates. Conventionally, EIS almost never attempt to include this important factor, let alone the spillovers to others from alumni presence in communities and the induced effects of alumni spending. Some but not all of the answers to the contemporary question mentioned at the outset of this chapter—the economic gains and locally generated spending from technology transfer and university-related business partnerships—would be accounted for by accurate inclusion of alumni data. There would remain to be added the accounts of businesses developed by alumni and of those that were begun only because of the resources represented in the institution. Nevertheless, EIS are the *basic* studies to understanding the economic impact of collegiate institutions on their communities or regions.

EIS tell us the immediate, or current-year, impacts of institution-related spending, viewed simply as college-associated individuals and the institution spending their budgets. Though much of that spending has a long-term investment purpose, the community or region still will realize an immediate gain. Sale of a piece of technical equipment may contribute to new local jobs and economic gain in the future when a new product is marketed; regardless, the sale will represent an immediate profit to a local firm. Estimating the collective impacts of institution-related higher education expenditures on a current-year basis is the major purpose of this section.

To this end were gathered, analyzed, and to some degree, standardized, the EIS of 74 two- and four-year institutions of higher education.[7] We employed two common measures in an attempt to estimate effects broadly. For 14 public two-year colleges the mean business volume (BV) to college budget ratio was 1.6 and the jobs created to budget (in millions of dollars) ratio was 55, expressed in 1988–1989 dollars.[8] This means that, on average, a community college budget of $10 million would generate local business volume of $16 million and would create 550 jobs in 1988–1989. For 50 four-year institutions the overall BV/budget ratio was 1.8 and the overall Jobs/Budget ($ million) was 53 (N = 31), expressed in 1988–1989 dollars. The highest BV/budget values were for private universities (value 2.3), but the sample was too small (N = 3) to justify inferences.[9] BV/budget ratios were 2.0, 1.8, and 1.4 for public college (N = 21), private college (N = 13), and public university estimates (N = 11), respectively.

This relative order of these effects is at some odds with theory, which holds that more complex and private institutions should contribute more to local/regional economies than do less complex and public ones because the former are characterized by greater regional specialization. It would be presumed that community colleges would demonstrate lower business volume/college budget ratios than would four-year schools, and among four-year institutions, that ratios for universities would be the highest. In fact, for our samples, although community colleges do demonstrate a lower BV/budget ratio than do four-year institutions overall (1.6 versus 1.8), jobs created are greater in community colleges.[10] Further, the public university and the private four-year college ratios are relatively lower than expected. Only the ratio for public four-year colleges, at 2.0, is about as anticipated. What explains these discrepancies with theory?

Economic base theory, the foundation of EIS, centers on attracting new resources to a community through regional specialization. According to this theory, locally derived moneys should not be counted in EIS because such moneys represent only local wealth transfer. The presumption in the literature is that less complex and public institutions are more likely to employ local resources than are more complex and private ones: Students are more likely to be local, as are sources of institutional revenues, in the former types of institutions.

One of the reasons the empirical data do not support the theory may be methodological. Few EIS appear to attempt to subtract out spending by local students or to subtract out locally derived institutional revenues.[11] Although there is no reason to believe this oversight to be more common in any particular institutional type, the effect would be more serious where these locally funded amounts are largest. Even if data were corrected only to adjust for local students who would not attend elsewhere in the absence of a local college, the effects should vary by institutional type. A related methodological problem may be that rigor may vary with institutional status. It may be that higher-status institutions have less reason to take methodological liberties with the data than do striving institutions. There does seem to be some evidence of fewer such liberties being taken in the case of public universities.

Another reason for the theoretical-empirical dissonance may be that the theory is incomplete. When one views the four components of business volume—employee, student, institutional, and visitor spending—plus multiplier (MP) effects, a complex picture unfolds and economic base theory does not capture everything.

First, the share of local spending varies greatly with local conditions. The local share of college spending was estimated in the EIS reviewed to range from 0 to 100 percent for 60 four-year institutions (see table 9–1). Although it is extremely unlikely that either figure is valid, it is true that this share varies with geographic location of the institution (degree of urbanization of the community) and that urbanization is associated with institutional type. Although rural versus urban location is important, the matter is not straightforward. For example, Coopers and Lybrand's (1985) estimate that the University of Miami makes 100 percent of its purchases locally appears more or less plausible, as does McGowan's (1988) estimate

Table 9–1. Matrix of Economic Impact Studies

(1) Author(s) (Pub. Date), Data Year	(2) Analysis Method	(3) College(s) Type	(4) "Community" or Region	(5) Surveys Collected	(6) % Local Expenditures	(7) % Student Spending	(8) Multipliers: Spending / Jobs	(9) Business Volume / College Budget	(10) Corrected Business Volume / College Budget	(11) Corrected Jobs / Budget ($ Million)	(12) Validity, Comparability	(13) Special Notes/Data Omissions (0)
Altmann[1] (1985) 1984	ACE	Pub. Coll.	Southeast IN	Yes	NA	NA	1.8 2.8	2.5	NC	7	1	Adjustments for induced student migration;* student expenditures high;* FT employees only.
Anonymous (1988) 1987–88	ACE	Pub. U.	San Diego, CA	No	NA	NA	1.4 —	1.1	NC		3	Inadequate documentation;* includes all employee wages as BV and capital expenditures; PT?
Berger[1] (1987) 1986	NA	Pvt. Coll.	Sante Fe, NM	NA	NA	.11	2.8 —	3.5	NC		2	Small pvt. coll.; hi MP;* documentation inadequate PT?
Billingsley et al. (1985) 1985	ACE	Pub. Coll.	Macomb, IL	Yes	NA	.43	2.0 3.8	1.4	NC	45	1	Modest documentation;* PT?
Bissonnette & Smith (1988) 1987–88	ACE	Pub. Coll.	Eastern WV	Yes	NA	.52	0.0 —	1.1	2.1		2	No MP;* documentation lacking;* PT?
Blalock (1984) 1983–84	EB	Pvt. Coll.	Evansville, IN	Yes	.18	NA	2.7 —	1.8	NC		1	Hi MP derived,* small local spending;* PT?
Booth & Jarrett[1] (1972) 1971–72	ACE	Pub. U.	Southern RI	Yes	.15	.21	1.8 1.6	.8	NC	64	2	Low local spending by all;* low student spending.*
Breslin[1] (1979) 1977–78	ACE	Pub. Coll.	Trenton, NJ	Yes	NA	NA	1.9 2.2	.9	.9	37	1	Visitors (0); jobs are "positions."
Burton & Carie[1] (1988) 1987–88	ACE	Pub. Coll.	Fresno, CA	No	NA	.41	2.4 5.4	3.8	NC		3	Values taken from other studies;* large jobs MP;* omits government effects provided.
Chawdhry[1] (1979a) 1976–77	ACE	Pub. Coll.	Calif., PA / 4 Co., PA	Yes	.08	.74	1.4 —	.5/1.2	NC	42/45	1	Small community;* local & 4-county estimates;* PT?

NA = not applicable or not available.
NC = not calculated.
n.d. = no date.

Chawdhry (1979*b*) 1976–77	ACE	Pub. Coll.	Suburban Pittsburgh, PA	—	NA	.62 —	1.4	1.1	NC		2	Conservative multiplier;* PT?
Consortium of Universities (1986) 1985–86	ACE(?)	Coll's. & U's.	DC area	Yes(?)	NA	.26	1.5 —	1.9	NC		2	For 11 D.C. area U's, pub. & pvt.;* PT?
Coopers & Lybrand (1985) 1983–84	ACE	Pvt. U.	Miami, FL	No	1.00	.14	4.7	3.9	NC		1	Hi MP;* local spending = 1.00;* low student spending;* no surveys;* PT?
Cox & Wyrick[1] (1985) 1984–85	ACE	Pub. Coll.	Springfield, MO	Yes	1.0	.58	2.4 —	7.2	NC		3	Hi student spending;* assumes 100% local purchases,* hi MP,* includes $4.7 M in unusual spending.
Davis & Morris (1986)	ACE	Pub. Coll.	Eastern NM	Yes	NA	.53	1.6 1.6	1.4	NC	52	1	Visitors & PT personnel (0); valid through slightly conservative approach.
Doti[1] (1987) 1986–87	Locally formulated	Pvt. Coll.	Orange Co., CA	Students only	.74	.10	2.2 —	1.1	NC		2	Method developed locally, not strictly comparable;* student spending small because only inclusion is room & board in auxiliaries.
Fisher (1981) 1979–80	ACE	Pub. Coll.	Northwest PA	Yes	1.0	.27	2.0 3.4	2.1	NC		1	Student jobs excluded;* jobs include PT employees as FT;* Hi jobs MP: 100% local expenditures by Coll.
Freiberg & Bichsel[1] (1985) 1982	ACE	Pub. Coll.	Chicago, NE IL	No	NA	.44	2.0 2.0	2.5	NC	75	1	Commuter college;* visitors (0), but minor; omit credit expansion and alumni earnings provided.
Fried (1980) 1980	ACE	Pub. U.	Fairbanks, AK	Yes	NA	.28	1.2 1.3	1.4	NC	67	1	Budget denominator is for FY 1979; small MPs.*
Fulton (1984) 1984	ACE	Pvt. Coll.	Boston–Newton, MA	Yes	NA	.40	0.0 —	1.1	2.1		2	No MP applied;* omits all other Boston area impacts;* documentation lacking; PT?
Gaulene (1985) 1984–85	ACE	Pvt. Coll.	New Orleans, LA	NA	.49	NA	2.5	2.4	NC	46	2	Lacks documentation;* hi MP;* PT?
Gonzaga U. (1988) 1988	NA	Pvt. Coll.	Spokane, WA	NA	NA	NA	—	1.3	NC		3	Lacks documentation;* PT?

Table 9–1. *Cont.*

(1) Author(s) (Pub. Date), Data Year	(2) Analysis Method	(3) College(s) Type	(4) "Community" or Region	(5) Surveys Collected	(6) % Local Expenditures	(7) % Student Spending	(8) Multipliers: Spending / Jobs	(9) Business Volume / College Budget	(10) Corrected Business Volume / College Budget	(11) Corrected Jobs / Budget ($ Million)	(12) Validity, Comparability	(13) Special Notes/Data Omissions (O)
Hanten & Stratton (1981) 1979–80	ACE	Pub. Coll.	Akron, OH	Yes	NA	.67	1.7 —	3.2	NC	48	2	Data corrected to conform to ACE method;* jobs MP corrected for inflation to 1980.*
Heffernan (1988) 1986–87	Locally Formulated	Pvt. U.	East LA, CA	No	NA	.07	2.0 —	4.4	NC		3	Method developed locally, not strictly comparable;* includes all U. spending;* student spending estimated and small because only inclusion is room & board in auxiliaries.
KPMG Peat Marwick (1989) 1989	NA	Pub. U.	San Francisco, CA	No	.65	.20	1.8 1.5	1.6	NC		2	Omits student resources from U. retirees, Lawrence Lab, visitors;* assumes local residents-employees spend 100% locally.*
Lange[1] (1980) 1979	ACE	Pub. Coll.	St. Cloud, MN	Yes	NA	NA	2.1 4.0	2.3	NC	61	2	Hi multipliers;* all employees (FT) included; expenditure values high.*
McEnany[1] (1979) 1977–78	ACE	Pvt. U.	Providence, RI & state	Yes	NA	NA	1.9 2.1	.9	.9	36	1	89% of students from out-of-state.
McGowan[1] (1988) 1988	ACE	Pub. Coll.	Spearfish, SD	Yes	.15	.64	1.9 3.6	1.3	NC		1	Rural town,* small local spending; PT?
Marietta Coll. (1986) 1985–86	NA	Pvt. Coll.	Marietta, OH	—	NA	.17	1.9 —	1.5	NC		2	Assumes all payroll spent locally;* lacks documentation;* PT?
May & Hauck[1] (1981) 1979–80	ACE	Pub. U.	Albemarle Co. (Charlottesville) VA	Yes	.20	.30	1.6 1.5	1.4	NC	54	1	Low value reflects high external spending due to rural area of U. Va.;* business lost not subtracted.

Miklausen & Smith (1975) 1973–74	ACE	Pub. Coll.	Shippensburg, PA	Yes	NA	.30	1.9 —	1.9	NC		1	Multiplier derived from actual expenditures; rural;* PT?
Mowen[1] (1979) 1977–78	ACE	Pub. U.	Stillwater, OK	Yes	.15	.50	1.8 1.7	1.3	NC	46	1	Low local spending;* jobs corrected for inflation;* PT?
Murray[1] (1971–72) 1971–72	ACE	Pub. Coll.	Brown Co., WI	Yes	.49	.46	1.9 1.9	2.4	NC	57	1	1971–72 study.*
Overturf[1] (1988) 1988	EB	Pvt. Coll.	Whittier, CA	Yes	.43	.17	3.4 3.4	1.6	NC	41	1	Hi MPs derived;* urban LA; visitors (O); limited to Whittier;* PT?
Palumbo[1] (n.d.) 1981–82	NA	Pvt. Coll.	Buffalo, NY	NA	.85	.19	—	1.6	NC		3	Inadequate documentation.*
Peat Marwick (1987) 1987	NA	Pub. U.	San Francisco, CA	NA	.41	.13	1.4 39/$ mill.	1.2	NC		2	Lacks documentation;* low MP;* v. small student spending estimates;* jobs estimated;* PT?
Peppers[1] (n.d.) 1983–84	ACE	Pvt. Coll.	Omaha, NE	No	NA	.46	2.0 2.0	2.0	NC	56	1	State of Nebraska is focus, but local effects are roughly equal; omits PT, credit expansion, and alumni earnings provided.
Planning Office (CMU) (1987) 1985–86	ACE	Pvt. U.	Alleghany Co., PA	No	.59	.06	1.5 —	1.2	NC	47	1	Urban, pvt. U. with small enrollments;* jobs corrected for inflation.*
Polzin[1] (1988) 1986–87	ACE	Pub. U.	Missoula, MT	Yes	NA	.67	0.0 —	1.5	2.9		2	No MP;* PT?
Posey[1] (1983) 1982–83	EB	Pub. Coll.	Atlanta, GA	Yes	1.00	NA	1.6 2.4	2.5	NC	73	2	Hi local expenditure ratio;* visitors & PT employees & (most) PT students (O); very hi student spending.*
Ripson (1985) 1984–85	ACE	Pvt. Coll.	Polk Co., IA	Yes	NA	.19	1.9 —	2.3	NC	61	1	Omits credit & govt. effects provided; PT?
Rosen et al.[1] (1985) 1983–84	ACE, I/O	Pub. U.	Dane Co., (Madison) WI	Yes	.24	.31	2.2 —	1.7	NC	44	1	Major state university;* omits govt. households & charities impacts provided; student employees included.
Rutgers (1985) 1981–82	ACE	Pub. U.	New Brunswick NJ	No	.19	.53	1.3 1.2	.3	NC	22	2	Relies on "spending averages" from other studies;* highly urbanized area = small local spending;* low MP.*

Table 9–1. *Cont.*

(1) Author(s) (Pub. Date), Data Year	(2) Analysis Method	(3) College(s) Type	(4) "Community" or Region	(5) Surveys Collected	(6) % Local Expenditures	(7) % Student Spending	(8) Multipliers: Spending / Jobs	(9) Business Volume / College Budget	(10) Corrected Business Volume / College Budget	(11) Corrected Jobs / Budget ($ Million)	(12) Validity, Comparability	(13) Special Notes/Data Omissions (O)
Salley[1] (1976) 1975–76	EB	Pub. Coll.	Atlanta, GA	Yes	1.00	NA	1.5 2.6	2.9	NC	90	2	Hi student & local spending values;* hi jobs multipliers;* PT employees & (most) PT students & visitors (O).
Salley[1] (1979) 1978–79	EB	Pub. Coll.	Atlanta, GA	Yes	1.00	NA	1.5 3.1	2.6	NC	85	2	Hi student & local spending values;* hi jobs multipliers;* PT employees & (most) PT students & visitors (O).
Schwartz et al. (1972) 1971	ACE	Pub. Coll.	Rural PA	NA	.04	.04	0.0 —	.5	1.0		3	No MP,* extremely low local expenditures and student expenditures;* PT?
Seeloff (1989) 1987–88	ACE	Pvt. Coll.	Lehigh Valley, PA	No	1.00	.10	2.0 —	1.5	NC		3	Modest documentation;* visitors (O); assumes 100% local spending, payroll & U expend;* no surveys;* PT?
Shaddix & Fielding[1] (1986) 1985	ACE	Pub. Coll.	Rural AL	Yes	.50	.60	2.2 8.2	4.2	NC	85	1	Very high jobs MP;* high student spending;* High local spending;* small budget for 7000 students;* PT?
Sharma[1] (1982) 1981–82	ACE	Pub. Coll.	Mankato, MN	Yes	NA	.56	1.9 3.6	2.3	NC	62	1	PT (O).
Showers (1989) 1988–89	ACE	Pub. Coll.	Western MO	No	.72	.27	3.5	3.5	NC		3	BV calc. by taking .72 (college budget + student spending) × 3.5 ("MP");* visitors (O); PT?
Soderlind[1] (1986) 1986	Keynsian; Basic/ Nonbasic	Pvt. Coll.	Northfield/ Twin Cities MN	Yes	NA	NA	1.3/1.8 —	.8/1.4	NC	24/17	2	40% are nonresident students; employs various economic base models.*
Stokes & Stokes[1] (n.d.) 1984–85	ACE	Pub. Coll.	Bridgeport, CT	Yes	NA	.43	1.9 4.4	.9	NC	34	1	Mid-sized, urban public college; PT?

Story & Longhurst[1] (1988) 1987–88	ACE	Pvt. Coll.	Rural OR	Yes	NA	.68	1.3 —	.6	NC	37	1	Rural area with small local spending;* spending limited to school district area.* Inflation adjusted.
Technical Systems (n.d.) 1985–86	ACE	Pvt. Coll.	St. Paul, MN	Yes	NA	.44	2.5 —	2.0	NC		2	Documentation lacking,* hi MP; PT?
TJS Associates (n.d.) 1986–87	NA	Pub. Coll.	Orangeburg, SC	Yes	NA	.00	3.0 —	3.0	NC		3	Hi MP empirically derived;* student and visitor expenditures (O);* PT?
University of Calif. Santa Cruz (1988) 1987–88	ACE	Pub. U.	Santa Cruz, CA	Yes	.49	.33	2.2 —	2.5	NC		1	Assumes 90% local spending by individuals; PT?
Univ. of Oregon (1988) 1987–88	ACE	Pub. U.	Eugene, OR	NA	NA	.24	2.0 —	1.8	NC		3	Assumes payroll 100% spent locally;* lacks documentation.*
University of Maine (1989) 1989	ACE	Pub. U.	Bangor, ME	Yes	NA	.52	1.8 —	2.1	NC		1	Study merely inflates values from 1975 study.
Wall (1989) 1988–89	NA	Pvt. Coll.	Ithaca, NY	No	NA	NA	—	2.6	NC		3	Estimates only; no formal study.*
Yi (1984) 1982	ACE	Pub. U.	Morgantown, WV	Yes	NA	.50	1.2 —	1.2	NC		2	Low MP;* documentation lacking;* PT?
Means					.50*	.39*	1.8*	1.8	1.8*	53*		

Notes:
Col. 1: [1] = economics/business faculty author or adviser.
Col. 2: ACE = American Council on Education. Employs a specific economic base model; EB = economic base, generically; I/O = input-output analysis.
Col. 3: Pub. = public; Pvt. = private; U. = university; Coll. = college.
Col. 5: No survey means that data were estimated.
Col. 6: % local expenditure is for nonsalary, noninternal, and nontax expenditures by college.
Col. 7: Percent of institutional, faculty/staff, student, and visitor spending that is student spending.
Col. 9: The sum of local college, employee, student, and visitor spending, including multiplier impact, divided by education and general expenditures (see col. 13 for exceptions).
Col. 10: Business volume corrected to standardize roughly, unusual treatment (see col. 13).
Col. 12: 1 = most valid/comparable studies; 2 = less valid/comparable but acceptable studies; 3 = invalid or noncomparable studies.
Col. 13: This column highlights study characteristics important to interpretation. Items marked (*) are most important to interpretation and often explain relatively high or low results unless effects tend to cancel out. (O) = Omitted by study author. Comments as to hi or low values are relative judgments usually based on identification of a questionable value in calculations. PT? = Part-time employees inclusion uncertain. BV = Business Volume; MP = Multiplier; FT = Full Time.
MEANS: * Excludes studies assigned value of "3."

that only 15 percent of purchases by Black Hills State College in Spearfish, South Dakota, are local. However, at first glance the fact that Bucks County Community College, located in suburban Trenton, New Jersey, makes only 10 percent of its purchases locally seems unlikely until one is made aware that in this EIS (Mahon 1979) "local" was defined as the college tax area; that is, purchases in nearby cities were excluded. In short, it is not only the presence or absence of local vendors that may be important but the presence or absence of nearby alternatives—not to mention the definitions employed. All these factors may vary by institutional type. Finally, in this regard, more complex institutions simply may not be able to make proportionately as many purchases locally. Research universities, for example, no doubt purchase expensive, sophisticated equipment in national, not regional or local, markets.

Second is the matter of student spending. To aid in examining student spending data in the EIS, student spending was calculated as a share of spending by all four groups. The student spending share ranged from 4 to 74 percent for the four-year sample. Although again the accounting stances taken by the EIS analysts may explain a sizable share of the differences, differences by institutional types appear more important. In general, private colleges, smaller institutions, and the more rural institutions are more likely than their counterparts to provide room and board for a large percentage of their students, resulting in relatively low community business volume from student spending. Relative proximity to large consumer markets, differences in student wealth, and definitional limits of "community" are other important determinants.

Finally, there is the unresolved matter of how spending by "local" students should be handled. Even if students who do not leave the community because of the presence of the local college are equated with students who come from elsewhere, it remains that private and more complex institutions tend to enroll more students who would, in fact, attend elsewhere if the local college did not exist.

Employee local spending is only somewhat more varied. The large issue here is how community is defined, because in many urban areas a large share of employees may commute considerable distances. Rutgers, for example, considers its employees' local spending to be small because most live outside the New Brunswick area (Rutgers 1985).

Visitor spending is usually relatively small in relation to the three preceding categories; nevertheless, differences may be of consequence. Community colleges, for example, often do not even bother to estimate visitor spending, whereas in large public and private universities the amounts involved may be quite substantial.

Related, but separate from all of these, are questions related to the size of the "multiplier" (MP). Multipliers are used in EIS to reflect the extent to which locally expended funds are respent in the local community (or to reflect number of additional jobs created per million dollars expended locally). Depending on the location of the college, plus other factors, locally spent money may "exit" the community faster or slower than in other cases. Generally, MPs are directly associated with the size of the geographic area, the population size, and diversity of manufacturers and suppliers present.

Most of the EIS reviewed simply borrow MPs from other studies, and the bases for selections made often are unclear. Nevertheless, to the extent that the factors that explain MP magnitudes are associated with institutional type, impacts on BV/budget and jobs/budget ratios should vary accordingly.

All these factors were examined in an attempt to understand the unexpectedly low BV/budget ratios for public universities and for private colleges. For the public universities, systematic explanations seemed to be in their small share of institutional budgets spent locally and, somewhat less, in the lower multipliers employed. The small share of public university local expenditures (.23 versus .50 for all four-year schools) is perhaps explained best by local unavailability of many needs of research universities plus more systematic and regulated purchasing procedures in these complex institutions. Regarding multipliers, for all four-year institutions, the average MP was 1.82, compared to 1.62 for the public universities overall, and was 1.48 for those public universities having extremely low BV/budget ratios. There was no apparent reason for these universities having employed small MPs, other than perhaps the exercise of greater methodological caution.

For private four-year colleges the explanation for the lower than expected BV/budget ratio appeared to be associated largely with their preponderant locations in rural areas and their residential nature. Both factors contributed to relatively small student spending in local communities, as room and board was more likely to be provided by the colleges. Local spending by the college itself also may have been limited by the local environments. MPs employed by private colleges were slightly above the sample average, even though smaller MPs appear more justified.

The higher jobs/budget ratios in community colleges than in four-year schools (55 versus 53) appear to be due largely to greater business volume generated directly by college and college-related expenditures in two-year schools for the samples of EIS in which the jobs/budget ratios were calculated. Community college jobs MPs employed were also slightly larger, being on average 2.2 for the community colleges compared to 2.1 for the four-year schools.

The business volume and jobs measures are, of course, not the only or even immediate effects of college-related spending. Caffrey and Isaacs (1971), whose instruments and techniques have served as the basis for the vast majority of collegiate EIS, list six additional economic impacts that could and occasionally have been translated into college-related pecuniary gains and losses: production of durable goods, expansion of the community credit base, the value of property connected to college activity, personal income, net effects on governments and taxes, and business lost due to business operations of colleges. (Note the omission of such benefits as earnings of alumni and effects of employee-induced businesses.) Although these additional effects should be included in EIS, they usually are not, and where they are included, accounting approaches are highly inconsistent.

Fortunately, the omissions do not appear to affect results of EIS seriously, in part because the BV/budget and jobs/budget ratios are somewhat redundant measures of some of the other impacts and in part because others of the six impacts are relatively trivial. Net effects on governments and taxes and "business lost," for example—while politically important—rarely amount to even a percentage point or two of the business volume effect, partially because gains and losses tend to cancel out. This can be illustrated nicely by pointing out, for example, that while a college presence results in more children to be educated (usually, easily the largest government impact of a college presence), those same children bring the community comparable state and federal school dollar allocations and their parents and other college employees pay substantial local property and other taxes that support the schools. Further, the presence of the college raises the tax yield on other property in the community. On balance, the notion of colleges and universities as drains on local economies and local taxpayers is largely a myth. Not only are effects on governments small, they appear more often to be positive than negative. Another controversial, contemporary view—that business is lost due to the presence of a college—may be similarly shortsighted. Most "losses" are represented by colleges' housing and feeding students, in selling them books and personal computers and the like. None of these "losses" could occur if the college were not present.

There are, however, definite social and economic regional/local costs associated with colleges and universities. No one can deny that collegiate institutions add to traffic problems and to concomitant pollution. Parking difficulties near campuses are long-standing. Families often are displaced as institutions expand, and all too often the victims are low-income persons without ready housing alternatives. Housing shortages are thus common near campuses, and available housing is more costly. In general, colleges and universities raise the cost of living wherever they are located, but of course they raise standards of living too. This is most readily seen in rural areas where a single college-possessing community may be prosperous in a sea of rural stagnation.

What Remains to Be Learned

There are important effects beyond those captured in conventional EIS, and it is these benefits that are of particular current interest. A few EIS have begun to include such factors, but no systematic approach exists to estimate their effects, nor have effects already counted been separated out (to avoid double counting). Several studies have included earnings of locally residing alumni (e.g., Peppers n.d.; Fulton 1984; Freiberg and Bichsel 1985), but none have subtracted out alumni earnings that are already captured in college employee wages or college spending. The University of Wisconsin, Madison, in one of the more complete and seemingly valid EIS, includes estimates of effects of all (employee) household earnings and effects on charities (Rosen, Strang, and Kramer 1985). The University of California, Berkeley, estimates the spending of university retirees (KPGM Peat Marwick 1989) and, like MIT (Bank of Boston 1989) and a few others, examines the economic impacts of businesses started by their alumni. These are, however, the exceptions rather than the rule, and, again, the data provided are not immediately useful for the purpose of cross comparison.

To date, EIS have focused primarily on single-year spending and have not looked closely at long-term university contributions to economic development, especially in the areas of technology transfer, industry-university partnerships and university investment in patenting, and commercial development of high technology. To capture the investment benefits of technology transfer, EIS procedures would have to be adjusted in several ways. First, they would have to be extended to cover the spending of the university community over a number of years, perhaps as many as fifteen. Second, they would have to establish techniques for tracing university impacts throughout the region. The accounting task is formidable; for example, how to treat companies that spin off from university research or how to consider private and public monetary contributions from state and local sources. A carefully developed EIS, however, should be able to track the local and regional economic impact of technology transfer.

Some have attempted to measure the economic benefits of phenomena such as technology transfer. Mansfield (1989), in a NSF working paper, calculated a social rate of return for academic research by measuring the related commercial value. His social rate of return, which he considered to be very conservatively estimated, was 28 percent. Rather than follow the movement of actual pieces of research from the university through the commercial development process, Mansfield arrived at this figure by using estimates, supplied by business people, of the contributions made by academic research to the development of business products and processes. Specifically, Mansfield randomly sampled 76 major American manufacturing industries and asked each firm's top executives to identify those products, developed between 1975 and 1978, that "could not have been developed (without substantial delay) in the absence of academic research carried out within 15 years of the first introduction of the innovation" (Mansfield 1989, p. 2).

Mansfield's approach is useful as a pioneering effort to understand the contribution academic research may make generally to economic development, but his work results in only crude estimates of the payoffs from relationships between firms and universities. Mansfield does not address the questions that are foremost in the minds of those interested in promoting technology transfer as a local or regional economic development strategy. His work says nothing about the impact of specific universities on their communities, nor does it speak to the organizational processes that universities use to initiate or enhance their contribution to economic development through technology transfer. Mansfield has, however, made a beginning.

Conclusion

Rate of return, growth accounting, and economic impact studies essentially do not deal with the question of such great current interest: how a university (or college) may collaborate with business or use its own means to advance economic development. University presidents and state governors have endorsed economic development strategies, as have groups such as the Business-Higher Education Forum, and even scientific organizations, such as the National Science Foundation. Technology transfer is probably the most widely promoted economic development strategy.

Although many states and communities are contemplating increased investment in university technology transfer programs, a number of questions are beginning to be raised about what effect they will have on the local economy. We review briefly now what is known about transfer of technology from the university to the commercial sector in order to see what we can learn about local and regional economic impacts. We begin by sketching out the technology transfer options that are available to universities and local communities.

There are two general types of technology transfer: corporate and campus cooperation and university investment in technology likely to lead to economic development.

Corporate and campus cooperation includes academic activities, such as training, consulting, and spinoff companies based on academic research, and a wide array of university-industry partnerships, ranging from very specific contracts between corporations and academic departments to federal or state funding of general joint efforts by businesses and university researchers to develop potential processes and products of benefit to the nation as a whole or to specific states and communities. University investment involves universities directly in steps that lead to commercial development or in commercial development itself. For example, universities are increasingly taking out patents on professors' research and creating "for-profit" corporations that hold equity positions in products or processes patented by professors.

Corporate and campus cooperation centering on training, consulting, and spinoffs is the means by which technology has traditionally been transferred. It is probably this kind of activity that is captured by Mansfield's work on the social rates of return (SRR) from academic research. Studies indicate that consulting is the mechanism by which technology is most frequently transferred (Peters and Fusfeld 1982). Training and consulting are the activities that businesses believe contribute most heavily to economic development. There are few studies of the economic impact of spinoffs. As is the case with Mansfield's work, studies that deal with training, consulting, and spinoffs do not usually speak to local and regional economic impacts.

Research associate programs are another form of corporate and campus cooperation. Although the associate concept was first initiated at MIT in the 1910s, many research institutions have only recently begun such programs. In a research associate program, corporations pay a university a fixed fee for the right to a "window" on university research in particular fields. Fees generally range from $5000 to $250,000 per corporation. Corporations have been eager to participate in these programs, especially when they are offered by universities renowned for their technological prowess or when the research is esoteric, costly, or further advanced than that in industrial laboratories. Again, there have been few studies of the local and regional impact of these programs.

Long-term research contracts between specific companies and academic departments are another type of corporate and campus cooperation. A number of very large, long-term contracts in biotechnology and pharmacology received a great deal of attention in the press in the early 1980s. Early on, there was hope that the private sector would become a major contributor to academic research; however, the number of large, long-term contracts between business and universities recently has declined sharply, and business is very clear that the private sector cannot make a substantial contribution to academic research, let alone substitute for the investment role played by the federal government. Generally, the business community does not see itself ever contributing more than 10 percent (David 1980; Slaughter 1989) as much as the federal government contributes for academic research, and doubts that this level will be reached in the near future.

Most of the large university-industry contracts call for secrecy and have not yet expired, so it is not yet possible to learn what they have contributed to economic development. However, the decline in this type of investment by the private sector, as well as the manifest private sector preference for short-term research contracts with universities, suggests that the payoff has been limited (Feller n.d.). When the economic impacts of this kind of investment in university research are investigated, the estimates probably will not be local or regional, since most of the companies that have engaged in this investment strategy have been national or multinational in scope.

University-industry partnerships are frequently funded by the federal government, very often through the NSF, the DOD, or DOE. These investments usually have a local or regional economic development dimension in that they frequently aim to upgrade or renew the strengths of local industry. Generally, the federal government deems these partnerships successful when funding responsibility is assumed by some other agent. It is hoped that private industry will assume sponsorship, but the endeavor is still seen as successful if state, local, or university sponsors step into the breech within a given number of years. To date there has been little assessment of these programs outside of that contained in technical reports submitted to sponsors.

This same general test of success is employed by state and local governments. Success is measured by decreasing dependence on government monies and by development of private sector businesses, especially private sector jobs. As in the case with federally sponsored partnerships, little assessment has taken place.

Unique types of federally sponsored university-industry partnerships are those that cannot be formed without special dispensation from antitrust law. These partnerships, such as Microelectronics and Computer Corporation, allow firms within an enterprise to pool their research efforts, usually in areas that have been deemed critical to the national economic interest in the global marketplace. In effect, these partnerships provide a U.S. industrial investment policy by targeting specific product lines. These partnerships are fairly recent and, to our knowledge, have not yet been assessed, but international market share is clearly the pertinent test of the success of these ventures.

Corporate and campus cooperation probably yields, as Mansfield suggests, a high SRR; however, such conclusions to date have been based principally on collaborations at a few eminent institutions, such as MIT, the University of North Carolina at Chapel Hill, and Stanford. The question of whether somewhat lesser universities lacking successful experiences in technology transfer programs can develop successful corporate-campus cooperation is a question that has not been addressed adequately. Nor have questions been answered regarding the sorts of local conditions necessary to facilitate corporate and campus efforts at economic development. Even less attention has been paid to the "costs" of high technology development within universities. For example, how does the increased entrepreneurial behavior impact the notion of the university as a community of scholars? Finally, the question of the disparate impact of corporate and campus cooperation on community citizens is not usually considered seriously. For example, in California, fruit growers benefited from university development of a grape-picking machine, but farm workers lost jobs. Not until some of these questions are answered empirically, with data gathered from a variety of locations over a significant period of time, will we be able to speak fully to the question of local and regional impacts of campus and corporate cooperation for technology transfer.

The second general type of technology transfer centers on university investment in research that is likely to lead to commercial product development. Since the change in the patent law in 1981, many research universities have established patent offices and begun encouraging their faculty to seek patents on products and processes developed through federally sponsored research. The time and energy spent in proving and defending these patents are seen as speculative investments that could greatly benefit the university, creating independent research funding from patent licensing and royalties. It is generally assumed that such patents will benefit local and regional economies by contributing to the creation of companies and resulting in new jobs.

At this writing, it is not at all clear that benefits will be captured locally, regionally, or, in some cases, even nationally. Evidence to date is limited and results are mixed. Insulin, which probably realized more royalties than any other university patent, was developed at the University of Toronto but was produced by Lilly in the United States. Although the University of Toronto benefited greatly, no additional jobs were created directly in Ontario. The insulin patent is probably not unique. Recent research on biotechnology commercialization indicates that national and multinational corporations are likely to buy up patent rights and small spinoff companies after the market possibilities of the product are well understood. These companies are as likely to move the production to their own plants as they are to continue operations pioneered close to a university.

Even if only the return to the university is considered, it is not clear that the payoff from patents is great. Ratios of patent disclosures to discoveries indicate that only one disclosure in 1000 can be expected to produce significant income, and only one in 500 will yield enough income to pay patent costs, which usually run about $10,000 (*Technology Transfer Newsletter* 1987). Even after patents are registered and proved, patent litigation, which almost invariably follows success, can be extremely costly (Noble 1976).

The vagaries of patent development are evident in one of the better known – and generally considered most successful – patent efforts, that of the university of Wisconsin Alumni Research Foundation (WARF). The WARF experience provides one of the longest standing records of patent returns to universities. WARF was started in the 1920s with patents for vitamin D irradiation of milk. Later WARF became the agency that held many patents proved by University of Wisconsin researchers. A study of WARF's history, however, revealed that most of the money accumulated came not from the handful of patents that resulted in royalties but from investment of royalty monies. Further, that return on investment was somewhat anomalous, in that the WARF investment program was guided successfully for over 25 years, through the depression, by a man who was head of the New York Stock Exchange (Blumenthal Epstein, and Maxwell 1986).

Another university investment strategy assumed to contribute to local economic development is investment in "for-profit" corporations that hold equity positions in products or processes patented by professors. Of course, such corporations may have no local presence, but usually local economic growth is expected. Investments are usually local, and the entity is often housed in a university-funded "incubator" before moving on to its own quarters in the community. This type of investment, however, is extremely risky. Thus far, one in ten have succeeded, when success has been measured as operation continuance for one year (Blake 1988).

University investment in technology transfer raises a number of additional questions. One is a question of opportunity cost. Whether public or private, all research universities receive important public subventions, ranging from tax exemptions to research funding. Allowing universities to invest in technology transfer prevents investment of public monies in other vehicles. The question is whether the university-as-investor contributes more to local and regional economic development than does training, consulting, spinoffs, and all manner of university-industry-government partnerships.

In considering technology transfer, we have assumed that this activity is consistent with the mission of the university. In fact, there have been virtually no studies of the many questions this assumption raises. For example, how does the required commitment of faculty time and university resources impact the quality of undergraduate instruction? How does attention to commercial research affect the nature and quality of graduate education? To what extent will universities be required to substitute self-generated funds for state and federal subsidies, resulting in no net gain for the institutions?

Endnotes

1. Terminology use here is conventional. By investment we mean resources put in use in the expectation that a profit will be realized at some future time. Consumption is the use or destruction of resources.

2. In this analysis we ignore the nonpecuniary benefits of higher education, which are numerous and large. See chapter 5 in *The Economic Value of Higher Education*, Leslie and Brinkman (1988).

3. Sheehan (1973, p. 62) first raised the question of cause and effect, whereas Chinloy (1980) and Psacharopoulos (1984) have raised the interaction question.

4. When one reads the economic development literature, it is clear that what is intended by the term is jobs creation.

5. The other, of course, is the benefit already discussed in rate of return and growth accounting studies: helping to create stocks of human capital.

6. There are several other accounts that may be important. For a thorough discussion see Caffrey and Isaacs (1971).

7. The two-year sample was limited to the EIS available in the University of Arizona library. The four-year sample was stratified by state and public/private institutions. Although *responses* to requests for EIS were in general accordance with the sampling, more public than private institutions and more colleges than universities reported that they had completed an EIS. The effective return rate was approximately 55 percent. Results reported here are for those EIS that met tests of validity *and* comparability to other studies.

8. Educational and general expenditures plus auxiliary enterprises. This estimate is an update of the figures reported earlier for 1985–1986 (Leslie and Brinkman 1988, pp. 93–95).

9. Differentiation between universities and four-year colleges conforms to the Carnegie taxonomy.

10. Because calculation methods often contained errors in the original works, jobs/budget ratios were recalculated using a standard algorithm; also, inflationary corrections were made.

11. This matter is not as straightforward as may appear at first glance. If no local college exists, some students will leave the community, taking their (otherwise) local spending and a share of their families' spending with them.

References

Altmann, J. L. (1985). *Indiana University Southeast's impact on the local economy.* (ERIC Document Reproduction Service No. ED 254 180).

Anonymous. (1988). *An analysis of the district's economic impact.* Sacramento, CA: The Los Rios Community College District.

Bank of Boston. (1989). *MIT growing businesses for the future.* Boston, MA: Economics Department, Bank of Boston.

Berger, G. (1987). *The economic impact of the College of Santa Fe.* Santa Fe: NM: The College of Santa Fe.

Billingsley, D., Hattwick, R., & Thistlethwaite, P. (1985). *The economic impact of Western Illinois University on McDonough County–1984.* Macomb: Center for Business and Economic Research, College of Business, Western Illinois University.

Bissonnette, K. K., & Smith, E. R. (1988). *A study of the economic impact of Shepherd College on its six county service area in the Northern Shenandoah Valley Region of West Virginia, Virginia and Maryland.* Morgantown: West Virginia University.

Blake, S. (1988). Presentation at the Economic Development Council Meeting, University of Arizona, Tucson.

Blalock, G. (1984). *The economic impact of the University of Evansville upon the local community.* Evansville, IN: University of Evansville.

Blumenthal, D., Epstein, S., & Maxwell, J. (1986). Commercializing university research: Lessons from the experience of the Wisconsin Alumni Research Foundation. *The New England Journal of Medicine 314*(25), June 19, 1621–1626.

Booth, G., & Jarrett, J. (1972). *The economic impacts of the University of Rhode Island.* Kingston: The University of Rhode Island.

Breslin, T. P. (1979). *The economic impact of Trenton State College on the local community* Trenton, NJ: Trenton State College (ERIC Document Reproduction Service No. ED 185 911).

Burton, G. E., & Carie, L. (1988). *California State University Fresno's economic impact on the valley reaches $.5 billion.* Fresno: CA: California State University, Fresno.

Caffrey, J., & Isaacs, H. (1971). *Estimating the impact of a college or university on*

the local economy. Washington, D.C.: American Council on Education.
Chawdhry, M. A. (1979*a*). *The economic impact of California State College on the local community*. California, PA: California State College.
Chawdhry, M. A. (1979*b*). *The economic impact of California State College on the local community*. Pittsburgh, PA.
Chinloy, P. (1980). Sources of quality change in labor input. *American Economic Review 70*, 108–119.
Consortium of Universities of the Washington Metropolitan Area. (1986). *4 billion dollars: The economic impact of the consortium universities*. Washington, D.C.: Consortium of Universities of the Washington Metropolitan Area.
Coopers & Lybrand. (1985). *Economic impacts of the University of Miami on the Miami metropolitan area and the State of Florida*. Washington, D.C.
Cox, L. G., & Wyrick, T. L. (1985). *Southwest Missouri State University's impact on the Springfield, Missouri economy, 1984–1985*. Springfield: Department of Economics, Southwest Missouri State University.
David, E., Jr. (1980). Industrial research in America: Challenge of a new synthesis. *Science 209*, July 4, 133–139.
Davis, D., & Morris, K. (1986). *Economic impact of Eastern New Mexico University*. Portales: Eastern New Mexico University.
Denison, E. F. (1962). *The sources of economic growth in the United States and the alternatives before us* (Supplementary Paper No. 13). New York: Committee for Economic Development.
Denison, E. F. (1964). Measuring the contribution of education (and the residual) to economic growth. *The residual factor and economic growth*. Paris: Organization for Economic Cooperation and Development.
Denison, E. F. (1984). Accounting for slower growth: An update. In J. Kendrick (Ed.), *International comparisons of productivity and causes of slowdown*. Cambridge, MA: Ballinger.
Doti, J. (1987). *The economic impact of Chapman College on Orange County*. Orange, CA: Chapman College.
Feller, I. (No date). University-industry research and development relations. Paper prepared for the Woodlands Center for Growth Studies Conference on *Growth policy in the age of high technology: The role of regions and states*.
Fisher, J. K. (1981). *The economic impact of Edinboro State College on Northwestern Pennsylvania–1979–80*. Edinboro: Edinboro University of Pennsylvania.
Freiberg, L., & Bichsel, D. H. (1985). *Northeastern Illinois University: A public asset–the economic impact of Northeastern Illinois University*. Chicago: Northeastern Illinois University.
Fried, N. (1980). *The economic impact of the University of Alaska on Fairbanks*. Fairbanks, AK: Fairbanks North Star Borough, Community Research Center Special Report No. 8.
Fulton, M. E. (1984). *A working partnership–Boston College and its neighbors*. Boston, MA: Office of Community Affairs, Boston College.
Gaulene, J. E. (1985). *The economic impact of Loyola University*. New Orleans, LA: Loyola University.

Gonzaga University. (1988). *Partners*. Spokane, WA: Gonzaga University.

Hanten, E.W., & Stratton, R.W. (1981). *Impact of the University of Akron on the economy of Summit County, Ohio*. Akron, OH: Center for Urban Studies, University of Akron.

Heffernan, A.M. (1988). *Annual financial report, 1986–1987*. Claremont, CA: Claremont University Center.

KPMG Peat Marwick. (1989). *University of California at Berkeley economic impact study*. Berkeley, CA: KPMG Peat Marwick.

Lange, M.D. (1980). *St. Cloud State University's impact on the local economy* (Report No. HE 0134.91). St. Cloud, MN: St. Cloud State College (ERIC Document Reproduction Service No. ED 197 696).

Leslie, L.L., & Brinkman, P.T. (1988). *The economic value of higher education*. New York: Macmillan.

McEnany, G.S. (1979). *The economic impact of Brown University on the city of Providence and on the state of Rhode Island*. Providence, RI: Brown University.

McGowan, F. (1988). *Public higher education's direct impact on the South Dakota economy*. Spearfish, SD: Black Hills State College.

Mahon, J. (1979). *The economic impact of Bucks County Community College on the local economy during fiscal year 1978–1979* (Report No. JC B00 02B). Newton, PA: Bucks County Community College, Office of Institutional Research (ERIC Document Reproduction Service, No. ED 179 276).

Mansfield, E. (1989). The social rate of return from academic research. Unpublished paper, University of Pennsylvania.

Marietta College. (1986). *Marietta College economic impact*. Marietta, OH: Marietta College.

May, E.G., & Hauck, M.E. (1981). *Impact of the University of Virginia on Charlottesville and Albemarle County*. Charlottesville, VA: Tayloe Murphy Institute, Colgate Darden Graduate School of Business Administration, University of Virginia.

Miklausen, A.J., & Smith, S. (1975). *The economic impact of Shippensburg University of Pennsylvania on Shippensburg*. Shippensburg: Shippensburg University of Pennsylvania.

Mowen, M.M. (1979). *The economic impact of Oklahoma State University on Stillwater, Oklahoma*. Stillwater: Office of Business and Economic Research, College of Business Administration, Oklahoma State University.

Murray, J.M. (1971–1972). *The economic impact of University of Wisconsin–Green Bay*. Green Bay: University of Wisconsin–Green Bay.

Noble, D. (1976). *America by design: Science, technology and the rise of corporate capitalism*. New York: Knopf.

Overturf, S. (1988). *The impact of Whittier College on the Whittier community: An economic impact report*. Whittier, CA: Whittier College.

Palumbo, G. (No date). *The Canisius impact*. Buffalo, NY: Canisius College.

Peat Marwick. (1987). *University of California, San Francisco economic impact*. San Francisco: University of California.

Peppers, L.C. (No date). *A partnership of value: Creighton University and*

Nebraska. Omaha, NE: College of Business, Creighton University.

Peters, L., & Fusfeld, H. (1982). Current U.S. university/industry research connections. In National Science Board, *University-industry research relationships*. Washington D.C.: National Science Foundation.

Planning Office, Carnegie-Mellon University. (1987). *The impact of Carnegie-Mellon University on the regional economy*. Pittsburgh, PA: Carnegie-Mellon University.

Polzin, P. E. (1988). *The University of Montana and Missoula: Economic interdependence*. Missoula: Bureau of Business and Economic Research, University of Montana.

Posey, E. I. (1983). *Georgia State University spending patterns and the Atlanta economy, 1983* (Institutional Research Report No. 84–2. Atlanta: Georgia State University, Office of Institutional Planning). (ERIC Document Reproduction Service No. ED 234 712).

Psacharopoulos, G. (1984). The contribution of education to economic growth: International comparisons. In J. W. Kendrick (Ed.), *International comparisons of productivity and causes of the slowdown*. Cambridge, MA: Ballinger.

Ripson, M. (1985). *Drake University—a study of economic impact on Polk County, Iowa*. Des Moines, IA: The Office of University Planning, Drake University.

Rosen, M. I., Strang, W. A., & Kramer, J. (1985). *The University of Wisconsin–Madison and the local and state economies: A second look*. Madison: Graduate School of Business, University of Wisconsin–Madison, Monograph No. 20.

Rutgers, The State University of New Jersey. (1985). *The contribution of Rutgers University to the economy of the Greater New Brunswick area*. New Brunswick, NJ: The Office of Budget and Resource Studies, Rutgers University.

Salley, C. D. (1976). *Georgia State University spending patterns and the Atlanta economy* (Institutional Research Report No. 77–8). Atlanta: Georgia State University, Office of Institutional Planning (ERIC Document Reproduction Service No. ED 135 320).

Salley, C. D. (1979). *Georgia State University spending patterns and the Atlanta economy, 1978* (Institutional Research Report No. 79–8). Atlanta: Georgia State University, Office of Institutional Planning (ERIC Document Reproduction Service No. ED 167 059).

Schwartz, H. E., et al. (1972). The economic impact of Mansfield State College on the local economy: An assessment. Mansfield State College.

Seeloff, L. J. (1989). *Lehigh University, economic impact on the Lehigh Valley*. Bethlehem, PA: Lehigh University.

Shaddix, P. W., & Fielding, W. T. (1986). *The economic impact of Jacksonville State University on Calhoun and Etowah Counties*. Jacksonville, AL: Center for Economic Development and Business Research, College of Commerce and Business Administration, Jacksonville State University.

Sharma, V. P. (1982). *Economic impacts of Mankato State University on the local area economy*. Mankato, MN: Department of Economics, Mankato State University.

Sheehan, J. (1973). *The economics of education*. London: George Allen and

Unwin.
Showers, R. (1989). *Economic impact study*. St. Joseph: Missouri Western State College.
Slaughter, S. (1989). *The higher learning and high technology: Dynamics of higher education policy formation*. Albany, NY: State University of New York Press.
Soderlind, S. D. (1986). *Economic consequences of St. Olaf College*. Northfield, MN: Department of Economics, St. Olaf College.
Stokes, C. J., & Stokes, K. B. (No date). *Economic impact of the University of Bridgeport on the Bridgeport area*. Bridgeport, CT: Division of University Relations, University of Bridgeport.
Story, H. J., & Longhurst, D. (1988). *The economic impact of Pacific University on the Greater Forest Grove–Cornelius area*. Forest Grove, OR: Pacific University.
Technical Systems, Inc. (No date). *Economic impact of the member institutions of the Minnesota Private College Council on the State of Minnesota–Individual Reports–FY 1986–College of St. Thomas*. St. Louis, MO.
Technology Transfer Newsletter. (1987). Tucson: University of Arizona, pp. 1, 4.
TJS Associates. (No date). *A study of the economic impact of South Carolina State College upon the Orangeburg community*. Summerville, SC.
University of California, Santa Cruz. (1988). *The University of California and its economic impact on the Santa Cruz community*. Santa Cruz: The University of California, Santa Cruz.
University of Maine. (1989). *The economic impact on the greater Bangor area of the activities of the University of Maine*. Bangor: Office of Financial Management, University of Maine.
University of Oregon. (1988). *Economic impact of the University of Oregon*. Eugene: Office of Public Affairs and Development, University of Oregon.
Wall, M. B. (1989). *Ithaca College*. Ithaca, NY: Ithaca College.
Yi, P. S. (1984). *A study of the economic impact of West Virginia University on the local community*. Morgantown: Office of Institutional Research, West Virginia University.

10 MEASURING THE REGIONAL ECONOMIC EFFECTS OF FEDERAL RESEARCH GRANTS

Rebecca Dorsett Goodman and William C. Weiler

A public university provides many benefits to its state. It provides diverse cultural and scholarly contributions to society at large. By instructing students in specific technical and general evaluative skills, it develops their human capital. Ideally, the end result is a sophisticated work force ready to meet the demands of a complex, modern economy. Jones and Vedlitz (1988) discuss how state government spending on higher education translates into higher income, income per capita, and net business establishments. Spending on a university is thus viewed as an investment in the state's economic future.

Universities also contribute more immediate economic benefits to their states by attracting funds from agencies outside the state, particularly the federal government. These federal funds are used to employ researchers and research support personnel at the university. Further, the distribution of those funds for salaries and supply and equipment purchases produces a chain of subsequent spending that generates income and employment beyond the initial impact. This chapter measures the economic impact of federal research grants on state's economy. By including only federal research dollars in our analysis, we can more clearly measure the economic stimulus of the university.[1] State research dollars, if not awarded to the university, will most likely be spent elsewhere in the state; the resulting economic benefits would not be unique to the university.

The estimation of the total economic impact of various types of university expenditures, including research grants, has been undertaken in a number of studies.[2] Our approach to measuring this impact incorporates two specific suggestions made by Bourque and Pedersen (1977). First, we assume that some goods and services are imported from other states. Assuming that no goods and services are imported will lead to an overstatement of the economic impact. Second, we are careful in how we associate institutional expenditures with spending categories in the input-output model. In addition to these two suggestions, we discuss the important subject of displacement, or the extent to which federal research grant expenditures represent a net increase in final demand rather than supplanting other state production. Our results demonstrate how different assumptions regarding displacement can lead to significant differences in the income and employment impacts.

This chapter discusses how these issues can be addressed with available data and input-output multipliers. The points are illustrated with the estimation of income and employment impacts within Minnesota that results from federally funded research grants in 1985–1986 at the University of Minnesota. The discussion of the input-output framework used in our analysis focuses on the benefits of using multipliers and other results from a two-region input-output model instead of the more common one-region model. The use of a two-region model is shown to be particularly beneficial when dealing with the issue of imports. Unfortunately, the base year of the two-region model utilized in our study is 1978. Since this is six years prior to the federal research grant data, our results will be distorted to the extent there were significant changes in price levels and productivity during this period. We do not provide analytic estimates of the extent of displacement but instead show the alternative impacts of assumptions regarding its levels. Our numerical results indicate that significant differences in the estimates of income and employment benefits can result from alternative resolution of the issues, particularly displacement. However, even conservative assumptions yield substantial benefits beyond the immediate impact of additional employment at the university.

The Two-Region Input-Output Model

Input-output theory stresses the interdependence of the producing sectors of a state's economy.[3] Since output from one sector may be an input to another, a change in demand for the output of a single industry effects each of the other industries in the state. The input-output framework permits us to estimate the total effect on sales and employment within Minnesota given the expenditures associated with federal research grants.

The total impact can be divided into two types of effects. Money received for university research is expended on staff salaries, supplies, and equipment. The direct effects are simply the first round of income and employment generated by these expenditures. These initial expenditures then generate a chain of further spending on additional goods and services. The indirect effects are the income and employment generated by these successive rounds of spending.

The fundamental identity of input-output analysis is that the gross output of an industry is the sum of its sales to each of the other industries for their use in output production and sales to final demands—consumption, investment, export, and so on. The formal algebraic representation of this relationship for n industries in a region is

$$X = AX + Y, \tag{10.1}$$

where: X = an $n \times 1$ vector of regional industry outputs in the producing sectors;

A = an $n \times n$ matrix of technical coefficients whose elements a_{ik} indicate the proportion of industry i's output absorbed in production of industry k's output (A is often called the transactions matrix) and;

Y = an $n \times 1$ vector of final demands.

We can solve equation (10.1) to relate industry outputs to final demands as

$$X = (I - A)^{-1}Y \tag{10.2}$$

where I is the $n \times n$ identity matrix. The elements b_{ik} of the matrix $(I - A)^{-1}$ are the interdependency coefficients that denote the change in output in industry i associated with a one-unit change in final demand for the output of the kth industry. Since expenditures from research grants constitute final demands, equation (10.2) allows us to estimate the total change in the output of each industrial sector resulting from externally financed research grant expenditures. The change in employment in an industry is then calculated by multiplying the left-hand side of (10.2) by the ratio of employment to output in that industry.

In determining the net impact of research expenditures on the Minnesota economy, we must allow for expenditures on products that are produced outside the state. In studies that use a one-region input-output model, the estimation of imports constitutes a serious problem. Although the data requirements of these models are not overly demanding, a one-region model treats imports as one of the elements of X—that is, as a single row in the transactions matrix. Hence, the imports in each industry are not determined within the model but must be estimated by other methods.[4]

Bourque and Pedersen (1977) suggest that the estimates can be obtained directly by examining university vouchers and personal consumption expenditure patterns to delete payments for goods and services purchased outside the state. However, the sample of vouchers required to produce accurate estimates would be large because expenditure patterns differ substantially depending on the area of research. Aside from being time consuming, this option will overstate the impact of the indirect effects because no adjustments are made for imports in industries involved in secondary transactions. Another alternative would be to assume that imports account for the same proportion of total expenditures in each industry and to calculate the proportion from the relation of imports to total final demand in all industries in the transactions matrix. This method can also result in serious distortions because the estimate may bear no relationship to the actual proportion imported in the specific industries associated with research contract expenditures.

In contrast to the one-region model, a two-region input-output model treats similar industries in other regions as distinct individual industries. A complete transactions matrix is constructed for both regions, along with matrices recording the trade flows between industries across the two regions. The total effects estimated from such a model are more reliable, since both the direct and indirect effects take account of the proportion imported from the second region for each specific industry. In our computations we use a two-region model, with Minnesota as one region and the rest of the United States as the other.[5]

Data Sources and Data Issues

The primary data sources for this study were University of Minnesota financial records. Using these records, we translated items of expenditures for research grants net of salaries into the input-output industrial categories.[6] We found that there was little ambiguity in relating university expenditure classifications to industrial category definitions. We did assume, however, that grant expenditures net of salaries largely were made through wholesalers in contrast to salary expenditures that would be made entirely through retailers.[7]

The manner in which university records were kept made two assumptions necessary. We could not easily distinguish federal grant purchases of particular goods and services categories from other grant purchases (state, local, business). Using the combined data, we took a fixed percentage of each category and assumed that pattern of expenditures from federal grants was not different from that of nonfederal grants. As federal grants constitute 60 percent of all grants, this assumption is unlikely to change our results. The second assumption involved the allocation of indirect cost recovery funds to expenditures items. Because indirect cost recoveries are merged with general operations and maintenance funds at the University of Minnesota, we allocated them according to the expenditures of all operations and maintenance funds.

The total salaries paid to researchers and research support personnel by rank or job title were also available from university records. Neither university records nor the data for the input-output model provided any clues regarding spending patterns from these salaries. To estimate expenditures by industrial category, we initially classified salaries into four income categories depending on the average salary in the rank or job title category. We then estimated the expenditures from each income category for a number of items based on the Bureau of Labor Statistics 1986 national survey of consumer expenditures patterns (1988). The survey expenditure items were then classified into the industrial categories of the input-output model.

Before estimating the impact of research grants on the Minnesota economy, one important issue must still be considered. The issue is the desirability of subtracting from in-state production activity related to the university's federally funded research grants all resulting displacements of other state production. It can reasonably be assumed that most of the resources, including personnel, that contribute to the university's research have alternative employment opportunities inside or outside Minnesota. This is certainly the case at full employment and is likely even during moderate unemployment. If the response to spending from a federal grant is primarily from resources that would otherwise be employed within the state, the grant's net effect on the state economy would be minimal. The larger the proportion of the resources, including personnel, purchased by grant expenditures that would otherwise be employed outside the state, the larger the impact of the grants on the state's economy.

The relative size of the displacement effect is not clear a priori. An argument suggesting that the displacement effect of federal research grants is large is that political forces may tend to provide each state with an aggregate share of federal spending. Hence, federal grant expenditures may only replace federal spending in some other program. However, this argument ignores the fact that much of the university research supported by federal grants requires critical specialized personnel, equipment, and facilities. Personnel, and to a lesser extent, equipment, are mobile, but facilities are not. For this reason federal research grants may enjoy some measure of political independence, with the implication that displacement effects are more modest.

Within the scope of this study we were unable to estimate these displacement effects directly, although it might be possible to investigate this issue further. In our results we computed alternative estimates of the income and employment impacts of federal research grants based on alternative assumptions regarding the unknown displacement effects. In all cases we assumed that the faculty employed as researchers on federal contracts would be employed in other states because of the national labor markets in which most researchers work. We assumed alternatively that 25, 50, and 100 percent of the expenditures for nonfaculty employees and for products and services purchased from grants represent net increases in resources expended in Minnesota. The usual (implicit) assumption made in other studies is that 100 percent of the research expenditures represent new resources attracted into the state. We show the results of this assumption only for comparison purposes because it always yields an overestimate of the local impact of these expenditures.

Income and Employment Estimates

Our results are displayed in two tables. The estimates in table 10–1 illustrate the distinction between the initial and total effects of research grants on income and employment in each of 34 industrial sectors of the Minnesota economy, including "University Research," under the 25 percent assumption described earlier. This type of data display is common to all studies of the economic benefits of university expenditures, although the displacement assumption used in constructing the table is specifically a result of the issues discussed here.

When interpreting the employment and expenditure impacts for each sector, two points should be noted. First, the columns for direct effects show the impacts of research grants alone, while the columns for total impacts show these initial impacts plus the effects of the succeeding chain of spending by the industries receiving the initial expenditures. Second, we can sum the separate employment effects in each industry to arrive at the total change in state employment resulting from research grants.

Table 10–1. Expenditure and Employment Impacts 1985–1986

Industry	*Direct Effect on Expenditures*	*Total Effect on Expenditures*	*Direct Effect on Employment*	*Total Effect on Employment*
Agriculture, forestry, fishing, mining	$ 179,120	$ 471,548	15	27
Construction	98,559	634,178	2	18
Food products	18,316	391,087	0	4
Textiles	2,039	44,235	0	3
Lumber & furniture	10,455	42,163	0	1
Pulp & paper	29,348	291,707	1	13
Printing & publishing	197,982	622,133	7	21
Chemicals	34,876	179,506	0	2
Petroleum refining, stone, clay & glass	68,839	353,524	2	6
Rubber products	540,245	568,346	14	15
Primary & fabricated metals	24,168	266,225	1	7
Machinery	2,258	120,640	0	3
Electronic & office machinery	452,675	562,287	11	13
Electrical equipment	19,199	194,212	0	5
Motor vehicles	4,197	56,613	0	1
Engineering, scientific, medical & dental equip.	192,967	258,618	9	11
Misc. manufacturing	27,700	84,069	1	3
Railroad, pipeline transportation	26,913	102,118	1	4
Local transit	527,523	560,302	26	28
Truck transportation	81,356	262,059	3	10
Water transportation	29,533	43,314	2	2

Table 10–1. (Cont.)

Industry	*Direct Effect on Expenditures*	*Total Effect on Expenditures*	*Direct Effect on Employment*	*Total Effect on Employment*
Air transportation	119,132	203,715	3	5
Transportation services	0	4,092	0	0
Communication, utilities	1,127,622	2,075,298	20	35
Wholesale trade	0	395,938	0	19
Retail trade	6,036,975	6,106,187	566	572
Finance, insurance, & real estate	4,763,055	7,077,139	113	175
Hotel, restaurants, personal services	1,859,498	2,426,865	193	245
Business services	806,548	1,709,480	25	52
Professional services	310,897	528,926	9	16
Medical & educational services	1,320,973	1,411,193	128	137
Federal government	64,841	245,156	0	0
State & local government	306,710	652,456	0	1
University research	23,363,512	23,363,512	924	924
Totals	—	—	2,076	2,378

Notes: In constructing this table adjustment was made for products and services purchased outside Minnesota. It was assumed that 25 percent of the expenditures for nonfaculty personnel, products, and services represented a net addition to expenditures that would be made in Minnesota in the absence of federal grants.

However, the expenditures cannot analogously be summed across industries because the total for one industry includes goods and services sold to other industries as inputs. This multiple counting of the same outputs makes the sum not meaningful as a measure of the change in total state output resulting from grant expenditures.

Clearly, the largest employment gain is in the retail trade sector. Because employment per dollar of retail sales is high, this sector includes about 45 percent of the employment impacts outside direct university employment. Other large employment impacts are in hotels, restaurants, and personal services (including local lodging and meals for consultants); finance, insurance, and real estate (space rental, payroll insurance premiums, and expenditures on housing); and medical and educational services.

The results in table 10–2 show the variation in the estimated economic impacts resulting from alternative assumptions regarding imports and displacement effects. The first row in the table incorporates the implicit assumptions made in most other studies. All expenditures are for products produced in the state, and all grant expenditures represent a net increase in federal spending in the state. The second row corrects for imports from outside the state. The last two rows include this adjustment plus assumptions about displacement of other state production.

Table 10–2. Direct and Total Employment Estimates Under Alternative Assumptions, 1985–1986

*Assumptions**		*Employment*		
Adjustment for Imports	*Net Increase in Resources Expended in Minnesota*	*Direct Research Employment*	*All Direct Employment*	*Total Employment*
N	100	1631	4754	5652
Y	100	1631	4624	5445
Y	50	1160	2522	2908
Y	25	924	2076	2378

* The codes for the assumptions are as follow. An N for imports indicates that all expenditures are assumed spent in Minnesota, and a Y indicates that expenditures have been adjusted for products in other states or countries. The number in the second column is the assumed percentage of the expenditures for non-faculty personnel, products, and services purchased from grants that represents a net increase in expenditures in Minnesota. In each case we assume that all faculty employed as researchers would otherwise be employed outside the state. The last row incorporates the assumptions used to construct table 10–1.

For each set of assumptions we show three employment estimates: the direct employment for "University Research," the direct employment in all industrial sectors including "University Research," and the total direct and indirect employment in all industrial sectors. The estimated total employment increase in Minnesota is at least 250 percent of the direct employment of research personnel at the university for all assumptions. These results indicate that calculating only the direct effects will seriously underestimate the true employment impact of research grants under any assumptions.[8]

However, the total employment estimates differ markedly depending on the assumptions used. The direct and total employment numbers in the first row are about 2.4 times as large as the comparable figures in the last row. In analyzing the differences we note that the failure to control for imports alone (compare the first two rows) yields only a modest (4 percent) increase in total employment. This occurs because salary expenditures, which are 60 percent of total grant expenditures, are primarily spent with retail merchants in the state and because about 75 percent of supply and equipment expenditures are spent for products produced in Minnesota. Almost all of the difference results from the different assumptions about displacement. These substantial differences in the estimated employment impacts may justify the expense of researching the degree to which spending from research grants results in resources drawn from competing uses outside the state.

Acknowledgments

This is a revised and updated version of an earlier study (Dorsett and Weiler 1982). We thank Daniel Pierro for computational assistance and Colleen T. Davidson for editorial assistance.

Endnotes

1. All dollars flowing into a university that would not otherwise be spent in its state represent a pure economic stimulus. Examples include grants from businesses, industries, and private individuals located outside the state. Had these data been accessible, we would have incorporated them into our calculations.

2. See Bonner (1968), Booth and Jarrett (1976), Lillis and Tonkovich (1976), and the references therein for a more complete discussion. Most of the authors use in their analyses multipliers developed from input-output models for estimation of the economic benefits of the particular types of spending. The study most similar to our work is by Lillis and Tonkovich (1976), which measured the impact of research grants awarded to Washington

State University on the Washington economy. Leslie and Brinkmann (1988), reviewing various types of economic impact studies, point out that input-output analysis yields accurate results but has stringent data requirements. Consequently, most authors use the economic base approach (the "standard" method of Caffrey and Isaacs, 1971). A cursory review of the literature since our original 1982 article shows no new input-output analyses.

3. Input-output analysis was developed by Leontief (1953). The discussion here is brief, but for an excellent description of the use of input-output theory in analyzing regional economic impacts, see Richardson (1973).

4. The question of allowance for purchases made outside the state is the most important issue raised in Bourque and Pedersen (1977). Lillis and Tonkovich (1976) implicitly assume that no goods and services are imported, which can result in a significant overestimate of both the direct and indirect effects.

5. This model was initially developed in 1966 by Donald Beard and others of the Northern Natural Gas Company. The two-region model has subsequently been updated using 1978 as the base year (see Hwang and Maki 1979).

6. Most of the industrial categories utilized are "two-digit" categories from the *Standard Industrial Classification Manual* (1967).

7. The issue of the classification of expenditures made from salaries is also raised in Bourque and Pedersen (1977).

8. Our results are all computed from the two-region model. It would be of interest to compare them to those from a one-region model, but a one-region model built with 1978–1979 data is not available for Minnesota.

References

Bonner, E. R. (1968). The economic impact of a university on its local community. *Journal of the American Institute of Planners 34*, 339–343.

Booth, G. G., & Jarrett, J. E. (1976). The identification and estimation of a university's economic impacts. *Journal of Higher Education 47*, 565–576.

Bourque, P., & Pedersen, D. (1977). The impact of importation of grant and research money on a state economy comment. *Journal of Higher Education 48*, 343–348.

Caffrey, J., & Issacs, H. (1971). *Estimating the impact of a college or university.* Washington, D.C.: American Council on Education.

Dorsett, R. A., & Weiler, W. C. (1982). The impact of an institution's federal research grants on the economy of its state. *Journal of Higher Education 53*, 419–428.

Hwang, H., & Maki, W. (1979). *User's guide to the Minnesota two-region input-output model* (REIFS Report No. 9). St. Paul; Department of Agricultural and Applied Economics, University of Minnesota.

Jones, B. D., & Vedlitz, A. (1988). Higher education policies and economic growth in the American states. *Economic Development Quarterly 2*, 78–87.

Leontief, W. (Ed.). (1953). *Studies on the structure of the American economy.* Fair Lawn, NJ: Oxford University Press.

Leslie, L. L., & Brinkman, P. T. (1988). *The economic value of higher education.*

New York: American Council on Education and Macmillan.

Lillis, C., & Tonkovich, D. (1976). The impact of importation of grant and research money on a state economy. *Journal of Higher Education 47*, 577–587.

Richardson, E. R. (1973). *Regional growth theory*. New York: Wiley.

U.S. Bureau of the Budget. (1967). *Standard industrial classification manual.* Washington, D.C.: Bureau of the Budget, Office of Statistical Standards.

U.S. Department of Labor. (1988). *Consumer expenditure survey series: Interview survey 1986*. Washington, D.C.: U.S. Department of Labor, Bureau of Labor Statistics.

11 THE AMBIGUOUS LINK: PRIVATE INDUSTRY AND UNIVERSITY RESEARCH

Roger L. Geiger

During the 1980s research relationships between universities and private industry assumed greater salience than ever before. One view, prominent in Washington, has identified these relationships as keys to enhancing the competitiveness of American industries. On the state and local levels, this same theme has been invoked for purposes of regional development. Both these expectations depend on *technology transfer*, the catchall term for moving the findings of university laboratories into the productive economy. Universities, for their part, have been increasingly eager to encourage these relationships, in part to augment support for research and also to curry favor with powerful constituencies. Faculty, most of whom stand outside of any ties with private industry, have been conspicuously distrustful of this trend. But industry, on the whole, has responded positively to the receptivity of academic laboratories. In each case, actions and rhetoric rest on expectations that are to some extent problematic. The expansion of research relationships between universities and industry during the 1980s has raised questions with respect to their cost, efficacy, and incidental effects. These matters need to be placed in a larger historical context, however, in order to distinguish the old from the new and what is valuable from what is worrisome.

The Historical Pattern

Academic and industrial research developed separately, each according to its own tradition. Only gradually in the first decades of the twentieth century were linkages forged between these two realms. Sustained, organized research by private corporations began in the two principal technological industries, electricity and chemicals. The first industrial laboratory was established in 1900 by General Electric, and AT&T followed in 1907. Research laboratories in the chemical industry were begun in 1902 by DuPont and in 1912 by American Cyanamid and Eastman Kodak.

Only the conduct of advanced research brought about the need of contacts with university science. At first, the chief concern of firms was with personnel – locating and hiring scientists with training in these emerging fields. AT&T began underwriting the costs of the electrical engineering course at MIT in 1913, Corning Glass sponsored fellowships in areas related to glass making, and DuPont's first support for universities came in the form of graduate fellowships. Industrial laboratories for testing, assaying, or tinkering preceded those for research (Mowery and Rosenberg 1989). Only later would industry develop an interest in basic research itself (Noble 1977; Weart 1976).

By the turn of the century the American university had emerged as the foremost locus of basic scientific research. A multipurpose institution, the university combined liberal and professional education with graduate study and research (Veysey 1965; Geiger 1990, 1986). It was the size and the wealth of the enterprise as a whole that allowed a handful of these institutions to afford the critical and costly inputs to the latter activities – eminent and highly paid professors with time for research as well as the libraries, laboratories, and other needed accountrements. The American university thus relied on its own resources to generate a capacity for research, but, because its revenues were largely derived directly or indirectly from instruction, it had few resources to devote to research per se. During the nineteenth century, universities had relied on separate endowments to support purely scientific work in observatories and museums. Individual professors had to find research support for themselves through gifts, subscriptions, or, more likely, their personal resources (Geiger 1986). Despite the growing affluence of the twentieth-century university, these conditions would not change: Universities would have to seek support for most academic research outside their walls.

For schools of engineering within universities and the independent institutes of technology, the natural constituency was private industry. Engineering education took off in terms of enrollments in the 1890s, but research was slower to develop. The Massachusetts Institute of Technology was precocious in this respect. It established a research laboratory and a graduate program in 1903. Then in 1908 it founded the Research Laboratory of Applied Chemistry, the first academic unit dedicated to performing research for industry (Servos 1980). It was not until after the First World War, however, that the research nexus between universities and industry was firmly joined.

The mobilization of American science for the war effort, brief though it was, caused a new and enduring appreciation for the place of research in an industrial economy. The new mood, moreover, received a permanent embodiment in the National Research Council (f. 1916). After the war, the NRC functioned as a kind of trade associaton for science, bringing together leaders from industry, government, foundations, and the universities. One of its chief concerns was to promote closer interaction between industry and university research (Geiger 1986, pp. 95–100). It propounded an uncomplicated view of this relationship: Basic research, the main function of universities, was the fount for applied research in industry and economic progress. The NRC also held that the support and direction of the nation's research should be the responsibility of private institutions rather than government. Accordingly, it urged industrial firms to support university research without regard for immediate commercial applications. An attempt was actually launched to realize this idealistic view. During the last half of the 1920s a campaign was conducted to raise a national research fund for universities through million-dollar contributions from major corporations. Only a few of the targeted donors could be cajoled into pledges, and the scheme eventually was swamped entirely by the depression (Davis and Kevles 1974). The NRC vision of American business supporting pure research in universities because of its long-range benefits for the economy would not set the pattern for this relationship.

The interwar years nevertheless did witness the emergence of a privately funded research economy for universities—recurrent external support for research available to universities in general. The bulk of this support came from the large, general-purpose philanthropic foundations that embraced the advancement of knowledge as a fundamental purpose (Geiger 1986). The several trusts that were consolidated into the Rockefeller Foundation (1929) provided most of the funding for research-related purposes in the 1920s, and the Carnegie Corporation also contributed. Their conception of the role of university research was consistent with that of the NRC; that is, they felt that the academy should concentrate on basic research and they tended to frown on direct university involvement with applied research for industry. If any institution embodied the "correct" relationship between industry and unviersities, it was the California Institute of Technology. It developed during the 1920s through extensive support from both foundations and individuals from the Southern California business community. Caltech focused largely on basic research, but it also cultivated fields that were relevant to local industries. Caltech was able to enter the ranks of research universities as a result of business-connected philanthropy rather than the provision of direct services to industry (Geiger 1986; Kargon 1982).

Even while the foundations were marking and underwriting the high road for academic research, an abundance of direct research relationships with industry also emerged. These relationships can be divided into two general types, depending on whether the collaboration was through individual scientists or within special organizations specifically designed for this end.

The use of academic scientists as consultants to industry developed out of the need for industrial laboratories to have access to advanced academic research. Such access depended, above all, on individual university scientists. They thus became the centerpoint in a larger sphere of activities (Swann 1988). Corporations had to make concerted efforts to learn who was doing what in their fields of interest, for example, visiting university labs, attending scientific meetings, and maintaining an active mailing list. Once potentially valuable individuals were identified, they could be utilized in several ways. Some served as special, per diem consultants brought in to help on specific problems, while others managed to become long-term, general consultants acting as advisers to an entire research department. From the latter type, in particular, the company expected more than advice on specific projects. The scientist's laboratory might be an important source for recruiting personnel, or fellowships might be awarded for research under that person's general supervision. In general, the more scientific research conducted in-house, the greater a firm's need to maintain contact with academic researchers. These contacts, then, comprised far more than direct support for research. Enterprising scientists in many subjects learned to enhance their own research programs with assistance from industry.

Specific university units for conducting industrial research developed separately according to different models. MIT's Research Laboratory of Applied Chemistry was a prototype. The Mellon Institute of Industrial Research, which was originally connected with the University of Pittsburgh (1913–1927), was another variation on this theme. In 1916 Congress failed to pass a bill that would have provided funding for engineering experiment stations, similar to the agricultural experiment stations supported by the Hatch Act (1887), but the attempt undoubtedly heightened the popularity of the concept. Many states established these units after the war, but the amounts of research actually performed varied widely. One of the most successful of these was the Department of Engineering Research at the University of Michigan, which performed $300,000 in contract research in 1929–1930 (National Resources Planning Board 1940, pp. 71–72; Kevles 1971, pp. 182–87; Uhlendorf 1958, pp. 1243–1251; Geiger 1986, 311*n*).

The engineering research units were able to develop and thrive by performing services for industry largely because they were separate compartments within compartmentalized institutions. They complemented the interests of some of the faculty in these areas and provided employment and experience for students. The institution benefited from these activities and from being able to acquire equipment it could not otherwise afford. Faculty in the purely academic portions of the university do not seem to have been perturbed by these undertakings. This kind of research relationship also forced institutions to deal systematically with externally funded research. At MIT, for example, the Division of Industrial Cooperation and Research was established to administer sponsored research, and at Michigan the Department of Engineering Research later evolved into such an office (Foster 1984; Swan 1988; and National Resources Planning Board 1940).

The two kinds of research links with industry had somewhat different intellectual bases and subsequent histories. In the research institutes universities offered some fairly mundane services that overlapped at least partially with those that might be purchased through independent laboratories or conducted in-house by large firms. Such research, in other words, did not depend on the expert knowledge of university faculty. Moreover, since these services tended to be closely linked with product development, they would be moved within the firm whenever feasible. Contacts with individual academic scientists, on the other hand, were more integral to the conduct of science-based industry because they buttressed internal research with expert advice and recruitment. There was thus a crucial difference between hired-out research services and ties with university scientists: As firms expanded their internal R&D efforts, the former would be superseded, while the latter would acquire increasing importance. In general terms, this seems to have happened. Except for the worst years of the depression (1931–1933), in-house industrial R&D expanded greatly during the 1930s. Consulting arrangements appear to have grown as well, particularly in technologically dynamic industries like pharmaceuticals, but the engineering research institutes saw their activity decrease in the early 1930s and never recovered their former vigor (Noble 1977, pp. 142–144; Geiger 1986, pp. 186–187; Blumenthal et al. 1986*a*, pp. 1621–1626). This decline is evidenced by cases such as that of the Engineering Research Institute at Michigan and the Research Laboratory of Applied Chemistry at MIT (Foster 1984; Uhlendorf 1958).

By the end of the interwar years, the relationship between industry and academic research had developed some clearly defined features. First and most important, university-generated knowledge seemed to have become a vital complement to the growing sphere of research within industry. Second, within the universities, research relationships had developed quite naturally within those fields of knowledge where interests and practices brought close interaction with industry. These included engineering, chemistry, pharmacy, medicine, and business economics. Third, for the universities as a whole, ways had already been found to exploit the connections with industry for institutional support. Here too, the universities exhibited organizational inventiveness: MIT pioneered these efforts with the Technology Plan; Caltech tapped business leaders through its Associates Plan; and the Wisconsin Alumni Research Foundation (WARF) was built on patent earnings. When changes in the tax laws made corporate philanthropy deductible (1935), another possibility was opened. Finally, despite multiplying links, there existed a strong sense of the appropriateness of keeping academic and commercial activities separate. An exceedingly sympathetic source wrote in 1940, "The proper relationship between the university and industry in the matter of industrial research is . . . a difficult one to determine and perhaps an even more difficult one to maintain" (National Resources Planning Board 1940, p. 39). This was perhaps most evident in the general hostility toward academic patenting and toward the indirect mechanisms that were erected to maintain this separation in situations, like WARF, where patenting was deemed expedient (Weiner 1987). These fundamental features of university–industry links remain relevant to the contemporary situation.

Industry Support for University Research: Stability and Change

During and after World War II university research was transformed by the infusion of previously unimaginable amounts of federal funding (Geiger forthcoming). Research relationships between industry and universities, however, were relatively unaffected by this great change because industrially sponsored university research arose from the nature and needs of industry-based research. To understand how industry utilized university research, then, requires some understanding of how industry transforms knowledge into products. This is a far more complex matter than is commonly assumed. Recent work by Richard R. Nelson (1989) on technological change offers some plausible and helpful distinctions on this subject.

Technology, according to Nelson, consists of both "generic knowledge," which is relatively public for those in the field, and "practiced techniques," which are acquired through investment and experience and hence are inherently private in nature. Generic knowledge consists of more than scientific theory; it comprises as well the understanding of the physical equipment and processes required to put knowledge to work. Many modern fields of academic inquiry, like computer science or chemical engineering, are based on the systematic study of such factors. Technique consists of hard-won knowledge of how to transform generic knowledge into actual products and is thus only transferable at a significant cost. Given key generic knowledge, Nelson found, the most important factor for firms in the development of products tended to be a head start in the lengthy efforts to fashion techniques. Development, in this sense, is thus a major focus of the process of technological innovation in industry. Patents play a circumscribed role in this process: They are necessary to protect innovations in those industries in which the composition of products (chemical or mechanical) is easily defined and delimited. More generally, where new generic knowledge functions as the springboard for a fast start on product development, patenting plays much less of a role.

One function of universities in this scenario is to contribute to the creation of generic knowledge. Numerous university departments exist to address the scientific underpinnings of technological fields, and these are the areas where collaboration flourishes. But the university's contribution should not be exaggerated. Nelson underlines the fact that firms must engage in their own R&D if they are to have the capacity to draw on the research of others; they must know what questions to ask and be able to understand the answers. Industrial research thus also contributes to the propagation of generic knowledge. Such knowledge is readily transmitted among those who comprehend the field. Academic and industrial scientists are trained in the same graduate schools, work on many of the same problems, read the same journals, and attend the same meetings. It would be odd indeed if industrial researchers did not tap into the work of their academic counterparts. For industry, university research supplements the generic component of technology, and even here the universities provide one link, although often a fundamental one, in a lengthy chain of effort.

This view of the relationship between academic research and industrial technology coincides with many of the depictions that appear in the literature (Mowery and Rosenberg 1989; Simeral 1983; Williams 1986). It is also consistent with the broad configurations of R&D activity. According to recent estimates, in 1989 industry performed 86 percent of development work in the United States and supported 62 percent of that with its own funds. Industry also funded nearly 39 percent of the nation's research (applied and basic), 93 percent of which was also performed internally. American universities, for their part, performed over half of the nation's basic research and 13 percent of the applied, but only 1 percent of development. The intersection of these two substantial efforts is nevertheless small: Over 6 percent of university research was funded by industry, and industry turned to universities for over 4 percent of its research needs (National Science Foundation 1989). The relationship between universities and industry clearly concerns research and not development. Table 11–1 accordingly depicts this historical relationship solely in terms of basic and applied research.

The consistent nature of industrial research is evident from these figures. For more than a generation industry's contribution to the national research effort has remained in the 30 percent range (column B). It touched the low end in the early 1960s, when the federal government vastly increased its support for research following Sputnik. Even during

Table 11–1. Industry Support for Research, Basic and Applied: 1955–1989

	A	*B*	*C*	*D*	*E*
	Industry Supported Research: National Total ($000,000)	*Industry Supported Research: % U.S. Research*	*Industry Supported Research: % of GNP*	*Industry Supported Research: % in Universities*	*University Research: % Support by Industry*
1955	773	38.1	0.19	3.10	8.0
1960	1,568	37.2	0.30	2.36	6.2
1965	2,115	30.7	0.30	1.84	2.8
1970	3,041	32.3	0.29	2.23	2.6
1975	4,222	33.9	0.26	2.51	3.3
1980	7,967	35.7	0.29	2.79	3.9
1985	14,583	38.1	0.35	3.35	5.8
1989 (est.)	17,760	38.7	0.34	4.79	6.6

Source: Adapted from National Science Foundation (1989).

these years, industrial research was stable as a proportion of GNP (column C). This last figure dropped to a low point in the mid-1970s. Then, from the late 1970s to the mid-1980s, industrial research exhibited a significant acceleration relative to total national research (which also rose) and GNP. There was a widespread belief that industrial support of basic research declined markedly in the 1960s, as evidenced by Roy (1972) and Smith and Karlesky (1977). Industrial spending for basic research was flat in real terms during the middle and late 1960s, and then declined about 15 percent by 1975. Total industrial spending for applied research grew moderately during these years.

The most variable feature of industrial research has been its relations with universities (columns D and E). Industry utilization of universities fell to a nadir in the late 1960s and then slowly recovered throughout the 1970s. It then continued to rise in the 1980s, particularly after 1985. This variability is the result of substitution. Industrial technology may have an inherent requirement for generic knowledge, but firms do not necessarily need to seek it in universities. They can adjust the amount of research they do in-house, and they can also turn to various commercial or nonprofit laboratories. Until 1975 industry funded more research in nonprofits than in universities. If only basic research is considered, nonprofit performance of industrial research was roughly comparable with that done by universities until the late 1970s, and actually exceeded universities from 1963 to 1970. Since about 1980 the balance has shifted markedly: In 1989 the university totals were more than double those for other nonprofits. The importance of industrial funding for university research has also grown during this span—from 3.3 percent for all university research in 1975 to 6.6 percent in 1989 (column E). More startling is the decided change in the historical pattern of research purchases by industry (column D).

Explanations for these changes may be sought on both sides of this relationship. Within industry the increased research activity has largely been due to the emergence or expansion of research-intensive industries. Industrial R&D held steady as a percentage of sales in the last half of the 1970s but then increased from 1.9 percent in 1979 to 3.2 percent in 1986—a remarkable jump in so short a period. The largest increases occurred, respectively, in scientific instruments, pharmaceuticals, electronic components, and computers. The twin revolutions in biotechnology and microelectronics are fully evident here. Biotechnology, in particular, has had an unusually close relationship with university research. In microelectronics, on the other hand, industry may have been in advance of universities throughout much of the 1970s, but in the 1980s the universities have also become an important source of generic knowledge. These industries have certainly led the increased intercommunication between industrial and university laboratories, and they have been followed to a lesser degree by others such as petroleum, chemicals, and communications. (These industrial categories reflect NSF bookkeeping. For a discussion of research in different industries, see Peters and Fusfeld, 1983, and for research spending within specific industries, see the "R&D Scoreboard," which has appeared periodically in special issues of *Business Week*.)

The changes in university attitudes toward industry-sponsored research have roots in the 1970s. Cutbacks in federal funding for academic research caused hardships for universities early in the decade, and these conditions gradually made academic scientists more receptive to programmatic sources of support (Geiger 1989). These changes were accompanied by a recognition among policy makers of the desirability of restoring closer industry–university cooperation for purposes of contributing to economic development (Smith and Karlesky 1977). Despite good intentions, actual research relationships expanded only modestly during the decade: Industry's contribution to university research rose from 2.6 to 3.9 percent; the academic component of industrial research rose from 2.23 to 2.79 percent (table 11–1). But in the 1980s, as indicated, progress was dramatic. Initiatives by universities to accommodate and encourage greater cooperation with industry proliferated early in the decade (Fairweather 1988). This activity was accompanied by widespread examination of the issue at the highest levels. In 1980 the National Science Board specifically directed its attention to "university–industry research relationships." The leading research universities called a private meeting in 1982 to assess these relationships, which was followed later in the year by a larger, public forum. Two years later these same concerns prompted the formation of the Government-University-Industry Research Roundtable under the auspices of the National Academy of Sciences (National Science Board 1982, and Rosenzweig 1983).

When the developments in industry and those within universities are considered together, a two-stage process of change seems to have occurred. From the end of the 1970s to about 1985, the growth of university-industry cooperation appears to have been driven by the large absolute and relative increase in industrial research generally (columns A and C). University initiatives to encourage this cooperation raised its relative share only modestly (column D). Since 1985, however, industrial research has shown no relative growth (columns B and C), but the university share of that research has risen markedly, surpassing historical norms. The most likely cause of this unusual development would seem to be the proactive approach of universities, often assisted by government policies.

These trends demonstrate that there is substance behind the oft-repeated rhetoric about the importance of university–industry ties in research. The 1980s witnessed not only a persistence of the historical relationship but also some unprecedented additions. Specifically, the dramatic growth in science-based, or high technology, industries has increased the industrial consumption of research. But the changes in academe appear to be more far-reaching. Universities have been actively promoting the services they can render to business. For consuming corporations, universities have transformed themselves from vegetable stands into supermarkets. The next section will examine those measures that universities have taken, and the following section will consider why they have followed that course.

The New Organization of University–Industry Research Relationships

The proliferation of relationships between industry and universities has created a problem of classification, which itself masks a deeper issue of comprehension and interpretation. Several typologies have been offered, but each is probably best suited to its athor's purposes (for examples: Peters and Fusfeld 1983; Johnson 1984; Fairweather 1988). Connections between university research and the realm of industry nevertheless seem to fall into two distinct categories. The first could be regarded as an enlargement and elaboration of the historical relationship: industry seeking generic knowledge from university research. Universities—with some help from government—have been amazingly resourceful in devising organizational arrangements to facilitate this kind of interaction. But certain features remain fundamental. First, these relationships for the most part involve large, established corporations. Second, insofar as these ties contribute toward economic development or industrial competitiveness, they do so through the intermediation of the internal research and development capacities of industrial firms. Third, universities benefit from these ties pricipally through the strengthening of their own research capacity in terms of support for research, faculty, and laboratories. Because these interactions are all predicated on the transfer of generic knowledge, they can for convenience be placed under the rubric of "gnostic relationships."

The second class of relationships is somewhat removed from academic inquiry and functionally closer to the world of commerce. These links tend to be oriented toward the entrepreneurial pole of industry, where new products and new companies are brought to the marketplace. These activities are frequently justified in terms of their contribution to economic development, and hence they are presumed to provide benefits to the state, region, nation, or all of mankind. On the other hand, they are explicitly intended to be financially advantageous to the universities that sponsor them. Given this character, they might be summarized as "commercial relationships."

Gnostic Relationships

The communication of generic knowledge takes place most effectually through the interaction of individuals, and accordingly the most fundamental form of university–industry interaction occurs through the use of *consultants*. Although these links are between firms and individual faculty members, universities have encouraged them as benefiting student placement and keeping faculty in applied fields in touch with real-world problems. Universities, in any case, are in a poor position to oppose consulting. Perhaps most important from the university's perspective, faculty consulting frequently generates more enduring research relationships (Peters and Fusfeld 1983). For that reason, some universities have attempted to market the consulting services of their faculty in an organized way by providing inventories of faculty research expertise to companies. Specially created university centers (see below) sometimes are designed to offer consulting services on campus under university auspices.

Industry has also systematized consulting arrangements by creating *science advisory boards*. They have been described as "intelligence units," intended "to provide a firm with a window on the latest developments" (Kloppenberg 1988, p. 229). Membership on a science advisory board usually guarantees university scientists substantial benefits for themselves and their research. The general aim of augmenting the awareness of industrial researchers can also be served by programs of *personnel exchange* that bring the latter into a university research environment. It has become commonplace, for example, for scientists of pharmaceutical firms to serve as adjunct professors. Knowledge transfer generally is facilitated by the personal interaction of industrial and academic scientists, and numerous mechanisms have been utilized for this purpose, but faculty consulting remains the primordial and most essential link of this kind.

A corporation generally funds university research in areas likely to produce generic knowledge germane to its own research and development efforts. The firm will then possess a comparative advantage for any commercial exploitation. Discoveries, in other words, may help to provide the head start that industry so values on the lengthy process of developing products. The basic form of industrial support for university research is *contract research*. More than half of industrial-supported university research takes this form, and most often support is provided to faculty who also serve as consultants. Support for graduate students is often included, and an important expected benefit is identifying potential employees among graduate students who have worked on the right kinds of problems. Most industrial contracts are for relatively small amounts and are made on a year-to-year basis. Compared with the rigmarole of applying for and accounting for government research grants, support from industry is made in a relatively informal and trusting manner. The critical factor is whether the research that is funded has value for the company's own R&D effort. This determination does not require elaborate reporting or justification by the recipient, but rather it depends more on the subjective assessment of company representatives (Peters and Fusfeld 1983).

It is of considerable advantage from the university's point of view if contract research can be enlarged to provide more general kinds of support and lengthened to permit greater continuity in a research program. One way in which this can be done is through establishment of *research consortia*, which in their most simple form consist of an agreement among several companies to support a particular vein of research at a single university. Even more permanence can be achieved through *cooperative research centers*. These fairly recent creations may be distinguished from other university research centers (see below) by the existence of *industrial affiliate programs*. Sponsoring companies pay an annual fee to support the center and in return have privileged access to research results.

Both cooperatives and consortia have several features in common. First, the sponsors are given a prominent role in determining the nature and direction of the unit. Second, they are often encouraged by public subsidies through state and federal programs, which are often an important factor in bringing them into existence. Third, they tend to be focused on generic research rather than investigations likely to produce proprietary techniques. If patents do arise, fourthly, the agreements usually stipulate that they will be available to the sponsors on a royalty-free, nonexclusive basis. Finally, cooperative sponsorship seems more likely to thrive in industries in which patents, and hence secrecy, do *not* play a crucial role. Microelectronics, for example, seems amenable to cooperative research, but the drug industry does not (Peters and Fusfeld 1983).

In the pharmaceutical industry, large firms have met the challenge of having continuous access to generic academic research by entering into multimillion-dollar *long-term research contracts*. Monsanto pioneered this kind of arrangement in 1974 when it committed $23.5 million for cancer research at the Harvard Medical School over twelve years. There were no followers, however, until the 1980s. Then numerous contracts of this kind were signed between 1980 and 1983 (Kenney 1986). Almost all of these contracts were in the biomedical sciences, the exceptions being in energy. In light of such massive investments, the sponsors required carefully defined benefis. Generally, these agreements call for a high degree of personnel exchange, designed to enhance the company's in-house research; they stipulate that the sponsor will have exclusive worldwide licenses for all patentable discoveries; and, to protect this commercial potential, the sponsor has the right to prevent the disclosure of discoveries for a specified period of time. Such long-term contracts are still sufficiently novel that it is not yet clear whether they emerged as a devide for firms to enter or "catch up" in a rapidly emerging field (i.e., biotechnology), or whether they are rather a manifestation of the enlarging sphere of interaction between universities and industry. Kloppenberg (1988, p. 196) interprets long-term research contracts as one part of a four-part strategy of multinational corporations, which also includes the rapid development of in-house capabilities in biotechnology; acquiring access through equity interest to new biotechnology firms; and attempting to shape federal policies and legislation affecting ownership rights in this area.

One of the most prominent developments of the 1980s was the proliferation of university *research centers* focused on specific technologies and designed to attract industry support. Such centers can vary in their extent from letterhead operations to large permanent laboratories. In their typical form (university centers are truly protean) an industrially oriented center is interdisciplinary in its makeup and fairly applied in its research undertakings. University faculty participate voluntarily in the centers, meaning that the larger centers must have a permanent non-academic staff. The centers offer faculty opportunities to conduct research that they find congenial, access to sophisticated equipment, and supplemental income, as well as opportunities for graduate students. Functionally, these centers are equivalent to the prewar engineering research centers, but they differ in having a specialized focus. They also have the potential of serving smaller firms that do not have large in-house research operations. If the overused phrase technology transfer is anywhere appropriate, it would be in these technologically oriented research centers (Peters 1989).

One particular model of research center has been encouraged by the National Science Foundation since the late 1970s. "Industry–university cooperative research centers" were established from joint university–industry proposals. NSF provided 50 percent of the funding for up to five years, after which the centers are expected to be self-financing. In 1986, for example, NSF provided $3 million, while industry and state governments contributed $15 million each. The successful centers have been based on "generic technologies," such as communications or computers, or on "generic industrial functions," such as material handling (Powers et al. 1988).

The NSF built on its experience with cooperative research centers by sponsoring more ambitious *engineering research centers* beginning in 1985. The essential purpose behind these units was the need to strengthen research in engineering, especially with respect to manufacturing, in order to contribute to the improved competitiveness of American industry. University–industry research cooperation was thus one of several factors in their creation. Fourteen centers were awarded on a competitive basis from 1985 to 1987. NSF currently provides about half of their support, while industry contributes a third. Corporations have been attracted to participate chiefly because they found an affinity with their own research interests and because of the certified high quality that comes through NSF sponsorship (U.S. General Accounting Office 1988).

Commercial Relationships

This class of relations between higher education and industry involves patents, real estate, nurturing and owning new businesses, technical assistance, and occasionally product development (Feller 1988). All of these endeavors are at least one step removed from the knowledge-generating activities of the university and are justified accordingly. That is, they are usually described as complementing the sacred trinity of teaching, research, and service, but they are also, and more importantly, rationalized in terms of their economic consequences. Organizationally, they generally require special units that stand outside of the regular academic structure. Finally, while historical precedents can be found for most of these undertakings, their scale, salience, and spirit have changed markedly during the 1980s.

This last point can be illustrated best in the case of *patents*. The Research Corporation, for example, was established as a philanthropic foundation in 1912 for managing academic patents and supporting scientific research. The Wisconsin Alumni Research Foundation (WARF) was the first entity of this nature operated by a single institution (1925). By the postwar era it was commonplace for research universities to have ownership of some patents that resulted from discoveries made on campus, but institutions still risked public opprobrium by acting too aggressively in this domain (Research Corporation 1987; Weiner 1986).

This attitude began to change gradually in the 1970s and was completely transformed in the 1980s. Some adjustments of the patent laws are at least partly responsible. The Patent and Trademark Amendment Act of 1980 made it possible for universities to receive patents for discoveries made during federally funded research. Court decisions also liberalized the criteria for patentable products, particularly biological products and processes (Kenney 1986), thus opening the way for such things as the patenting of the Harvard mouse in 1988. The general liberalization of patent policy has stemmed from the wish to encourage more patenting and the development of more new products. The first of these goals has certainly been achieved. Under these new conditions, universities realized, if they did not profit from the discoveries of their faculty, someone else would.

During the 1980s almost every research university reexamined its patent policy. There has been a general movement away from employing external patent management organizations, like the Research Corporation, in favor of internal management. Some universities confide the actual business of patent management to an affiliated foundation, like WARF; but almost all have established internal offices for patenting (with titles that often include "technology transfer"). The function of these offices is to develop policies on intellectual property rights, or the division of the spoils. These units justify themselves, however, by ensuring that the university learns of and stakes its claims to all potentially valuable discoveries. More than half of the leading research universities now require their faculty to waive rights over patents to the university. Overall, this has created a new environment in which universities have become more and more aggressive in identifying, securing, and defending proprietary rights over patents (Peters and Fusfeld 1983; Rhoades and Slaughter 1989; Feller and Seshadri 1990; Spector 1989; Weiner 1986). This is a dediced shift from their accustomed role of disseminating knowledge in a disinterested manner.

The establishment by universities of *research parks*—actually, industrial parks catering to high-technology or science-intensive industries—resembles patenting in the recent rush of activity. The first such development was started by Stanford in 1951, in part to capitalize on its abundance of land, but the 1980s saw this concept widely replicated among research universities. A research park is essentially a form of real estate development. When successful, it brings visible economic benefits to the community it terms of firms and jobs. But like any such venture, success requires a keen appreciation of the real estate market, the intended clientele, and the costs of development.

High-technology firms are in theory attracted to university research parks because of the potential advantages of interacting closely with university scientists, having a ready supply of well trained personnel, and obtaining access to university libraries and facilities—what might be called "propinquity effects." Research parks are frequently described as places to nurture small, fledgling science-based companies; however, the presence of a large corporate tenant is particularly highly valued by the landlord because it provides a financial anchor and a magnet for client firms. Universities usually justify research parks with the argument that they will augment the university research mission: Interaction with tenant firms will purportedly produce faculty consultation and research contracts. A second attraction is rental income, although the financial attractiveness of these ventures is an issue that involves the murky economics of the parks (see below). In practice, universities probably have to choose to emphasize one outcome or the other. That is, if income is the objective, institutions are likely to consign the park to a real estate developer, and thus cede substantial control over the tenants (hence, making it more of a straight industrial park). If research interactions are the chief motivation, the university will wish to retain control over tenants, and the investment may not pay for itself in rental income for decades, if at all (Dimancescu & Botkin 1986; Powers et al. 1988; Peters and Fusfeld 1983).

Research parks are frequently associated with *business incubator programs*, but these latter efforts involve a far more complicated issue of university involvement with encouraging, financing, and owning new companies. Business incubators in themselves can be rather modest undertakings. Facilities for fledgling companies are typically first made available in unused, academically inhospitable space. The program usually offers relatively low rent, on a sliding scale, and some shared business services. The crucial benefits flow from propinquity effects: access to the university for equipment, advice, and research assistance. The successful new companies are expected to eventually move out, ideally to the university research park. Most incubator programs are located in public universities and are likely to receive public subsidies as part of overall economic development policies. But private universities too have a large stake in their ambient economies. Rensselaer Polytechnic Institute, for example, established an incubator to encourage the growth of high-technology industry in the Troy area, which it felt would complement its ambitions to become a nationally prominent engineering school. RPI receives a 2 percent equity interest from the firms it accepts into its incubators and may acquire a larger stake. One of the functions of incubators is thus to allow universities to get in at the ground floor of potentially lucrative investments. Still, probably the most important reason for public and private institutions to sponsor incubators is to improve opportunities for students and faculty by thickening the research density of the immediate environment (Rosenzweig 1983; Peters and Fusfeld 1983).

Universities have been tempted to tap directly into the wealth that may be engendered on their campuses through *venture capital funds*. Some institutions have simply provided venture capital to development-stage companies on an ad hoc basis. Such investments are a matter of endowment management—the weighing of potential risks and rewards for the university's investment portfolio. Universities that have wished to enter this area systematically, however, have generally utilized separate affiliated foundations. The Foundation for Advanced Science and Technology of the University of Pittsburgh, for example, is intended to provide venture capital and obtain equity in firms connected with the university's research center and incubator (Powers et al. 1988).

There are additional possibilities for universities to commercialize the results of their research. Case Western Reserve University has created University Technology, Inc. as a wholly owned but separately incorporated subsidiary. Its essential purpose is to screen technologies produced by university faculty and develop commercialization strategies for those with promise. The largest payoffs are expected to come from licensing university patents to companies prepared to invest in further research and development at the university. The outcome should be both royalty income and additional university research. Arrangements of this kind can become quite complicated as universities strive to derive income and research support from actual commercial activity without contaminating their academic core. One arrangement worked out by Stanford and UC Berkeley involved working with venture capitalists and sponsoring corporations to establish a nonprofit research center and the for-profit corporation Engenics (Rosenzweig 1983; Kenney 1986).

Another type of commercial relationship would be the provision of *technical assistance* by university-related units to small businesses with limited internal science and engineering capacity. Such assistance is usually part of a state-supported program, and it is well removed from academic research in content and delivery. Typically, technical assistance is confided to a special unit with its own staff. The justification for being connected with universities at all, other than administrative convenience, is to provide the field staff with access to university faculty for their more challenging problems. For universities, technical assistance programs are essentially services that allow state businesses to utilize university resources in a small way. They can, however, assume a larger role. The Georgia Tech Research Institute, formerly the state's engineering experiment station, simultaneously maintains field stations throughout the state while also being a major contractor of Pentagon research. It accounts for two-thirds of Georgia Tech's research expenditures (Feller 1988; Powers et al. 1988; Rosenzweig 1983).

This simplified typology of the commercial relationships of universities does not adequately convey some of their most important features. First would be organizational complexity: These arrangements overlap, interpenetrate, and complement one another, and in the process they reinforce the same underlying purposes. Second, they exist for the most part on the periphery of the university, insulated by organizational boundaries from the academic core. (For an example of commercial relationships intruding closer to the core, see Rhoades and Slaughter, 1989.) Some institutions, in fact, serve identical functions without being part of a university at all; the Industrial Technology Institute in Ann Arbor, for example, has propinquity with the University of Michigan, but no formal ties. Third, insofar as these relationships are intended to augment economic activity, they are of deep interest to governments. Explicit state policies to promote economic development lie behind much of this activity, and some draw on federal programs as well (Feller 1989). University behavior in this case cannot be isolated from government interest and subsidization. Fourth, commercial relationships involve the university in fields of endeavor in which they must compete with other kinds of organizations, including for-profit firms. In the final analysis, one must evaluate why universities have made these links with industry, how effective the university has been in the different facets of these links, and what the consequences have been for its core functions.

The Entrepreneurial University

The American university has three salient rationales for cultivating research ties with industry: to foster economic development, to augment its own research activities, and to increase institutional revenues. When making actual decisions about research undertakings, however, these considerations are likely to remain separated. The multiple missions of the university serve well for purposes of public relations, but they create ambiguity by providing multiple criteria for judging relative success or unsuccess. In the case of rationales for research, it would seem that the university's gnostic relationships have a profile different from that of its commercial relationships.

The remarkable success of American universities in expanding the amount of research interaction with industry, particularly in the latter part of the 1980s, has been due to the new organizational arrangements and entrepreneurial spirit. As Fusfeld (1983) put it, "While industry has been receptive, it is clear that the university is selling, not receiving" (p. 14). On the other hand, university aggressiveness has not seemed to alter the fundamental relationship to date. The proportion of industry-supported university research that is basic in character increased slightly during the 1980s—from about 60 to 62 percent. This compares with a change in total basic university research from 66 to 68 percent. Universities have a competitive advantage when it comes to basic research, and it would appear that industry has continued to seek basic or generic knowledge from academic sources in order to complement internal R&D activities. In other words, the new gnostic research relationships of the 1980s seem to have enhanced the historical relationship between industry and university research.

The economic benefits of gnostic research relationships are difficult to isolate with any certainty because they are mediated through the much larger internal R&D efforts of firms. It is unclear furthermore whether such benefits can be captured by a region or even a nation, given the multinational character of many of these firms. There are nevertheless several reasons to believe that these relationships have been productive. Given the increasing scientific content of many industrial technologies, firms have been compelled to broaden their coverage of generic scientific and technological knowledge. Relying on universities to do this seems to provide broad coverage inexpensively because of the substantial subsidization of university research (even without explicit public programs) and its generally low-cost structure. Collaboration with universities also enhances the human capital of the internal R&D enterprise—an important secondary effect. Perhaps for these reasons, collaborative research within universities seems to be more effective than cooperative ventures between corporations that do not involve universities (Mowery and Rosenberg 1989). Finally, the pervasive rise in spending for university research in itself testifies to the economic value of these ties.

For universities, close ties with large science-based industrial firms benefit more than just research. The research support is important in itself, but it tends to fall quite unevenly across institutions. By one reckoning, 86 percent of industrial research support found its way to schools of engineering, medicine, and agriculture (Fusfeld 1983). Of greater value to the institution as a whole would be the other forms of support that stem from industry. Private industry provides voluntary support to a wide range of institutions, and for a variety of purposes. But there can be no mistaking the close relationship between the institutions that do research for industry and those receiving large amounts of voluntary support from industry (table 11–2). For eight of the dozen largest performers of industrial research, gifts from industry exceeded funds for research; and for nine of them the proportion of gifts from industry was more than 1.5 times the national norm. Not included are substantial but unquantifiable gifts from individuals who have derived their wealth from university-assisted industries. Voluntary support may in fact be the most important payoff resulting from university links with industry.

The gnostic relationships of universities are long-standing and appear to be fruitful for both parties, but the increased emphasis that they have received in the 1980s has focused attention on their possible negative consequences. Sheila Slaughter, for example, believes that a spreading corporate mentality threatens to subvert the leadership of American universities (Slaughter 1989; Dickson 1984; Kloppenberg 1988). The discussion here will be confined to situations that could affect the behavior of university faculty. The chief discernible problems concern potential threats to the free flow of information, academic freedom, and the allocation of faculty effort.

Table 11–2. Universities with Largest Industry Support for Research, 1986–1987

	Industrial Research Support ($000,000)	*% of Total Research*	*Industrial Voluntary Support ($000,000)*	*% of Total Voluntary Support*
MIT	35	13.3	49.7	49
Georgia Tech	24	20	9.6	39.5
Penn State	20	12	18.1	37
U. of Washington	18.6	10	29.4	38
Cornell	17	7	33.7	22.5
Carnegie-Mellon	16	19	18.4	56
U. of Michigan	14.4	6.4	13.3	21.7
UCLA	14.4	7.6	23.1	39.5
Texas A&M	13.4	6	21.6	41.5
Washington U.	12	12	10.6	9.6
North Carolina St.	12	12	12.6	54
U. of Arizona	11.6	8.4	12.8	34
Total U.S. Higher Ed	764.1	6.4	1819	21.4

Sources: "Innovation in America," *Business Week*, 1989 Special Issue (August): 56–57; Council for Aid to Education, *Voluntary Support of Education, 1986–87* (1988).

Secrecy may be antithetical to Robert K. Merton's norms of science, but it has long existed in varying degrees in American universities. Probably many researchers have experienced stages in their work when they were reluctant to disclose findings until they were in a position to complete them and claim due credit. A more extreme case, classified military research, has been rejected on principle by many universities, and where it exists on campus it has tended to be physically segregated, thereby minimizing the impact on collegial relations. The long-term research contracts in biotechnology, however, seem to have produced more deleterious effects. The distinctive features of these relationships are that patentable discoveries are the expected outcome of this particular species of corporate-financed research and that these hypothetical properties are already owned by the sponsors. Ordinarily, in academic research, patents emerge after the fact and hence affect collegial relations little during the research process. In this new situation, competition for profit is inherent in the research place, and scientists have become reluctant to share ideas that might prove commercially relevant at a later date. Numerous accounts attest to the chilling effect that this has had in academic laboratories involved with biotechnology (Kenney 1986; Blumenthal et al. 1986*b*; Kloppenberg 1988). Some of the controversy has focused on the sponsor's right to preclude the publication of findings. This matter is relatively minor, however, and can usually be governed by procedures acceptable to both sides. Far more damaging to the academic ethos is the reluctance to cooperate fully with colleagues during the actual research process.

In American universities the individual tenure-track faculty member is essentially sovereign when it comes to research commitments. Relationships with industry, then, depend on the willingness of faculty to accept and perform such research. One widespread concern has been that industrial funds have been steering academic research from basic to applied questions. It has just been seen that no such trend is evident in official accounts. On the other hand, the reliance on external funding for university research has meant that some degree of steering has always been present (Geiger forthcoming). Where one firm funds a substantial part of a department's research, its influence would clearly be considerable. This has been the case in aeronautical engineering, for example, and is undoubtedly true under the large, long-term research contracts. Perhaps more worrisome is the fact that the structures created to serve industry, to be effective, require the participation of university faculty. Empirical studies have found university administrators often more enthusiastic about endeavors like special centers than were faculty. This disjunction implies a conflict of interest, as administrators wish to see faculty initiatives toward industry located within, rather than outside, these new structures (Peters 1989).

Behind this conflict lies the matter of faculty work. The productivity of the university is largely based on the finite quantity of faculty time and effort. The more time faculty devote to technology transfer in special centers, or to promoting propinquity effects, the less will be available for teaching and fundamental investigation. It is in this sense that linkages to industry might be construed as inimical to university teaching (Fairweather 1989). In general, it is not the process of searching for generic knowledge with support from industry that seems likely to divert faculty from their academic duties but rather the attempt to commercialize such research. The pursuit of patents is likely to entail a different course of research than the endeavor to publish journal articles, and continual involvement with patenting will surely preclude other lines of research (Feller 1990). In this sense, the pitfalls just discussed stem more from the pressure to commercialize gnostic research relationships than from the fact of doing research under industrial support.

The motivations for universities to become involved in commercial relationships are usually presented in straightforward terms, but in fact they contain a series of seldom acknowledged trade-offs: While the potential for profits exist, these ventures contain risk and hence the possibility of loss as well; while they may augment the dollar volume of research performed, such research may contribute little to the core academic purposes of the institution; and while these activities may further economic development, they also draw universities into activities where they have few or no comparative advantages. It thus become difficult to judge university participation in these nonacademic activities by any one criterion, and it is virtually hopeless when, as is usually the case, the criteria are confounded.

There are compelling political reasons for universities to participate in activities related to economic development. For private institutions, particularly engineering schools, these undertakings may be congruent with institutional mission, project a positive public image, and frequently allow the institution to qualify for public funds. State-supported institutions share these same motives, but for them there is a larger stake: They perceive their appropriations for general operating expenses to be related to their apparent contributions to the general economic weal (Feller 1989). Perceptions are important here because tangible evidence of economic development is difficult to isolate.

What is at issue here is principally the extent to which university programs spur economic development through the creation and assistance of new firms, through expediting the commercialization of university discoveries (patents), or by providing technical assistance to firms with little internal capacity for R&D. The notorious examples of success in such cases are probably misleading, for reasons that will be explored momentarily. Proponents of these programs often make explicit claims for their economic benefits: The director of the Penn State technical assistance program avers that $17.10 in benefits flows from each dollar expended; North Carolina estimates that its Microelectronics Center (which is heavily subsidized) has created 6000 new jobs (Powers et al. 1988; SRI International 1986). Such claims ignore the multiplicity of factors impinging on economic activities, nor can they account for the complex matter of opportunity costs. Certainly the creation of an additional business or patent does not constitute ipso facto economic development. Many economists remain dubious of the claims. Feller (1984) could find no connection between state programs encouraging commercial relationships and actual economic development and, in fact, doubted that subsidized activities would succeed where market inducements were lacking. Mowery and Rosenberg (1989) interpreted the "weight of anecdotal evidence" to mean that commercial relationships "that focus on applied development work or on technological 'deliverables' [were] less successful" than what this chapter has termed gnostic relationships. High-quality universities in their traditional roles seem to contribute to the size and the quality of the job structure (Jones and Vedlitz 1988), but a systematic case seems to be lacking that would justify university participation in short-term economic development.

Universities have also looked to commercial relationships for additional sources of income; however, the distinctive characteristics of universities make it difficult to judge whether any specific activity produces a profit or a loss. Universities are either public or nonprofit organizations; they are heavily subsidized by state or philanthropic support; internally they operate through considerable cross-subsidization; and one of their principal goals is to optimize prestige, as emphasized in Garvin (1980) and Bowen (1980). Universities are also in a distinctive situation with respect to the markets in which they conduct commercial relationships. When this topic is considered, it is the great successes that spring to mind—the Stanford Research Park, WARF, or the high-tech firms that have prospered in Silicon Valley or around Route 128 in Boston. These are misleading examples; they represent universities or individuals capitalizing on unusual circumstances. Universities, it has been frequently pointed out, have no comparative advantage when it comes to ordinary real estate development, patenting, or founding companies. But they do possess another kind of advantage, that of having privileged access to extraordinary opportunities that emerge as secondary outcomes of their normal activities. The outcomes that these great success stories mirror, in fact, largely spring from these serendipitous opportunities.

In large measure, the behavior of universities in the commercial realm has exhibited a form of economic opportunism. Universities have positioned themselves to take advantage of the infrequent discovery or development in their midst that has significant commercial potential. The crucial distinction has been that, whereas before about 1980 much of this activity was not systematic, during the 1980s it was institutionalized to a significant extent. There have been tangible forces that have pushed universities toward parks, patenting, and firm formation, as explained earlier, but there has also been a kind of bandwagon effect at work. As this has occurred, the comparative advantage of opportunism becomes more tenuous as universities become involved in ongoing commercial activities. Research parks need tenants, patent offices must patent, and incubators ought to incubate. The more that universities engage in such activities, the more their situation resembles that of other market participants. On average, university performance in these areas has not inspired confidence in their competence.

Universities are no neophytes in real estate. By their very existence, major research universities exert a significant effect on local real estate markets, and they have been inescapably involved in those markets as they grew. Nevertheless, developing research parks has proven to be a long-term commitment with an uncertain payoff. One study reached the judgment that three parks failed ("attracted no industries or substantially fewer than planned") for each clear success (Powers et al. 1988). Another estimated that just four of fourteen parks were producing the benefits that had been expected (Peters and Fusfeld 1983). Establishing a research park requires a substantial initial investment. Of course, in cases where these funds are provided by a public agency, the university's own commitment is less. With perhaps forty parks currently under development, prospective tenants have both choice and bargaining power, which could have the effect of requiring even larger initial investments. Then too, considering the variety of programs universities wish to sell, a firm desiring propinquity with a given university is by no means constrained to do so through a research park. A considerable length of time is usually required before the cash flow from a park will cover its expenses; another similar period is normal before the park will yield a profit. Although the many recent park projects have not yet had time to prove themselves, it seems unlikely that the majority will be of pecuniary benefit to the sponsoring university or substantially enhance technology transfer. The factors contributing to success—available land, nationally recognized science programs, past successes, financial inducements, and anchor projects—make it appear that the greatest opportunities have already been seized (Powers et al. 1988).

The economics of opportunism are even more evident in the case of university patenting. Only a very few patents yield substantial amounts of income, while the vast majority produce no income at all. Yet, patenting involves considerable expenditures. Maintaining a one-person patenting office costs over $100,000 per year, each patent application costs from $5000 to $10,000, and successful patents have to be defended in court (Blumenthal, Epstein, and Maxwell 1986*a*). For these reasons, it has made good sense economically for universities to engage outside patent management organizations. But universities have recently opted instead for internal control over the patent process and the potential income. University foundations have been the preferable mode of control, but such a course also presupposes sufficient capital to cover overhead expenses. The aggressive stance that universities have adopted toward patenting is usually justified in terms of economic development: Patenting brings discoveries into the commercial realm by making it possible for firms to appropriate the rewards from their investments in development costs. Probably individual universities are more concerned with their own returns from patenting than these supposed social returns. For the few universities that have significant income from patents, this income is still dwarfed by the other support they receive for research. Nevertheless, excess patent income (above costs) is particularly valuable because it can be used for discretionary purposes. Thus universities seem willing to invest in patents largely in the hope of hitting the jackpot. Peters and Fusfeld (1983, pp. 38–39) identified only eight universities with more than $500,000 in income from patents in 1981, although income from patents seemed to be rising (Blumenthal et al. 1986*a*; Feller and Seshadri 1990). The lure of big profits seems to outweigh the less tangible destractions that aggressive patenting brings, particularly the latent conflict with the university's role as a disinterested arbiter of knowledge.

The university's disinterested status is further occluded when it seeks to profit from its opportunities to invest in fledgling companies. But in this area, too, the university's hand was to some extent forced. The commercialization of biotechnology began in the late 1970s when venture capitalists teamed with university biologists to form the initial companies. Once again, those who first seized the opportunities reaped spectacular gains (Kenney 1986, pp. 93–106; Kloppenberg 1988, pp. 193–196). These unrepresentative examples inspired university administrators to seek ways to participate in really large profits by acquiring equity interest, although here too they preferred to conceal self-interest under the cloak of economic development. In this case, however, the economics of opportunism are even more problematic: The payoffs are uncertain and the threat to the academic mission is considerable.

At the beginning of the 1980s Harvard was sorely tempted to accept an equity interest in a biotech company established by university faculty. After considerable agonizing and debate, Harvard declined. Through all the pros and cons, one fact stood clear: The university's academic integrity was the sine qua non of its mission, and even the appearance of a conflict with commercial interests could not be tolerated (Bok 1982). Considering Harvard's stake in remaining a worthy object of philanthropy, this decision should not appear surprising. But as the decade progressed, this kind of resolve weakened throughout higher education. Increasing numbers of universities were encouraging their faculty to exploit their expertise by forming companies, and even Harvard found a way to refuse its equity and have it too—through a venture capital limited partnership. Still, a fundamental incompatibility of purpose remains evident between academic and commercial institutions (Etzkowitz 1983; Fairweather 1988; Feller 1990).

The incompatibility of purpose becomes visible in the everyday operations of the university. Faculty who become entrepreneurs, although they tend to be overachievers, can hardly find the time to fulfill all the unremunerated chores of academic citizenship. Moreover, the two roles that they fill require decisions about graduate students, laboratory use, the research funding in which interests inherently conflict. Many faculty entrepreneurs eventually leave the university when their firms become commercially successful. This situation represents a triumph for the university's mission of economic development but a loss for academic purposes (Bok 1982; Etzkowitz 1983; Richter 1989).

Finally, the university's absence of comparative advantage may be most glaring in this area. Backing development-stage companies is one of the most free-wheeling and risky arenas of capital finance. Unless the university's opportunistic advantage allows it to score a blockbuster success, it is likely to fare poorly among more nimble private investors whose motives are pure (greed). In the worst case, universities can find themselves throwing good money after bad to keep a failing investment afloat. For example, according to the *Chronicle of Higher Education* (January 10, 1990), Boston University has invested $60 million, equivalent to 36 percent of the university's endowment, in Seragen, a development-stage biotech firm. It provides more than $12 million per year for operations, and has written off more than $26 million. A risky investment by any standard, this action clearly transcends the normal bounds of prudence that govern university investments.

Toward a Balanced View

Much of the ambiguity that has enshrouded the research and research-linked relationships between industry and universities derives from the fact that this is such a large and complex arena. This chapter has attempted to clarify the subject by employing the available data to establish historical patterns and by separating these relationships into two basic types. Several conclusions stand out. The 1980s witnessed an unprecedented acceleration of industry-sponsored university research. This growth during the first half of the decade corresponded with an increase in total industry-sponsored research. The growth in the latter half of the decade almost certainly was due to the lagged effects of the numerous university programs and facilities established to encourage interaction with industry. The preponderance of this research represents gnostic relationships, in which generic knowledge is sought through academic research to complement the internal R&D of (mostly) large, technology-based firms. Industry is the consumer here, and although universities have expanded what they have to sell, it is purchases by industry that drive this relationship. Gnostic relationships have been on the whole highly advantageous for universities. Despite possible friction in areas such as expectations of patenting and the faculty commitments to centers, universities on balance stand to increase their volume of research, support for infrastructure, and overall gifts to the institution.

Commercial relationships, in which universities have entered the marketplace to profit from internal research or to provide services to industry, have also proliferated during the 1980s. The environment has clearly become more permissive for this kind of university behavior, even though a conflict of values is still apparent. Universities have been expected to contribute in various guises to economic development, but commercial relationships, in particular, generate conflicts with fundamental academic norms. Both sets of values are important. Universities are dedicated to public service and depend on public and charitable subsidies for their operations. They consequently cannot afford to be perceived as withholding key resources from a cause like economic development. On the other hand, academic norms are embodied in the faculty and are crucial to their morale and behavior. The incentives for institutional behavior in the

1980s, it has been argued, have been preponderantly on the side of broadening commercial relationships, and, despite criticism, this trend has not yet threatened academic norms sufficiently to provoke significant backlash. Absent such negative feedback, university behavior can be expected to continue to drift in this same direction. But to what effect?

The university's role in economic development is largely a by-product of its primary, and economically most valuable, missions of educating students and extending fundamental knowledge. The case for the importance of the university role in economic development rests on two pillars: that industry has been underinvesting in generic research and thus could profitably utilize additional research from universities, and that discoveries of potential commercial value were being made in universities but were not reaching the market because of the inefficiency of linking mechanisms. The first pillar points toward gnostic relationships. The sustained expansion of industry-supported research through the mid-1980s would seem to indicate the validity of this case (although the recent leveling might then mean that optimal levels have now been reached). The second pillar implicates commercial relationships. Here, convincing evidence would seem to be lacking that special exertions are required to bring university discoveries to market. But valid or not, individual institutions still have positive incentives to pursue these relationships. The perverse economics of opportunism indicate that universities will continue to hope for large payoffs from research parks, patents, or stakes in new firms, despite the fact that the more that try, the worse the average return will be. Such a scenario, nevertheless, does not necessarily portend disaster for American universities.

The expansion of commercial activities is likely to encounter negative feedback at some future point. Either financial disappointments or dissonance with academic norms could force a moderation or encapsulation of these programs on the part of universities. The importance of this feedback is emphasized by Nelson and Nelkin (1986, p. 45), who expect that "there is a lot of winnowing that will go on," as both sponsoring companies and universities discover that some of the current arrangements are uneconomic. To dwell on the inevitable failures, however, is to miss the great strength and resilience that universities possess.

The American university has historically reconciled the many and contradictory demands placed on it by evolving complicated organizational arrangements. "The patterned isolation of its component parts" at the beginning of the twentieth century, which Veysey (1965, p. 338) noted, has advanced to bewildering complexity at the century's end. The panoply of centers, institutes, and foundations that has been noted in the preceding discussion has evolved as a natural way of accommodating activities that are loosely related to the academic core of the university. These units have proven, on the whole, to be an appropriate and effective means of establishing systematic linkages between industry and university research. Should the explicitly commercial linkages cause future embarrassments, the wisdom of these arrangements will become more apparent. Specifically, universities are likely to conclude that when they are induced to pursue complementary social goals, like economic development, they should do so insofar as possible in units well removed from the academic core, and also with funds provided for these purposes by external sources. On such terms, there is no reason why the American university cannot continue on its imperial course, establishing its presence in new realms of activity. James Killian (1985) has described the research universities as one of the central institutions of American society, and the expansion of ties with business during the 1980s only confirms that role. In a society increasingly dependent on knowledge, the university's incongruous and ambiguous entanglements with nonacademic organizations seem destined to grow, not contract.

Acknowledgments

I would like to thank William Becker, Michael Dooris, James Fairweather, and Irwin Feller for helpful comments on an earlier draft of this chapter.

References

Blumenthal, D., Epstein, S., & Maxwell, J. (1986*a*). Commercializing university research: Lessons from the experience of the Wisconsin alumni research foundation. *New England Journal of Medicine 314*, 1621–1626.

Blumenthal, D., Gluck, M., Louis, K., Stoto, M., & Wise, D. (1986*b*). University-industry research relationships in biotechnology: Implications for the university. *Science 232*, 1361–1366.

Bok, D. (1982). *Beyond the ivory tower* (pp. 141–42, 160–66). Cambridge, MA: Harvard University Press.

Bowen, H. (1980). *The costs of higher education* (pp. 1–26). San Francisco: Jossey-Bass.

Chronicle of Higher Education. (1990). January 10, pp. 29, 32.

Davis, L. E., & Kevles, D. J. (1974). The National Research Fund: A case study in the industrial support of academic science. *Minerva 12*, 207–220.

Dickson, D. (1984). *The new politics of science* (pp. 56–106). Chicago: University of Chicago Press.

Dimancescu, D., & Botkin, J. (1986). *The new alliance: America's R&D consortia.* Cambridge, MA: Ballinger.

Etzkowitz, H. (1983). Entrepreneurial scientists and entrepreneurial universities in American academic science. *Minerva 21*, 198–233.

Fairweather, J. S. (1988). *Entrepreneurship in higher education: Lessons for colleges, universities, and industry* (ASHE-ERIC Higher Education Report No. 6). Washington, D.C.: Association for the Study of Higher Education.

Fairweather, J. S. (1989). Academic research and instruction: The industrial connection. *Journal of Higher Education 60*, 388–407.

Feller, I. (1984). Political and administrative aspects of state high technology programs. *Policy Studies Review 3*, 460–466.

Feller, I. (1988). *University-industry partnerships: Promise or promiscuity*? Unpublished manuscript. Institute for Policy Research and Evaluation, Pennsylvania State University.

Feller, I. (1989). *The impacts of state technology programs on American research universities*. Unpublished manuscript. Institute for Policy Research and Analysis, Pennsylvania State University.

Feller, I. (1990). Universities as engines of R&D-based economic growth: They think they can. Institute for Policy Research and Evaluation, Pennsylvania State University.

Feller, I., & Seshadri, S. (1990). The evolving market for university patent rights. Institute for Policy Research and Evaluation, Pennsylvania State University.

Foster, L. (1984). *Sponsored research at MIT, 1900–1968*, vol. 1, 1900–1940. Unpublished manuscript. Institute Archives and Special Collections.

Fusfeld, H. I. (1983). Overview of university-industry research interactions. In T. W. Langfitt, S. Mackney, A. P. Fishman, & A. V. Glowasky (Eds.), *Partners in the research enterprise: University-corporate relations in science and technology* (pp. 10–19). Philadelphia: University of Pennsylvania Press.

Garvin, D. (1980). *The economics of university behavior*. New York: Academic Press.

Geiger, R. L. (1986). *To advance knowledge: The growth of American research universities, 1900–1940*. New York: Oxford University Press.

Geiger, R. L. (1989). The historical development of American research universities since World War II. Paper presented at the AAAS annual meeting, January.

Geiger, R. L. (1990). The American university and research. In R. Overman & J. Campbell (Eds.), *The university research enterprise within industrialized nations: A comparative perspective* (pp. 15–33). Washington, D.C.: National Academy of Sciences.

Geiger, R. L. (Forthcoming). *Research and relevant knowledge: American research universities since World War II*. New York: Oxford University Press.

Government-University-Industry Research Roundtable [GUIRT]. (1986). *New alliances and partnerships in American science and engineering*. Washington, D.C.: National Academy Press.

Johnson, L. G. (1984). *The high technology connection: Academic/industrial co-*

operation for economic growth (ASHE-ERIC Higher Education Research Report No. 6). Washington, D.C.: Association for the Study of Higher Education.

Jones, B.D., & Vedlitz, A. (1988). Higher education policies and economic growth in the American states. *Economic Development Quarterly 2*, 78–87.

Kargon, R.H. (1982). *The rise of Robert Millikan*. Ithaca: Cornell University Press.

Kenney, M. (1986). *Biotechnology: The university-industrial complex*. New Haven: Yale University Press.

Kevles, D.J. (1971). Federal legislation for engineering research stations: The episode of World War I. *Technology and Culture 12*, 182–87.

Killian, J.R., Jr. (1985). *The education of a college president: A memoir*. Cambridge: MIT Press.

Kloppenberg, J.R., Jr. (1988). *First the seed: The political economy of plant biotechnology, 1492–2000*. New York: Cambridge University Press.

Mowery, D.C., & Rosenberg, N. (1989). *Technology and the pursuit of economic growth*. New York: Cambridge University Press.

National Resources Planning Board. (1940). *Research–A national resource* (Vol. 2). *Industrial Research*. Washington, D.C.: Government Printing Office.

National Science Board. (1982). *University-industry research relationships*. Washington, D.C.: National Science Foundation.

National Science Foundation. (1989). *National patterns of R&D resources: 1989*. Washington, D.C.: Author.

Nelson, R.R. (1989). What is private and what is public about technology. *Science, Technology, and Human Values 14*, 229–241.

Nelson, R., & Nelkin, D. (1986). Observations after the conference. In GUIRT, *New Alliances and partnerships* (pp. 43–45). Washington, D.C.: National Academy Press.

Noble, D.F. (1977). *America by design: Science, technology, and the rise of corporate capitalism*. New York: Alfred Knopf.

Peters, L. (1989). Organizational innovation and the evolution of academic values. (Paper presented to Research Perspectives on Research Universities Workshop, Pennsylvania State University, April 14–15).

Peters, L., & Fusfeld, H. (1983). Current U.S. university/industry research connections. In *University-industry research relationships: Selected studies* (pp. 7–16). Washington, D.C.: National Science Board.

Powers, D. R., Powers, M. F., Betz, F., & Aslanian, C. B. (1988). *Higher education in partnership with industry: Opportunities and strategies for training, research, and economic development*. San Francisco: Jossey-Bass.

R&D scoreboard. (1989). In innovation in America, *Business Week*, Special Issue, August, p. 180f.

Research Corporation. (1987). *A 75th anniversary report*. Tucson: Author.

Rhoades, G., & Slaughter, S. (1989). *Professors, administrators, and patents: The management of technology transfer*. Unpublished manuscript. Tucson: University of Arizona School of Education.

Richter, M. N., Jr. (1989). University scientists as entrepreneurs. In D. W. Breneman & T. I. K. Youn (Eds.), *Academic labor markets and careers* (pp. 165–173). Philadelphia: Falmer Press.

Rosenzweig, R. M. (1983). The Pajaro Dunes conference. In T. W. Langfitt, S. Mackney, A. Fishman, & A. V. Glowasky (Eds.), *Partners in the research enterprise: University-corporate relations in science and technology*. Philadelphia: University of Pennsylvania Press.

Roy, R. (1972). University-industry interaction patterns. *Science 178*, 955–960.

Servos, J. W. (1980). The industrial relations of science: Chemical engineering at MIT, 1900–1939. *Isis 71*, 531–549.

Simeral, W. G. (1983). The evolution of research and development policy in a corporation: A case study. In T. W. Langfitt, S. Mackney, A. P. Fishman, & A. V. Glowasky (Eds.), *Partners in the research enterprise: University-corporate relations in science and technology* (pp. 91–98). Philadelphia: University of Pennsylvania Press.

Slaughter, S. (1989). *The higher learning and high technology: Dynamics of higher education policy formation*. Albany: State University of New York Press.

Smith, B. L. R., & Karlesky, J. J. (1977). *The state of academic science*. New York: Change Magazine Press.

Spector, B. (1989). Universities' patent policies vary. *The Scientist 3*, October 2, 26.

SRI International. (1986). *The higher education-economic development connection*. Washington, D.C.: American Association of State Colleges and Universities.

Swann, J. P. (1988). *Academic scientists and the pharmaceutical industry: Cooperative research in twentieth-century America*. Baltimore: Johns Hopkins University Press.

Uhlendorf, B. A. (1958). The engineering research institute. In *The University of Michigan: An encyclopedic survey* (Vol. 4, pp. 1243–1251). Ann Arbor: University of Michigan Press.

U.S. General Accounting Office. (1988). *Engineering research centers: NSF program management and industry sponsorship*. Washington, D.C..

Veysey, L. (1965). *The emergence of the American university*. Chicago: University of Chicago Press.

Weart, S. R. (1976). The rise of prostituted physics. *Nature 262*, 13–17.

Weiner, C. (1986). Universities, professors, and patents: A continuing controversy. *Technology Review*, February/March, 33–43.

Weiner, C. (1987). Patenting and university research: Historical case studies. *Science, Technology and Human Values 12*, 50–62.

Williams, B. (1986). The direct and indirect rôle of higher education in industrial innovation: What should we expect? *Minerva 22*, 145–71.

IV HIGHER EDUCATION AS SOCIAL INVESTMENT FOR EQUITY

In this final section of the book, chapter 12 reviews evidence in the literature relative to whether the outcomes of higher education contribute to equity in our society. Three different higher educational outcomes—that is, educational, occupational, and income attainments—are examined relative to equity factors of socioeconomic status, gender, and race (or ethnic background). The evidence suggests that those at the lower socioeconomic levels have been least well served by higher education. On the other hand, for women and minorities the literature indicates that higher education has proven capable of appreciably improving their socioeconomic status.

12 EQUITY ISSUES IN HIGHER EDUCATION OUTCOMES

Melissa S. Anderson and
James C. Hearn

In the United States a college education has long been viewed as a passkey to advancement, prosperity, and economic security. Over the course of the nation's history, higher education has become accessible to more and more people. What was in colonial times an experience closed to all but the white male offspring of the nation's most educated and prosperous Christians has become an experience open to virtually any high school graduate from virtually any background (Trow 1970). During this transformation, the higher education system came to be seen as not only a provider of social and economic opportunity for individuals but also a critical element in the national quest for equity of opportunity across socioeconomic, gender, and racial/ethnic groups. Yet it is important to acknowledge and to examine critically the difference between higher education's undeniable legal-bureaucratic openness to the masses and the functional-operational openness of its benefits to all. Accordingly, this chapter reviews evidence from the research literature to assess how well higher education is performing its role as "the great equalizer" for society.

We consider here the extent to which the benefits of higher education are enjoyed by all college attendees, regardless of socioeconomic background or ascriptive characteristics. We first approach equity issues by focusing on educational attainment itself, asking: Are any two students of equivalent abilities, academic achievements, and ambitions likely to complete the same level of formal postsecondary education? This question does not address issues of equity in access (Who can attend?) or choice (Can an individual attend the institution of his or her choice?). Instead, our approach focuses on equity of educational attainment as an outcome of the higher education system.

We also seek to assess equity in higher education by considering whether people who attend college are all equally able to translate their advanced education into occupational and income benefits. There is ample evidence that a college education does indeed boost an individual's occupational and income attainment. How it does so is the subject of a continuing competition among various theories of the education-employment connection. Human capital theories suggest that higher education, by teaching important skills to students, makes them more employable—and employers know it (Becker 1964). Alternative views do not assume that the connection between what is learned and what is required for employment is quite so direct. Certification theories (Mincer 1974; Freeman 1986) suggest that higher education may or may not make students more employable but that employers assume that it does. Screening theories (Arrow 1973) likewise take actual enhancements of employability to be irrelevant but emphasize that employers can use educational attainment as a cheap and easy measure of employability. Chartering theories (Meyer 1977) claim that employers and other social arbiters accept, without much inspection, the graduates of colleges as having certain socially valued characteristics that signify their employability. However college graduates manage to reap benefits from their education in terms of later occupational status and income, the question here is, Are all college attendees, regardless of socioeconomic background or ascriptive characteristics, equally successful in turning their educational attainments into occupational and economic benefits?

It is important to stress that the focus in this chapter is on only one of the several ways in which women, minorities, and those from lower SES backgrounds may be disadvantaged in the nation's competition for educational credentials, occupational status, and income. We do not address here the below-average rates at which individuals from these backgrounds enter college. That is a major social problem, but the focus here is on what happens to those who do attend college. The concern is primarily with the below-average rates at which individuals from these backgrounds attain college degrees. We are also concerned with the possibility that their college credentials may benefit them in ways different from the ways such credentials benefit white males from middle- and upper-class backgrounds. Specifically, we investigate the equity question of whether equal educational crendentials lead to unequal outcomes, to the benefit of those already advantaged by circumstances of birth and upbringing.[1]

We review the literature on higher education outcomes using three different equity criteria: educational attainment, occupational attainment, and income attainment. In doing so, we focus on three equity-related factors: socioeconomic status (SES), gender, and race (or ethnic background). We consider the effects of these three factors on educational attainment *per se*, and on the relationship between educational attainment and subsequent occupational and income attainment. Our review is structured by the following questions:

Educational Attainment: Is attainment of higher education equally likely for college attendees who have equivalent abilities, academic achievement, and ambition but who differ in socioeconomic status? in gender? in race or ethnic background?

Occupational Attainment: Are occupational outcomes equally enhanced for college attendees who have equivalent abilities, academic achievement, ambition, and educational attainment but who differ in socioeconomic status? in gender? in race or ethnic background?

Income Attainment: Are income outcomes equally enhanced for college attendees who have equivalent abilities, academic achievement, ambition, and educational attainment but who differ in socioeconomic status? in gender? in race or ethnic background?

Our primary interest is in presenting evidence that addresses the equity issues we have raised in the context of controls for differences in academic ability and achievement, as these are important factors in higher education outcomes. To supplement our understanding of these patterns, we will also consider SES, gender, and racial/ethnic differences related to the quality of institution attended, the major field of study, and the career path pursued.

Educational Attainment

We turn first to educational attainment *per se*. The equity question here is, To what extent do socioeconomic status, gender, and race/ethnicity contribute to the level of education a student attains, over and above the effects of academic ability and achievement? Researchers have used a number of different measures of educational attainment, including years of schooling completed, credit hours or years in attendance at various levels of postsecondary education, and degree completion (Kerckhoff

1980). We use the term *educational attainment* to signify the level of formal education completed at a given time. Our concern with equity outcomes leads us furthermore to consider qualitative differences in higher education obtained from different kinds of institutions.

Socioeconomic Status

In a meritocratic system educational attainment would be determined primarily by such factors as academic ability and academic achievement, not by socioeconomic background. Family socioeconomic status would not have significant effects on education completed, except perhaps through its effect on prior academic credentials. To the extent that parental educational attainment, parental occupational status, and parental income affect a student's educational attainment over and above their effects on the student's academic success, there is evidence of socioeconomically based inequities. The question here is, How does socioeconomic status affect educational attainment?

Extensive research reveals that socioeconomic background does indeed influence the level of education completed in the United States. Historical investigations have suggested that SES influences on educational attainment were stable over the first half of the twentieth century (Mare 1981). Studies of more recent cohorts find that socioeconomic background continues to affect educational attainment, over and above the effects of ability and academic achievement. In summarizing a collection of recent reviews, Kerckhoff reports that educational attainment varies by socioeconomic status background, even among students of similar ability (Kerckhoff 1980). A similar review by Wise and Steel (1980) came to the same conclusion: "While socioeconomic status is strongly related to academic abilities in high school, path analyses of the attainment process have generally found that SES has an influence on attainment independent of academic abilities" (p. 116).

The mechanism by which these socioeconomic influences operate is not clear, however. A review of research results from the National Longitudinal Surveys of Labor Market Behavior led Herbert S. Parnes and Malcolm C. Rich (1980) to lament this confusion, noting that parental SES reflects

> financial ability, "tastes for education," the presence of "role models" in the home, and "home-produced human capital," the last of which may be partially reflected in conventional measures of "ability." When education (or occupation) of head of household is the only variable representing SES in a model, it is presumably standing for all these things. That each of them is probably inde-

> pendently influential is suggested by the fact that studies have produced significant coefficients for various combinations of: parental income, father's education, mother's education, father's occupation, mother's occupation, presence of reading material in the home, number of siblings, and parental encouragement. Nevertheless, the relative importance of these factors and the ways in which they reinforce one another are as yet unclear. [Pp. 179, 186]

Various studies have attempted to untangle this complexity by focusing on the effects of particular aspects of family socioeconomic status. For example, Graham and McMahon (1987) produced econometric estimates of the amount of education undertaken by U.S. males and found that family disposable income is a highly significant explanatory factor. Others, following the lead of Blau and Duncan (1967) in their classic study of this question, have focused on the influences of nonmonetary aspects of SES, such as father's education and father's occupational status.

Research by William H. Sewell and his colleagues during the 1960s examined the effects of all these aspects of family socioeconomic status on educational attainment. Known collectively as "The Wisconsin Study," their analyses were based on survey responses, measures of intellectual ability, and measures of family, school, and community status of the high school class of 1957 in Wisconsin. From a 1964 follow-up survey they report: "Using a socioeconomic index, which included parents' income, father's and mother's educations, and father's occupation, we found enormous differences in the educational attainments of the socioeconomic groups. These differences are large no matter how we define educational attainment—whether as continuation in any kind of post-secondary education, college entry, college graduation, or professional and graduate education" (Sewell and Hauser 1980, p. 68). Specifically, they found that a student in the top SES quarter of their sample had a 2.5 times greater chance of obtaining postsecondary education than a student in the bottom quarter; the high-SES student's advantage was four to one for entering college, six to one for college graduation, and nine to one for obtaining graduate or professional education (Sewell and Hauser 1980). Even controlling for ability, Sewell and associates found definite effects of SES on educational attainment. For example, within the top quarter of the sample with respect to ability, a student in the highest SES quarter was twice as likely to attend or graduate from college as a student in the lowest SES quarter (Sewell and Hauser 1980).

These findings lead inevitably to the conclusion that the members of the Wisconsin cohort found it difficult to escape the effects of their socioeconomic origins in their pursuit of higher education. The effects of socioeconomic background operated independently of ability and sex at every stage of the higher education process. Those who overcame the handicap of status origin at one transition point found themselves again disadvantaged at the next transition point. There are, of course, many ways in which these processes operate. Importantly, with measured ability held constant, low-SES persons are less likely to make early application to college, to make multiple applications, to know about the possibilities of scholarships, to go to college immediately after high school graduation, or to attend high-quality colleges; moreover, low-SES persons are more likely to drop out of college, and they are less likely to return to college if they do drop out (Sewell and Hauser 1980).[2]

Educational attainment is not just a matter of quantity of education obtained; there are important differences in the quality of education offered by various postsecondary institutions. Though it is difficult to evaluate the instructional effectiveness of a given college or university, it is clear that the diversity of the United States higher education system provides a wide range of educational experiences. Two years spent at a large, underfunded community college are likely to produce a very different education from that provided by a highly selective, prestigious, liberal arts college (London 1978). Not surprisingly, the quality of institution attended may also be affected by socioeconomic background. In his analysis of data on 1980 high school graduates from the National Center for Education Statistics High School and Beyond Data Base, Hearn (in press) investigated student background effects on two measures of the quality of institution attended: college selectivity and institutional expenditures per student. He found positive SES-based effects on both of these college quality variables, over and above their effects on mediating variables such as academic ability, achievement, and expectations. Similar findings are presented in Karabel and Astin (1975), Alexander and Eckland (1977), and Hearn (1988).

We conclude that socioeconomic status influences educational attainment in the sense that students of similar ability but different SES are not equally likely to obtain a college degree and are not equally likely to attend a prestigious institution. These differences in educational attainment are therefore likely to magnify the advantages of high-SES students over low-SES students.

Gender

The second equity issue relating to educational attainment concerns the distribution of male and female students across levels of educational attainment. The question here is, Do men and women with similar academic abilities and achievements attain similar levels of education?

The overall proportions of undergraduate degrees awarded to men and to women, and changes in these proportions, are simple measures of educational attainment by gender. Trent (1984) reports these proportions as derived from Higher Education General Information Survey (HEGIS) data: Between 1975–1976 and 1980–1981 the percentage of bachelor degrees awarded to women rose from 45.4 to 49.7. One can reasonably conclude that women do not lag far behind men in degree completion. Nevertheless, more refined multivariate analysis is necessary to address the fundamental question of gender equity in educational attainment.

Fortunately, comparison of the processes of educational attainment for men and for women has received considerable attention in the research literature. Some researchers conclude that the processes are essentially the same for both. A study by Antos and Mellon (1978), based on a subsample of the National Longitudinal Survey of Labor Market Behavior, found that for both men and women several aspects of socioeconomic status influenced the number of years of school completed. They report strong, positive effects on educational attainment for IQ, mother's education, and father's occupational status. When the male and female subsamples were combined in a regression equation, the dummy variable for sex proved nonsignificant. In a study of status attainment for women and men, based on a 1967 sample of women (Longitudinal Study of Labor Market Experience of Women) and a 1962 sample of men (Occupational Changes in a Generation), Treiman and Terrell (1975) conclude, "To sum up our conclusions for employed whites, we have seen that the process of educational attainment is virtually identical for males and females. Although both parental education and parental occupational status have significant effects on how much education one attains, the educational level of the like-sexed parent is most important, followed by the educational level of the opposite-sexed parent; father's occupation is less important than either parent's education" (p. 178). Such evidence suggests essentially equitable attainment outcomes for men and women.

Others, however, have found differences in the influences on men's and women's educational attainment. Kerckhoff (1980) notes that, despite female students' tendency to do better in school, SES background plays a greater role in women's access to higher education than men's. In follow-up research on Wisconsin students of the high school class of 1957, Sewell and Hauser (1980) found that educational aspirations in the senior year of high school, as well as perceptions of parental encouragement with respect to further education, are more strongly related to socioeconomic status of origin for females, while these factors are more strongly linked to ability for males. From such evidence, Kerckhoff concludes: "When we recognize that perceived encouragement and aspirations have independent effects on attainments (net of both SES and ability), the male–female differences in attainments come to have greater meaning. Evidently these differences are at least in part a function of sex-linked differences in socialized aspirations, due to influences which occur outside the school as well as within it" (p. 262).

Wise and Steel (1980) agree that there are gender differences in educational attainment processes. They used Project TALENT data, based on the high school classes of 1960 through 1963 with several follow-ups, to investigate gender-related effects on educational attainment. Their findings indicate that socioeconomic status and academic aptitude have independent effects on college attendance and have different effects for men and women: "For males, the effect of socioeconomic status on college attendance was somewhat weaker than the effect of academic aptitude, but for females, college attendance was determined as much by socioeconomic status as by academic abilities. This difference is primarily due to the fact that females with low socioeconomic [status] and moderate or high abilities attended college only half as often as males with low socioeconomic status and moderate or high abilities" (p. 117).

As already noted, educational attainment can be differentiated by the status or quality of the institution attended, since these factors influence subsequent returns to higher education. There is evidence that, other factors being equal, men are somewhat more likely to attend higher-quality institutions; for example, Hearn's research on attendance at selective colleges found that women are likely to attend less-selective colleges and colleges that have lower per-student expenditures (Hearn in press). Sandell's research (1977), based on the National Longitudinal Surveys, indicates that on average men attend colleges of higher quality than women. For men, ability, family income, and father's education all had positive effects on the quality of institution attended, while for women only family income and father's education had positive effects and even these proved less consistently related to college quality. Sandell observes, therefore, that typical earnings functions that control only for number of years of education, without considering differences in college quality, are likely to overstate the "pure" sex differential in earnings.

There is also evidence of a gender-related difference in the effects of attendance at a community college on eventual educational attainment. Grubb (1989) describes an "educational advancement" effect for men;

that is, community colleges promote an increase in postsecondary education among those who otherwise would not attend at all. For women, he found evidence that community colleges have an "educational moderation" effect, reducing aspirations for B.A. degrees. There was, moreover, no evidence that community colleges produce educational moderation effects for men or educational advancement effects for women (Grubb 1989).

With regard to institutional selectivity, there are indications that socioeconomic status has different effects on educational attainment for men and women. Alexander and Eckland (1977) found that SES has a greater impact on the quality of college attended for women than for men. They also note, however, "Unlike our findings for men, women's access to select colleges is not at all affected by their secondary school's status composition ... suggesting that the mechanisms by which socially select high schools enhance the educational prospects of their students are in this respect salutary only for men" (p. 181). Individual SES thus affects women more than men, but high school SES composition affects men more than women. Furthermore, the effects of college context on post-baccalaureate educational attainment also appear to be stronger for men than for women (Alexander and Eckland 1977). The differential impacts of SES on men and women therefore appear to operate distinctively at the individual level and at the contextual level.

Gender differences in field of study are also apparent. While not necessarily a reflection of different levels of educational attainment, unequal distributions of men and women across college majors may have consequences for later occupational status and income differentials. Trent (1984) documents a number of these differences: Males continue to dominate scientific and technical fields, particularly business and engineering; females show an advantage in education and health professions; though comparisons of 1975–1976 and 1980–1981 data show shifts in major field distributions, males in engineering continue to show up to a 10-to-1 advantage over women, while women in education still show at least a 2-to-1 advantage over men. Trent notes that in neither year was there significant overlap of the top fields for men and the top fields for women (p. 294). This subject area segregation in men's and women's educations undoubtedly contributes to occupational segregation, a point that will be discussed further later in this chapter.

Evaluating equity of educational attainment by gender appears to be more complicated than in the socioeconomic background case. Although some evidence suggests that similarly gifted men and women achieve similar levels of education, there are indications that attainment cannot be so simply described. Differences in quality of college attended and choice of major field must be also considered, in relation to educational equity and in relation to their effects on later occupational status and income.

Race/Ethnicity

Minorities continue to lag behind whites in a variety of raw descriptive indicators of educational attainment, although the standing of some groups relative to whites has improved somewhat since 1970 (NCES 1989). From a multivariate causal perspective, however, racial/ethnic equity with respect to educational attainment is achieved when any two students of different racial or ethnic groups, with similar academic abilities and records, attain equal levels of education on average. This perspective takes into account the unequal distribution of educational and socioeconomic advantage among whites and minorities. The equity question in this case is, How do race and ethnicity affect educational attainment, once other factors are taken into account? The descriptive and multivariate perspectives on racial/ethnic equity in educational attainment are explored next.

Overall, average educational attainments of minority groups have increased over time. For example, Farley (1980) notes that in 1950 the college graduation rate for blacks was approximately 1 in 30 and the corresponding rate for whites was 1 in 12; by 1977 the rate for blacks was 1 in 8, while for whites it was 1 in 4. Such simple statistics illustrate the expansion of higher education for both blacks and whites, as well as the more rapid increase in graduation rates for black students. They also, however, illustrate the fact that the gap between the proportion of blacks and of whites with college degrees has more than doubled since 1950, from about 5 percent to over 12 percent (Farley 1980, p. 13). Trent (1984) cites evidence from the Higher Education General Information Survey on Degrees Granted that, though more blacks are completing college, the persistence rate for blacks still lags considerably behind that for whites.

Hines (1988, p. 81), citing recent U.S. Department of Education statistics, agrees that we are not moving forward on minority participation in higher education. He notes that in 1976 blacks represented 9.1 percent of total enrollments in higher education and Hispanics 3 percent—by 1984 these percentages were 8.7 for blacks and 3.8 for Hispanics. Blacks earned 820 research doctorates in 1986, 27 percent less than the number earned by blacks in 1976. Hirschorn (1988) notes a related trend: Doctorates earned by blacks declined 26.5 percent within a recent decade. There are similar problems in the completion rate for minorities: Between 1976 and 1984 the number of black college graduates dropped more than 10 percent, from 26,000 to 23,000 (Collison 1987). Finally, there is evidence that more young minority men are choosing not to complete college: The current college completion rate for whites is 59 percent, compared to 42 percent for blacks, 31 percent for Hispanics, and 39 percent for Native Americans (State Higher Education Executive Officers 1987, p. 18).

Trent (1984) stresses that the most pressing problems in minority attainment appear when summary statistics are disaggregated: "Blacks, for example, show small increments in degree attainment overall, but black males have decreased in their share of all degrees, decreased their progress toward parity using the population age cohort, and, like all other males, received a smaller share of within-race degrees in 1981 compared with five years earlier" (p. 302). Eckland and Alexander (1980) illustrate another way in which summary statistics can be misleading. Using data from the National Longitudinal Study of the High School Senior Class of 1972, they found that in 1976 virtually equal proportions of whites and nonwhites in this group were still enrolled and working toward a degree. The reason, however, for the equivalent proportions was that substantially more whites had graduated "on schedule," while substantially more minorities had dropped out; among males the completion rates were 36 percent for whites, 27 percent for blacks, and 14 percent for Hispanics (Eckland and Alexander 1980). Similar conclusions may be drawn from more recent data (NCES 1989).

Clearly, many factors influence the educational attainment process, and conclusions reached without controls for these factors are unsatisfactory. Wise and Steel (1980) showed, for example, that blacks obtain as much education as whites who have similar socioeconomic status and measured ability. Suter (1980) found that blacks who graduate from high school are even more likely than white high school graduates to go to college. Eckland and Alexander (1980) report that when such factors as SES and ability are controlled, blacks have higher educational aspirations, receive more parental encouragement, are more likely to be in the college preparatory curriculum, and have higher grades than their white counterparts.

To study the effects of personal, background, and educational effects on the attainment process for students in various racial/ethnic groups, Portes and Wilson (1976) examined data from the Youth in Transition Project of the Institute of Social Research of the University of Michigan, derived from a nationwide sample of high school boys. They found that, compared to white students with similar ability and parental status, black students have higher educational attainment levels. This difference, however, can be accounted for by effects of other variables, such as performing better in school, receiving more parental encouragement, and having higher self-esteem and educational aspirations than comparable whites. Portes and Wilson conclude that the lower levels of educational attainment by blacks are due to exogenous institutional disadvantages, not to pure racial discrimination:

> Blacks are able to move upward in the system primarily through individual self-reliance and ambition; whites, while being able to use this same channel for mobility, have at their disposal an additional set of institutional "machinery" which can, in effect, carry them along to higher levels of attainment, net of positive subjective orientations. [P. 430]

There is evidence that socioeconomic status has a weaker influence on educational attainment for blacks than for whites. To study racial differences in the processes of educational and occupational attainment, Porter (1974) used Project TALENT data with follow-up data. Though the generalizability of his results is reduced somewhat by an overrepresentation in his subsample of students with above-average socioeconomic background and academic abilities, his findings provide evidence on the relationship between race and socioeconomic status: For blacks, unlike whites, socioeconomic background had no direct effect on educational attainment, acting only indirectly through occupational aspirations. Sewell and Hauser (1980) also note three studies that find that SES is a much less important determinant of aspirations and attainment for blacks than for whites. Rather, for blacks, the crucial factor in educational attainment is high school performance. They report, furthermore, that the differential effect of SES for blacks and whites is evident at almost every successive stage of the status attainment process. Treiman and Terrell (1975) report similar race differences in the effects of SES:

> What is distinctive about the black equations is that father's occupational status plays no role in educational attainment for either males or females. Thus for blacks, educational attainment appears to depend exclusively upon parental education; whatever educational advantage (or disadvantage) whites derive from their parents' occupational status is not shared by blacks of either sex. [P. 1978]

Interestingly, Freeman's analysis (1976) suggests race differences in SES effects on education are either declining or sensitive to age levels. He used the National Longitudinal Surveys to compare the effect of SES on number of years of schooling completed for blacks and for whites of different ages. Comparing the 17- to 27-year-old cohort of 1969 to the 48-

to 62-year-old cohort of the same year, he found the difference between blacks and whites in the effect of socioeconomic background on educational attainment was considerably smaller in the former cohort than in the latter.

Insofar as majority and minority students are represented in different proportions at institutions of varying quality, college destination may be a factor in equity of educational attainment. Trent notes that a minority student is considerably more likely to enter a two-year institution and, once there, is less likely to complete a four-year degree (Trent 1984). Estrada (1988) reports that Hispanic students are six times more likely to be enrolled in a two-year institution than in a four-year institution. A minority student's choice of institution may be based on criteria different from those influencing whites. For example, according to the freshman surveys administered by the Cooperative Institutional Research Program at the University of California, Los Angeles, Hispanic students are more likely than white students to be influenced in their choice of postsecondary institution by the preferences of their relatives, the geographic proximity of the institution, and offers of financial aid (Carnegie Foundation for the Advancement of Teaching 1988).

Historically black colleges have played an important role in the educational attainments of black students. A study by Pascarella, Smart, and Stoecker (1989) shows that controlling for other influences (including social origins, high school attainments, initial aspirations, institutional quality, and collegiate academic and social experiences), black men attending black institutions have early educational, occupational, and economic accomplishments not significantly different from those of black counterparts at white institutions. For black women, however, attending a predominantly black institution had positive net effects on educational attainment.

What can we conclude about race and ethnicity effects on educational attainment processes? It appears that, in general, students of different races who have similar ability and achievement levels attain comparable educational levels. It is clear, however, that this inference masks substantial inequities across racial groups in earlier academic credentials and educational preparation.

Occupational Attainment

The second set of equity questions to be covered here focuses on equity-related differences in the effects of educational attainment on occupational attainment. In terms of occupational status, attainment refers to the level of prestige associated with an individual's employment position, as measured by Duncan's Socioeconomic Index (1961) or some other indicator of perceived status. While there is much evidence that education has a significant, positive effect on the level of occupational status achieved, this benefit may not be enjoyed equally by all. The fundamental question here is, Do all groups of people realize the same adavantage from their educational levels in terms of occupational attainment? The issue addressed in this section is not the direct relationship between, say, gender and occupational attainment. Neither is it the direct relationship between educational attainment and occupational attainment. It is, instead, the effect of gender and other background and ascriptive characteristics on the relationship between educational and occupational attainment.[3]

Socioeconomic Status

There are many reasons one might suppose that family socioeconomic status may affect the impact of education on occupational attainment. A high level of parental occupational attainment may contribute to a student's understanding of the processes of entry into high-status occupations. The generosity of wealthy parents may provide the means to travel or to make contacts that may pay off in terms of later occupational prestige. The equity question here focuses on the effects of parental SES in turning educational attainment into occupational status: Does educational attainment affect occupational attainment in the same way for people of different socioeconomic origins?

As Fagerlind (1987) points out, in a meritocracy, education is assumed to be the dominant factor in social mobility. This assumption has been challenged in the last twenty years by interpretations of research findings suggesting that education is not as strong a factor in intergenerational occupational mobility as a purely meritocratic process would imply. Hurn (1979) notes:

> A consistent finding of recent research on occupational attainment is that the socio-economic status of parents allows us to predict the future status of children with the same levels of educational credentials. Such research has uncovered consistent relationships between parental status and their children's status after educational attainment is held constant. . . . High status groups, therefore, enjoy a double advantage: not only are they a great deal more successful in obtaining high levels of educational credentials for their children, they are also more successful in translating these credentials into high status occupations. [P. 102]

In the 1960s research based on the Wisconsin Study showed clear differences by father's occupational status in the effects of educational attainment on status of first occupation (Hauser 1973). Hauser found that the correlation between father's status and the occupational return to education was .93 over nine categories of father's occupational status: "In short, the data suggest that a year of education is worth more to the son of a rich man than to the son of a poor man in the status of his first job" (p. 133). This conclusion, however, does not take account of ability differences in the correlation between father's occupation and son's years of schooling. From analyses of the 1964 follow-up of the Wisconsin Study, Sewell and Hauser (1980) report that the effects of virtually all socioeconomic status variables on son's occupational status are mediated by other variables, particularly son's educational attainment. In other words, much of the effect of SES on occupational outcomes is indirect. Nevertheless, Sewell and Hauser (1980) do report that in their sample father's occupational status affected occupational attainment directly. Useem and Karabel (1986) found that socioeconomic status affects occupational status over and above the effects of educational attainment. Specifically, they found that a person with an upper-class background is more likely to become a top corporate manager than is a similarly talented and educated person from a lower-class background.

Other aspects of the effects of SES background on occupational status involve the influence of college quality. To some extent, SES of origin affects occupational attainment by affecting the quality of higher education institution attended. For example, Useem and Karabel (1986) note that in the case of senior managers of large corporations in the United States, nearly all of whom have graduated from college, distinctions among colleges and universities have become increasingly important. Though some researchers have found that college selectivity shows only minor effects, if any, on occupational status (Griffin and Alexander 1978; Trusheim and Crouse 1981), others identify significant effects of SES on occupational status through college quality. Tinto (1980) has presented evidence that the influence of a person's alma mater on his or her career path is greater for someone with low SES of origin than for someone with high SES of origin. This finding suggests that institutional prestige may have differential sponsorship impacts for persons of different social status. Tinto cautions, however, that these sponsorship effects are not universal for all graduates, even within a given social status. Rather, sponsorship is largely "a latent capacity of institutions which can be activated by able and ambitious persons within the institution" (p. 481). He suggests that while the advantages of a degree from a highly selective institution are in part a matter of being in the right place at the right time, being able to be in the right place at the right time is not independent of socioeconomic or high school origins (Tinto 1980).

Therefore, although social origins affect students' access to prestigious institutions, and graduation from such institutions affects occupational outcomes, the impact of graduation from such a school is not uniformly, significantly positive. That impact depends on such factors as an individual student's background, ability, and ambition. It also depends on the type of degree obtained.

We conclude that not only is educational attainment affected by socioeconomic background but also that its effect on occupational status is SES-related. It appears that education does not overcome the effects of such factors as parental education, occupation, and income on eventual occupational status.

Gender

Another equity issue has to do with gender effects on a person's ability to turn educational attainment into occupational status. The question here is, Does educational attainment affect occupational attainment in the same way for men and women?

In terms of occupational prestige, Treiman and Terrell (1975) found that a year of education results in approximately equivalent increases in occupational prestige for men and for women. They found, moreover, that for both sexes, occupational prestige depends significantly on educational attainment but not on parental socioeconomic status, with two exceptions: Father's occupation affects a man's occupation, and mother's education affects a woman's occupation. Spaeth (1977) reached a somewhat different conclusion, however, in his research on the occupational attainments of a sample of 1961 college graduates. He found that although the levels of occupational achievement of female and male college graduates are similar, the dispersions in expected and achieved occupations are narrower for women than for men. Importantly, women also appear to have lower returns in occupational status to their educational investments (Spaeth 1977).

This finding is corroborated by the more recent work of Sewell, Hauser, and Wolf (1980). From their analysis of a 1975 follow-up of Wisconsin students of the high school class of 1957, they conclude that the effect of a year of postsecondary education on the status of first jobs is nearly twice as large for men as for women: "While educational attainment ... has a larger effect on initial job status than does any other variable, women clearly obtain a lower payoff for their schooling than men at the time of initial labor force entry. ... With less than a college education, women obtain higher-status first jobs than men; with a college degree or post-graduate education, men obtain higher-status first jobs than women" (p. 575). They further explain that part of the difference in occupational attainment is rooted in different patterns of employment across the life cycle. Women, who are more likely to interrupt employment and later reenter the labor market, rely on educational attainment at mid-life. Men tend to rely on their more continuous careers and occupational experiences.

It is interesting to consider the combined effects of gender and race on the education–occupation linkage. Rosenfeld (1980) analyzed data from the National Longitudinal Surveys of Labor Market Experience of Young Women and of Young Men to investigate sex and race difference in career dynamics. Her findings include the following:

> White men receive greater returns to their human capital than white women. They receive higher returns in terms of both status and wages to their years of formal schooling. ... While nonwhite men receive lower human capital returns than white men, they actually do better than white women, with the exception of somewhat lower wage returns to education. ... Nonwhite women, the "double minority," receive higher status returns to their education than does any other group, and wage returns almost as high as those of white men. ... Poorly educated nonwhite women receive very low status, while well-educated nonwhite women (and, on the average, these women do have education beyond high school) have their credentials recognized. For them, education seems to be the key to high attainment. [P. 604]

Occupational segregation by gender may be an indication of inequitable returns to occupational status from educational attainment. Various researchers have documented substantial sex segregation across occupational fields. McPartland and colleagues (n.d.), for example, found extensive occupational segregation by sex, particularly among people with low levels of education. These researchers investigated occupational sex segregation by determining the average proportion of a person's co-workers of the same sex. For males, these proportions were 89 percent for high school graduates, 73 percent for workers with some college, and 71 percent for college graduates. For females, the proportions were, respectively, 82 percent, 79 percent, and 71 percent. Thus, while higher levels of education are associated with less occupational exclusivity with respect to gender, it appears that there remains a distinction between occupations dominated by men and those dominated by women.

Gender differences in occupation show up not only across fields but also across longitudinal career patterns. Sewell and Hauser (1980) relate their findings to gender-based patterns of advancement. First, women's initial advantage in occupational status may result from the fact that they are more likely than men to hold entry-level white-collar jobs. Second, as Wolf and Rosenfeld (1978) have also suggested, female-dominated occupations may be easier to reenter after interruptions in employment yet do not offer as much opportunity for upward mobility. Third, even in female-dominated occupations, women are less likely than men to advance to positions of authority (Sewell and Hauser 1980).

Rosenfeld's study (1979) of career patterns suggests other differences in the occupational attainment processes of men and women. Her findings demonstrate that men tend to be employed continuously, to pursue the same general line of work, and to rise in occupational status. Women tend to experience less continuity of employment and less upward mobility in occupational status, but, like men, they tend to stay within the same general occupational area over the career course. A human capital explanation for these differences would attribute women's lack of upward mobility to differences in women's and men's employment patterns. Alternatively, structural arguments would find causes of differential occupational attainments in the differing structures of occupational opportunities available to men and women. Rosenfeld notes, "The structural arguments, however, do not require that one believe that women are somehow forced into certain types of jobs. Because of 'socialization' or a 'rational' decision made weighing time required for home and family responsibilities, women might choose such jobs. The point is rather that once in such secondary, female jobs in the competitive sector, women will be limited in their opportunities for advancement in a way unrelated to their employment behavior" (p. 304).

Differences in men's and women's abilities to convert educational attainment into occupational status are thus difficult to evaluate. They are complicated by job segregation and differences in career paths. They are also dependent on the time of measurement, and it is here that our limitations in understanding this issue are most confounding. Too many of our data sources are prohibitively old. More recent and more comprehensive data are absolutely imperative before firm conclusions can be drawn.

Race/Ethnicity

We now turn to the effect of race and ethnicity on the relationship between educational attainment and occupational attainment. Basically, we ask whether similarly educated people of different races or ethnicities are equally able to translate educational attainments into occupational attainments: Does educational attainment affect occupational attainment in the same way for people of different racial and ethnic groups?

Blau and Duncan's research (1967) documented what they referred to as the "double handicap" for blacks relative to whites: (1) Advantages of parental achievement do not so easily convert to advantages for offspring, and (2) advantages obtained on the way to economic achievement, such as educational achievement, do not so easily convert to occupational and income advantages. The persistence of substantial occupational segregation by race/ethnicity, and the fact that blacks and Hispanics are more often underemployed and less often overemployed than whites of their same sex and education level (McPartland et al., n.d.) suggest that educational attainment indeed has differential effects on the occupational attainment of majority and minority groups.

A direct consideration of differential occupational returns to education by race appears in the work of Jencks and his colleagues (1979). They address the question, Does an extra year of schooling raise a white man's occupational status more than it raises a nonwhite's? They cite five studies in which the expected status advantage of a college graduate over a high school graduate is larger for nonwhites than for whites. They interpret this evidence as follows: "This does not mean that nonwhite BAs work in higher-status occupations than white BAs. It simply means that nonwhites without college degrees are at even more of a disadvantage relative to whites than nonwhites who finish college. As a result, college graduation is more valuable to nonwhites than to whites, even though secondary schooling is less valuable" (p. 174).

As one might expect, disaggregation within race provides intriguing information. There is evidence that minority graduates' ability to convert their educational attainments into occupational status differs by gender. For example, Treiman and Terrell (1975) found that black women are more able than black men to convert educational attainment into occupational status.

We conclude that education is worth more to blacks in terms of occupational status benefits. It should be remembered, of course, that this finding also implies that blacks with lower educational attainment levels are disproportionately disadvantaged in terms of occupational status. In other words, the marginal returns to education appear greater for blacks than for whites, and access to that extra education is therefore critical to achieve this potential racial advantage. What is unknown is the extent to which increases in educational attainments among minorities would decrease the relative returns to that extra education. What is also unknown is the nature of occupational returns to education for racial/ethnic groups other than blacks; too few studies of that topic have been undertaken.

Income Attainment

The third set of equity questions to be discussed involves the effects of educational attainment on income attainment. The fundamental question is, Do all groups of people realize the same income advantage from obtaining certain levels of education?

Several points should be made about the nature of schooling's effects on income. First, there is evidence from the research literature that the processes and outcomes of income attainment differ from those of occupational attainment. High-status occupations and high-income positions are positively, but not highly positively, correlated. One indication of the distinction is found in Sewell and Hauser's work (1980). They report that about half of the effect of education on earnings is a direct effect, while the other half is indirect, through occupational status (Sewell and Hauser 1980). Second, there is evidence, described in the following sections, that differences in returns to higher education for various groups may not exhibit the same patterns for income attainment as for occupational attainment. Third, schooling can affect income outcomes in several ways. For example, a 1977 earnings model examined by Solmon (1981) shows strong effects of years of schooling—with economic advantages for completing college, postundergraduate education, selectivity of institution, and high grades. Relatedly, major field also can have a significant impact on earnings: In Solmon's (1981) analysis, arts, humanities, and social science graduates were at the bottom in terms of income, with engineering and professional majors at the top. Finally, schooling effects vary over time. Murphy and Welch (1989) note the extraordinary fluctuations in returns to college education: from 50 percent in the 1960s, to 46 percent in the early 1970s, to 32 percent in the late 1970s (according to Freeman's work (1980) on overeducation), to 70 percent in the early 1980s. Next we review that effects of SES, gender, and race/ethnicity on income outcomes.

Socioeconomic Status

Parental educational attainment, occupational status, and income all have the potential for affecting the relationship between education and earnings.

The equity question here is, Does higher education affect income attainment in the same way for people of different socioeconomic origins?

In terms of individual returns to higher education, there is evidence that parental economic status has a positive effect on a student's ability to translate educational attainment into subsequent income. Research based on follow-ups of the Wisconsin Study reveals that the effect on earnings of average parental income during the four years following the son's graduation from high school was larger than the effect of any other variable. Sewell and Hauser (1975) conclude, "Thus, there appears to be little doubt that the intergenerational effect of parental income cannot in any large measure be explained by the differing abilities, social psychological characteristics, educational attainments, or occupational achievements of the sons of wealthy or poor families" (p. 24).

Beyond individual returns to higher education, one way to frame the equity of outcomes question is in terms of intergenerational transfer of wealth across population subgroups. The overall system of higher education can then be viewed as inequitable to the extent that it enables advantaged groups to pass privileges on to their offspring in disproportion to meritocratic standards of reward. This issue is part of a familiar debate in the economics of higher education. Hansen and Weisbrod's study (1969) on equity in the California higher education system of the 1960s concluded that "the current method of financing public higher education leads to a sizeable redistribution of income from lower to higher income" (p. 77). This situation resulted from a system in which public higher education was heavily subsidized for all residents, regardless of economic status. Other researchers (e.g., see Pechman 1970) came to the reverse conclusion. Their results are based on a different approach to calculating the net benefits for various income classes. Rather than determining net benefits for median students in income classes, as Hansen and Weisbrod did, they distributed benefits across income classes in proportion to the distribution of students at each level of institution (e.g., two-year and four-year institutions), and they distributed taxes in a similarly proportional way (Nelson 1982). Net benefits then proved negative for high-income groups and positive for low- and middle-income groups.

Nelson (1982) explains that analysis of redistribution effects of higher education subsidies is complicated by the fact that all cohorts in society contribute to higher education, while intergenerational transfers are assessed by considering students and their parents. These parents are likely to be at their career peak in terms of earnings, and thus students' families will naturally have higher than average incomes. Nelson describes the dilemma thus: "Even if the tax side is included . . . the implications for redistribution remain unclear, since all age groups are contributing to the subsidies. Because of the difficulty in evaluating the equity of these intergenerational transfers, the net-benefit approach produces a perplexing situation: evidence of income redistribution cannot be judged for its equity, and evidence of equity does not provide information on income redistribution" (p. 219).

Returning to individual-level effects of SES on the education–income connection, there is some evidence that college quality and major field of study have some impact on the relationship between educational attainment and income attainment. In a model proposed by Griffin and Alexander (1978), college selectivity and college major proved to be the only appreciable mediators of parental income effects. In other words, part of the impact of parental income on offsprings' income outcomes was through its effects on the characteristics of college attendance, like college selectivity and student major choice. In this way, they suggest, college attendance characteristics may serve to maintain SES inequalities across generations. For example, a major in business or engineering yields substantial earnings returns, net of occupational position (Griffin and Alexander 1978).

Several qualifications to the general impact of college quality on earnings have appeared in the literature. Solmon's (1985) work shows that, for white males with above-median IQ, college quality has an increasing impact on earnings over time, with a greater impact on income for high-ability students. Trusheim and Crouse (1981) found that college selectivity has a significant impact on the income of a mid-career male in a given year but that college social prestige does not. The advantage of college selectivity is realized through a boost in early income levels, since neither college selectivity nor social prestige affects income growth over time. That is, of two men with similar incomes by age 39, the one who graduated from a more selective college will not on average earn more in the future. Finally, Smart (1988) has noted differential influences of college characteristics on income for those employed in private firms and public agencies.

Gender

Turning to gender differences, we now consider differences in the ways men and women realize economic benefits from educational attainment: Does educational attainment affect income attainment in the same way for men and for women? Male college graduates earn more than female college graduates, due to a variety of factors, including major choices. Studies of the earnings of young adults suggest, however, that earnings advantages of the college-educated (as opposed to others with less education) are more substantial among women than among men (NCES

1989; Becker 1992; Berger 1992). Equally striking are the changes in relative income returns to education. Murphy and Welch (1989, p. 20), in a recent analysis of returns to college for men and women in four different time intervals, found women's disadvantage relative to men to be decreasing over time.

In reviewing such evidence on returns to college degrees, Solmon, Bisconti, and Ochsner (1977) and Solmon (1981) note that gender differences in income attainment tend to be due in part to background variables such as grade point average, institutional selectivity, sector of employment, and years of employment. Solmon (1981) notes important sex differences in his analysis of 1977 earnings functions: "In 1977, the same three majors, business, engineering and the physical sciences, led to relative income advantages for members of both sexes. However, the pay-off to women in these fields was greater than the pay-off to men in all cases" (p. 625). This difference, Solmon suggests, is probably attributable to the higher demand for women in these fields, possibly in response to affirmative action policies. Solmon also found further evidence of sex differences: (1) More years of education pays off more for older women than for older men; (2) high grades had a significantly positive effect on the earnings of women but did not enter the equation for men; (3) low grades had a negative effect on earnings for members of both sexes; (4) college selectivity was significant, with somewhat greater effects for women.

There are many similarities in the educational and occupational attainment processes of men and women, but income attainment processes exhibit great differences. Alan King (1977) has examined data on never-married women who are employed as professionals, to determine whether women's earnings rise more slowly with experience because women tend to be in fields where all workers experience a slower rise in earnings or because their earnings patterns differ from those of male co-workers in the same fields. He concludes that the flatter experience–earnings profile and lower mean earnings of professional women are due only to a minor extent to their employment distribution among the professions.

With respect to the effects of college quality on earnings, Mueller (1988) found that selectivity has significant direct and indirect effects for both men and women. The direct effects are similar for both sexes, while the indirect effect is twice as large for women as for men. Solmon's recent work (1985) suggests that, while college quality appears to matter less than undergraduate degree attainment for white men, college quality is the more important factor for white women. This effect is apparent after controlling for undergraduate major, grade point average, employment sector, and length of employment.

It appears that gender-related differences in the effect of education on income are more pronounced than in the educational or occupational attainment cases. As before, however, it is not only the differences in the education-attainment relationship but also the processes by which these differences arise that are important. Also, as in the case of occupational status returns, the complexity of measuring returns, and the different career and family patterns of men and women, make definitive conclusions difficult (Becker 1992). If one must summarize this work, it appears that both the years and nature of college education have greater influences on women than on men and that the marginal payoff to further education of this kind is greater for women than for men.

Race/Ethnicity

Race and ethnicity also clearly figure into patterns of income attainment. In 1980 Farley wrote that the average black family's income was 59 percent of that of the average white family or equivalent to the white family's average income of the mid-1950s. What Farley referred to as a "lag of about one full generation" in income attainment is due to many factors, including differential effects of educational attainment on earnings for different racial/ethnic groups. The equity question here is, Does educational attainment affect income attainment in the same way for people of different races and ethnicities?

Chiswick (1987) used 1970 U.S. census data on adult men born in the United States to document racial/ethnic group differences in the education–earnings relationship. As a proxy for the rate of return from schooling, he calculated the estimated percentage increase in earnings for an additional year of schooling for various race and ethnic groups. These estimates range from 4.4 percent for blacks to 8.0 percent for Jews. He also demonstrated the interaction of race and sex with respect to income returns to education. The ratio of black earnings to white earnings for college graduates is greater than that for women but less than that for men. He suggests that the greater returns for black women may be due to their greater labor market experience (Chiswick 1987).

Jencks and colleagues (1979) found that whites receive considerably higher dollar returns to education than nonwhites. Since proportional "returns" to education are not significantly different for whites and nonwhites (that is, the ratio of nonwhite to white earnings is approximately the same at each level of education), and since nonwhites generally earn less than whites, equal percentage returns imply greater absolute returns for whites. Jencks and colleagues also describe different effects of years of schooling and undergraduate degree attainment on economic success for nonwhites: "The implied ratio of nonwhite to white earnings fell as education increased from zero to fifteen years. But non-white returns to a B.A. were so much higher than white returns that the earnings of those with B.A.s were almost equal for the two groups" (p. 199). The results of Featherman and Hauser (1978) are similar: Although the ultimate advantage of blacks with B.A.s over others with B.A.s was minimal, blacks with less than a B.A. were at a substantial disadvantage compared to others. Findings from more recent data support the general observation that a college education is worth more to minority than to majority students in terms of income attainment. For example, earnings ratios for college graduates versus high school graduates have been greater for blacks than for whites at least through the 1983–1988 period (NCES 1989; also see Murphy and Welch 1989).

Our conclusion here must be similar to that for gender differences: It appears that both the years and nature of college education have greater influences on blacks than on whites and that the marginal payoff to further education of this kind is greater for blacks than for whites. Regarding other racial/ethnic groups, the evidence is sadly insufficient.

Summary

Our basic concern here has been whether graduates of similar academic ability and achievement are able to benefit equally from higher education in terms of their attainment of further education, occupational status, and income, regardless of their socioeconomic origins and other ascriptive characteristics. Our criterion for the analysis was straightforward: We may consider the outcomes of higher education to be equitable to the extent that, controlling for such factors as ability and achievement, educational attainment and its effects on occupational status and income are independent of college attenders' socioeconomic and ascriptive backgrounds. To determine whether higher education produces similar benefits for all students, we have considered three kinds of equity questions in relation to socioeconomic, gender, and racial/ethnic groups.

The first set of equity questions relates to educational attainment. It is clear that socioeconomic background does affect educational attainment, over and above its effect on ability and achievement in class. Offspring of wealthy, high-status, or well-educated people appear to be disproportionately advantaged in educational attainment. Differences in attainment patterns for men and women are less clear-cut. Here, the significant distinctions are in the mechanisms by which background and academic factors influence educational attainment; that is, background and educational experiences influence educational attainment in different ways for male and female students. For example, socioeconomic background appears to be a more significant factor in educational attainment for women than for men. With respect to racial differences, there is evidence that blacks show some advantage in educational attainment when ability and achievement are controlled. This finding, however, must not obscure the fact that disadvantages in earlier educational experiences continue to hinder blacks' overall opportunities to attain educational parity with whites.

The second set of equity questions deals with the effects of educational attainment on occupational attainment. The outcomes of higher education may be considered equitable in this sense if graduates with similar ability, academic achievement, and educational attainment are able to benefit in similar ways in terms of occupational attainment. Socioeconomic background appears to have significant influence over a graduate's ability to realize occupational benefits from educational attainment; that is, such factors as parental education, income, and occupational status affect one's occupational status over and above the effects of one's educational attainment. Again, the differences between benefits for men and women are more complicated. It is not accurate to say that men or women are disproportionately able to translate educational attainment into occupational status. In fact, there is evidence that men and women both experience advantages in realizing the occupational benefits of education, though at different career stages. More importantly, such factors as job segregation and differences in lifetime career patterns influence the way women and men benefit occupationally from their college degrees. With respect to differences across racial groups, it appears that education is worth more to blacks in terms of occupational status benefits. This finding, however, also implies that blacks with lower educational attainment levels are disproportionately disadvantaged in terms of occupational status.

The last set of equity questions we have considered has to do with the effects of educational attainment on income level. As in the previous two cases, socioeconomic background shows the most distinct pattern of influence; that is, SES appears to affect the education–income relationship in important ways. Gender and racial/ethnic effects are somewhat unclear, but it appears that in terms of returns to attendance, pursuing higher education is worth less at the margin to white males than to those from other groups and that the raw advantages of white males in income in the years after college attendance have been decreasing in recent years.

Discussion

The evidence suggests that equity problems seem most severe for those from the lower socioeconomic classes. Repeatedly, the research literature suggests that coming from a socioeconomically disadvantaged background limits educational attainments and limits the positive effects of college attendance on occupational and income attainments. Colleges seem to serve their poorest, most deprived students less well than we all would like. Clearly, the dream of college as the great equalizer does not hold completely true for those whom Thomas Jefferson and Andrew Jackson envisioned as its most likely potential beneficiaries (Hearn 1992). The effects of gender and race/ethnicity on college outcomes seem less deleterious, and in some ways these effects are positive. For women and minorities, college has indeed proven capable of appreciably improving their life chances. The woman or minority high school graduate who does not attend stands at a shockingly clear disadvantage to one who does. Note that the evidence does not imply that women and minorities attain as much as or more than white males in their college outcomes, but only that women and minorities will tend to do as well as or better than comparably credentialed white males, will tend to attain a greater payoff to choosing college attendance over nonattendance than males attain, and are gradually closing the gap on white males in raw returns to college attendance.

A number of qualifications must be attached to our analysis. First, we have focused largely on the outcomes of postsecondary education, rather than on the ways people come to enter the postsecondary system or to persist in it. That there are unequal entry and persistence rates in the system should not be ignored. It is one thing to say, for example, that certain minorities stand at no substantial disadvantage relative to comparable whites in their higher education outcomes, but quite another to say that we have an racially equitable system of education. The high school dropout rate among blacks, in particular, is shockingly high (see Hurn 1979), and those blacks who do reach and attend college are preselected in significant ways. What is more, the dropout rate of minorities in higher education is higher than that of others (see Tinto 1987), so those blacks who graduate from a four-year college are further preselected. To ignore this point is to misread grossly the implications of this chapter.

Second, methodological complications continue to attenuate the definitiveness of conclusions drawn from existing data. Most of the effects discussed here result from long-term processes that can be best examined with longitudinal research designs. Such studies are not only costly but are also subject to difficulties in analysis and interpretation. For example, sample attrition can seriously bias conclusions. Different groups (e.g., blacks and whites) often have significantly different rates of sample attrition in longitudinal surveys. Recent developments allowing more precise estimations of the effects of sample attrition (e.g., Heckman 1979) hold particular promise here.

Third, we have focused in this chapter only briefly on certain important public policy issues, such as the question of whether low tuition in public higher education really benefits the lower classes once the regressiveness of most state tax systems is taken into effect. Instead, we have focused more on individual-level longitudinal analyses and largely ignored the question of how governments' taxing and state subsidy policies affect returns for those from various backgrounds. Some further discussion of the returns on social investments in public higher education is imperative.

Implications for Further Research

Our review of empirical evidence on the equity of higher education outcomes across socioeconomic, gender, and racial/ethnic groups suggests a number of directions for further research on educational equity issues. First, continued attention to longitudinal studies will be extremely valuable. Because the effects of education on occupational status and income levels are potentially realized over the course of a career, it is important to trace the economic status of graduates over the long term. Although current longitudinal projects will continue to provide valuable information, it is important that new studies be initiated at intervals because of cohort effects on career patterns. Social changes, such as emerging employment patterns of women, affect the way a college cohort's educational attainment influences its opportunities for economic advancement.

Second, there appears to be a need for more research on the equity effects of higher education across racial groups. The need arises in part because advances in educational attainment of some minority groups have fluctuated in the last two decades, from significant gains to subsequent declines. Conclusions about minority participation in higher education based on the enrollment patterns of a decade ago need to be adjusted in light of later enrollment shifts. Another reason for further research in this area is that scholars are increasingly aware of distinctions among many racial and ethnic groups that may have implications for students' ability to translate education into economic benefits. Specifically, the simple dichotomy between black and white students that appears in many earlier studies does not fully capture the experience of the several minority populations either in educational attainment or in education's effects on occupation and income.

Third, more attention to the effects of qualitatively different educational experiences is warranted. Since there is evidence that college degrees differ in their effects by such factors as institutional quality and major field, it is likely that a wealth of useful information could be obtained from more detailed studies of the linkages between different forms of collegiate education and subsequent economic benefits.

Fourth, definitive conclusions on the equity effects of higher education are dependent on having more recent and more comprehensive data than are now available. For example, women trailed men in college enrollment appreciably until the 1970s, but by 1976 they had passed men in enrollment rates (NCES 1989). Yet much of the scholarly work we have on the topic of gender differences in long-term educational effects on attainment dates to earlier periods. For example, the Project Talent data and the Wisconsin data of Sewell and his colleagues are based on the teenagers of the 1950s and early 1960s. Given major societal changes since that time, particularly with respect to women and minorities, the inadequacy of those sources to reflect current realities of educational effects is apparent.

Finally, we suggest that changes in the student population call into question the causal models usually employed in studies of the effects of higher education. The student who enters college at age 18, attends full-time, and graduates after four years is becoming a rarity. As more nontraditional students, particularly older students, enter colleges and universities, it becomes more difficult to treat educational attainment as a precareer factor. Instead, it may be more appropriate to model the interactive effects of education and employment throughout the career cycle.

Acknowledgments

The authors gratefully acknowledge the editors' helpful comments on an earlier version of this chapter.

Endnotes

1. In the terms of multivariate modeling we are concerned with SES, gender, and race/ethnicity differences in the strength of the educational attainment coefficient in explaining eventual occupational and income attainments.

2. Not all studies, however, have shown important, causally distinct effects of SES. A study by Kohen, Nestel, and Karmas (1976) showed that, when ability, enrollment in a college preparatory curriculum, and choice of a four-year (versus two-year) college were controlled, socioeconomic status had no discernible effect on grade completion at any level of college.

3. It should be noted at the outset that few studies have sought to examine systematically the particular effects of higher education on occupational outcomes. Instead, most research in this area has relied on simple indicators of years of education attained, and thus higher education effects tend to be confounded with effects of education in general. To the extent possible, distinctive effects of higher education are reviewed here. When such data are not available, the next-best alternatives are pursued.

References

Alexander, K.L., & Eckland, B.K. (1977). High school context and college selectivity: Institutional constraints in educational stratification. *Social Forces 56*(1), 166–188.

Antos, J.R., & Mellon, W.S. (1978). The youth labor market: A dynamic overview. Mimeo. United States Bureau of Labor Statistics.

Arrow, K.J. (1973). Higher education as a filter. *Journal of Political Economy 2*, 193–216.

Becker, G.S. (1964). *Human capital.* New York: National Bureau of Economic Research.

Becker, W.E. (1992). Why go to college?: The value of an investment in higher education. In W.E. Becker & D.R. Lewis (Eds.), *The economics of American higher education.* Norwell, MA: Kluwer Academic Publishers.

Berger, M.C. (1992). Private returns to specific college majors. In W.E. Becker & D.R. Lewis (Eds.), *The economics of American higher education.* Norwell, MA: Kluwer Academic Publishers.

Blau, P.M., & Duncan, O.D. (1967). *The American occupational structure.* New York: Wiley.

Carnegie Foundation for the Advancement of Teaching. (1988). Trendlines: Hispanic students continue to be distinctive. *Change*, May/June, 1988, pp. 43–47.

Chiswick, B.R. (1987). Race earnings differentials. In George Psacharopoulos (Ed.), *Economics of education: Research and studies.* Oxford, England: Pergamon Press.

Collison, M. (1987). More young black men choosing not to go to college. *Chronicle of Higher Education*, December 9, p. 1.

Duncan, O.D. (1961). A socioeconomic index for all occupations. In A.J. Reiss (Ed.), *Occupations and social status.* Glencoe, IL: The Free Press.

Eckland, B.K., & Alexander, K.L. (1980). The National Longitudinal Study of the High School Senior Class of 1972. In A.C. Kerckhoff (Ed.), *Research in sociology of education and socialization: Longitudinal perspectives on educational attainment* (Vol. 1). Greenwich, CT: JAI Press.

Estrada, L. F. (1988). Anticipating the demographic future. *Change*, May/June, pp. 14–19.

Fagerlind, I. (1987). Status attainment models and education. In G. Psacharopoulos (Ed.), *Economics of education: Research and studies*. Oxford: Pergamon Press.

Farley, R. (1980). The long road: Blacks and whites in America. *American Demographics 2*(2), February, 11–17.

Featherman, D. L., & Hauser, R. M. (1978). *Opportunity and change*. New York: Academic Press.

Freeman, R. B. (1976). *The black elite: The new market for highly qualified black Americans*. New York: McGraw-Hill.

Freeman, R. B. (1980). The facts about the declining economic value of college. *The Journal of Human Resources 15* (1) (Winter), 124–142.

Freeman, R. B. (1986). Demand for education. In O. Ashenfelter & R. Layard (Eds.), *Handbook of labor economics* (Vol. 1). Amsterdam: Elsevier Science Publishers.

Graham, J. W., & McMahon, W. W. (1987). Personal earnings variation and education. In G. Psacharopoulos (Ed.), *Economics of education: Research and studies*. Oxford: Pergamon Press.

Griffin, L. J., & Alexander, K. L. (1978). Schooling and socioeconomic attainments: High school and college influences. *American Journal of Sociology 84*(2), 319–347.

Grubb, W. N. (1989). The effects of differentiation on educational attainment: The case of community colleges. *The Review of Higher Education 12*(4) (Summer), 349–374.

Hansen, W. L., & Weisbrod, B. A. (1969). *Benefits, costs, and finance of public higher education*. Chicago: Markham.

Hauser, R. M. (1973). Socioeconomic background and differential returns to education. In L. C. Solmon & P. J. Taubman (Eds.), *Does college matter?: Some evidence on the impacts at higher education*. New York: Academic Press.

Hearn, J. C. (1988). Attendance at higher-cost colleges: Ascribed, socioeconomic, and academic influences on student enrollment patterns. *Economics of Education Review 7*(1), 65–76.

Hearn, J.C. (1991). Academic and non-academic influences on the college destinations of 1980 high school graduates. *Sociology of Education 63*(4), 158–171.

Hearn, J. C. (1992). The teaching role of contemporary American higher education: Popular imagery and organizational reality. In W. E. Becker & D. R. Lewis (Eds.), *The economics of American higher education*. Norwell, MA: Kluwer Academic Publishers.

Heckman, J. J. (1979). Sample selection bias as a specification error. *Econometrica 47*, 153–61.

Hines, E. R. (1988). *Higher education and state governments: Renewed partnership, cooperation, or competition*? (ASHE-ERIC Higher Education Report No. 5). Washington, D.C.: Association for the Study of Higher Education.

Hirschorn, M. W. (1988). Doctorates earned by blacks decline 26.5 percent in

decade. *Chronicle of Higher Education*, February 3, p. 1.
Hurn, C. J. (1979). *The limits and possibilities of schooling: An introduction to the sociology of education*. Boston: Allyn & Bacon.
Jencks, C., et al. (1979). *Who gets ahead: The determinants of economic success in America*. New York: Basic Books.
Karabel, J., & Astin, A. W. (1975). Social class, academic ability, and college "quality." *Social Forces 53*, 381–398.
Kerckhoff, A. C. (1980). Looking back and looking ahead. In Alan C. Kerckhoff (Ed.), *Research in sociology of education and socialization: Longitudinal perspectives on educational attainment* (Vol. 1). Greenwich, CT: JAI Press.
King, A. G. (1977). Is occupational segregation the cause of the flatter experience-earnings profiles of women? *Journal of Human Resources 12*, 541–549.
Kohen, A. I., Nestel, G., & Karmas, C. (1976). Success and failure in college: A new approach to persistence in undergraduate programs. Mimeo. Columbus: Center for Human Resource Research.
London, H. (1978). The perils of opportunity: The working-class community college student in sociological perspective. In Herbert S. Sacks & Associates, *Hurdles: The admissions dilemma in American higher education*. Saddle Brook, NJ: Stratford Press.
McPartland, J. M., Braddock, J. H., II, Crain, R. L., & Dawkins, R. L. (No date). *New evidence on race and sex inequalities from the survey of employers linked to the National Longitudinal Survey*. Center for Social Organization of Schools, Johns Hopkins University.
Mare, R. D. (1981). Change and stability in educational stratification. *American Sociological Review 46*(1), February, 72–87.
Meyer, J. (1977). The effects of education as an institution. *American Journal of Sociology 83*, 55–77.
Mincer, J. (1974). *Schooling, experience, and earnings*. New York: National Bureau of Economic Research.
Mueller, R. O. (1988). The impact of college selectivity on income for men and women. *Research in Higher Education 29*(2), 175–191.
Murphy, K., & Welch, F. (1989). Wage premiums for college graduates: Recent growth and possible explanations. *Educational Researcher 18*(4), May, 17–26.
National Center for Education Statistics [NCES]. (1989). *The condition of education: Postsecondary education* (Vol. 2). Washington, D.C.: U.S. Government Printing Office.
Nelson, S. C. (1982). Equity and higher education finance: The case of community colleges. In W. W. McMahon & T. G. Geske (Eds.), *Financing education: Overcoming inefficiency and inequity*. Urbana: University of Illinois Press.
Parnes, H. S., & Rich, M. C. (1980). Perspectives on educational attainment from the National Longitudinal Surveys of Labor Market Behavior. In A. C. Kerckhoff (Ed.), *Research in sociology of education and socialization: Longitudinal perspectives on educational attainment* (Vol. 1). Greenwich, CT: JAI Press.
Pascarella, E. T., Smart, J. C., & Stoecker, J. (1989). College, race and the early

status attainment of black students. *Journal of Higher Education 60*(1), January/February, 82–107.
Pechman, J. (1970). The distributional effects of public higher education in California. *Journal of Human Resources 5*(3), 361–370.
Porter, J.N. (1974). Race, socialization and mobility in educational and early occupational attainment. *American Sociological Review 39*(3), 303–316.
Portes, A., & Wilson, K.L. (1976). Black-white differences in educational attainment. *American Sociological Review 41* June, 414–431.
Rosenfeld, R.A. (1979). Women's occupational careers: Individual and structural explanations. *Sociology of Work and Occupations 6*(3), August, 283–311.
Rosenfeld, R.A. (1980). Race and sex differences in career dynamics. *American Sociological Review 45*, August, 583–609.
Sandell, S.H. (1977). The demand for college quality. Paper presented at the Meeting of the American Educational Research Association, New York.
Sewell, W.H., & Hauser, R.M. (1975). *Education, occupation, and earnings.* New York: Academic Press.
Sewell, W.H., & Hauser, R.M. (1980). The Wisconsin longitudinal study of social and psychological factors in aspirations and achievements. In Alan C. Kerckhoff (Ed.), *Research in sociology of education and socialization: Longitudinal perspectives on educational attainment* (Vol. 1) Greenwich, CT: JAI Press.
Sewell, W.H., Hauser, R.M., & Wolf, W.C. (1980). Sex, schooling, and occupational status. *American Journal of Sociology 86*(3), 551–583.
Smart, J.C. (1988). College influences on graduates' income levels. *Research in Higher Education 29*(1), 41–59.
Solmon, L.C. (1981). New findings on the links between college education and work. *Higher Education 10*, 615–648.
Solmon, L.C. (1985). Quality of education and economic growth. *Economics of Education Review 4*(4), 273–290.
Solmon, L.C., Bisconti, A.S., & Ochsner, N.L. (1977). *College as a training ground for jobs.* New York: Praeger Publishers.
Spaeth, J.L. (1977). Differences in the occupational achievement process between male and female college graduates. *Sociology of Education 50*, July, 206–217.
State Higher Education Executive Officers. (1987). *Focus on minorities: Synopsis of state higher education initiatives.* Denver: Education Commission of the States.
Suter, L.E. (1980). Elementary and secondary school progression, high school graduation, and college entrance of the American population: 1950 to 1978. In A.C. Kerckhoff (Ed.), *Research in sociology of education and socialization: Longitudinal perspectives on educational attainment* (Vol. 1). Greenwich, CT: JAI Press.
Tinto, V. (1980). College origins and patterns of status attainment: Schooling among professional and business-managerial occupations. *Sociology of Work and Occupations 7*(4), November, 457–486.
Tinto, V. (1987). *Leaving college: Rethinking the causes and cures of student*

attrition. Chicago: University of Chicago Press.

Treiman, D. J., & Terrell, K. (1975). Sex and the process of status attainment: A comparison of working women and men. *American Sociological Review 40*, April, 174–200.

Trent, W. (1984). Equity considerations in higher education: Race and sex differences in degree attainment and major field from 1976 through 1981. *American Journal of Education*, May, 280–305.

Trow, M. (1970). Reflections on the transition from mass to universal higher education. *Daedalus 99*(1), 1–42.

Trusheim, D., & Crouse, J. (1981). Effects of college prestige on men's occupational status and income. *Research in Higher Education 14*(4), 283–304.

Useem, M., & Karabel, J. (1986). Pathways to top corporate management. *American Sociological Review 51*, April 184–200.

Wise, L. L., & Steel, L. (1980). Educational attainment of the high school classes of 1960 through 1963: Findings from project TALENT. In A. C. Kerckhoff, (Ed.), *Research in sociology of education and socialization: Longitudinal perspectives on educational attainment* (Vol. 1). Greenwich, CT: JAI Press.

Wolf, W. C., & Rosenfeld, R. A. (1978). Sex structure of occupations and job mobility. *Social Forces 56*, 823–844.

Index

MIX
Papier aus verantwortungsvollen Quellen
Paper from responsible sources
FSC® C105338

If you have any concerns about our products,
you can contact us on
ProductSafety@springernature.com

In case Publisher is established outside the EU,
the EU authorized representative is:
Springer Nature Customer Service Center GmbH
Europaplatz 3, 69115 Heidelberg, Germany

Printed by Libri Plureos GmbH
in Hamburg, Germany